Central Africans, Atlantic Creoles, and the Foundation of the Americas, 1585–1660

This book establishes Central Africa as the origin of most Africans brought to the English and Dutch American colonies in North America, the Caribbean, and South America in their formative period before 1660. It reveals that Central Africans were frequently possessors of an Atlantic Creole culture that included adaptation of Christianity and elements of European language, especially names and material culture. It places the movement of slaves and creation of the colonies within an Atlantic historical framework, showing interactions among Africa, Europe, and all of the Americas. It explores the development of attitudes toward race, slavery, and freedom as they developed in the colonies of England and the Netherlands, and it revises earlier discussions on these issues. The book suggests ways in which this generation of Africans helped lay the foundations for subsequent development of African-American culture in all the colonies of these countries.

Linda M. Heywood is Professor of African American Studies and History at Boston University. She is also W.E.B. DuBois Fellow at Harvard University and formerly a Whiting Fellow at Columbia University as well as Professor of History at Howard University and Cleveland State University. She is the author of *Contested Power in Angola* (1999) and editor of *Central Africans and Cultural Transformations in the American Diaspora* (2001). Professor Heywood has published in the *Journal of African History, Journal of Modern African Studies, Journal of Southern African Studies,* and *Slavery and Abolition.*

John K. Thornton is Professor of African American Studies and History at Boston University. He is also W.E.B. DuBois Fellow at Harvard University and formerly Carter Woodson Fellow at the University of Virginia, as well as Professor of History at Millersville University and Allegheny College. He is a former lecturer at the University of Zambia. He is author of *The Kingdom of Kongo: Civil War and Transition, 1641–1718* (1983), *Africa and Africans in the Making of the Atlantic World, 1400–1800* (2nd edition, 1998), *The Kongolese Saint Anthony: Dona Beatriz Kimpa Vita and the Antonian Movement, 1684–1706* (1998), and *Warfare in Atlantic Africa* (1999). He has published in, among other journals, the *Journal of African History, History in Africa, Cahiers d'etudes africaines, William and Mary Quarterly, American Historical Review, The Americas,* and the *International Journal of African Historical Studies.*

Central Africans, Atlantic Creoles, and the Foundation of the Americas, 1585–1660

LINDA M. HEYWOOD

Boston University

JOHN K. THORNTON

Boston University

CAMBRIDGE
UNIVERSITY PRESS

CAMBRIDGE UNIVERSITY PRESS
Cambridge, New York, Melbourne, Madrid, Cape Town,
Singapore, São Paulo, Delhi, Tokyo, Mexico City

Cambridge University Press
32 Avenue of the Americas, New York, NY 10013-2473, USA

www.cambridge.org
Information on this title: www.cambridge.org/9780521779227

First published 2007
Reprinted 2011

A catalog record for this publication is available from the British Library.

Library of Congress Cataloging in Publication Data

Heywood, Linda Marinda, 1945–
Central Africans, Atlantic Creoles, and the Foundation of the Americas, 1585–1660 /
Linda M. Heywood, John K. Thornton.
   p.   cm.
Includes bibliographical references and index.
ISBN 978-0-521-77065-1 (hardback) – ISBN 978-0-521-77922-7 (pbk.)
1. Africans – America – History – 17th century.   2. Blacks – America – History – 17th
century.   3. Creoles – America – History – 17th century.   4. African Americans – History
– 17th century.   5. Community life – America – History – 17th century.   6. Great Britain
– Colonies – America – History – 17th century.   7. Netherlands – Colonies – America
– History – 17th century.   8. Slavery – America – History – 17th century.   9. America –
Social conditions – 17th century.   10. America – Race relations – History – 17th century.
I. Thornton, John Kelly, 1949–   II. Title.
E29.N3H49   2007
306.3´620899674107 – dc22   2006101961

ISBN 978-0-521-77065-1 Hardback
ISBN 978-0-521-77922-7 Paperback

In memory of Alix Thornton Ehlers,
Mary Elizabeth Thornton, and
Robert L. Thornton

Contents

Preface

This book was conceived during a watershed conference held at Williamsburg, Virginia, in 1998 that was intended to explore the ways in which historians might use newly refined data on the slave trade made available by the DuBois Institute and a Cambridge University Press publication of a database of slave shipping records. The records made easier the task of linking patterns in the slave trade to the settlement of slaves in the Americas. One of the possibilities that occurred to us as we interacted with other scholars and reviewed the data was the possibility of linking specific events in Africa with their consequences in America. What stood out for us was the amazing wave of Angolans coming to the Americas at just the time that the English and Dutch were establishing their colonies.

This realization that there was what might be termed an "Angolan wave" dovetailed with a work that Thornton had just published on the Angolan background of the first shipload of Africans to arrive in Virginia. As our joint research would soon reveal, their background of enslavement in Angola, shipment to the Spanish Indies on a Portuguese vessel, and capture by English or Dutch privateers was not unique but in fact typical of the history of the entire first generation of Africans coming into the new colonies of the English and the Dutch. Heywood, for her part, was completing a study of the strongly Creole background of Angolans and the influence that this background had on the cultural connections among Portugal, Angola, and Brazil, which she subsequently followed up with a major conference on the Central African roots of American cultures in 1999, published by Cambridge University Press in 2001. We were also already jointly working as consultants for the African Burial Ground project in New York, where we were struck by the remarkably uniform and Angolan background of the first Africans to be enslaved in that early Dutch colony. Just as we began our project, we also became consultants to the Jamestown–Yorktown Foundation's new exhibition to commemorate the 400th anniversary of the founding of the first permanent English colony in North America and especially its African component. Because we were both involved in teaching courses on the history of the Atlantic and the African diaspora, we saw the potential for uniting these disparate insights into a single project.

The circumstances of our initial interest in the project led us to explore English and Dutch colonization and our work at Jamestown and New York had started us off. After we had engaged the project for some time we realized that French colonization probably followed the same lines, and, where relevant, a few references to French activities are included. However, filling out the picture for the French would require much more time than we were prepared to spend. We hope that others will take up this challenge and see the degree to which our preliminary guess is correct.

Acknowledgments

Our research has taken us to many archives and libraries; a first trip to England helped us locate materials on the English end of the colonization in the Public Record Office and British Library, and three more trips to English repositories extended this. However, one of the most important research collections that we visited was the Engel Sluiter collection at the Bancroft Library at the University of California at Berkeley. The Sluiter documents, collected from a wide range of archives in Spain, Portugal, and the Netherlands in particular, were almost entirely relevant to our study, and we spent literally hours on end doing nothing but transcribing or summarizing documents. No one should approach this topic without stopping at this collection, which has filmed copies of the original texts, transcriptions, and often (for Spanish and Portuguese documents) summaries and translations.

A long stop in Portugal allowed us to work jointly on the massive collection of documents at the National Library and the Archives of Torre do Tombo, as well as the Overseas Historical Archive. In 2002 we spent three weeks in Angola working in archives and visiting Mbanza Kongo and Massangano, historic locations that were important sites in the story we were telling. In 2004 we returned and went back to Massangano and also to N'dalatando, giving us a visual sense of the areas we were writing about. We conducted interviews on both trips in Portuguese, Kikongo, and Kimbundu. In 2004 we visited Rome and did research in the Vatican archives, as well as in the Archives of the Propaganda Fide. Other trips took us to Bermuda and Barbados, as well as local archives in Virginia, Pennsylvania, New York, Maryland, and Massachusetts. We spent many hours at the Library of Congress in Washington, DC, as did graduate students working with Heywood.

The professional staffs of a number of libraries and archives were of great assistance to us. In particular we thank the librarians and staff at Arquivo Nacional de Torre do Tombo, Arquivo Histórico Ultramarino, and Biblioteca Nacional de Lisboa in Lisbon; the Public Record Office, Scottish Record Office (who held their offices open for us one day), and the British Library in the United Kingdom; the National Archives of Bermuda; and the National Archives of Barbados. The staff of the Secret Archives and Library in the Vatican were helpful and provided us with important microfilmed documents. We are similarly glad for the help of the archivists of the Royal Archives and Library in Stockholm and the National Archives (formerly the General Royal Archives) in the Hague. We are grateful to Rosa Cruz e Silva for her friendship and support in our research trips and our work at the Arquivo Histórico Nacional de Angola, of which she is director. In the United States we thank the staffs of the Virginia State Library and the Pennsylvania Historical Society, where the Amandus Johnson Papers opened up the entire Swedish archives; the New England Historical Genealogical Society; the New-York Historical Society; the New York Public Library; and the New York State Archives, especially Charles Gehring, whose knowledge of the Dutch documentation was very helpful. We consulted materials in a variety of other libraries, such as those at Howard University, Millersville University, Columbia University, Boston University, and Harvard University.

A number of colleagues were very supportive of our project. Thomas Davidson of the Jamestown–Yorktown Foundation was always a good intellectual sounding board, as well as a fine companion during our trip to Angola in 2004. We owe a special thanks to Tim Hashaw for generously sharing his own detailed research on the first generation of Africans and their descendants in Virginia in the exchange of long and numerous e-mails about it. Emily Rose also provided us interesting discussion and leads for the early history of the Virginia Company. Karen Kuperman shared her resources generously and was also a good source of intellectual stimulation. M. K. Thornton was very helpful with Latin documents, providing us with a complete translation of Antonio Franco's valuable chronicle as well as some lesser ecclesiastical documents. Allison Blakely kindly supplied us with copies of documents he had acquired at the United Amsterdam Archive, as did Jelmer Vos. Wim Kooster provided us with references and discussions on our project at an early stage, Douglass Deal generously shared his own notes and transcriptions of Virginia documents with us, and John Coombs provided us with a copy of his doctoral dissertation on colonial Virginia.

We have benefited from the assistance of a number of research assistants. At Millersville University and at Howard we received help from Gregory Brechenko and Wanda Porter. Special thanks go to Andrea Mosterman, who helped to locate Dutch documents and provided assistance in transcribing them and at times in translation.

We received quite a bit of financial assistance for our travels and research. Howard University funded Heywood's travel to London, Bermuda, Barbados, Lisbon, and Luanda from 1998 to 2002, whereas Thornton received funds from Millersville University for travels to Lisbon and Luanda. Boston University provided funding for both of us to purchase microfilm and to travel to Rome in 2004 and to Florence in 2005. The National Park Service generously funded Thornton's share of travel to Berkeley, whereas the Jamestown–Yorktown Foundation assisted our travel to Luanda in 2004. The Mariner's Museum of Newport, Virginia, funded some of our travel to London and Lisbon, as did the Gilder Lehman Foundation of Yale University.

Introduction

The emergence of postcolonial, postmodern, and subaltern studies since the early 1980s has reshaped the way historians view the history of the Atlantic and the African diaspora. Although an older school focused on slavery and the attitudes of the European and Euro-American elites toward Africans, newer research has tried to recover the world of the slaves themselves, with a developing interest in culture and identity. Africans and their descendants are increasingly being considered in the same vein as working-class Europeans, indentured servants, and other migrants. Historians have also begun to reexamine the history of Native Americans as historical actors, with interesting internal social dynamic and a long engagement with European settlers. Although work has proceeded rapidly on European peasants, sailors, urban workers, and even the underclass or their American counterparts, Africa has yet to achieve similar coverage, even though a number of new works have recognized that Africans in the Americas can be subjected to the same sort of detailed research.

This work seeks to explore the specific origins of the Africans who formed part of the founding generation of English and Dutch America. Because most of them came from Central Africa, an area with a century-and-a-half-long history of intense interaction with Europe that was unique to this zone, their role as founders and creators of African American culture is enhanced.

Our approach addresses a number of shortfalls in the study of the relationship between Africa and the Americas. First, our study concentrates on a detailed examination of the history of a specific region in Africa over a limited period, including a careful examination of who was enslaved at what time. This helps to overcome the common assertion in American history that the exact background of Africans is either unimportant or cannot be ascertained. It is possible to know much more about the African military and the commercial, religious, cultural, and social background of slaves arriving in the Americas than just their port of embarkation or their alleged ethnic identity as revealed in ships' records or American bills of sale, inventories, or court records. Although these records provide a starting point from the American side, only a full and careful examination of a variety of sources dealing with the African side can present a complete understanding of who had been enslaved and their social and cultural background.

West Central Africa is richly documented by first-hand original eyewitness sources written both by Europeans and by Africans – in all several thousand pages of materials help to illuminate this region in the seventeenth century and allow a highly nuanced understanding of the intricacies of politics, commerce, and culture. The maps that illustrate Chapter 4 show the fruits of what close reading of these sources can do. What our investigation reveals is the degree to which Central Africans were bearers of an Atlantic Creole culture and the extent to which many of those who were actually enslaved, transported, and eventually integrated into the estates and homes of American colonists bore this culture. Their knowledge of European material culture, religion, language, and aesthetics made it easy for them to integrate into the colonial environment, especially in the fluid frontier situation that existed between the 1580s and 1660.

A second problem we addressed is to place the particular group of Africans in the larger setting of the Atlantic world. It is only through this sort of regional framework – by understanding the complexities of Spanish and Portuguese financial and colonial dealings, the struggles in the Low Countries, naval campaigns, and colonization that were a part of the war, religious dimensions of missionary work, and ideological contestations – that the status of Africans in this period can be appreciated. English and Dutch privateers carried their pirated captives to colonies from the sweltering Amazon basin to snowy New England and to a dozen islands and coastal enclaves in the Caribbean and South America. Here, too, a comparative and Atlantic approach allows us to see the wide variety of situations that African captives faced once they arrived in America.

A third problem is addressed by taking insights drawn from the larger framework and using them to explore the local situations of Africans. For the most part, the lives of the early Africans in English and Dutch colonies are poorly documented; the records are scattered and often uninformative. But using a wide lens and seeing a comparative focus, as well as centering the Central African background, makes possible a richer understanding of the world they lived in and helped to create. In addition, it reveals their strategic position at the moment when the developing English and Dutch slave trade brought thousands of West Africans, with very different cultural backgrounds to the same colonies. A new cultural dynamic would soon be in play.

Finally, we are able, using the knowledge gained from our focused study to reexamine the attitudes that Europeans developed in their dealings with Africans from this region. The set of circumstances that brought Central Africans to the Americas during the crucial period that slavery was emerging in the English and Dutch colonies also coincided with the publication of several detailed books about the region that revealed its Creole character. No other region of Africa was so well and so favorably described. This conjuncture had a profound influence on the origins of race relations in the American colonies of England and the Low Countries.

Atlantic Basin

Privateering, Colonial Expansion, and the African Presence in Early Anglo-Dutch Settlements

In the late rainy season of 1619, a woman named Angela began a new period of her life. Enslaved in one or another of the wars that gripped West Central Africa, she was taken to Luanda, the coastal capital of the Portuguese colony of Angola.[1] There, she and thousands of other war captives were lodged in squalid conditions in the courtyard of one of the many merchants' houses that sprawled along the narrow beach that separated the bay from rocky cliffs. From the courtyard one could see the residences of the Portuguese elite on the hills to the south, the governor's palace, and the Jesuits' church. Soon she and 350 of her fellow captives were rowed across the sound that separated Luanda's beach to the "island," a long, low spit of land that protected the harbor.[2] She was paraded before Portuguese officials at the Casa da Mina's counting house and noted for tax purposes and then loaded aboard the waiting frigate *São João Bautista*. Captain Manuel Mendes da Cunha was to guide his ship across the Atlantic to the Mexican port of Vera Cruz and sell its human cargo to eager Spanish merchants, who would use the newly arrived Angolans as personal servants, plantation workers, or perhaps porters.

Angela's name tells us that she was baptized and thus may have been spared the otherwise meaningless ministrations of priests who were

---

[1] John Thornton, "The African Experience of the '20. and Odd Negroes' Arriving in Virginia in 1619," *William and Mary Quarterly* 55 (1998): 421–34.

[2] This description of Luanda is taken from notes and maps in the Fernão de Sousa documents, c. 1626, Beatrix Heintze (ed.), *Fontes para a história de Angola do século XVII* (2 vols., Stuttgart, 1985–1988), 1: 172–84, including "Mapa da baía de Luanda," 12 October 1626, and "Planta da fortificação de Luanda," 12 October 1626, and maps photographically reproduced and transcribed.

required by law to baptize all slaves who were not already Christian before they boarded the waiting slave ships.[3] Christianity was already old in this region of Central Africa, and Angela may well have been among the 4,000 Christian porters who had been enslaved by rampaging mercenary soldiers in Portuguese service during the war Portugal was waging against the African kingdom of Ndongo – the Bishop of Angola would lodge a vain complaint against the affair in August.[4] Or she may have been captured in a civil war in the Christian kingdom of Kongo. The journey to America was a long one, and food supplies ran low. Water was in short supply and the number of deaths steadily mounted. Most of the miserable cargo, held below decks for long periods, were now sick. The *São João Bautista* stopped in Jamaica and sold off 24 younger children, took on supplies, and probably allowed its unwilling passengers a respite on land.[5]

A short time later, as they were passing Campeche on the coast of Yucatán, just a few days before their destination, sails were spotted. They were two English ships operating in consort, the *White Lion*, under Captain John Colyn Jope, a privateer carrying a letter of marque from Vlissingen (Flushing), Holland, and its companion, also a privateer, the *Treasurer*, under English Captain Daniel Elfrith, carrying its marque from the Duke of Savoy in Italy. Both had license to capture Spanish shipping and to take whatever they deemed valuable. The *White Lion* sent a pinnace with 25 men to board the *São João*, taking off some of its cargo of tallow and wax and 50–60 of the slaves, including Angela. They then released Captain da Cunha to deliver the remaining 122 people of his cargo at Vera Cruz.[6]

---

[3] The Catholic Church was seriously examining the question of the validity of these baptisms at the time, testimony that describes in detail the methods of the Church in Angola; see Alonso de Sandoval, *Natvraleza, Policia, Sagrada i Profana, costvmbres i ritos, disciplina i catechismo Evangelico de todos Etiopes* (Seville, 1627) mod. ed. Angel de Valtierra as *De Instauranda Aethiopum Salute: El mundo de la esclavitud negra en America* (Bogota, 1956), pp. 348–54.

[4] Bishop Manuel Bautista Soares, "Copia dos excessos que se cometem no gouerno de Angola que o bispo deu a V. Magestade pedindo remedio delles de presente, e de futuro," 7 September 1619, in António Brásio (ed.), *Monumenta Missionaria Africana* (1st series, 15 vols., Lisbon, 1952–1988), 6: 370.

[5] For details of the ship, and its itinerary up to its capture, Engel Sluiter, "New Light on the '20. and Odd Negroes' Arriving in Virginia, August, 1619," *William and Mary Quarterly* 3rd series, 54 (1997): 396–8.

[6] These two ships and the capture are described in Public Record Office (henceforward PRO), Records of the High Court of Admiralty (henceforward HCA) 1/48, Deposition of Richard Stafford of Staplehurst, Kent, 23 July 1620, summarized in Peter Coldham,

Angela was sent to the *Treasurer*, which took her under scarcely better conditions than she enjoyed on the *São João Bautista* northward to the new English colony of Virginia. Jope and the *White Lion* sailed ahead and delivered "twenty and odd Negroes" to Virginia toward the end of August. Those on the *São João Bautista* who were taken to Captain Jope's *White Lion* became the "twenty and odd Negroes" who are traditionally described as the founders of the African presence in English America. John Rolf described them as being brought to Virginia by a "Dutch Man of War" (Jope's marque from Flushing made them Dutch in his mind) that the "Governor General brought for victuals."

When the *Treasurer* arrived at Point Comfort four days later, Captain Elfrith discovered that the Duke of Savoy had made peace with Spain, thereby canceling his privateering marque. Samuel Argall, who had arranged for Elfrith's voyage, had been replaced as governor of Virginia by Edwin Sandys, who was at odds with Elfirth's master, the Earl of Warwick, and who also feared that the privateer would evoke the hostility of Spain and might lead to retaliation.[7] Concerned that he might now be charged as a pirate and hung, Elfrith quickly set sail for Bermuda, where Miles Kendall, the vice governor, was more favorable to privateers. Kendall gave Captain Elfrith grain and allowed him to land his Angolan cargo.[8]

Angela and 28 of her surviving companions were then seized by the governor, Samuel Butler, and unceremoniously lodged in the longhouse at St. Georges, a sort of jail. Some were sold off to various Bermudan colonists, whereas most of the rest were put to work on behalf of the Company.[9] In February 1620, Angela and about half a dozen other survivors of the *São João Bautista* were back in the *Treasurer*, a leaky, tired old ship that returned her to Virginia before overturning and sinking in

---

English Adventurers and Emigrants, 1609–1660 (London, 1984). Our thanks to Tim Hashaw and Michael Jarvis for this reference. Note that Maruice of Nassau began giving out letters of marque in early in 1619; see Archivio General de Simancas, Estado 1090, Archduke Alberto to King, 28 February 1619.

[7] Virginia Court Session, 31 May 1620 in Susan M. Kingsbury (ed.), *The Records of the Virginia Company of London* (4 vols., Washington, DC, 1906–1935), 1: 367.

[8] The *Treasurer*'s case is complex and became the subject of an extended lawsuit in England; Magdalene College, Oxford, Ferrar Papers, Doc. 403 Court of 19 January 1620 and 24 July 1624 (our thanks to Thomas Davidson for this reference).

[9] John Dutton to the Earl of Warwick 20 January 1619/1620, Vernon A. Ives, *The Rich Papers: Letters from Bermuda, 1615–46* (Toronto, Buffalo, London, 1984), pp. 141–2; PRO HCA 1/48, Testimony of Richard Stafford of Staplehurst, 3 June 1620, summarized in Coldham, p. 181. Dutton puts their number at 29, Stafford gives 25, we have favored the Dutton number as being closer in date to the events.

a creek off the James River.[10] Angela appeared on the 1625 muster list as one of four "servants" laboring on the estate of Captain William Pierce at "James Cittie," the main town of Virginia, helping to raise cattle and pigs and perhaps performing some personal services.[11]

Angela's experience was typical of many Central Africans arriving in the emerging Dutch and English settlements in the first decades of the seventeenth century. During the early years of the English and Dutch colonies, the Africans who formed part of the laboring class arrived largely as a result of piracy on the high seas, as the English and Dutch attempted to wrest the Atlantic commerce and territories in the Americas from Catholic Spain and Portugal. For the Protestant aggressors, successful settlement in their own colonies was achieved by taking land that Catholic Spain and Portugal had nominal and real claims to since the mid-sixteenth century and capturing Africans that merchants from these nations had acquired as slaves for their colonies.

Like Angela, the overwhelming majority of the Africans who are identified in the records, and who became the founding generation of Afro-American populations in the English- and Dutch-speaking world of the seventeenth century, came from West Central Africa. Whether they supported the privateering war against Spain or not, both English and Dutch colonists benefited from the African captives that privateers supplied.

---

[10] HCA 13/44, Testimony of John Wood of Wappington, Middlesex, summarized in Coldham, p. 13. The *Treasurer* was noted as being scarcely seaworthy in January 1620; Nathaniel Butler, *The Historye of the Bermudaes or Summer Islands* (ed. J. Henry Lefroy, London, 1882; reprint, New York: Burt Franklin, 1892 [Lefroy wrongly attributed the authorship of this work to John Smith]), pp. 157–8, and Dutton to Warwick, *Rich Papers*, p. 142; but Richard Staplehurst, a witness, said it departed nevertheless for Virginia in February before capsizing (Coldham, p. 181). Their number must not have been too many, for Jupe delivered "twenty and odd" slaves to Virginia in August, and a census of March 1620 reveals the presence of 32 Africans in the colony, William Thorndale, "The Virginia Census of 1619," *Virginia Genealogical Society* 33 (1995):168 (Thorndale argues that the census was conducted in 1619 but provides convincing evidence that it was made in 1620). Allowing for minimums, and no mortality, they could not have exceeded 12. In other testimony over the recovery of this cargo, one witness mentions that the number brought to Bermuda were divided by thirds, and Angela and her companions may have been among one of the thirds, thus being nine; Magdalene College, Oxford, Ferrar Papers, Doc. 403, Court of 24 June 1622.

[11] The census of 1625 gives details of the holdings of William Piercey in James Cittie, see PRO Colonial Office (CO) 1/3, fol. 24, published in Annie Lash Jester and Martha Woodruff Hiden (eds.), *Adventurers of Purse and Person: Virginia 1607–25* (Princeton, 1956), p. 29. It lists her name as "Angelo, a Negro Woman in the Treasurer." We have altered the name to make it feminine (we have examined the original text and found it correctly transcribed from an unambiguous original), expecting that Angela did not pronounce the final vowel of her name, a tendency found in both Portuguese and Kimbundu, and the scribe simply heard it as "Angelo."

Before the English and Dutch developed a regular slave trade with Africa, privateers preying on Portuguese shipping were their sole suppliers of African labor.

Early Portuguese Activities along the Atlantic African Coast

At the time of Angela's capture and export, the Portuguese were the only European power engaged in the Atlantic slave trade. The Portuguese not only supplied their own colonies of São Tomé and Brazil with African slaves but also had a de facto monopoly to supply the Spanish Indies with African captives. The Portuguese thus had 150 years of experience in developing the Atlantic slave trade.

Africans living on the coast of Senegal first encountered Portuguese mariners who visited their coast in 1444 as ruthless marauders who captured fishermen and coastal people and took them back to Europe to sell as slaves. The Portuguese arrived in the African waters armed for war after pioneering voyages solved the navigation problems that dogged earlier attempts. But the Senegalese coastal inhabitants who used shallow draft vessels outmaneuvered the sea-going ships in the waters of the coast and its estuaries. They fought the Portuguese with lance and sword, but it was their poisoned arrows, which neutralized Portuguese armor, that won the day and left Portuguese crews decimated.[12] In the face of defeat, during the 1450s and 1460s Portugal abandoned raiding and set up commercial relations with African rulers through formal diplomatic means. African rulers, who negotiated the nonaggression treaties with the Portuguese royal envoy Diogo Gomes, agreed to sell gold, other commodities, and some of the captives they had captured and enslaved in their own wars or had purchased from other rulers and merchants in exchange for European and North African merchandize.[13] Portugal cultivated diplomatic relations with the rulers of the whole coast, from Cukuli Mbooj of Great Jolof in Senegal to Nzinga Nkuwu in Kongo, and by the mid-sixteenth century Africans had come to expect European visitors interested in buying captives to follow local African law and customs and accept African authority.[14] Although Portuguese claimed monopoly over African trade,

---

[12] John Thornton, *Warfare in Atlantic Africa, 1500–1800* (London, 1998), pp. 44–51.

[13] Diogo Gomes, "De Inventione africae maritimae et occidentalis videlicet Genee per infantem Heinrichum Portugallie," in Brásio, *Monumenta* (2nd series, 5 vols., Lisbon, 1958–1985), 1: 214–15.

[14] John Thornton, *Africa and Africans in the Making of the Atlantic World, 1440–1800* (2nd edition, Cambridge, 1998), pp. 36–40; Elbl, "Cross-Cultural Trade," pp. 165–204.

the Africans had never accepted these claims and welcomed anyone willing to trade.

Portugal valued this trade in people and in African commodities like gold, ivory, and pepper enough to obtain a Papal Bull and even threatened to put sailors who visited the coast without a license in the sea.[15] This breakthrough allowed them to begin the purveying of African captives as slaves from the whole Atlantic coast of Africa, first to western Europe and then to island colonies off the African coast, to the Spanish colonies in the Americas, and finally to their own colony in Brazil.[16] As a result of commercial vigor, diplomatic tenacity, and navigational experience, the Portuguese had become the only European country to buy slaves routinely and deliver them to the Americas by the end of the sixteenth century.

English and Dutch Interlopers and Privateers on the African Coast

Portugal's claims were not unchallenged, and almost as soon as Portuguese sailors showed the way, their Iberian rivals, the Castilians, and other Europeans were visiting the African coast, though these visitors were more interested in commodities other than slaves. Castilian ships were visiting Africa as early as 1475, and it was through Castilian auspices that Dutch sailors, like Eustace de la Fosse, an Antwerp-based merchant whose ship sailing to the Gold Coast (modern Ghana) in 1479 was captured by the Portuguese while seeking gold, learned about the African trade.[17] Thus North Atlantic seafarers were sailing to Africa only a few years after the first Portuguese sailors came there, well before the founding of the first permanent Portuguese base in sub-Saharan Africa at São Jorge da Mina on the Gold Coast in 1482.

English merchants started later. An attempt to promote English trade to Africa, again under Spanish auspices, stalled by 1488[18] and only barely

We have identified Cukuli Mbooj as the ruler known to Alvise da Mota as Zucholino, following Jean Boulègue, *Le Grand Jolof (XIIIe-XVIe siècle)* (Paris, 1987), pp. 148–9.

[15] Thornton, *Africa and Africans*, pp. 21–42. Also see Ivana Elbl, "Cross-Cultural Trade and Diplomacy: Portuguese Relations with West Africa, 1441–1521," *Journal of World History* 3 (1992): 165–204.

[16] Maria da Graça Alves Mateus Ventura, *Negreiros Portugueses na rota das Índias de Castela (1541–1556)* (Lisbon, 1999).

[17] For details, see P. E. H. Hair, *The Founding of the Castelo de São Jorge da Mina: An Analysis of the Sources* (Madison, 1994), p. 2 and 50, no. 21. A good overview of early travel can be found in the older but still useful work of John W. Blake, *European Beginnings in West Africa, 1545–1578* (London, 1937, reprinted as *West Africa: Quest for God and Gold, 1454–1578* (London, 1971) and a large collection of documents in *Europeans in West Africa, 1450–1560* (2 vols., London, 1942).

[18] Kenneth R. Andrews, *Trade, Plunder and Settlement: Maritime Enterprise and the Genesis of the British Empire, 1480–1630* (Cambridge, 1984), p. 58.

began in the late 1530s.[19] Most English efforts in the Atlantic went through Spanish hands, because treaties allowed English merchants free access to Spanish territories, especially the Canary Islands, where they were already working by 1526. From there, English merchants were free to trade with other Spanish colonies or to defy Portuguese claims and deal with Africa and Brazil. William Hawkins, one of the earliest Englishmen to engage in the Canary trade, visited Brazil as early as the 1530s and 1540s,[20] and shortly thereafter the English began a number of voyages to the Gold Coast in violation of Portuguese claims to monopoly.

Africans who met these English adventurers on the Gold Coast sold them gold and not slaves. They welcomed them and the opportunity to break Portugal's monopoly, which drove down the prices for their gold. It was in this spirit that the people around Accra greeted Thomas Wyndham, an English pioneer in the Gold Coast trade in 1553, offering to allow the English to build a trading post and support them against the Portuguese.[21] Although these friendly relations kept up along the Gold Coast, elsewhere Englishmen would come to obtain slaves.

John Hawkins, son of the pioneering William Hawkins, is often probably correctly credited with being the first Englishman to bring Africans to the Americas as slaves, but he was more a pirate than a trader. John went beyond his father by not only ignoring Portuguese claims but also establishing a new pattern of illegal trade in Spanish America. Spanish settlers in the Caribbean islands were enjoying a boom in the production of sugar and needed slaves to work their estates, but the Spanish Crown imposed a monopoly on their import and regulated the flow of African workers. The island colonies were regarded as marginal and most of the slaves ended up in the richer colonies of Mexico and Peru, whereas the islanders paid high prices and received few slaves. Working through merchant contacts in the Canaries, Hawkins was assured that "Negroes were very good marchandise in Hispaniola, and that store of Negroes might easily bee had upon the coast of Guinea, resolved with himselfe to make triall thereof...."[22]

[19] Andrews, *Trade*, pp. 101–2.
[20] Andrews, *Trade*, pp. 59–60.
[21] Richard Hakluyt, *Principal Navigations, Voyages, Traffiques of the English* Nation, (London, 1589, 2nd expanded edition, 3 vols., London, 1599–1600, cited), vol. 2, part 2, pp. 10–13; see also P. E. H. Hair, *East of Mina: Afro-European Relations on the Gold Coast in the 1550s and 1560s* (Madison, 1988), for relations of the later voyages of Towerson, along with translations of relevant Portuguese documents.
[22] Kenneth R. Andrews, *Spanish Caribbean: Trade and Plunder, 1530–1630* (New Haven and London, 1978), pp. 110–12. The quotation is from Richard Hakluyt, *Principal Navigations* 3, p. 500.

The region of modern Sierra Leone that attracted Hawkins's interest was troubled in the 1550s – an invading group from the interior that claimed to be part of the forces loyal to a rebel princess in the Empire of Mali had attacked from somewhere along what would become the border of modern-day Liberia and Sierra Leone and were fighting their way northeast. Known as Manes, they recruited thousands of local people into their ranks as "Sumbas," who were noted for their brutality and, according to widespread rumor, were cannibals. These dreaded invaders conquered the disunited towns of the coast and established their own chain of states. In the process most of the region was involved in wars as conquests and rebellions marched together.[23] Where there was war, there were captives, and Spanish merchants in the Canaries knew of these wars. In the mid-sixteenth century they sent ships to Magarabomba on the coast to purchase captives and brought shiploads of unfortunate prisoners back to the Canaries to work in sugar mills.[24]

Knowing these facts Hawkins set sail for Sierra Leone in 1562 and was sufficiently successful that he followed this one with three more voyages lasting until 1568. Hawkins's activities in Sierra Leone show an evolution from ground piracy to sea piracy. Here Hawkins acquired his slaves in a variety of ways – sometimes he landed groups of armed men who captured or sought to capture the inhabitants, but more often he joined his own forces to those of Mane and other armies and assisted them in attacks. Finally, Hawkins also captured Portuguese ships carrying captives under contract to the Caribbean and took them. Once in the Caribbean, he sold the slaves and other African merchandize to Spanish settlers in Hispaniola or the coast of modern Colombia.[25]

Dutch merchants came into the Atlantic slave trade though a different route. In the sixteenth century, when Hawkins was sailing to the Canaries, Dutch traders from Antwerp were already deeply involved in the sugar trade of Brazil, thanks to the decision of Portugal to use the town as a center for redistribution of its Asian and Atlantic sugar and spices.[26]

[23] The story of these invasions is told in near contemporary English and Portuguese sources, as well as traditions among the descendants of these invaders in early Portuguese accounts. There are several attempts to match these to other known African events, this account follows the work of Paul E. H. Hair, presented in footnotes to his English translations of these sources.

[24] Manuel Lobo Cabrera, *La Esclavitud en Las Canarias Orientales en el siglo XVI: Negros, Moros y Moriscos* (Tenerife, 1982).

[25] Andrews, *Spanish Caribbean*, pp. 113–33.

[26] Hermann van der Wee, *The Growth of the Antwerp Market and the European Economy (14th-16th Centuries)* (3 vols., 1963), 2: 125–31.

Antwerp interests invested in Brazilian sugar and Dutch merchants like Erasmus Schetz and his descendants owned a number of estates in southern Brazil.[27] By 1600 this interest would grow so much that a large portion of the sugar trade from Brazil was carried in Dutch ships working through the empire.[28] Some of these merchants included Portuguese Jews, who were persecuted by the Inquisition and fled to the more liberal atmosphere of the Low Countries, especially Antwerp (and then, during the Dutch Revolution in the 1570s and 1580s, further relocated to Amsterdam). It was through these connections that the first Dutch became involved in the slave trade, not by raiding but by working through the Spanish Empire. Antwerp- and Amsterdam-based merchants, many of whom were Jews, held contracts to deliver slaves to the Spanish American empire and Brazil, which they did by the hundreds, if not the thousands. By the late sixteenth century, records of their transactions show up in Amsterdam archives[29]; a report of 1611 lists a dozen of the "most important" Jewish merchants, based in Portugal, Antwerp, Amsterdam, Porto, and Brazil, who were visiting the coast of Angola, from which came "many trading ships with ivory and slaves which they carry to Brazil and [the] Indies, and from there they carry much money in reals."[30]

English and, later, Dutch successes in obtaining slaves for their colonies in the early part of the seventeenth century were due in large part to the dramatic change and transformation that English and Dutch activities in the Atlantic underwent in the late sixteenth century, leading to more emphasis on the piratical elements of Hawkins's voyages and less on the commercial side. The causes of this transformation were connected primarily to new political configurations in Hapsburg Spain and reactions to it in northern Europe. Beginning in the late 1560s, Philip II of Spain attempted to tighten Spanish control and impose Catholic orthodoxy over the Low Countries, which his father had inherited from the Dukes of Burgundy as part of the Hapsburg family's domains earlier in the century.

[27] José Gonçalves Salvador, *Os Cristãos-Novos e o comérico no Atlântico Meridional* (São Paulo, 1978), pp. 42–57.

[28] Engel Sluiter, "Dutch Maritime Power and the Colonial Status Quo, 1585–1641," *Pacific Historical Review* 11 (1942): 29–42.

[29] Ernst van den Boogart and Pieter C. Emmer, "The Dutch Participation in the Atlantic Slave Trade, 1596–1650," in Henry Gemery and Jan Hogendorn (eds.), *The Uncommon Market Essays in the Economic History of the Atlantic Slave Trade* (New York, San Francisco, and London, 1979), pp. 355–75, the reference to the early voyage comes from the Amsterdam Notarial Archives for a trip to São Tomé in 1596, p. 354.

[30] Dom Pedro de Castilho, "Avisos para o Conselho de Estado," 9 November 1611, Brásio, *Monumenta* 6: 47.

His efforts violated local customs and privileges and eventually led to open rebellion so that in 1581, six northern territories declared their independence and established the nucleus of the Dutch Republic amid war and civil strife. In 1585, the States General of this unsteady new country invited England to send it a governor, and Queen Elizabeth I agreed to do so. England was now fully engaged in a war against Spain, most dramatically manifested by the dispatch of the Spanish Armada in an attempted sea attack on England in 1588.

The struggle over the Low Countries was waged on sea as well as land, but both England and the Dutch Republic lacked funds for state-sponsored navies of any size. Private groups, not all of them with savory reputations, took up the cause of naval warfare. The English and Dutch were not pioneers in this type of private naval pillage; Protestant French privateers in the 1560s had been active in the Americas during the Franco-Spanish wars, though the end of war had put a stop to the official privateering.[31] Nevertheless, French Protestant ports like La Rochelle continued to harbor seamen who wanted to take on the Spanish, with or without official recognition. The "Sea Beggars," among the earliest partisans of Dutch independence, made frequent raids against Spanish shipping in the English Channel and the coasts of Europe and were already raiding in the Caribbean in 1569. A Spanish report of 1571 warned that Prince William of Orange, the rebel leader, was mustering 18 ships to join a large French force at La Rochelle for a major attack on the Caribbean and aimed at taking Santo Domingo and Cuba, though this did not come to pass. The Sea Beggars attached to this fleet were said to have 100 cannons borrowed from the Tower of London.[32]

Although Elizabeth I was reluctant to promote this sort of large-scale venture officially, she was prepared to overlook efforts by private Englishmen to attack the Spanish. John Hawkins, with his experience in African and Caribbean navigation and a history of anti-Spanish violence, became a promoter of private English raiding by the "Sea Dogs." His protégé, Francis Drake, raided Spanish ports and shipping in the Panama

---

[31] Charles de la Roncière, *Histoire de la Marine Française* (6 vols., Paris, 1909–1932), vol. 3.

[32] Archivio General de Simancas, Estado 824, fol. 172 Emformasão de viaje que faz o Comde Llodovico, irmão do Prince d'Orange, e mais comfederado com armada que faze na Rochella e outras partes, c. 14 February 1571, in Kervuy de Lettenhove (ed.), *Relations politiques des Pays-Bas et de l'Angleterre, sous le rege de Philippe II* (vol. 6, Brussels, 1888), pp. 92–3; Museu Naval, (Madrid) Coleccion de MSS Navarete, MS 480, vol. 25, fol. 114.

region in the 1570s. Although Drake's operations were the best known, at least 14 other privateering voyages were sent out, half of them supported by Hawkins.[33] When the Spanish "arrested" English shipping in Cadiz in 1585 in response to the war, English merchants clamored for the right to obtain reprisals from Spain, and Elizabeth began issuing letters of marque to allow them to attack Spanish shipping on the high seas. The aggrieved merchants soon joined the "Sea Dogs" seeking reprisals, along with pirates looking for legitimacy, adventurers, patriots, and fanatics.[34]

Privateering wars, whether by the French pioneers, or the English and Dutch, took on a definite pattern, which defined how the Protestant powers would eventually establish a presence in the Americas. Although the economic side of these ventures allowed that any cargo of value would be seized, the privateering war would establish precedents for the use of African slaves as workers in colonies the Dutch and English would establish in the Americas. One aspect of privateering entailed the capture of African captives and other commodities from Portuguese slave ships, which became fair game after 1580, when the Spanish and Portuguese Crowns were united. When the English and Dutch established colonies, the captives from the privateering wars would be among some of the early colonists.

The privateers began by seizing any Spanish shipping they could to injure Spain and recompense aggrieved merchants who financed the effort. Beyond inflicting damage, however, naval thinkers hoped, as French leaders in the 1560s had before them, to capture the Spanish silver fleet, which carried the recently discovered wealth of Mexico and Peru to Europe.[35] This silver was vital to war; nearly 40 percent of all the Spanish expenditures of this revenue went to Flanders, and as the war heated up, another 20 percent or so was spent in defense of Spain's coasts and in the Atlantic.[36] English and Dutch strategists realized that the flow of silver was vital to Spain's war in far-away Flanders, and the fleet provided both a strategic and commercial prize of inestimable value. Whatever its significance

---

[33] Kenneth R. Andrews, *The Spanish Caribbean: Trade and Plunder, 1530–1630* (New Haven and London, 1978), pp. 134–46.

[34] Kenneth R. Andrews, *Elizabethan Privateering: English Privateering during the Spanish War, 1585–1603* (Cambridge, 1966), pp. 3–52.

[35] Andrews, *Spanish Caribbean*, pp. 84–87; 128–30; 134–50.

[36] See graph in Ferndand Braudel, in Sîan Reynolds (trans.), *The Mediterranean and the Mediterranean World in the Age of Philip II* (2 vols., New York, 1972 [1966]), 1: 476–82, and chart, p. 477.

neither country was in a position to attempt anything quite so difficult in the late sixteenth century as to capture the silver fleet.

With this background of official support, in 1585 fairly large-scale privateering began and continued unabated until both England (in 1604) and the Netherlands (in 1606) signed truces with Spain, though smaller scale privateering continued. Between 1585 and the signing of the truces, English and Dutch privateers made war in any way they could against any Spanish targets that they could. They captured ships and took their cargos, and they landed troops and looted cities, often in cooperation with communities of former slaves, called *cimarones*, who had fled their Spanish masters and lived in remote areas. Dutch planners, like their French predecessors, discussed taking the silver fleet.[37] Drake's famous attacks on Panama had been made with the help of *cimarones* although the Spanish had all but eliminated them in the 1580s.[38] But the idea of seeking the help of runaways was not forgotten, for later English and French privateers operating in the West Indies also made regular contacts with runaways on those islands, sometimes even selling them slaves. The cooperation was sufficiently close that the Spanish governor of Jamaica in 1595 was concerned that the slave population would rise up if the English attacked the island.[39] In the pearl fisheries along the north coast of South America, especially at the island of Margarita (off Venezuela), English privateers would capture the slaves who fished for pearls and then ransom them back to their masters. In 1593, a fleet of four English galleons captured slaves at Toro, in Venezuela, and resold them to their former masters,[40] a feat that was more or less repeated by Francis Drake at the Venezuelan ports of La Hacha and Cumaná in 1595.[41] In fact, in 1600, a Spanish soldier in Margarita boasted of having rescued slaves from capture by privateers.[42]

The capture and resale of Africans taken from Portuguese slave ships formed one of the routes to recompense damages and fit the older pattern that Hawkins had established of selling slaves illicitly in Spanish colonies.

---

[37] Resolution of the States General, 27 June 1606, in *Resolutië*, 13: 552; see also discussion on 4 July, p. 557.

[38] Andrews, *Spanish Caribbean*, pp. 136–45.

[39] Archivio General de Indias (Seville) (henceforward AGI), Santo Domingo (henceforward SD) 51, Lope de Vega Portocarrero to King, 20 May 1595.

[40] British Library (BL) Additional MSS (Add MSS) 36316, fol. 75v, Testimony on Dutch, 13 September 1593–23 Feb 1594.

[41] "Hakluyt, *Principal Navigations* 3, pp. 585–86; BL Add MSS 36 317, Roque de Montes treasurer of Cumana to King, 30 December 1597.

[42] AGI SD 185, Service Record of Pedro Diaz de Orrego, Sgt Maj Margarita, of events over past 20 years, 16 May 1600.

However, unlike Hawkins, the privateers of the late sixteenth century captured their slaves on the high seas and near the coast but did not land troops on the African coast. After 1560, in fact, all the African captives taken from Portuguese vessels and sold by Englishmen were taken at sea. In 1565, a Portuguese renegade, Bartolomeu Bayão, serving as captain of an English ship, captured a slave ship with 125 people near Cape Verde, perhaps expecting to take them to the Spanish Indies.[43] But the Indies were not the only destination, for in 1594 the English ship *Red Lion* captured a Lisbon-bound Portuguese ship, the *São João Bautista*, from São Tomé that carried some 60 slaves as well as a cargo of sugar. The *Red Lion* subsequently delivered 24 of the slaves to Venice and sold them there.[44]

Although English trade expanded in Africa in this period, it did not involve trading in slaves. The late-sixteenth-century Guinea traders, such as Anthony Dassel, who developed trade with Senegal in the 1590s, although not averse to seizing ships bearing slaves on the high seas, did not seek to develop a slave trade with African rulers, even as they negotiated for other commodities.[45] Richard Jobson's visit to the Gambia in 1620–1621 revealed this attitude toward the purchase of slaves in Africa, as opposed to the seizure of those already enslaved on Portuguese vessels. Jobson's trip was to consider possibilities for trade, and when a Mandinka merchant offered him slaves, he refused, saying "we were a people who did not deale in such commodities, neither did wee buy or sell one another, or any that had our owne shapes."[46] His statement made sense only when applied to purchases in Africa, for long before he wrote, Englishmen were willing to capture slave ships and sell their cargos to anyone who might buy.

Privateering in the Americas

By the 1590s English privateers shifted these operations more to the American side, where the opportunities to capture ships passing through the well-known and limited shipping corridors were increased. As a result, the origins of the African slaves were much more widespread than in earlier phases. Ships from Angola or from the Gulf of Guinea joined those of Sierra Leone or Senegal and Cape Verde among the prizes. American

[43] Kenneth R. Andrews, "Thomas Fenner and the Guinea Trade, 1564," *Mariner's Mirror* 38 (1952): 312–14.

[44] PRO HCA 13/31, 23 January 1594.

[45] Andrews, *Trade, Plunder and Settlement*, pp. 112–13.

[46] R. Jobson, *The Golden Trade* (London, 1623).

side operations had the additional advantage of placing captures near prospective markets, either in the Spanish Indies, other established points or eventually the emerging colonies of the English and Dutch. Christopher Newport, sailing in the *Golden Dragon*, did exactly this in 1591, when he captured "a Portugall ship of Lisbone of 300 tuns which came from Guinie, and was bound for Cartagena, wherein were 300. Negros young and olde" near Dominica in the West Indies. This cargo was taken to Puerto Rico, along with the Portuguese ship's captain, "for that he hoped to helpe us into some money for his Negros there." Although the plan did not work exactly as designed, Newport did sell the entire cargo on the western end of the island.[47] English privateers, like Thomas Cavendish, operating off the coast of Brazil in 1591, captured slave ships ferrying people from one end of the colony to the other, taking their slaves and probably smuggling them to people in other parts of the coast.[48]

French and English smuggling of this sort was common, a complaint to the Spanish official from Hispaniola in 1594 attested to two years of smuggling that had delivered a total of 359 slaves illegally to various residents.[49] In 1595, English privateers robbed the Spanish ship *La Concepción* of a variety of goods, including slaves.[50] When Anthony Shirley's small fleet of seven vessels reached Jamaica in 1597 after a number of pillaging exploits, it had five prizes already, one of which included a cargo of slaves, destined to sell anywhere that smuggling could be done.[51] Cuban officials complained in the same year about the persistent habit that people on the coast of that island had of dealing with French, Dutch, and English privateers and selling them slaves.[52] The trading continued, however, as in 1598 English privateers captured two other cargos of slaves, though exactly where they sold their cargoes is unknown.[53] In 1600 the *Phoenix* captured a prize of 130 slaves traveling from Guiana to Cartagena, off

---

[47] "A true report of a voyage undertaken for the West Indies by M. Christopher Newport...the Golden Dragon, Admirall, Prudence, and Margaret, and the pinnace Virgin, 12 February 1591," in Hakluyt, *Principal Navigations* 3, p. 567.

[48] Gonçalves Salvador, *Cristãos Novos*, p. 66, citing testimony in the Livro de Denuncias de Bahia, 1591, p. 195. The brief account of this voyage, "The Last Voyage of Thomas Candish intended for the South Sea..." in Hakluyt, *Principal Navigations*, 3, 842 mentions taking one ship with slaves, but fails to explain what happened to them.

[49] AGI SD 51, Miguel Aleman de Ayalá to Crown, 23 September 1594, fols. 2–2v.

[50] AGI Contaduria 1055, entry of 7 July 1595 and 23 June 1597.

[51] AGI SD 177, Fernando de Milgarejo to King, Jamaica, 15 August 1597, fol. 33.

[52] AGI SD 155, "Sobre rrescates y rresistencias que ynbia el Lic do Barela juez, 10 September 1597.

[53] Andrews, *Elizabethean*, Appendix, p. 269; Kenneth. R. Andrews, "English Voyages to the Caribbean, 1596–1604: An Annotated List," *William and Mary Quarterly* 31 (1974): 250.

Barbados, and then sold them for 60 ounces of pearls in the island of Margarita.[54] In 1601 Captain William Parker, after ransoming Margarita for 500 pounds of pearls, captured 370 slaves from a ship from Angola bound for Cartagena and sold them in Panama.[55]

The activities of Dutch privateers are less well documented in this earlier period, though they came to be important. What documentation does exist suggests that they fell immediately into the same patterns as those of the English and French pioneers. They seized prizes of all sorts, and when they managed to take slave ships they followed the lead of their allies. A privateering vessel brought 130 captives to Zeeland in 1596, and when local dignitaries found them to be Christian (perhaps because they had an Angolan connection) they ordered them freed.[56] Because one of these Zeelanders, Pieter van der Hagen, wanted to use the Portuguese pilots captured in the same vessel to guide a voyage to the West Indies, it seems likely that they were taken from Portuguese ships carrying slaves to the Americas.[57] It would be a powerful argument in favor of taking captives to the Caribbean instead of Europe. On 27 July 1606, the *Roode Hart*, of Doderecht, captured a Lübeck ship, in Portuguese service, carrying sugar, ivory, cotton, and 90 slaves. It subsequently sold the slaves to an English vessel that probably took them across to America.[58] Again, in 1606, a Jewish captain of Portuguese origin who had once lived in Angola, but now served as a privateer with a Dutch marque, captured ships near Angola, including some Jesuit priests.[59] Furthermore, Dutch ships provided some 500 slaves to Spanish planters in Trinidad in 1605, taken from a slave ship from Angola.[60]

---

[54] Andrews, "English Voyages," p. 248.

[55] Purchas, *Pilgrimmes* xvi, p. 293.

[56] As stated in the resolution of the States of Zeeland, 15 November 1596, quoted in J. H. de Stoppelaar, *Balthasar de Moucheron: Een bladzijde uit de Nederlandsche Handelgeschiedenis tijdens den Tachtigjarigen Oorlog* (The Hague, 1901), pp. 61–2.

[57] Resolution of the States General, 23 November 1596, in N. Japikse (ed.), *Resolutiën der Staten-General van 1576 tot 1609* [and continuing] (15 vols., The Hague, 1915–) 9: 333; L. C. Vrijman, *Slavenhalers en Slavenhandel* (Amsterdam, 1943), p. 16.

[58] "Journael van mijn voyagen gedaen naer Capbe Verde, van daer naer Guinea . . . begonnen de eerste mael in de Maendt November in den Jaere 1605," in Klaas Ratelband (ed.), *Reizen naar West-Afrika van Pieter van den Broecke, 1605–1614* (The Hague, 1950), entry of 27 July 1606. Entry dates are cited in the English translation, in J. D. La Fleur (ed. and trans.), *Pieter van den Broecke's Journal of Voyages to Cape Verde, Guinea and Angola 1605–12* (London, 2000).

[59] Fr. Francisco de Góis to Antonio Mascarenhas, 10 July 1606, Brásio, *Monumenta* 5: 191–5, from Fernão Guerreiro, *Relação Anual*, a similar letter is printed, from ARSI *Lus* 79, fol. 65–68bis in *MMA* 5: 203–12.

[60] British Library (henceforward BL), Sloane MSS 3662, John Scott, Untitled manuscript collection, fol. 45. This section published in Vincent Harlow, *Colonising Expeditions*

Privateering, Colonies, and African Slavery

The English and Dutch Protestants did not confine themselves merely to privateering but soon turned their attention to establishing colonies. The naval war in the distant Caribbean could be made easier by taking and holding American bases in the form of colonies, and these would be more likely to be self-sustaining if they had agricultural settlements to sustain them. It was in this context that African slaves became part of the first settlers in the earliest Protestant colonies.

The French were the first Protestant power to attempt to build colonies in the Americas. Gaspard de Coligny, Admiral of France, saw colonies as important bases for French interests and privateering and sent men to found "Antarctic France" in the Rio de Janeiro region, which lasted from 1556 to 1566,[61] and created another short-lived colony in "Florida," first at Santa Elena Island in modern South Carolina in 1562–1563 and then in the area of Jacksonville, Florida, in 1564–1565.[62]

The English would follow suit as they joined the war. In 1578, Queen Elizabeth I issued a license to Humphrey Gilbert to found a colony in America, specifically in areas "not actually possessed of any Christian prince or people."[63] This in fact meant North America, away from Spanish power and the war, and was conceived primarily to control fishing rights to the northern regions. Gilbert's expedition managed to capture a vessel along the way in its voyage of 1583 but founded no permanent colony.[64] Walter Raleigh, who took over the patent from Gilbert, used it to found a colony at Roanoke, on the North Carolina coast, in 1585.[65] Raleigh's fleet, under the command of Richard Grenville, attacked Spanish ships and pillaged goods in Puerto Rico and Hispaniola, while en route to "Virginia," showing clearly the connection between the sea war and colonization.[66] The Spanish, for their part, recognized this settlement as

---

to the *West Indies and Guiana, 1623–67* (Hakluyt Society, 2nd series, no. 56, London, 1925), p. 125; on the origins of these slaves, see Cornelis Goslinga, *The Dutch in the Caribbean and on the Wild Coast, 1580–1680* (Gainesville, 1971), p. 341.

[61] For an overview of French activities in Brazil, see John Hemming, *Red Gold: The Conquest of the Brazilian Indians, 1500–1760* (Cambridge, MA, 1978), pp. 119–38. French also frequently left merchants and sailors to live among the Native people, a second form of colonization.

[62] Eugene Lyon, *The Enterprise of Florida: Pedro Menéndez de Avilés and the Spanish Conquest of 1565–68* (Gainesville, 1976), pp. 19–70.

[63] Hakluyt, "Sir Humphrey Gilberts Letters Patent," *Principal Navigations* 3, p. 135.

[64] Hakluyt, *Principal Navigations* 3, 246–51.

[65] Ivor Noël Hume, *The Virginia Adventure: Ronoake to Jamestown, an Archaeological and Historical Odyssey* (Charlottesville, 1994), pp. 20–53.

[66] Hakluyt, *Principal Navigations* 3, pp. 251–53.

a privateering base, observing that "this settlement and fort of theirs at Jacan [the Spanish name of Roanoke], directly west of Bermuda...from which position they can readily attack the fleet at any season."[67]

Dutch plans during the war were similar to those of the other Protestants, if not more ambitious. Already in 1600 the Dutch were thinking about establishing a colony in Brazil to carry war there, using Native Americans trained in European techniques to attack. An attempt to create such a colony by Pieter van Caerden in 1603 quickly failed, as did a more ambitious attempt by his brother Paulus to capture Pernambuco in 1606.[68] If carrying the war directly into Brazil might fail, in 1603 Zeelanders did build two forts, Fort Nassau and Fort Orange, on the eastern side of the Xingu River, which probably were also linked to eventual settlement and certainly with local trade.

Roanoke was the first place that plans for employing African slaves captured by privateers would be attempted by the English. Francis Drake used it as a stopping point on his large-scale raid on the Caribbean the same year, at the same time also bringing 250 captured African slaves to create an agricultural work force. But the new colony could not yet either supply Drake or absorb the slaves, and so Drake carried the whole group, including the settlers, back to England.[69]

The importance of buttressing the more permanent agriculturally based colonies with the labor of slaves was clear. The Dutch made no attempt to settle in North America at this time and concentrated their initial efforts on the "Wild Coast" – the Amazon and Guianas. Dutch merchants began visiting the region in 1595 and in 1596 founded a short-lived colony at Essequibo.[70] The English followed suit; in 1605 Charles Leigh left some 35 people as a colony at Wiapoco at the mouth of the Amazon, which was promptly supplied with African slaves by a Dutch ship under the command of Isaac Duverne.[71] The same year, Walter Raleigh founded another colony, this time in Trinidad, and like his counterpart on the Amazon, benefited from the arrival of 470 "men and women Negroes" carried by Duverne.[72] These multitudes of Africans had to come from

---

[67] Diego Fernández Quiñones to the Crown, September, 1586, in Irene A. Wright (ed. and trans.), *Further English Voyages to Spanish America, 1585–94* (London, 1949), p. 204.

[68] Goslinga, *Dutch in Caribbean*, p. 53.

[69] David B. Quinn, "Turks, Moors, Blacks and Others in Drake's West Indian Voyage," *Terrae Incognitae* 14 (1982): 93–100.

[70] Goslinga, *Dutch in the Caribbean*, p. 58.

[71] "The Relation of Master Iohn Wilson...from Wiapoco in Guiana 1606," in Samuel Purchas, *Purchas His Pilgrimmes* (London, 1625), vol. 4, chapter 14, p. 1262.

[72] BL, Sloane MSS 3662, Scott, fol. 45 in Harlow, *Colonizing Expeditions*, p. 125.

recently taken prizes, surely not from any African trading connections, for Duverne was admiral of a privateering fleet that fought the Spanish off Cuba late in 1605.[73] Neither of these colonies flourished in spite of their demographic strength, for in the end, Spanish efforts, in alliance with Carib and Arawak inhabitants, destroyed them both. But a pattern of creating colonies and supplying them with African labor taken from prizes of slave ships was already established for the English and Dutch.

Privateering, Commerce, and Colonies

Merchants from the Low Countries and England followed the routes opened by the privateers and looked to establish commercial colonies. Like the privateering fleets, colonies needed to be self-supporting, and if possible even profitable, so that merchants would finance them. Merchants were not necessarily interested in the fruits of attacking shipping but were interested in the new products that came from the tropical Atlantic world, like salt, sugar, sasparilla, and especially tobacco. They had purchased these products from Spanish markets before the Spanish stopped the commerce, and they had dealt with them during the days of the early trade in Spanish territory, now they might have to go to the New World or Africa and acquire them themselves.

The privateers opened up knowledge about the Caribbean that was exploited by private merchants, who began visiting the Caribbean in fairly large numbers at the end of the sixteenth century. The Dutch, for example, began sending ships to the Caribbean to engage in the pearl, hide, salt, and tobacco trade with Spanish settlers, especially in the islands of the eastern Caribbean and the mainland of modern-day Venezuela as well as the "Wild Coast" of South America.[74] Dutch smugglers were active in the trade of hides even in the well-defended islands of the Greater Antilles, as

---

[73] Engel Sluiter, "Dutch Spanish Rivalry in the Caribbean Area, 1594–1609," *Hispanic American Historical Review* 27 (1948): 190.

[74] The best source for these voyages are the contract documents found in the Gemeent Archief Amsterdam (henceforward GAA) Notary Archives (NA). However, they give few details of intentions or routes, and even of destination, for example, in 1610 among others there are, GAA NA no. 196, fol. 276v (a voyage to the West Indies for salt) 16 January 1610; no. 119, fol. 68 (the *Griffoen* to the West Indies), 16 April 1610; no. 119, fol. 114 (the *Halve Maen* for the West Indies), 3 May 1610; no. 196, fol. 517 (the *De Jonge Tobias* to the West Indies), 12 July 1610; no. 120, fol. 90–90v (a voyage for the West Indies "and other nearby places"), 26 July 1610; no. 122, fol. 58 (the *De Brouwerije* to the West Indies), 12 October 1610; no. 196 (the *St Jacob* to Saint X.toffel de la Havana in the West Indies), 16 December 1610.

numerous Spanish complaints show. Engel Sluiter estimated that by 1600 some 120 Dutch ships a year visited the southern Caribbean to trade in salt or, at times, to simply extract it from the islands of the coast of Venezuela.[75]

In 1602 English merchants followed the Dutch salt hulks and tobacco dealers to the southern regions of the West Indies and the hide trade to the larger islands, even though King James I's prohibition of privateering in 1604 and the end of the war in 1605 made them defenseless, and the Spanish executed even merchants as pirates.[76] Thomas Curry, one of these merchants who operated in Trinidad for the tobacco trade from 1609 to 1611, when captured by the Spanish gave detailed testimony on his activities, as was probably typical of many others. He clearly operated in collusion with Spanish settlers in all his dealings, and his dossier contained many letters from these settlers.[77]

At the same time, English merchants began looking to North America for commercial openings. The possibility of trade in sassafras, for example, led to voyages to New England in 1603, and soon a fur trade with Native American suppliers, managed though coastal factories was in operation. Temporary settlements were founded, like the one on the Kennebec River in Maine in 1602 – a follow-up expedition in 1606 was captured by the Spanish in spite of the peace accords, its commercial intentions, and its northern destination. The Virginia Company's colony at Jamestown in 1607 was the first colony of this period in North America to be successful, rapidly followed by the Company's second colony in Bermuda (1609). Meanwhile, Dutch visitors to North America also engaged in commercial ventures, focusing on the New York area after Henry Hudson's voyages in 1609. In 1614 they established their first colony, far up the Hudson River at Fort Orange, later to become Albany. As trading around the mouth of the Hudson became more developed, the Dutch began to consider colonies, in 1620 discussing the possibility of sending the group of English Puritans settled in Leiden, who were, in the words of the debate, "well versed in the Dutch language" to New Netherland,[78] even proffering a warship to protect them as they lay between English and French colonies[79] – although in the end they went to Plymouth under English auspices.

---

[75] Goslinga, *Dutch in the Caribbean*, pp. 54–5.
[76] Andrews, *Trade, Plunder and Settlement*, pp. 284–7.
[77] AGI SD 54, fols. 6v-46, Inquiry into activities of Thomas Curry, 11 July 1611.
[78] Algemeen Rijksarchief (ARA) Staten General Resolution (St. Gen. Resol.), 62, 12 February 1620.
[79] ARA St. Gen. Verlog, 62, 27 February 1620.

Commercial settlements in the West Indies in this period were less successful, because they were closer to Spanish positions and the Spanish continued to treat the English and Dutch as military threats and the traders as pirates. Dutch and French traders captured in Jamaica trading illegally were garotted in 1608, for example.[80] Similar Spanish reports from Jamaica still called these traders from England, France, and Holland "corsairs,"[81] and 30 English traders were hung in Trinidad and the Guianas in 1608, with more expected for the next year.[82] Indeed, in 1611, John Digbe, the English ambassador to Spain, reported that the Spanish had altered their policy dealing with smugglers from one of sending them to Spain to trial to one of immediately trying and hanging them in the Caribbean.[83] In was in this context that Caribs, operating in collusion with Spanish, wiped out the earlier attempts to found colonies on the "Wild Coast" and Trinidad in 1605 and 1606.

If the Protestant merchants escaped hanging by the Spanish, they might still meet a worse fate at the hands of the Native American inhabitants of the Caribbean. An attempt by Bristol merchants to found a colony on Grenada in 1609 was destroyed by Caribs the next year.[84] In 1609, Robert Harcourt sought to develop another colony at Wiapoco to replace the failed 1604–1605 colony, which was initially designed to promote trade with Native people rather than direct production, but the colony seems to have failed by 1611. The 280 Zeelanders who landed there were driven out by Caribs in 1615, but another Zeeland attempt was underway the following year. When this colony became troubled Aret Andrianszoon Groenewegen, a Dutch Catholic from Delft who had served in the Spanish forces in Flanders and was then Spanish factor in their small settlement at San Tomé (on the Orinico), decided to help the failing colony in 1616. Under his leadership this colony became the first permanent Dutch colony in the Guiana region.[85]

Although many of these earlier attempts at establishing colonies were short-lived because of Spanish hostility, and Native American raids, the

[80] AGI SD 53, Geronimo Gomez de Sandoval to King, S Domingo, 23 April 1609.
[81] AGI SD 177, Jamaica, letter 25 June 1608, fol. 32.
[82] AGI SD 100, Pedro Suarez Coronel, Gov of La Margita to King, 2 September 1609.
[83] PRO State Papers (henceforward SP) 94/18 (Spain), John Digbe to Government in London, 23 December 1611. The governor of Cuba noted that he planned to hang all English, "in accordance with Your Majesty instructions" that he caught trading in the area, AGI SD 100, Gaspar Ruiz de Pereda to King, 18 December 1612, fol. 2.
[84] BL Sloane MSS 3662, fol. 53v-52, John Scott (in this section the foliation proceeds backwards), 53.
[85] BL Sloane MSS 3662, fol. 40, Scott, in Harlow, *Colonizing Expeditions*, p. 139. For more biographical information on him, see Goslinga, *Dutch in the Caribbean*, pp. 79–81.

general pattern was clear. Merchants from northern European countries were intent on acquiring American commodities either by trade with the native inhabitants or Spanish settlers or having their own settlers produce them. These colonies, although they were commercially established, would play a strategic role when war with Spain resumed.

Given the consistent Spanish resistance to any attempts by northern Europeans to trade or settle in the Americas, both colonies and shippers had necessarily to take military precautions. These precautions effectively continued the role of privateering even in peacetime. It is not surprising that English and Dutch ships did not desist entirely from piracy, becuase their crews might be hung, with or without a letter of marque. Dutch authorities in fact began issuing defensive letters of marque for salt boats and traders allowing them to engage in hostilities if attacked in 1611.[86] The Rotterdam Admiralty seized goods of the Dutch *Vergulden Craen* on accusation that it appeared he had been engaging in piracy during his West Indian voyage in 1609–1610.[87] English corsairs also returned to more piratical ways; in 1610 one managed to capture a slave ship and delivered its cargo to Cuba as they might have during the war.[88] Likewise, a French pirate took at least 10 prizes in a cruising voyage of 1612, including at least some with slaves, which he landed off Cuba for sale to settlers.[89] The next year another French pirate captured an additional slave ship from Guinea with 208 slaves, which were delivered to Spanish colonists in central America.[90]

The English

The creation of a few successful Dutch and English colonies in North America, Bermuda, and the Wild Coast during the period of commerce would change the way in which privateers operated when war once again broke out. Now, it was possible to sell slaves captured on the high seas to these fledgling colonies rather than take the considerable risks of selling them as contraband to Spanish colonies in the Caribbean or South America. This made the capture of slave ships more attractive and rapidly increased the numbers of African slaves held in some of the English and Dutch colonies.

[86] Koniglijk Huis Archief, Commissie Boek Prince Maurice of Orange, a 74. "Commissie, Omme naer Oost ende West Indien ende andere vreemde landedn te vaeren."
[87] GAA NA 119, fols. 198v-199, testimony of 30 July 1610.
[88] AGI SD 100, Gaspar Ruiz de Pereda to King 14 April 1610, fol. 1v.
[89] AGI SD 100, Gaspar Ruiz de Pereda to King, 18 December 1612, fols. 1–2.
[90] D. García de Girón, 6 February 1613 in Tronchis Veracoechea, *Documentos*, p. 144.

Even while peace was holding in Europe before 1619, English and Dutch privateers began returning to the Caribbean to prey on Spanish ships, either from the tradition of self-defense of traders or as aggressive seekers after plunder. The new English colony of Bermuda became an important center for this new trade, even before the truce had ended.

The Spanish maintained that Bermuda was in actuality a piratical base, or at least an important English naval base. In 1613, a Spanish shipper from the Canaries claimed that he had been robbed on this way to the Caribbean by English from Bermuda and Jamestown (the two operated under the same company at the time), although the governor thought he had actually delivered his goods there, it reflected a general belief that the colony was a naval base.[91] The same year, a Spanish report noted the fortification of the island and worried that it would be strategically placed to harass shipping.[92] This was no doubt the source of contraband slaves still coming into the Spanish Indies from English and Dutch raiding. In 1610 the governor of Jamaica reported that more than 1,540 slaves had been delivered by smugglers to his island.[93]

The Spanish fears were no doubt enhanced by the fact that Robert Rich, the second Earl of Warwick, was an important backer of the Bermuda venture, and at the same time, he and his associates were deeply committed both to war against Spain and to privateering. Not only was Rich well connected with the merchant community of England, but many of his associates had alliances with equally militant Dutch familes, such as Jan de Moor or William Courteen, whose family was found in both countries.[94] Rich's ships had created an international scandal in 1615 when they captured a ship belonging to the Mughal Emperor of India, greatly straining English relations with that potentate.[95] Rich would waste no time in using his base in Bermuda to bring the same spirit back to the Caribbean.

This new phase of privateering was intense, for the Spanish ambassador to the Netherlands complained, with some exaggeration and some

---

[91] AGI SD 272, Gaspar Ruiz de Pereda to King, 28 August 1613.

[92] AGI SD 270, 9 January 1613, Don Diego Sarmiento de Acuna Conde de Gondoma.

[93] AGI 78-2-2, tomo 6, fol. 172, Audienca de San Domingo, 12 December 1610.

[94] For further details on these families, especially on the English side, see Robert Brenner, *Merchants and Revolution: Commercial Change, Political Conflict and London's Overseas Traders, 1550–1653* (Cambridge, 1993), pp. 171–5; for the Dutch equivalents, see Goslinga, *Dutch in the Caribbean*, pp. 31–37.

[95] W. Frank Craven, "The Earl of Warwick, a Speculator in Piracy," *Hispanic American Historical Review* 10 (1930): 461–2.

concern in 1615 that "I am informed that during the last ten years the English have captured more prizes belonging to the subjects of the king my master, than during the twenty years of the war."[96] Initially, the English Crown was reluctant to grant letters of marque, but many privateers went out with letters from wherever they could get them. Two of Rich's ships, for example, cruised the Caribbean in 1616–1618 and took several prizes and went to Savoy.[97] When Daniel Elfrith sailed for the Spanish Main to capture the slave ship *São João Bautista* in 1618, he carried his marque from the same Duke of Savoy. Others obtained their letters from Dutch authorities, and for this reason, like Jope in 1619, for example, they were mistaken for Dutch by English colonists.

One of the earliest Bermuda-based privateers, the English captain Walsingham captured two Spanish ships loaded with silver in 1615.[98] That same year another Bermuda-based ship, the *Hopewell*, under Captain John Powell, captured a Portuguese sugar cargo, although he lost it to a French rover a bit later.[99] Powell subsequently captured, in 1617, a "good store of Negroes," undoubtedly from a Portuguese prize, the first large group of African slaves shipped to the island, whom Robert Rich believed would allow tobacco growing to take off.[100] Before this, there had only been one or perhaps two Africans on the island, brought from the Venezuelan region to help in pearl fishing, and most likely a free person, because one was referred to as "Symon, the Negro," probably so called because he was the only African on the island at the time.[101]

Captured slave ships began arriving more regularly after this. Powell may have taken three prizes with as many as 30 slaves in 1617, and the next year the African cargo of another ship arrived with Daniel Elfrith.[102]

[96] ARA St. Gen. 6900, Diego Sarmiento de Ocuña to English Privy Council, 22 April 1615.
[97] *Calendar of State Papers*, 1617–19 (vol. 15, London, 1909), no. 376, p. 223; Pierre Contarini, Venetian Ambassador to the Doge and Senate 31 May 1618.
[98] ARA St. Gen. 6900, 22 April 1615, Letter from Spanish Ambassador, Diego Sarmiento de Ocuña, Conde de Gondomar.
[99] Butler, *Historye of the Sommer Islands*, pp. 85–6.
[100] Robert Rich to Nathaniel Rich, 25 [19?] May 1617, Ives, *Rich Papers*, pp. 17, 25.
[101] Butler, *Historye*, p. 84, on arrival of first African on the *Edwin*. The idea of getting slaves to fish pearls from the Venezuelan coast is mentioned in Captaine Danille Tucker's Commission, 15 February 1615/1616 in Lefroy 1: 115–16. On Symon's court see Bermuda Colonial Records (henceforward BCR), 1 (1616–1640), no pages. These pages are now in fragments and cannot be read. Lefroy published a summary (1: 127) without the quotation, which was still readable in 1975 when Packwood inserted it in his book, *Chained to the Rock: Slavery in Bermuda* (Hamilton, 1975), p. 5.
[102] Miles Kendall to Robert Rich, 17 January 1619/1620, in Ivens, *Rich Papers*, p. 122; see also Butler, *Historye*, pp. 145–6.

Elfrith brought the slaves taken from the *São João Bautista* on his ship the *Treasurer*, including Angela (see above), who went to Virginia in 1619. Elfrith's consort was John Jope's *White Lion*, which delivered Virginia its first Africans. But Elfrith was not alone, for a pirate named Kirby also brought a cargo of slaves taken from a prize in 1619, of which the deputy governor Miles Kendall received a share of 15.[103] Elfrith's Anglo-Dutch joint venture was matched by Captain Powell, who fell in with Frans Lonckes, though they lost their ship and ended up stranded on the island. Nevertheless, the undercargo of the Dutch ship, Pieter Barentz, noted that Bermuda was inhabited by Englishmen and enough slaves to make a noticeable impression.[104] In 1620 Daniel Elfrith was again capturing slaves to be delivered to Bermuda, for in October of that year he (and another ship operating in consort with him) had brought more slaves to populate the tobacco estates of Robert Rich.[105] Bermuda's reputation as a privateering center had grown as well. The court of Virginia determined in 1620 that Bermuda, a colony that was becoming a haven for "men of war and Pirates with whom the inhabitants are growne in great liking, by reason of the commodities they bring [and] the robbinge of the Spaniard (as being a type of antichrist)," would provoke the Spanish to attack them.[106]

Africans, numbering probably at least 100 by 1620, formed a sizable part of the population of the island. A public ordinance of 1622 required masters of "Negroes" to send them for public works,[107] and the Company also employed them in salvaging operations.[108] The new Africans brought in from prizes soon helped the tobacco crop take off. One of Powell's African slaves, Francisco, was regarded as a master tobacco grower, and Robert Rich hoped to buy him to train his own workers.[109]

Bermuda was not the only colony to see its black population increase as a result of privateering, though it is the best documented. English commercial colonies in the Amazon also benefited from slaves carried there probably by privateers, many under the patronage of the Rich family. A French traveler passed one such settlement in 1622 and found a settler named

[103] Miles Kendall to Robert Rich, 17 January 1619/1620, in Ivens, *Rich Papers*, p. 123; Butler, *Historye*, p. 144.
[104] van Wassenaer, *Historisch verhael*, 12 deel, fol. 39v, 1626; for the English side of this voyage, see Lewis Hughes to Nathaniel Rich, 12 August 1619, Ivens, *Rich Papers*, p. 138.
[105] John Dutton to Earl of Warwick, 17 October 1620, Ivens, *Rich Papers*, pp. 202–3.
[106] Virginia Court Session, 31 May 1620 in Kingsbury, *Records* 1: 367.
[107] Bermuda Colonial Records (BCR), Fragments, Box A, "A warrant to the Tribes for election for sending fitt men for supply of the Castle," no pagination.
[108] Butler to Jacobb, the Ship Carpenter and Sommerseate, 24 June 1622, Lefroy 1: 252.
[109] Robert to Nathaniel Rich, 22 February 1617/1618, Ives, *Rich Papers*, p. 59.

Henry Johnston growing tobacco with three Africans.[110] A Portuguese reconnaissance of 1623 along the Amazon noted the presence of English settlements there since 1609 (probably Harcourt's settlement), including holding many "negros of Angola."[111] This reconnaissance also reported numerous Dutch settlements north of Pará, holding, "many negros which they sieze from the Angola ships going to the Indies."[112] Another Portuguese expedition, this time commissioned to wipe these settlements out in 1625–1626, noted the production of over 800,000 pounds of tobacco and many more Angolan slaves who were taken off by the victorious army.[113] In spite of Portuguese hostility and occasional success, however, various English, French, Irish, and Dutch settlements remained in the Amazon region.

One of these English settlements had been planted with 100 men by Roger North in 1620 with the support of Robert Rich, whose activities in Bermuda were critical to that island's development. Among the would-be settlers was Thomas Warner, who, finding the settlement risky, returned by way of the Lesser Antilles and made friends with Tegreman, a powerful leader ("king") of the Caribs of St Christopher (now St Kitts). In 1623–1624, Warner returned to St Christopher with colonists and founded the first English colony in the Caribbean.[114] In 1626 Captain Combes was sent "with about sixty slaves to plante" on 1,000 acres of land then owned by Lord Carlisle.[115] These slaves were probably Africans, because when the Spanish captured the island in 1629 they noted "some negros" among the captives, who they distributed among themselves.[116] Although the deposition, made 20 years after the fact, seems to suggest these slaves

[110] Sloane MSS, 179 B, f. 8; see Mrs. Robert W. DeForest, *A Walloon Family in America Lockwood de Forest and his forbearers, 1500–1848 together with a Voyage to Guiana being the Journal of Jesse de Forest and his Colonists 1623–25* (2 vols., Boston and New York, 1914), p. 237.

[111] "The report which António Vicente Cochado makes of the discovery of the river Amazon and Cabo do Norte...Lorimer from original in Guedes, *Brasil-costa norte*, pp. 37–9.

[112] BL, Add 13977 Papeles varios de Indias, Symão da Sylueira, *Relação Summaria das cousas do Maranhão* (Lisbon, 1624, rare printed folio), fol. 492.

[113] "Informação de Luiz Aranha de Vasconcellos sobre o descobrimento do Rio das Amazonas, 1626 in *Documentos para a historia da conquista e colonisação da costa de leste-oeste do Brasil* (Rio de Janeiro: Officina Typographhica da Bibliotheca Nacional, 1905, pp. 232–3.

[114] "Relation of the first settlement of Saint Christopher and Nevis, by John Hilton chief gunner and storekeeper...," 1675, in Harlow, *Colonizing Expeditions*, pp. 1–3.

[115] "A brief collection of the depositions...," 1647, Deposition of Morice Thompson, in Harlow, *Colonizing Expeditions*, p. 26.

[116] Spanish letter of 15 October 1630, captured by Dutch fleet and published in Dutch translation in de Laet, *Jarlikjk Verhael* 99 [Port trans. 223].

came from England, in all probability their ultimate origin must have been from privateering voyages of English (or Dutch, who had permission to trade with the island)[117] ships conducted by the very same men who were prominent in founding the colonies, many of whom were associated with Rich's interest in Bermuda and elsewhere.

In 1627, Henry Powell, another Rich associate with connections to the Amazon ventures, proceeded to settle Barbados, leaving his son John Powell, the same sea rover who first brought slaves to Bermuda in 1617, on the island. Henry also held a letter of marque to privateer and captured some 8–10 slaves from a "Spanish" (Portuguese) prize to help the colonists.[118]

As these colonies struggled to maintain themselves against Spanish hostility and also yield profits from the sale of tropical products (mostly tobacco), Rich and his associates began moving toward the western end of the Caribbean and established a privateering/planting base at Providence Island off the coast of Nicaragua in 1631.[119] That same year they also took on the new island colony of Tortuga (which the Company called Association Island) that had been founded in 1630 by John Hilton, who came there from St Christopher.[120]

The backers of the island project quickly sought to include slaves taken by privateers among the settlers. The Company that created the colony wrote to its governor in 1633, "If 20 or 40 Negros could be possessed ... They might be very usefull for Publicke work" but, remembering the experience of Bermuda, where a too-large number of Africans had led to problems, added " ... but not so many that too great a number may as yet be dangerous in the Island."[121] These slaves were clearly to come from privateering, and if not by English ships, then by Dutch vessels, which were cruising the Caribbean in force at the time, as in 1633 Captain Cannock was advised to procure negroes from any Dutch ship,[122]

---

[117] Algemeen Rijksarchief (henceforth ARA), Records of the Oude West Indische Compagnie (henceforth OWIC) 20, fol. 89, Zeeland Chamber Session of 2 January 1627.

[118] "An Abstract of some Principle Passages concerning Sir William Courteen," in Harlow, *Colonizing Expeditions*, p. 30.

[119] This project has been carefully studied in two books, A. P. Newton, *The Colonizing Acitivities of the English Puritans* (New Haven, 1914) and Karen Ordahl Kupperman, *Providence Island, 1630–41: The Other Puritan Colony* (Cambridge, 1994).

[120] "Relation of the First Settlement of St. Christopher ... John Hilton," 20 April 1675, in Harlow, *Colonizing Expeditions*, pp. 12–13.

[121] PRO CO 124/1 Book of Entries of the Governor and Company of Adventurers for the Plantation of the Island of Providence, fol. 47v, Letter to Captain Bell, April 1633.

[122] PRO CO 124/1, fol. 58v, Instructions to Captain Cannock, July 1633.

although in 1634 the Company was exploring the possibilities of bringing Africans over from Bermuda to work the crops.[123] It was probably
from privateering ventures that the first Africans were brought in and distributed by the Company in 1635, however.[124] By 1636 there were some
150 Africans on the island, and already at least 36 had run away, some
of whom had been purchased from the Dutch from as far away as Tortuga.[125] Some, however, were acquired in other ways, for the Company's
ship *Expectation* traded at the Mosquito Coast (Central America) with
Native Americans there in 1636 and also acquired 14 Africans.[126] The next
year Giles March was reprimanded for staying too long on the Mosquitos
without instructions, and then for other misdemeanors, while putting off
Africans at Bermuda.[127] These may have come from trading with Spanish
or Native Americans who held or had captured them, but it is likely that
vessels operating off the Central American coast also captured incoming
slave ships. Two years later, for example, Captain William Jackson, operating under a Providence Island Company marque, captured a slave ship
just off Trujillo in the area; no doubt he was following an established
practice.[128] Certainly the privateering licenses issued for Company ships
from 1636 onward specified the disposition of "any prize of Negroes"
that they might take. The *Blessing*, for example, was to consort with any
Dutch ship that it might meet, and captures of slave ships were certainly
anticipated.[129] At the same time the *Happy Return* was instructed to
deliver Africans from prizes to Company colonies, Bermuda, Virginia,
"or any other place that shall benefit the Company."[130] Indeed, sometimes English ships visited the Dutch colonies as well, for one ship brought

[123] PRO CO 124/1, fol. 67, General letter to Captain Philip Bell, August 1634 (signed 30
       July).
[124] PRO CO 124/2, fol. 133, Court held at Sir Ben Rudyerds chamber, 22 March 1635. Our
       assessment is based on notices concerning privateering that preceed these details.
[125] PRO CO 124/2, fols. 133–33v, Committee for [Providence] Island and Brookehouse
       6 March 1636. See also fol. 144, Ordinary Court held for the Island [Providence],
       Brookehouse, 23 June 1636, on payment to the Dutch West India Company for delivery
       of 6 Africans.
[126] PRO CO 124/2. fols. 151v–5, Committee Meeting, 26 June 1636; BL Add 63854 B,
       fol. 238, Mr. Jessop's letter book, transcript, W. Jessop to Mr. Wentworth, August 1637.
[127] PRO CO 124/2, fol. 150, Court held at Brookehouse, 21 June 1637.
[128] BL Sloane MS 758, Nathaniel Butler Diary, 31 May 1639, cited in Kupperman, *Provi-
       dence Island*, p. 278.
[129] PRO CO 124/2, fol. 95, Instructions to be given to Captain William Rous of Blessing,
       May 1636.
[130] PRO CO 124/1, fol 104, Instruction to Captain Newman on Happie Return, June 1636;
       similar commissions were made through 1638, see fols. 104–33v *passim*.

two prizes of hides taken off Cartagena to New Netherland in 1636, having first obtained a Dutch commission that allowed them to visit the
colony.[131] The ship was probably that of Samuel Axe, who, it was noted
in Providence Island Records, often took Dutch commissions to engage
in privateering (as early as 1635) and sold at least three Africans to the
Dutch director Twiller van Wouters that year, probably from those or
other prize ships.[132]

By the late 1630s Providence Island had largely replaced Bermuda as a
center for privateering and soon held a large number of Africans, prompting extraordinary security concerns. In 1641, when the Spanish captured
the island, it had a population of 381 Africans compared with 350 English
settlers, and the ratio had recently been reduced by removals and the
killing of some 50 of the Africans after a conspiracy.[133] As the African
population surpassed the Europeans, and as runaways and eventually
revolts broke out, the Company sought to reduce this population and
replace Africans with English indentured servants. Slaves taken to and
from Providence Island were carried to other colonies like Bermuda and
St Christopher; it was from Providence that the first slaves were taken to
Puritan colonies in New England, at least as early as the early 1630s.[134]

Often Providence Island received Native Americans from New England
in exchange, as they did after the Pequot War in 1637. New Englanders
envisioned exchanging problematic Native Americans for Africans on a
regular basis. As late as 1645 Emmanuel Downing thought of this as
a regular strategy, in referring to a war against the Narrangansetts in
a letter to John Winthrop, that "if it is a just war the Lord should deliver
them into our hands, we might easily have men, women and children
enough to exchange for Moores, which will be more gainful pillage for
us than we conceive, for I do not see how we can thrive until we get into
a stock of slaves."[135] The idea of exchanges prevailed even on a smaller
scale, so that keeping Indians in prison was deemed less desirable, thus
"the magistrates of the Jurisdiccon [considering a plot in 1646] deliuer

[131] David P. de Vries, *Korte Historiael*, p. 145.
[132] Return of Wouter van Twiller's Property in New Netherland, 22 March 1639,
O'Callaghan, *Documents* 14: 19, on Axe's activities and his connections to Dutch commissions and letters of marque, see Kupperman, *Providence Island*, pp. 191, 197, 283.
[133] AGI Santa Fe (SF), 223, Francisco Díaz Pimenta to Crown 11 September 1641, cited in
Kupperman, *Providence Island*, p. 172, an earlier Spanish report put the numbers of
Africans on the island at 1600.
[134] See the excellent reconstruction in Kupperman, *Providence Island*, pp. 169–77.
[135] Emmanuel Downing to John Winthrop, 1645, *Calendar of State Papers, Colonial 1574–
1660* PRO London 1860, vol. 1, quoted in Luis B. Wright, *The Atlantic Frontier* (New
York, 1947), p. 123.

vp the Indians seased to the party or parties indamaged, either to serue or be shipped out and exchanged for Negroes."[136] This penchant for the exchange of problematic Native Americans might explain the decision to send some Africans ("Caniball Negros") from New England to Providence Islands in 1638.[137]

A center of privateering as well, Tortuga soon had a population of Africans. In 1634 the Providence Island Company believed that as many as 30 Africans could be purchased on the island.[138] In fact, Tortuga had about 100 Africans on it when the Spanish took the island in 1635.[139]

The Dutch

Just as English privateering had begun before the end of the truce, Dutch privateers, many of whom had found advantages by war with Spain, began to return to the war in the mid-1610s. Already in 1610, the *Guldene Craen* was seized by the admiralty authorities in Rotterdam upon its return from the West Indies on suspicion of "roving," though the captain and owners protested their innocence.[140] Likewise, in 1611 a Dutch vessel captured Francisco Gomes, a "free Negro," while he was fishing at the Cape Verde region of Africa and then continued, following the same tradition, to the Caribbean.[141] That same year, a Dutch ship was operating in consort with three English vessels when they captured a Portuguese slave ship and delivered 23 of its cargos to Maroons in Hispaniola.[142]

---

[136] Plymouth Court, Session of 15 September 1646, David Pulsifer (ed.), *Records of Colony of Plymouth in New England* (12 vols., 1855, reprint New York, 1968) 9 (1643–51): 71.

[137] PRO CO 124/1, fol. 124v, Instructions to the Swallow, 3 July 1638. The timing suggests that these might have been Pequots, though there is no clear precedent for calling Native Americans "negros" at this period. One should note that in 1625 Samuel Purchas published an account of Andrew Battell on Angola that was likely to have been read in New England by 1638. Given the frequency of Angolan background for Africans delivered to all the colonies in the period it seems possible that people in New England feared that their captives may have been from the Imbangala visited by Battell and represented as cannibals.

[138] PRO CO 124/1 fol. 73v, Instructions for Robert of London, 30 July 1634.

[139] Francisco de Tajagrando and Diego Nunez de Peralta, to Crown, 24 June 1640, Wright, *Nederlandsche Zeevaarders*, p. 66, a report on the Spanish campaign notes the capture of 49, but many escaped. An Irish priest who was captured from a Spanish vessel noted meeting 44 others in the island who had escaped, AGI, Seccion 5, Indif gen, leg 1872, first published in the original Spanish in T. G. Mathews in *Carribean Studies* 10 (1989): 89–106; Bernard O'Brien's account, 1636, Lorimer translation, p. 419.

[140] GAA NA 119, 198v-99, Deposition of 30 July 1610.

[141] AGI SD 54, Gomez de Sandoval to King, 15 July 1611.

[142] AGI SD 54, fol. 6v, Declaraziones de Agustin Brito y Guillermo Pereyra, frances, 25 March 1611.

While the English focused their colonial activities in growing tobacco, the Dutch concentrated their efforts on the salt trade. Whereas the Dutch saw the trade as peaceful commerce, the Spanish regarded the Dutch traders as pirates and continuously attacked them. The overall effect was to make Dutch trade more like privateering, and many of their ships were heavily armed, like the ship engaged in exploring trade with Trinidad in 1611.[143] Others carried defensive commissions that allowed them to capture prizes if attacked. In 1616 Dutch officials issued a secret letter of marque to a Dutch ship seeking the "Green Island" off the coast of Honduras said to be full of gold. With this letter the captain took a Spanish prize, leading to a protest by the Spanish.[144] The pace of privateering then accelerated as the period of truce drew to a close. The Spanish agent in the Netherlands reported in 1618 that five privateers left Zeeland for the Indies, saying that "they are poor with the truce" and another was scheduled to leave in just two weeks.[145] The next year, the agent promised the authorities in Spain that he would obtain a copy of a letter of marque given by the Prince of Orange to "go out and rob"[146] In fact, in 1619 the States General of Zeeland began issuing letters of marque for merchants seeking recompense for losses to Spanish from their peaceful trade (mostly the salt trade) in the West Indies.[147] The Dutch privateers joined with Bermuda-based English privateers during these years.[148] Jope, the English privateer who delivered Angela to Bermuda, held a Dutch commission from the Prince of Orange.

If English privateering centered around Robert Rich and his associates, the Dutch privateering interests coalesced in the formation of a permanent company, the West India Company, in 1621. Spanish agents in Brussels were well aware of the intentions of the Dutch to send large fleets from the time the Truce ended, as revealed by a report suggesting that 18 ships would be dispatched to Cuba and that it was possible that slaves and maroons on the island might assist them in conquering it.[149] Although

---

[143] GAA NA 124, fols. 196v-98, Deposition of 21 October 1611.

[144] ARA St. Gen. 5464, Admiralty of Rotterdam to States General, Rotterdam, 9 December 1616, 18 October 1617; GAA NA199 f. 264v, Deposition of 1 September 1617. On the "Green Island" see ARA St. Gen. 4567, Admiralty doc 1 June 1618.

[145] AGS Estado 1089, News from Holland, 19 July 1618.

[146] AGS Estado 1090, Archduke Alberto to King, 28 February 1619.

[147] ARA St. Gen Resol. 568, fol. 607; actual letters are found, for example, fol. 681 Dierck Ruyter of Middelburch and Francois de Cesne van Leyden, 19 December 1619; vol. 569, fol. 34v, letter for Pieter Courten, 29 January 1620.

[148] van Wassenaer, *Historisch verhael*, 12 deel, fol. 39v, 1626.

[149] AGI Indifferente General 1869, Gaspar de Pereda to King, Brussels, 4 March 1622.

initially the Company was envisioned as a monopoly company for these sorts of enterprises, in fact, Dutch privateers also operated outside the Company's purview. Nevertheless, by 1624, the Company, having gained solvency, began a massive campaign against Spanish and Portuguese shipping and colonies in the Caribbean, Brazil, and Africa. In addition to raiding, the Company planned to take colonies. In 1624 a fleet of 23 ships and three yachts, bearing 3,200 soldiers and sailors captured Bahia, a rich Brazilian captaincy, but lost it again to a determined Luso-Spanish relief expedition the next year.[150] The local Portuguese forces also repelled a simultaneous attack, led by Piet Heyn, on Luanda, which they correctly perceived as the principal source of slaves for Brazil.[151] These initial operations established the main pattern for the Dutch, who hoped to seize Brazil and Angola, pillage Spanish possessions on land in the Caribbean, and capture whatever prizes could bear profit. The West India Company kept a detailed chronicle of these captures, published from the ships' own books by Johannes de Laet in 1644, showing 69 ships captured in 1624, 18 in 1625, 29 in 1626, and 55 in 1627. Included among the cargoes captured by the Dutch fleets was the Spanish silver fleet, taken by Piet Heyn off Cuba in 1628. The Dutch thus achieved many of their goals – Pernambuco, Brazil, was taken in 1630 and held for over a dozen years, Angola fell in 1641 and was held for seven years, whereas parts of São Tomé fell into their hands from 1641 to 1649, but in the long run, Portugal recovered its lost territory and independence from Spain by mid-century.[152]

In their operations, the Company also envisioned capturing slave ships on the high seas and distributing their cargoes wherever there was a demand to Spanish or Portuguese colonies, as had been done earlier, or in newer colonies to be founded by the Company. Jewish merchants living in the Low Countries with connections to the Portuguese slave trade were well aware of their intentions, for in 1621, as the Company's charter was being drawn up, Diogo Nunes Belmonte, one of the more prosperous of these Luso-Jewish merchants, took out insurance on a variety of ships in the Angolan slave trade to protect his interests on both the sea and in Angola.[153]

[150] Charles Boxer, *The Dutch in Brazil, 1624–54* (Oxford, 1957), is still an excellent introduction to the Dutch activities in Brazil.
[151] For Dutch operations in Africa, see Klaas Ratelband, *Nederlanders in West-Afrika, 1600–1650: Angola, Kongo en São Tomé* (Zutphen, 2000).
[152] For details of the West India Company's plans and their operations in the Caribbean, see Goslinga, *Dutch in the Caribbean*, pp. 89–311.
[153] ARA Loketkas, Admiraltriteit 33: 1.

When the Company captured Bahia in 1624, they quickly turned to raiding the Portuguese trade from Angola; as early as 1 July 1624, a ship from Angola with 220 slaves was taken at sea and delivered to the newly seized colony on behalf of the Company.[154] The Company recognized from its Brazilian experience that obtaining slaves on the high seas would be a good starting point for colonies; not surprisingly, the Company, when contemplating new colonies in the Amazon in 1626, ordered its ships to cruise the Angolan coast looking for slavers to capture.[155] They continued cruising the coast of Brazil looking for prizes of slaves for any sort of sale, though often they could not persuade the Portuguese to buy them. When Admiral Cornelis Corneliszoon Jol captured an Angola ship with 600 slaves in 1626 he felt he could not dispose of them and so let the ship continue its journey, and in 1627, the people of Pernambuco could not purchase all 600 slaves captured and delivered there by Dirck Simonszoon van Uytgeest.[156]

But the same year, Piet Heyn managed to capture a ship with 370 slaves that he sold to the Company's benefit in Brazil.[157] Many of the Company's captures of slave ships were eventually delivered to Brazil, especially after the Dutch captured Pernambuco in 1630.

The Company also made captures in the West Indies, for example, in February 1627, one squadron captured a ship bearing 150 slaves off Tobago and took it along. It was probably delivered to English colonies at Saint Christopher, newly established in the region, and the Zeeland Chamber of the Company authorized its ship to do this.[158] In June, the fleet captured another ship, inbound from Angola with 125 slaves off Cuba. The decision on this occasion was to take only a part of the slave cargo and to let the others go. One of the ships of that fleet, the *Bruynvisch*, subsequently visited the new Dutch colony at New Amsterdam on its return trip, possibly delivering the first Africans to that colony.[159] In 1628,

---

[154] Joannes de Laet, *Iaerlyck Verhael van de Verrichtighen der Geoctroyeerde West-Indische Compagnie* (modern edition, S. P. L'Honoré Naber, 3 vols, Hague, 1931–33) 1, p. 28.

[155] ARA OWIC 20, Minutes of Zeeland Chamber, 21 December 1626, cit Martin, *Loango Coast* p. 54, n 3.

[156] de Laet, *Iaerlyck Verhael* 160–1, 2, p. 31.

[157] de Laet, *Iaerlyck Verhael* 1, p. 160, 2, p. 2.

[158] ARA OWIC 20, Zeeland Chamber Session of 2 January 1627.

[159] de Laet, *Iaerlyck Verhael*, 2, p. 26, 30, 34; also WIC 20, Zeeland Chamber Session of 6 December 1627. Some Africans, Paulo Angolo, Big and Little Manuel, Manuel de Gerrit de Reus, Simon Congo, Antony Portuguese, Gracia, Piter Santome, Jan Francisco, and Little Antony, whose names suggest an Angolan origin, sued for freedom in 1644, claiming they had served 18–19 years (implying that they had arrived in 1626, because there was no colony in 1625), A. J. F. van Laer, *New York Historical Manuscripts:*

the fleet under Pieter Andriaenszoon Ita tried to capture another slave ship off Cuba but accidentally sank it with all its cargo.[160]

The Company's ships also delivered slaves captured at sea to its newly established colonies in other areas of the Americas. In 1627, for example, the Company promised to deliver Africans as workers in their patent to Abraham van Pere, who intended to settle in the Guianas.[161] The same year, Jan van Ryen, settled at the Wiapoco nearby also demanded African slaves from the Company, arguing that Dutch settlers would not work.[162] Jan de Moor, a Zeeland leader, asked that workers for his small, newly established colony in Tobago be supplied from prizes taken in 1628,[163] and the Company obligingly ordered its ships to deliver prizes of slaves to the island.[164] The Company promised the New Amsterdam settlers that it would supply them with "as many blacks [*Swarten*] as it possibly can" in 1629, and in 1634 they specified that 12 men and women for each colonist would be taken "out of the prizes in which Negroes shall be found."[165] Prizes were indeed delivered again, for in 1630, Michael Pauw received no less than 50 Africans, 20 men and 30 women, for his patroonship established in Pavonia (which included the eastern parts of modern New Jersey and Staten Island). These had been sent on the *Bruynvisch* from Pernambuco in Brazil, where they had been "captured in the last prize."[166] Apparently that prize was a Portuguese slaver, inbound from Angola with 280 slaves, landed in July.[167]

Sometimes it was not fleets of privateers capturing Portuguese vessels that brought slaves to the various Dutch colonies. Settlers in David de Vries' colony, founded in 1636 on the Wild Coast (Guiana), believed they

---

Dutch (4 vols., Baltimore, 1974), 1: 212. For doubts that there were Africans in 1626, see Robert J. Swan, "First Africans into New Netherland, 1625 or 1626?" *De Halve Maen* 66/4 (1993): 75–82.

[160] De Laet. *Iaerlyck Verhael* appendix p. 12 (the appendix only occurs in the 1644 original edition).

[161] Goslinga, *Dutch in Caribbean*, pp. 102–3.

[162] AJF van Laer, *Documents Relating to New Netherland 1624–1626 in the Henry E. Huntington Library* (San Marino, CA, 1924), p. 29.

[163] ARA OWIC 20, Minutes of the Zeeland Chamber, 27 April and 17 August 1628, fols. 137v, 147v.

[164] ARA OWIC, 2, Secrete notulen, kopien van uitgaande brieven, fol. 19.

[165] On the 1629, "Uryhheden ende Exemptien voor de Patroonen, Meesters ofte particulieren..." in A. J. F. van Laer, *The Van Rensselaer Bowier Manuscripts* (Albany: SUNY, 1908), p. 153 (Dutch text on 152); in 1634 in E. B. O'Callaghan (ed.), *Documents relative to the Colonial History of the State of New-York; Procured in Holland, England and France, by John Romeyn Brodhead* (14 vols., Albany, 1856–1887), 1: 91.

[166] ARA OWIC 44, Servantius Carpentier to Directors XIX, 25 September 1630. On the Pavonia colony, Van Laer, *Van Rensselaer Bouwier*, pp. 50, 55, 158.

[167] De Laet, *Iaerlyck Verhael*. 2, p. 147.

would benefit so much from the cargo of a slave ship they captured when it stopped to take on water supplies that they were persuaded by some Englishmen and sailors among them to abandon the colony and take their slaves to an English Caribbean colony. The English convinced the Dutch that because they were going to an English territory, the English should be the captains and the Dutch servants. Arriving at the colony the English then "sold the prize, and the sailors as servants."[168]

Origins of African Slaves in the Age of Privateering, 1560–1640

The African origins of the many slaves captured by privateers from the first Hawkins voyages in the 1560s onward varied but gradually came to be overwhelmingly Angolan, until the Angolan element completely dominated them by the first decades of the seventeenth century. This increasingly West Central African bias meant that the original African laborers in the new colonies that the English and Dutch established in America after 1605 were virtually all from this region of Africa.

The original Africans captured by the English and Dutch were not from West Central Africa. This was because in the mid-sixteenth century, Cape Verde–based traders dominated the trans-Atlantic slave trade, and it was into this stream that Hawkins entered in the 1560s when he began preying on ships going to the Spanish Indies off the coast of Sierra Leone. At this time the delivery of slaves to the Spanish Indies was managed by the Spanish Crown through a system of contracts (*asientos*), given somewhat haphazardly to various bidders, most of whom had contacts in the Portuguese slave trade. Spanish records reveal that during the period 1544–1550 all the ships carrying slaves to labor in the sugar estates of the islands or to work in Mexico and Peru left from Cape Verde, carrying captives who originated from the coast and the interior regions between modern-day Sierra Leone and Senegal.[169] Indeed, according to the somewhat spotty records, all slave ships recorded in Spanish sources before the mid-1580s were from Cape Verde. Portuguese shippers who drew on slave markets in the Lower Guinea region (served by their colony in São Tomé) and Angola delivered them primarily to the sugar estates of São Tomé or Brazil. Through smuggling or other means, a few of the people from these latter regions did occasionally make it to the Spanish Indies, for an inventory taken in 1549 in Mexico shows that although 78 of the

---

[168] De Vries, *Korte Historiael*, p. (Jameson, p. 196).
[169] Mateus Ventura, *Negreiros Portugueses*, Annex 1, pp. 121–33, drawn from records in the Casa de Contratación, the Spanish licensing agency.

83 people (94 percent) enslaved on its sugar estates were "Brans, Zapes, Biafaras, Gelofe [Wolof], and Mandingas," all drawn from the region around Cape Verde, they also included one North African, two "Manicongos," and two "Mozambiques" from West Central and South Eastern Africa, respectively.[170] Shipping from São Tomé must also have visited Española during this period, for the inventory of a sugar estate there in 1547 shows that 5 of the 20 people whose origins can be determined came from the Bight of Benin area (Lucumis, Calabaris, and an Ambo) so that only 80 percent were from Upper Guinea.[171] In a breakdown of the African ethnic origins of 276 slaves reported from several statistical studies for Mexico, 90.2 percent were from Upper Guinea, 5 percent were from West Central, and 2.5 percent were from Lower Guinea.[172] Inventories and bills of sale from Peru reveal a similar breakdown. In reference to the African ethnic origins of 207 slaves from 1548 to 1560, only 21 (10.1 percent) were from Angolan areas or Mozambique, smuggled, no doubt, through Buenos Aires to the mining regions, and a handful (4 or 2 percent) were from the Lower Guinea region served by Portuguese shipping based in São Tomé.[173] Thus the earliest English privateers were drawn into the already-established pattern of the slave trade that took people from the Upper Guinea coast in Africa to the Spanish Indies.

In the following period, however, the ethnic origins of the slaves shifted dramatically from a near monopoly of Upper Guineans to a near monopoly of West Central Africans. Moreover, from around 1580 to the 1620s the number of captives exported from Africa increased significantly. The dramatic increase and the ethnic dominance of West Central Africans were due in large part to a number of related causes. First, the colonization of Angola in 1575 and the wars that followed greatly increased the number of people exported from the region. Second, the decline of sugar production in São Tomé, which had been the primary target of West Central African exports, led to a great expansion of exports directed to Brazil and other American destinations. Third, after 1595 the Spanish Crown began to systematize the delivery of slaves to its American colonies by giving an *asiento* to a single holder and finally *asientos* were held by people with especially strong Angolan connections.[174] The king granted the entire slave trade to single contractors for long periods of time. Pedro

---

[170] As presented in Curtin, *Atlantic Slave Trade*, p. 98.
[171] Published in J. Inchaustegui Cabral, *Reales Cedulas y correspondencias de governadores de Santo Domingo* (5 vols., Madrid, 1958), 1: 236–9.
[172] Patrick J. Carroll, *Blacks in Colonial Vera Cruz*, 2nd ed. (Austin, 2001), pp. 158–9.
[173] Curtin, *Atlantic Slave Trade*, p. 97.
[174] Magalhães Godinho, 4, pp. 161–81; Vila Vilar, *Hispanoamerica*.

Gomes Reinel, who held the *asiento* from 1596 to 1601, freighted some 116 ships between 1597 and 1601 whose African origins can be ascertained. Angolans made up about half of the 20,478 slaves he delivered to various Spanish colonies, whereas the percentages from the remaining regions varied from 6 percent from São Tomé to 26.5 percent from Guinea and 20.6 percent from Cape Verde.[175]

This varied pattern prevailed for a few years but soon changed to a new one dominated by Angolans. Fiscal records from the port of Vera Cruz from 1604 to 1614 show the new distribution: a majority of Angolans, with 7,124 of the 9,638 slaves (73.9 percent) entered this port.[176] The Angolan domination underwent an even more sensational increase in the following years, after Antonio Fernades d'Elvas won the *asiento* in 1615. To fulfill his obligations to the Spanish Crown, which he held until 1621, he acquired the contract of Angola, which gave him exclusive rights to export slaves from Angola.[177]

Successive *asiento* holders exploited similar connections in Angola and the Spanish Indies. Taking the number of ships licensed to deliver slaves to America for which African ports of call are known – 428 ships in all between 1616 and 1640 – 364 (85 percent) purchased their slaves in Angola. In some years, 1625, 1627–1628, 1630–1632, and 1637–1639, all the ships were from Angola. Even in the intervening years the numbers originating in Angola topped 90 percent; only in 1626 did the number of ships from Angola account for just half.[178] A sample of 274 slaves found in Mexican inventories from 1632 to 1657 show that 86.7 percent derived from West Central Africa.[179]

It was from this overwhelmingly Angolan stream of captives going to the Spanish holdings in the Caribbean and Central America that Anglo-Dutch privateers took the Africans they would use in their emerging American colonies, just as the privateers of the Hawkins years delivered people from Upper Guinea to the Spanish Indies. Both of the slave ships whose provenance are known and that were taken by English privateers came from Angola. The first was the *São João Bautista*, which was bearing Angela and other Angolan captives to Vera Cruz before her capture and transport by way of Bermuda to Virginia. The other was "an Angola man" bearing "manie Negroes" captured by Captain Arthur Guy of the *Fortune*

[175] Drawn from Quadro 2 in Vila Vilar, *Hispanoamerica*.
[176] Drawn from Quadro 3 in Vila Vilar, *Hispanoamerica*.
[177] Heintz, "Ende," pp. 111–20; Magalhães Godinho, 4, pp. 164–7.
[178] Drawn from Quadro 1 in Vila Vialr, *Hispanoamerica*.
[179] Carroll, *Blacks*, pp. 159–61.

in 1628. The Angolans taken on this occasion were also delivered to Virginia.[180] Spanish records provide fuller details of the English raiding. In 1639 the then-*asiento*-holders Melchor Gomez Angel and Christofo Mendoza de Sosa made a deposition to the Spanish Crown concerning their losses to English privateers. They said that the slaves were discharged "in the Indies." They came from "the port of Angola which is the principal one from which the slaves come out." Between 1631 and 1639, according to this disposition, the English had taken some sixteen ships on this route.[181] This loss probably represented 2,400 slaves, as the average ship transported at least 150 slaves. It is likely that the Providence Island Company's ships, the principal privateers of the period, were responsible for many of the captures.

Although the records of English privateering activities are scant, the Dutch records provide a fuller overview. Johannes de Laet, the chronicler of the Dutch West India Company, compiled detailed annual accounts of the activities of each of the Company's ships between 1624 and 1636 based on her captain's log. These logs record captures, burnings, groundings, and other attacks on some 16 slave ships and the transfer of 2,356 slaves to Dutch hands. Because this is the same number of ships as the English had taken in roughly the same period, we can assume that the total number of slaves entering English hands must have equaled that of the Dutch (roughly 2,500). Of these, we know the provenance of ten of the Dutch ships, and all but one were from Angola – roughly the same 90 percent ratio found in the trade as recorded in Spanish fiscal documents. The other ship, which hailed from Cape Verde, delivering a cargo of 400 slaves to Cartagena, was stopped but allowed to continue its journey with its full cargo. Of the five ships with no provenance, we can assume that at least four were from Angola, because, again, slave ships originating from Angola represented 90 percent of all slave ships crossing the Atlantic during these years.[182]

The Dutch continued privateering, but in 1635, both Zeeland and Amsterdam chambers decided to send ships to Angola to purchase slaves; the Amsterdam ship (*Windhout*) was to cruise and capture prizes, whereas

[180] PRO HCA Instance and Prize Courts Examinations 13/47, fols. 106, 560–60v; PRO State Papers. Domestic. Charles I, letters and papers 16/103, John Ellzey to Mr. Nicholas Esq., 13 May 1628.
[181] AGI Indiferente General, 2796, "Declaracion por causas nuevamerte sobre venidas algunas de los condiciones que Melchor Gomez Angel y Christofo Mendoza de Sosa . . ." 28 February 1639, fol. 33.
[182] de Laet, *Iaerlyck Verhael*, Appendix, pp. 11–13 (details in text).

the Zeeland ship (*Eendracht*) was to "get blacks," perhaps, like the *Wind-hout*, by prize taking or perhaps to buy slaves.[183] The *Eendracht* had taken an earlier voyage, perhaps on the same route, as it delivered "some soldiers, blacks, and other persons" at New Netherland around 15 April that year.[184]

From Privateering to Slave Trading, 1638–1660

Both the origin of the slaves and the numbers of slaves in Dutch and English hands would change when the two powers decided to obtain slaves by purchase on the African coast as well as by taking them from Portuguese vessels. As early as 1626 the Zeeland chamber of the West India Company was contemplating purchasing slaves in Angola to take to their newly founded colonies in the Amazon.[185] However, there is no reason to believe that any such trading took place, and it was not until 1637 that the Dutch began to purchase slaves directly from African sellers on the African coast. The English followed soon afterward. Initially, trading supplemented privateering, but eventually trading became the primary source of slaves. Although both nations had, as we have seen, extensive commercial operations in Africa from the mid-sixteenth century, neither had purchased more than a handful of slaves, if any during this long period. This remarkable fact is documented most tellingly in a survey of the trade of the West India Company in Africa from 1623 to 1636 prepared for Swedish authorities considering the formation of an African company. This was a time when privateers were delivering thousands of captive Africans to Dutch and English colonies in the Americas. This list includes 102 voyages, going primarily to "Guinea" and "Cape Verde" but also including occasional mentions of "Senegal," "Gambia," and "Angola." It provides a detailed enumeration of the cargoes of the ships and their value and includes gold, hides, ivory, cloth, wax, Sierra Leone wood, cloth, and grain but no slaves. The document notes that the Portuguese bought

---

[183] ARA OWIC 14, fol. 3, Amsterdam Chamber resolution, 4 January 1635; also ARA OWIC 8, fols. 192v–193v (details for the Windhout); ARA OWIC 20, fol. 523, Resolution of Zeeland Chamber, 1 October 1635 (Eendracht), the wording is ambigious "sal gesonden worden naer Guinea ende Angola om Swarten." The Amsterdam Chamber's instructions to the Windhout are more detailed and make it clear that prize taking was the method of choice; the Zeeland Chamber left no detailed notes.

[184] GAA NA 917, 1 December 1635, p. 309v quoted in Rink, *Holland on the Hudson*, p. 130 n 22.

[185] ARA OWIC 20, Minutes of the Zeeland Chamber, 21 December 1626.

slaves in Cacheau, Gambia, and especially Angola in the regions of Bengo, Dande, Kongo, Luanda, and Ambres [Ambriz] but gives no indication that the Dutch were purchasing slaves in this or any other location.[186]

The Dutch sent what appears to be their first slaving voyage to Africa in 1637, when they dispatched the *Nassau* for "Angola" and included 200 pairs of handcuffs, though the fate of this voyage is unknown.[187] The choice of West Central Africa as a place to purchase slaves was fairly clear to Dutch authorities. The Dutch noted that the Portuguese trade was substantial in the region, and their merchants had established relations with the Central African kingdoms of Kongo and Loango and with the ruler of Kongo's coastal province of Soyo. In addition, the Estates General had concluded a more formal alliance with the king of Kongo. The first fully documented voyage was completed in September 1638, when the *St Michiels* arrived in Brazil from "Sonho-Zerri a Congo [Soyo-Nzari a Kongo]" with 72 slaves.[188] The Dutch also sent two more ships that year to purchase slaves, bought mostly at Nzari, where there was "no lack of ivory or slaves." With this initial success, Jan Maurits van Nassau wrote that the Dutch should focus their efforts on buying slaves in Angola, as they would have the best luck there.[189] On 5 May 1639 the *St. Michiels* delivered 150 of 155 slaves bought in Mpinda to Pernambuco.[190] Three more shiploads from Kongo left for Brazil that year, bearing 329 slaves.[191] Based on this record, the Dutch believed in 1639 that they could eventually be able to get 200 slaves a year in Loango, with another 100 from Soyo.[192] In 1640, the Dutch had about 150 slaves at various places along the north bank of the Congo River, which they wanted to send quickly to Brazil as they were sick and dying from lack of food. A year later the Dutch factor sent out first 600 slaves on the Leyden and then made a second voyage in the same year, delivering 155 more.[193]

---

[186] Universitetsbiblioteket Uppsala, L 123, fols. 59–65, "Handel op alle de kusten van Africa van Cap: Spartell tott Cab: de bona Esperanza," The list of voyages is on fols. 63v–64 and the commodities on fol. 64v.

[187] ARA OWIC 23 fol. 763v, Minutes of Zeeland Chamber, 12 November 1637.

[188] ARA OWIC 56, no. 33, Frans van Capelle, "Corte beschrijvynge vat gepasserde in Rio Congo" 1641, but based on a diairy. The arrival in Brazil was noted in OWIC 68, Notulen van Brazilië, 22 September 1638.

[189] ARA OWIC 8, fol. 213, Jan Maurits van Nassau to XIX, 30 June 1639.

[190] ARA OWIC 68, Notulien van Brazilië, 5 May 1639.

[191] ARA OWIC 68, Notulien van Brazilië, 5 May, 24 June, 25 October 1639.

[192] ARA OWIC 8, fol. 268, Jan Maurits to XIX, 28 November 1639.

[193] ARA OWIC 56, no. 33, Capelle, "Corte beschrijvynge."

Having enjoyed some success in their initial trade in Loango and Kongo, the Dutch decided to try trading for slaves in West Africa. Initially, they were pessimistic about the "Guinea trade," as they described the commerce in West Africa, thinking that longer voyages would result in higher mortality, and they were skeptical about health conditions in the "Bight."[194] Late in 1639, a Dutch ship delivered 688 slaves from Allada in Brazil, and they were exporting slaves from Calabar in the same year.[195] Dutch authorities were confident that their capture of Luanda, the capital of the Portuguese colony of Angola, in 1641 would bring them a bonanza in slave exports as they believed they could simply take over the existing Portuguese trade, which they estimated would total over 15,000 per year. The Angola trade proved disappointing, however, and as a result, they continued to exploit their opportunities in the West African trade. Over the course of the next few years, from 1639 to 1646, when the Company stopped sending ships to Angola and opened the trade to "ships belonging to the colonists," the West India Company traders delivered more than 11,000 West Africans to Brazil, somewhat less than the number delivered from Angola.[196]

Following their expulsion from Angola in 1648 the Dutch shifted their slave-trading activities again to Soyo, Angola, and West Africa. The loss of the First West India Company's records as well as the scattered records that free trade generated make it difficult to reconstruct the volume and direction of Dutch trade from about 1645 to 1660. The records of the free traders that are available show them purchasing slaves from a variety of areas, including the *Eendracht*, which purchased 200 slaves in Calabar in 1648, the *Propheet Daniel*, which purchased 400 slaves in Allada in 1649, the *Geele Son* and the *Geele Engel*, which purchased a total of 731 slaves between Angola and Allada in 1653, and the *Vergulde Valck*, which purchased 675 slaves in Angola in 1660.[197] Other records for the period from 1658 to 1660, when the trade had a "sudden revival," show

---

[194] ARA OWIC 56, Jan Maurits and Council to XIX 31 May 1641.

[195] ARA OWIC 8, fol. 252, Jan Maurits to XIX, 22 October 1639, which mentions not only the dispatch of slaves from Allada but also the purchase of beans for slaves from Calabar.

[196] For statistics, see Johannes Postma, *The Dutch in the Atlantic Slave Trade, 1600–1815* (Cambridge, 1990), p. 21. The table is not entirely complete but is representative. We have modified this through our own research in the "Brieven en Papieren uit Brasil" section of ARA OWIC and in correspondence with David Eltis and Jelmer Vos, working on the 2nd edition of the Slave Trade Database.

[197] These notices are made from notarial entries in the GAA, NA as follows: 1690A, fol. 599, 16 April 1648 and fols. 1099–12, 9 June 1648 (*Eendracht*); 2113A, fol. 25, 30 August

a total of 13 free trader ships transported 3,718 slaves from various areas in Africa.[198]

The Dutch supplied many of their purchased slaves to the English colonies from the 1650s, not only to Barbados but also to Virginia. Even in 1650, the *Tamandare*, bringing prize slaves from Brazil to New York, ended up supplying Virginia, a circumstance that led Dutch settlers in New Amsterdam to complain that its slaves "slipped through our fingers," according to the remonstrance of 1650, apparently to Virginia, and, again, in 1652 a "Negro boy" was sold to Virginia. Moreover, in 1652 many, at least 50 and perhaps more, of the Africans who arrived on the ship *Witte Paert* were sold to Edmund Scarburgh, a Virginia settler.[199]

The English started later than the Dutch in sending out ships to buy slaves directly on the African coast. Although a real shortage of records makes any discussion of the English trade problematic, it seems quite likely that, like the Dutch, their trade with Africa before about 1640 was entirely in commodities like woods, gold, and ivory.[200] English merchants who decided to purchase slaves in Africa began their activities at Calabar, for the first known voyage, made by the *Star* of London in 1641, took Africans from that port to Barbados and carried more to St. Christopher.[201] Once they began, however, the English went into slave trading with considerable force; in January 1642 James Browne of Barbados noted that 500 slaves were "daily expected."[202] A bit later that year, another Barbados planter wrote of securing new slaves against the next slave ship to arrive, already implying a regular traffic in slaves.[203] This increasing rhythm is revealed by the arrival of the *Mary Bonaventure* in 1644, which delivered at least

---

1649 and 1819, fol. 800, 29 September 1651 (*Propheet Daniel*); 1355, fol. 72, 11 May 1657 (*Geele Son* and *Geele Engel*); 1515, fol. 26, 5 October 1660 (*Vergulde Valck*).

[198] Postma, *Dutch in Atlantic*, p. 354.

[199] Geurt Tyssen vs Judich Verlettes and Anna Heckx, 9 September 1652, Gehring, *Council Mintues* 5: 45.

[200] For a discussion of the early British slave trade see Larry Gragg, "'To Procure Negroes': The English Slave Trade to Barbados," *Slavery and Abolition* 16 (1995): 65–84; and *Englishmen Transplanted: The English Colonization of Barbados, 1627–1660* (Oxford, 2003), pp. 113–31.

[201] National Archives of Barbados (NAB) Recopied Deed Book (RB) 3/2, pp. 202–3, Contract of Nicholas Crispe of London Samuel Chrispe and John Wood of London merchants, last day of February 1642. The ship then left, still bearing "negroes" as its cargo, perhaps to be sold in St. Christopher. The port of Calabar is a supposition, based on the observation of the Dutch factor at São Tomé that an English yacht bound for Barbados passed the island in 1641, OWIC 57, Journal of Jan Claesz Cock, 8 May 1642 [Journal runs from 2 December 1641].

[202] Scottish Record Office (SRO), Hay Papers, James Browne to A. Hay, 17 January 1641/2.

[203] NAB, RB 3/1, p. 132.

229 slaves to Barbados planters.[204] In 1645 multiple ship arrivals were attested, when Emanuel Dowling wrote about this remarkable trade (for the time) to his cousin John Winthrop. In fact, a study of the registers of the Dutch factors on the Gold Coast reveals that from February 1645 to January 1647 some 19 English slave vessels, many of which carried 100 slaves or more, stopped along the coast, bound mostly for Calabar or Allada.[205] Barbados slave owners were pleased with this increased trade and found it was meeting their needs, as did Edward Longville, who made a contract in 1647 to deliver "true able and sufficient working negroes" contingent on the arrival of the "good shippe *John and Catherine.*"[206] The pace increased markedly in the next decade for between 1652 and 1657, no less than 80 English ships traded for slaves along the coast of Lower Guinea.[207]

Beginning in 1644, New England merchants like the Winthrops quickly became involved in this African trade along with traders of England. In 1645 the city fathers of Boston found themselves obliged to return Africans who had been illegally captured in Sierra Leone to their home-lands via the *Rainbow*, which had taken the bulk of its captive passengers to Barbados.[208] In 1650 John Allen of Charlestown (then in Boston) acquired property in Barbados along with rights in the ship *Fortune*, which was trading in "Guinea" in 1649.[209] Indeed, the interests and property of New Englanders and Barbadians were intimately connected.[210]

Barbados was also feeding the other English colonies with slaves; its first vessel, the *Star*, continued on to St Christopher to deliver other slaves, and this became a common pattern later. In 1647, Captain Daniel Pierce of Barbados, with the ship *Swallowe*, arrived in Virginia and sold Captain Yardley four Africans.[211] By 1650 slaves were arriving as far afield as Boston thanks to the New England connections with the slave trade, as Samuel Maverick, a slaveholder on Noodles' Island (in Boston Harbor)

---

[204] NAB RB 3/1, Contracts, 30 July 1644 and 31 July 1644, p. 419; also 15 August 1644, p. 432.
[205] Gragg, *Englishmen*, p. 122. The Dutch registers were published by K. Ratelband, *Vijf Dagregisteers uit het Casteel S. Jorge da Mina* (Hague, 1950).
[206] NAB RB 3/2, Contract 23 November 1647, p. 286.
[207] Gragg, *Englishmen*, p. 122.
[208] Gragg, *Englishmen*, pp. 123-4.
[209] 10 (4) 1650, Liber I, *Suffolk Deeds*.
[210] Gragg, *Englishmen*, p. 124.
[211] Alice Granbery Walter (ed.), *Book "B" Lower Norfolk County Court Records* (Baltimore, 1994), p. 109. Walter, *Lower Norfolk B*, p. 109. Two years later, Nathaniell Powndall of Bristol sold negroes to Captain Francis Yardley for use of Captain Nicholas of London a mariner and commander of merchant frigate in 1649.

purchased slaves from Barbados-based John Parris, owner of the *Fortune*, which traded in Guinea.[212] Thus in 1654 the *Samuel* of Barbados, which was bound from Africa, was to deliver Africans by the pinnace *Hope* "elsewhere in the Caribee islands."[213]

The early English slave trade focused on West Africa, particularly Calabar, which is frequently mentioned as a port of call in the early records. However, English merchants, like their Dutch counterparts, also engaged in the Central African trade. Even during the Dutch occupation of Luanda, English merchants were hoping to deliver Angolan slaves to Spanish territories. In 1642, two English merchants offered the Spanish 2,000 slaves obtained from the Dutch in Angola, threatening to give them to the breakaway Portuguese if the offer was refused, though it and a similar offer by Ferdinand Franklin were indeed refused.[214] English traders even tried to deal with the Portuguese when the Dutch were ousted, for in 1658 an English ship with a Dutch captain carried 1,200 slaves and 22,000 pounds of ivory from Angola to Brazil in which "all of the officers and some of the ordinary seamen bought negro slaves at Luanda to adventure for their own account."[215] The example, of the *Hopewell*, seized by the Portuguese governor in 1659, and its crew held in Angola for two years may have discouraged the English from continuing to trade in Luanda, though certainly English merchants did begin trading at Loango and Kongo, beyond the reach of Portuguese power.[216] One English merchant who traded in Calabar in 1660 noted that Africans from that port were not as valued as Angolans, presumably also carried by English traders as well.

The growing dominance of trading in Africa as a source of slaves eclipsed but did end the capture of slaves by privateers. One of the most famous of the later privateers, William Jackson, led a number of successful voyages in 1642–1645 that captured a good number of slaves, many of which he delivered to Bermuda.[217] In 1646 the Dutch West India Company was still issuing instructions for the disposal of prizes by its ships,

---

[212] *Suffolk Deeds* Liber I, (Boston), p. 262.

[213] NAB RB 3/2, Contract 29 March 1654, p. 629.

[214] Georges Scelle, *L'traite negrere aux indes de castile* (Paris, 1906) 1: 484.

[215] C. R. Boxer, "English Shipping in the Brazil Trade, 1640–65," *Mariner's Mirror* 37/3 (July 1951), p. 214.

[216] PRO HCA 13/73, 27 June 1659.

[217] Vincent Harlow, *The Voyages of Captain William Jackson (1642–45)*, Cambden Miscellany, v. XIII, Camden Third Series, 34 (London, 1924), which includes a number of primary sources. There are also Spanish accounts of his voyages, AGI SD 215, Auto por donde se tomo so declarasion al prisonero que se quedo de la harmada ynglessa, 15 December 1642; and William Jackson to Governor of Venezuela, 21 February 1643 (showing the capture of African slaves).

including slaves. Even as late as 1653 the Company renewed these regulations covering prizes and slaves, primarily for the benefit of Brazil.[218]

With regular trade and the sporadic raids by the privateers, and as the Spanish *asiento* trade opened up and brought West Africans as well as Central Africans, those Africans arriving in the English and Dutch Americas came from a much wider geographic range than during the initial period of colonization. Richard Ligon, visiting Barbados in 1648–1649, noted that slaves were obtained from every part of Africa: "Guinny and Binney, Catechew, Angola, River Gambia."[219] The era of Angolan dominance in the slave trade was eclipsed shortly after 1641 but was never ended. Although English and Dutch traders now focused considerable interest on purchasing Africans in Allada and Calabar, they did not stop buying them in Central African as well. Though a detailed statistical breakdown of origins is not possible before the 1670s, the impression that one gets from the scattered sources is one of great diversity that included both West and Central Africans.

Thus from 1585 to 1640 a remarkable series of circumstances had created a situation in which the English and Dutch obtained almost all, if not all, of the first enslaved Africans from West Central Africa. West Central Africa itself had a unique place in the larger story of the Atlantic world, for it was the one region in Africa where people had been deeply involved with European culture and where enslavement for the Atlantic trade was commonplace, as the story of Angela, the young Christian woman whose journey to Virginia began this chapter, attests.

[218] "Resolution of the West India Company to Encourage Privateering," 15 September 1653, *New York Colonial Documents* 14: 214.
[219] Richard Ligon, *A True & Exact History of the Island of Barbadoes* (London, 1657), p. 46.

2

The Portuguese, Kongo, and Ndongo and the Origins of Atlantic Creole Culture to 1607

There was a marked contrast between the West Central Africans who came to dominate the slave trade during the first half of the seventeenth century and the earlier groups from Upper Guinea or those from Lower Guinea coast who would later dominate the trade. Unlike these other areas, the West Central Africans came from a region of Atlantic Africa that had an intense engagement with European culture unlike the earlier generation of Africans coming from Upper Guinea. The relationship between West Central Africa and Europeans predated the founding of the Portuguese colony of Angola in 1575 by nearly a century and resulted in a unique blend of African and European political practices and cultural synthesis that Ira Berlin aptly named "Atlantic Creole."[1] In addition to the engagement with European culture, West Central Africans shared quite similar linguistic, social, cultural, and political forms, making for a much more uniform set of beliefs and practices than any of the other regions of Atlantic Africa. It was this shared heritage and the long and complex interactions of Central Africans with the Portuguese and later with the Dutch that made for the emergence of a distinct Atlantic Creole culture in Central Africa.

From the Central African perspective, the integration into the Atlantic world began in 1483, when the kingdom of Kongo first encountered

[1] Ira Berlin, "From Creoles to African: Atlantic Creoles and the Origins of African American Society in Mainland America," *William and Mary Quarterly* 53 (1996): 251–88; modified and updated in *Many Thousands Gone: The First Two Centuries of Slavery in North America* (Cambridge, MA, 1998) and *Generations of Captivity: A History of African American Slavery* (Cambridge, MA, 2003), pp. 23–49. This concept has proven controversial, as discussed in Chapter 5.

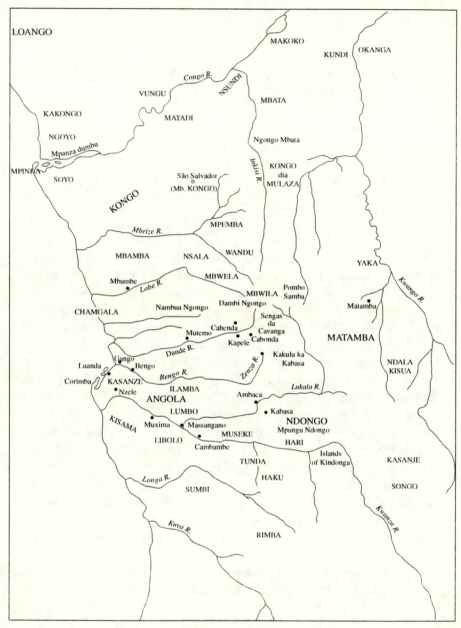

LOANGO

MAKOKO

KUNDI   OKANGA

Congo R.

NSUNDI

VUNGU

MBATA

KAKONGO

MATADI

NGOYO

Ngongo Mbata

Mpanza dumbu

MPINDA

SOYO

São Salvador
(Mb. KONGO)

KONGO
dia
MULAZA

Inkisi R.

KONGO

MPEMBA

Mbrize R.

MBAMBA   NSALA   WANDU

MBWELA

YAKA

Mbumbe   Lobe R.

MBWILA   Pombo
Samba

Kwango R.

CHAMGALA   Nambua Ngongo   Dambi Ngongo

Matamba

Sengas
da
Cavanga

Mutemo   Cahenda

Cabonda

MATAMBA

Kapele

Dande R.

Zenza R.

Kakulu ka
Kabasa

NDALA
KISUA

Giango
Luanda   Bengo   Bengo R.

Corimba   KASANZE

Lukala R.

Nzele   ILAMBA

ANGOLA   Ambaca

LUMBO   Kabasa

KISAMA   Muxima   Massangano   NDONGO
Mpungu Ndongo

LIBOLO   MUSEKE

Cambambe   HARI

Islands
of Kindonga   KASANJE

TUNDA

Longa R.   HAKU   SONGO

SUMBI

Kuva R.   Kwanza R.

RIMBA

West Central Africa

FIGURE 1. Mbundu Blacksmiths. Source: Ezio Bassani, "Un Cappuccino nell'-Africa nera del seicento. I disegni de Manoscritti Araldi del Padre Givanni Antonio Cavazzi da Montecuccolo," Quaderni Poro 4 (1987).

Portuguese explorers, expanded when its southern neighbor, Ndongo, initiated its own contacts with Lisbon in 1518, and continued when Portugal sought to contact a third African kingdom, Benguela, in 1546. The Portuguese conquest of Angola, which began in 1575, created dramatic new developments for all three kingdoms. In about 1580 yet another kingdom, Loango, contacted Portugal with a request for missionaries and joined the integrated region.[2]

---

[2] The best overviews of events in this period, based on a close and careful reading of the original sources, are in Graziano Saccardo [da Legguzzano], *Congo e Angola con la storia dell'antica missione dei Cappuccini* (3 vols., Venice, 1982–1983), and Ilídio do Amaral, *O Reino do Congo, os mbundu (ou Ambundos), o reino dos "ngola" (ou de Angola) e a presença portuguesa, de finais do século XV a meados do século XVI* (Lisbon, 1996), and *idem, O Consulado de Paulo Dias de Novais. Angola no último quartel do século XVI e primeiro do século XVII* (Lisbon, 2000). There is also the aging survey in English in David Birmingham, *Trade and Conflict in Angola: The Mbundu and Their Neighbours under the Influence of the Portuguese, 1483–1790* (Oxford, UK, 1966).

From a Portuguese perspective, its contacts with Central African kingdoms grew out of its expansion into Africa, and the establishment of
colonies on off-shore islands, like São Tomé in 1485, or, more significantly, in the Central African mainland in Angola from 1575. The surge
of tens of thousands of captives exported on Portuguese shipping after
1605 and the uniquely Afro-Atlantic culture of many of those Africans
was a product of this interaction. The Portuguese monopoly of commerce
was altered when Dutch and English merchants began visiting the region
in the early seventeenth century.

Geography and Demography, Language and Ethnicity

West Central Africans who entered the Dutch and English colonies either
through piracy or trade were drawn from ports on a coast that was
bounded by Pointe Noire, in the modern-day Republic of Congo (Congo-
Brazzaville), in the north and Benguela, in modern-day Angola, roughly
1,000 kilometers to the south. The coast was a broad and generally flat
strip that bounded a highland interior. The flat lands varied from some
200 kilometers deep along the Congo and Kwanza Rivers to 45–75 kilometers between these broader areas. Several large rivers emerged from
inland regions and cut and divided the highlands into distinct sections:
the Congo River to the north extended lowlands far inland, though its
valley became narrower and the sides steeper as one moved inland. To the
south, the Kwanza River also cut through the highlands, making a broad
plain at the coast that narrowed to a deep canyon in the interior. Farther
inland there was a great bend in the Kwanza as the northward-flowing
river turns west to the coast, and this bend defined the southeastern border of the area.[3] Both the Congo and the Kwanza were broad enough
to allow ships to penetrate into the interior until they reached a fall line
in the highlands, though during this period the Kwanza was more often
used as a shipping corridor linking highlands and the Atlantic than was
the Congo. Smaller rivers that flowed from the first range of highlands
were also sometimes important strategically or for supporting agriculture,
such as the Mbidizi (Ambriz, M'brige), Dande, and Bengo Rivers north
of the Kwanza, or the Longa to the south, though none of these rivers
bore any shipping by ocean-going vessels.

The Kwango River in the interior of Kongo and Angola formed the
northeastern boundary of the region. In the north the Kwango flowed

---

[3] Ilídio do Amaral, *O Rio Cuanza (Angola), da Barra a Cambambe: Reconstituição de
    aspectos geográficos e acontecimentos históricos dos séculos XVI e XVII* (Lisbon, 2000).

through a fairly deep canyon that opened out in a broad lower lying area, known today as the Baixa de Cassange and in the seventeenth century as the Great Kina, defined by steep cliffs on its western side. Beyond the Kwango and the upper Kwanza soils were thin and sandy, and rainfall was less than abundant, making it a zone of low population density and less interaction. It would not be until later in the seventeenth century that the more populated regions that lay beyond the Kwango entered into contact with the Atlantic coast, through the western expansion of the Lunda Empire into the zone.

The density of population along the coast and the northeastern Kwango frontier depended on the quantity and regularity of rainfall. Along the coast, rainfall and population both decreased as one moved south from the mouth of the Congo River, making for sparser and sparser coastal populations the further south one moved. Although the population of the coast around the mouth of the Congo River was fairly dense, the coast south of the river toward Luanda suffered increasing aridity, and Luanda itself, valuable for its fishing and navigational aspects, did not support a dense population before the arrival of the Portuguese, in addition to the fishermen who lived on the coastal spit of land called the island of Luanda. South of the Kwanza the coastal population became even more sparse, and the scattered population tended more to nomadism.

Rainfall and population increased inland from the coast: generally as one reached about 30 kilometers inland there were settled populations and small towns, but the densest population and largest settlements were in the highlands, typically at elevations above 500 meters. In 1483 the most important of these was the kingdom of Kongo, with its capital at Mbanza Kongo, a substantial city located on the western edge of the interior highlands. Kongo's expansion and conquests had given it most of the coast as well: its province of Soyo controlled the moderately densely populated mouth of the Congo River, and its province of Mbamba controlled much of the south coast, especially the island of Luanda and its surrounding area, valuable because *nzimbu* shells, which circulated widely as money, could be fished in great quantities there. According to titles that Kongo's king Afonso I presented in 1535, it claimed a vast region stretching from the coast north of the Congo to the arid plains south of the Kwanza, though it did not have uniformly even control. But the country did control a large area directly – something on the order of 100,000 square kilometers with as many as 350,000 people regularly paying taxes and accepting justice from the kings in Mbanza Kongo. Beyond this nuclear region, defined roughly by the Congo River on the north, Luanda Island and the Dande River on the south, and both banks of the Inkisi River on the east, Kongo's control was much less direct and its authority more contested.

The kingdom of Ndongo, whose capital region of Kabasa was located in the highlands between the Kwanza and its effluent the Lukala River, did not emerge as a political force independent of Kongo until the second decade of the sixteenth century. It was not as centralized as Kongo, even though its rulers would seek to increase their power. The rulers of this kingdom pushed their authority toward the coast, especially in the arid lands of Kisama, which lay south of the Kwanza, where rich mines of rock salt were found. Ndongo's claims by the mid-sixteenth century included about half the territory and the population that Kongo ruled directly.

The third highland region, lying south of the Kwanza, was the likely capital region of the kingdom of Benguela, known in 1546 to lie somewhere near the headwaters of the Longa River. Very little is known about the size and structure of the kingdom of Benguela, beyond it being a major enemy of Ndongo in the 1560s and being more or less destroyed in the late sixteenth and early seventeenth centuries.[4] The highland region in which the kingdom lay was densely populated, at least as densely as the core regions of Kongo and Ndongo and perhaps even more so. Certainly the region was the demographic center of West Central Africa in later periods and remains so even today.

In the interior there were some other powerful, but much less known, kingdoms. On Kongo's northeastern border was the Teke kingdom, or Nziko, cited as a powerful force even at the start of the sixteenth century.[5] Although Kongo fought against Teke in the sixteenth and seventeenth centuries, there is little documentation about its internal structure or even the exact extent of its territorial domains. It was famous for producing cloth from tree bark, and its exports of varying qualities spread far and wide.[6] South of Teke were the "Seven Kingdoms of Kongo dia Nlaza," a confederation of states that was independent of Kongo, whose ruler was called "Emperor" in 1561 and who controlled a substantial area between

[4] What little is known is reviewed, along with some speculation about its exact location, in Beatrix Heintze, "Wer war der König von Benguela?" *In Memoriam António Jorge Dias* (Lisbon, 1974), 1: 185–202.
[5] Mentioned as "Anzica" under a king called "Emcuquaanzico" (Nkuku a Nziko) in Duarte Pacheco Pereira, *Esmerlado de Situ Orbis* (ed. Augusto Epiphânio da Silva Dias, Lisbon, 1905), book 2, chapter 3, p. 136, a text originally written around 1506.
[6] Most detail is given in a late-sixteenth-century description by Duarte Lopes, edited and published in Filippo Pigafetta, *Relatione del Reame di Congo e circonvincine contrade*...(Rome, 1591, mod. ed. Giorgio Cardonna, Milan, 1978, marking pagination of original), pp. 14–18.

Kongo and the Kwango, before being absorbed into Kongo's province of Mbata at the end of the century.[7]

Matamba was another kingdom located east of Ndongo, in the broad stretch of lower land bounded on the east by the Kwango River, called the Baixa de Cassange, whose north portion it dominated. Matamba was nominally tributary to Kongo at least by 1530, when it is first mentioned as "one of my noblemen" by King Afonso I, but probably was never really dominated by Kongo.[8] Local traditions recorded in the 1660s maintained that an unnamed king of Matamba had rebelled from Kongo at some unspecified time and had grown to take over many other lands and vassals, establishing his capital at Mocaria Camatamba.[9] Matamba was ruled by a "Great Queen" in the 1560s who wanted very much to enter into direct contact with Portugal and enjoyed an exaggerated reputation for having substantial mines of silver and other minerals.[10]

Although the major kingdoms all had capitals in the highlands when the Portuguese arrived, one kingdom, Loango, developed on the coast during the course of the sixteenth century. The coast north of the Congo received enough rainfall to support a kingdom, and although early-sixteenth-century observers noted the dense population they made no mention of a large state.[11] The polities of the early sixteenth century were small, lying north of the Congo River (Vungu) or along the coast (Ngoyo and Kakongo) but there was not yet a Loango.[12] But by mid-century Loango was noted and was attracting the attention of international traders by the 1570s.[13]

In addition to the larger states and emerging kingdoms, there were still a number of smaller entities that were not under the control of any of the larger states. One such group of smaller polities (sometimes called the Dembos) lay in the borderland between Kongo and Ndongo, still in the

---

[7] Apontamentos de Sebastião de Souto, c. 1561, in António Brásio, ed. *Monumenta Missionaria Africana* (*MMA*) (15 vols, Lisbon, 1952–98) 2: 480.

[8] Afonso to João III, 28 January 1530, *MMA* 1: 540. Matamba is also listed among Afonso's titles in 1535, *MMA* 2: 38; on the other hand, in 1561 Sebastião Souto, a priest in the Kongo court, wrote about Matamba as if it were an independent territory, see Apontamentos de Sebastião de Souto, c. 1561, *MMA* 2: 479–80.

[9] MSS Araldi (Modena) (MSS Araldi), Giovanni Antonio Cavazzi da Montecuccolo, "Missione evangelica al regno di Congo" (MS of 1665–68), vol. A, Book 1, pp. 5–6 and Book 2, pp. 42–3.

[10] De Souto, *MMA* 2: 479–80.

[11] Pacheco Pereira, *Esmeraldo* (ed. Silva Dias), book 3, chapter 1, pp. 132–3.

[12] Afonso to Paulo III, 21 February 1535, *MMA* 2: 38.

[13] A good account of its early history and international relations is found in Phyllis Martin, *The External Trade of the Loango Coast, 1576–1870* (Oxford, 1972).

land of Mbundu, but not under the authority of either power. This border area had broken terrain, and the jagged mountains provided fortified residences that allowed local rulers called *sobas* to defend themselves against determined enemies, even though they often might declare vassalage to Kongo or Ndongo temporarily when threatened. Some of these smaller powers might engross more than one *soba*; certainly Mbwila, located in the flatter land of the valley of the upper Bengo-Zenza River, was one. Others dominated a mountain and its surrounding valleys, like Nambu a Ngongo on the front range of the highlands.

Although the region was divided into a multiplicity of kingdoms and smaller political entities, in the entire region only two languages, Kikongo and Kimbundu, were spoken. These languages were members of the same subfamily of Bantu family of languages, and speakers of each language understood each other with a little difficulty. The similarities were noticeable enough as to lead the sixteenth-century chronicler Duarte Lopes to declare that "the language of the population of Angola is the same as the language of the people of Kongo." He went on to add that the differences were similar to those that existed between "neighboring nations as between Portuguese and Castilians or between Venetians and Calabrians."[14]

Although language served as one component in manifesting identity, it was not always the determining factor. Thus although Kikongo was spoken in the kingdom of Kongo as well as in neighboring kingdoms, and people who lived in the kingdom of Kongo had a clear attachment to the Kongo state, in reference to kingdom of Loango one observer wrote that "the language and people are quite different from those of Kongo or Angola."[15] The Mbundu people, however, although living in politically fragmented units all spoke Kimbundu and regarded this as providing them with a common identity. Overall, however, political attachment was visible in people's identity with rulers and political units rather than with language.

In addition to language, the people of Kongo and Ndongo shared similar religious concepts, especially concerning the role of deities and ancestors. Ethnic differences were not linked to differences in religion, however, as many of the traditions connected Kongos and Mbundu to a common origin. Thus despite the loyalty that Kongos and Mbundus

---

[14] Pigafetta, *Relatione*, p. 24.
[15] BL Add. 15183, fol. 10.

showed to their political leaders, this in no way was comparable to the ethnoreligious conflicts evident in western Europe at the time or the deep, long-lasting hatreds that surfaced in colonial and contemporary Africa and in the more recent history of Europe.[16]

Central African States: Political Structure

A. Kongo

When Central Africans first became involved in the emerging Atlantic world, the kingdom of Kongo was well placed to fashion the way in which this integration took place. Kongo was the most highly centralized state in the region, which put its rulers in position to influence political, cultural, and religious innovations in Kongo and the wider region and also allowed them to negotiate Portuguese activity from a position of strength.

Kongo's ability to deal with the Portuguese from a position of strength was based on its long experience of dominating its neighbors and controlling its subjects.[17] This development began long before Diogo Cão arrived at the mouth of the Congo River in 1483. A century earlier, in the late fourteenth century, Lukeni lua Nimi, ruler of a petty state (*wene*) named Mpemba Kasi near the modern town of Matadi, south of the Congo River, made an alliance with his neighbor Mpuku a Nsuku, ruler of another small polity in the Inkisi River valley called Mbata. Each agreed to support the claims to rule of the other's descendants against competing claimants, thus insuring unbroken succession in their own lines. From this beginning, the alliance forced or persuaded half a dozen neighboring states to join the growing kingdom; renamed Kongo after Lukeni lua Nimi founded a new capital at Mbanza Kongo on a flat mountain overlooking the coastal lowlands. By concentrating population around their capital, successive kings

[16] See, John Thornton, "La Nation angolaise en Amérique, son identité en Afrique et en Amérique," *Cahiers des Anneaux de la Mémoire* 2 (2000): 241–56.

[17] The strength, size, security of travel, wealth, and loyalty of subjects to the king were all stressed in the only two brief fifteenth-century accounts of the country, the first by the Portuguese chronicler Rui de Pina, published in Carmen M. Radulet, *O cronista Rui de Pina e a "Relação do Reino do Congo"* (Lisbon, 1992), including both the Italian version of Pina's account of Kongo (1492) and the later official Portuguese account (1515) based on an inquest with six witnesses from the returning Portuguese fleet, see fols. 99ra–100rb of the Italian text (Portuguese translation on facing pages), and the second left by the Milanese ambassador to Lisbon, 6 November 1491, in Adriano Cappelli, "A proposito di conquiste africane," *Archivio Storico Lombardo*, series. III, 5 (1896): 416–17, based on his gleanings from the same fleet.

of Kongo created a demographic base from which they drew soldiers and supplies allowing them to overwhelm further opposition.[18] The growth of power in the kings' hands permitted them to replace rulers in the conquered lands with a subservient class of governors, serving at the king's pleasure for terms of three years, drawn primarily from the ruler's family and its clients.[19]

The centralizing power of Kongo's rulers was evident in the actions of Nzinga a Nkuwu, seventh in this line of rulers, in office when the Portuguese arrived. He was able to give out the formerly independent subunits of his kingdom, long converted to provinces of various sizes, to his family and supporters as sources of income, which they called *rendas* when they began writing in Portuguese.[20] His son Mvemba a Nzinga (baptized as Afonso) recalled that when he and others displeased his royal father in about 1508, the king "took away our renda," which was the province of Nsundi, "leaving us like a man blown by the wind."[21] When Afonso became king he also gave out and took back *rendas* at will, for his own kinsmen held most of them in 1526.[22] This system of income grants in the gift of the king gave kings substantial control over all their officials but also led to ferocious competition when kings died.

The alliance with Mbata, whose leaders were not chosen by the king,[23] also illustrates the experience that rulers had in maintaining domestic

---

[18] John Thornton, "Mbanza Kongo/São Salvador: Kongo's Holy City," in David Anderson and Richard Rathbone (eds.), *Africa's Urban Past* (London, 2000), pp. 67–9.

[19] John Thornton, "The Origins and Early History of the Kingdom of Kongo, c. 1350–1550," *International Journal of African Historical Studies* 34 (2001): 1–31, reconstructing the early history largely from traditions.

[20] Most of our knowledge of Kongo institutions and government in the first half of the sixteenth century comes from Kongo sources; the letters of king Afonso I are crucial, as are a few letters of his successor, Diogo I, and legal inquests conducted by Kongo monarchs; see the 1550 inquest for politics of giving and taking rendas, Auto de Devasa de D. Diogo I, in *MMA* 2: 248–62.

[21] Afonso to João III, 5 October 1514, *MMA* 3: 295. That the province was "Isunde" or Nsundi is revealed in a later text, Francisco de Santa Maria, *O ceu aberto na terra* (Lisbon, 1697), cap. 19, excerpt in *MMA* 1: 95 based on earlier documentation that is no longer extant.

[22] Afonso to João III, 18 March 1526, *MMA* 1: 461. In response to this letter and other now lost ones, King João III of Portugal encouraged Afonso to make up books of rendas so that he could keep track of his nobles' obligations – and also so he "would not take their lands, making with them contracts and conditions with them..." undated letter written perhaps as late as 1529, *MMA* 1: 530.

[23] Afonso to João III, 18 March 1526, *MMA* 1: 461, makes it clear that he did not control this province's ruler. Mbata gradually lost its privileges in the seventeenth century, see John Thornton, *The Kingdom of Kongo: Civil War and Transition, 1641–1718* (Madison, 1983), pp. 38–46.

alliances, for when Afonso seized power from one of his brothers in 1509, upon the death of Nzinga a Nkuwu, Dom Jorge, ruler of Mbata, who was, according to Afonso, "the head of our kingdom," supported him against enemies who sought his support in overthrowing the new king.[24] Such negotiations were the regular stuff of Kongo domestic politics.

Other features of Kongo politics included an elaborate judicial system, the earliest account of Kongo describing its ruler as "exercising greatest justice" especially in cases of adultery, theft, and treason.[25] The king, according to an inquiry of 1492, could exercise ultimate judicial power and could order "death and the confiscation of all goods" for all who failed to obey a royal decree.[26] A royal "inquisitor" came from Kongo to Soyo to investigate stolen goods in 1517,[27] and a judicial inquest of 1550 reveals that royal judges held courts (*nkanus*) and dispensed justice in the provinces.[28]

Royal power was also maintained in the practice of religion.[29] Nzinga a Nkuwu maintained a "house of idols" (probably *nzo a ukisi* in Kikongo) most likely dedicated to territorial deities at his capital and reflected a host of other such deities who were found at "temples" also in Soyo, Nsundi, and surely throughout the kingdom.[30] The snake imagery found

---

[24] Afonso to Manuel I, 5 October 1514, *MMA* 1: 299.

[25] Milanese Ambassador, 6 November 1491, in Capelli, "Conquiste africane," p. 416.

[26] De Pina, Untitled Chronicle, 1491, fols. 93rb–93va (ed. Radulet), *Cronista*, pp. 116–17.

[27] Act of Inquest of Afonso I, 22 April 1517, *MMA* 1: 393–7.

[28] The inquest itself was held at Mbanza Kongo, but in the course of testifying about a treason plot, one witness recalled that the governor of Mpemba decided he could not join the conspiracy as there was "a mucano in his lands and he was without people" *MMA* 2: 257. Mucano in sixteenth-century Kongo was a legal inquest or court proceeding, and there is no evidence in the original text (Arquivo Nacional de Torre do Tombo (ANTT) Corpo Cronotógico (CC) II 242/121), which we have consulted directly, to read the term as *mocambo* as Brásio suggests in the editor's apparatus.

[29] For a discussion of religion in Central Africa, based largely on sixteenth- and seventeenth-century sources see, John Thornton, "Religious and Ceremonial Life in the Kongo and Mbundu Areas, 1500–1700," in Linda M. Heywood (ed.), *Central Africans and Cultural Transformation in the American Diaspora* (Cambridge, 2001); other details and a somewhat different interpretation are found in Ann Hilton, *The Kingdom of Kongo* (Oxford, 1985), pp. 24–31.

[30] Afonso destroyed this house in 1509 and triggered opposition throughout the kingdom, Afonso to Manuel I, 5 October 1514, *MMA* 1: 296. The Mwene Soyo ordered that all "idols and temples" be burned in his lands, de Pina, Untitled Chronicle, 1492, fol. 92va (ed. Radulet), *Cronista*, pp. 112–15. Even before, Afonso burned "idols" in Nsundi, suggesting that these territorial shrines existed there as well, João de Barros, *Asia* (Lisbon, 1552), Decade 1, Book 3, Chapter 10, fols. 35–6. This account was surely written from other original documents, for a very similar account appeared in Martin Fernandez de Enciso, *Suma de Geographica* (Seville, 1519). The probable ultimate source is a letter

on the clothing of the ruler of Soyo in 1491 also probably reflected a protective deity as well as his patronage.[31] There was also a sacred grove containing the graves of former kings in the capital, surely related to the central African practice of veneration of ancestors, also kept under royal patronage.[32] The king, however, as ordinary Kongolese, could resort to use of charms for good or evil. When Nzinga a Nkuwu was told by jealous rivals that his son Mvemba a Nzinga (Afonso) was flying around at night through magical powers and visiting the wives of others, he arranged to discover the truth by sending a "fetish" in Afonso's name to one of the wives, who then revealed Afonso's innocence by returning the charm to the king.[33] The power that the kings had over religious practices could readily be transferred to other religious traditions like Christianity.

Kongo and Portugal, 1483–1600: Cultural Dimensions

In 1483 when the Portuguese navigator Diogo Cão and his crew reached Soyo, Kongo's province at the mouth of the Congo River, they were seeking to create Christian allies and link with other Christians to be found in Ethiopia or India. They found a willing partner for military and cultural exchange in Kongo. Although the Mwene (Lord of) Soyo was the first Kongolese official to meet them, he immediately forwarded the mission on to the capital of Mbanza Kongo. When they did not come back soon Cão took some notables from Soyo to Lisbon, promising to return them later. Among the group was Kasuta, a noble of the royal house, who was baptized as João da Silva. Kongo's ruler, Nzinga a Nkuwu was interested in Portugal and its culture as a result of his conversations with the Portuguese who he kept at his court, so that in 1485 when Cão returned the nobles, including Kasuta, to Kongo, Nzinga Nkuwu was ready to initiate a major cultural initiative. He chose Kasuta to be his official ambassador to Portugal and instructed him to request priests, carpenters, and stonemasons to build a "house of prayer" as these were in Portugal, farmers to teach them to till the soil with plows, and women to teach the baking of bread. He also sent some children from Kongo to learn to read and write

written by Afonso I in 1509, alluded to in his letter to Manuel I of 5 October 1514, *MMA* 1: 294–5, but now lost.

[31] De Pina, Untitled Chronicle, 1492, fols. 89rb–90va (ed. Radulet), *Cronista*, pp. 106–9. On the snake and its imagery, see Hilton, *Kingdom of Kongo*, pp. 12–17, 51. Hilton's "*mbumba* dimension" corresponds to our cult of territorial deities.

[32] Afonso recalled the cutting down of this forest in 1509 much later, in discussing a church that was later built at the site; Afonso to João III, 25 August 1526, *MMA* 1: 479–80.

[33] de Barros, *Asia*, decade 1, book 3, chapter 10, fols. 35–6.

and become Christian to create a bilingual and bicultural group to spread the new ideas throughout his kingdom.[34] In 1491 this group returned to Kongo with a major mission, including the various priests and farmers. Both the Mwene Soyo and Nzinga a Nkuwu accepted baptism, the king becoming João I of Kongo on 3 May 1491. The Kongolese who had gone to Lisbon with Kasuta established a school, and one of their number wrote the first letter of a Kongo king in October of that year.[35]

It was under these conditions that the first Atlantic Creoles emerged, formed both in Central Africa and in Portugal, beginning a process that would continue in the following years. Because Nzinga a Nkuwu had initiated the contact with Portugal, he and Kongo's later rulers established the system that kept cultural transfer under Kongo's control.[36] Kongo's initiative was one of the most ambitious bilateral cultural programs in the period of European expansion, especially because it was not accompanied by any attempt at conquest or forced conversion. The morning of his baptism, Nzinga Nkuwu and his court, along with thousands of followers, celebrated what is known as a *nsanga*, a military dance done at major occasions, which included dancing, playing music, and doing their "customary games."[37]

If Nzinga a Nkuwu started the Kongolese version of Atlantic Creole culture, it was his son and successor, Afonso I Mvemba a Nzinga (1509–1542), who carried the process even further. He realized early on that not all European ideas and technology were valuable. Thus he quickly abandoned European agricultural techniques that proved unsuitable to tropical Africa and restricted stonemasonry and carpentry to the churches and the houses of a few Kongolese nobles. Afonso also experimented with Portuguese legal forms but rejected most of them and made few changes to the legal structure of the country. After studying the Portuguese law code, he laughingly asked Baltasar de Castro, a Portuguese legal advisor, what was the penalty in Portuguese law "if anyone puts his foot on the ground."[38]

---

[34] De Pina, *Chronica*, caps. 57 and 58; Kasuta is written in this source as Caçuta, but in the Italian version of the original report (ed. Radulet), fols. 87ra–87rb *Cronista*, pp. 100–3 his names is given as "Chrachanfusus." For a detailed reconstruction, see do Amaral, *Reino do Congo*, pp. 21–6.

[35] De Pina, Untitled Chronicle, 1492 (ed. Radulet), fol. 88rb, *Cronista*, pp. 104–5; see also João I of Kongo to João II of Portugal, October 1491 in *ibid*, fols. 99vb–100ra, pp. 132–3.

[36] Regimento to Simão de Sousa, 1512, *MMA* 1; 222–5.

[37] Rui de Pina, Untitled Chronicle, 1492 (ed. Radulet) fols. 95va–95vb, *Cronista*, pp. 122–3.

[38] Damião de Góis, *Chronica de Dom João II* (Lisbon, 1545), part IV, chapter 3, *MMA* 1: 375.

Christian conversion and literacy were the hallmarks of Atlantic Creole culture as it emerged during the reign of Afonso. By 1516, he funded and established a school system involving more than 1,000 students of noble families that created a literate elite.[39] In deciding to adopt Christianity, he fell in with a long-standing Portuguese desire. According to the royal instructions given to Gonçalo de Sousa, Portugal's first official ambassador to Kongo in 1491, the embassy was to "take the Faith of Jesus Christ Our Lord" to Kongo and that it was to "destroy and the temples and idols and false images of their gods, and finish all the rites and habits of sacrifice and heresy."[40] Later directives, such as instructions to the embassy of 1512, opened with discussions of the religious dimension of their efforts and included more instructions on political affairs and a request that Kongo nobles come to Portugal to study, joining others already in the country.[41]

The element of Christian identity that set Kongo's Atlantic Creole culture apart from Portuguese culture was its mixing of Christian ideas with local religious concepts. This was initially rooted in internal political turmoil. Afonso became king in 1509 after winning a battle against his half-brother Mpanzu a Kitima, who represented a strong element that opposed Afonso's deep Christian convictions. Afonso believed that the miraculous spectral appearance of Saint James Major and the Heavenly Host was responsible for his victory. He referred often to this miracle and incorporated it into the official coat of arms and seal of Kongo, which he adopted in 1512.[42]

As Afonso consolidated his control over the country, he pushed Christianity and a cultural program that extended the Atlantic Creole identity much farther than his father's limited goals. Afonso did not so much impose a European form of Christianity on his people as Africanize Christianity to fit Kongo beliefs. Traditional Kongolese religion focused on two sorts of otherworldly beings, deities with territorial jurisdiction and the souls of dead ancestors.[43] Afonso identified Christianity with both elements of the older religious tradition. Shortly after taking power, he

---

[39] Rui d'Aguiar to Manuel I, 25 May 1516 published in Damião de Goís, *Chronica delRei D. Manuel I* (Lisbon, 1556), book 4, chapter 3 in *MMA* 1: 361.

[40] Rui de Pina, Untitled Chronicle, 1492 (ed. Radulet), fols. 86ra-86va, *Cronista*, pp. 98–101. The official chronicle of 1515, had made this mission much less harsh and unyielding, see de Pina, *Chronica*, cap. LVIII.

[41] Regimento of D. Manuel to Simão da Silva, 1512, *MMA* 1: 232–4, 237–44.

[42] Afonso to the Lords of his Realm, 1512, *MMA* 1: 256–59.

[43] Thornton, "Religious and Ceremonial Life."

destroyed the "house of idols" in Mbanza Kongo, a center of worship of national deities, and immediately built a church on the site.[44] Subsequently the term *nzo a ukisi* (which readily translates as "house of idols") became the Kikongo term for a Christian church.[45] At the same time, he built a church dedicated to São Miguel on the site of the royal graves and their forest, so important during his father's time as a center of worship of the ancestors of the elite.[46] This church was locally known also as *mbila*, meaning "grave," and was used as a noble cemetery as before.[47] Afonso himself was buried there, and it was still a center of devotion hundreds of years later.[48]

Afonso continued the engagement with the European side of Christianity even as he incorporated African ideas. He sent noble children to study theology in Portugal, including his own son, Henrique, who went to Europe in 1512, was made a bishop of Utica in 1518, and was reassigned to Kongo in 1521. Henrique assisted his father in creating an Atlantic Creole Christianity that would be acceptable in both Europe and Africa. Educated Kongolese joined with well-educated Portuguese priests who resided in Afonso's court in this enterprise. Afonso read deeply in European theology, quizzing his advisors from Portugal on every detail, until one of them, Father Rui d'Aguiar, a theologian, wrote, "he knows the Prophets and preaching of our Lord Jesus Christ and all the lives of the saints, and all things of the holy mother Church better than we ourselves do."[49] From this careful reading Afonso and his advisors developed a whole theology of vocabulary that became commonplace. *Nkisi*, the Kikongo term referring to physical receptacles in which the spirits of deities or ancestors manifested themselves and which the Portuguese often called "idols," was used for an important linguistic transformation. The translators of Christian terms into Kikongo used an abstract form, *ukisi*, to mean "holy" in Portuguese and Latin. This grew from and continued the idea that the objects of worship in the royal "house of idols" that Afonso destroyed

---

[44] Afonso to Manuel I, 5 October 1514, *MMA* 1: 296.

[45] As attested in the dictionary of 1648, where "templus" is rendered as *nzo a ukisi*, see further John Thornton, "Perspectives on African Christianity," in Vera Hyatt and Rex Nettleford (eds.), *Race, Discourse, and the Origin of the Americas* (Washington, DC, 1995).

[46] Afonso to Joao III, 25 August 1526, *MMA* 1: 476.

[47] Christovão Ribeiro, 1 August 1548, *MMA* 15: 161.

[48] Jesuit priests complained that King Diogo prevented them from saying a mass in Afonso's honor at his grave in the church "Ambiro", Jorge Vaz to Capitan of S. Tomé, 11 February 1549, *MMA* 2: 228.

[49] Rui d'Aguiar to Manuel I, 25 May 1516 in de Goís, *Chronica, MMA* 1: 361.

in 1509 remained sacred when it became a church. The new vocabulary transformed such items as the Holy Bible into a "book with the characteristics of idols" (*nkanda a ukisi*) or a Christian priest (*nganga a ukisi*) into a "religious specialist with the characteristics of idols." Saints were converted into ancestors' souls (*moyo*), so that the Holy Spirit was called *Moyo Ukisi* and the Holy Trinity came to be rendered as "three people" (*antu a tatu*), focusing on their ancestral nature.[50]

Afonso sought to spread the Atlantic Creole Catholic religion throughout his realm, and by 1516 he had already established a network of missionary schools under Kongolese teachers, funding this through demanding a tithe.[51] As Kongo expanded, Kongolese missionaries spread Kongo influence into neighboring countries. When the kingdom of Ndongo sought its own Portuguese alliance and missionaries in 1518, and the king of Ndongo imprisoned the missionary, Afonso had him rescued in 1526 and dispatched his own priest, Afonso Anes, to continue the missionary work.[52]

Afonso's successors maintained the Christian identity of Kongo and continued his policies. None failed to proclaim their fidelity to the Church in their correspondence from Afonso's day onward, and anti-Christian factions never again disrupted life in Kongo. Although Afonso had elaborate plans to extend Christianity systematically through all his domains, using up to 50 priests and more,[53] the religion was still quite limited, mostly to the elite in a few locations, at the time of his death in 1542. Jesuit priests who came to Kongo a few years after Afonso died noted unbaptized adults within a few miles of the capital city and Mpinda, Kongo's major port.[54] Afonso's successor, Diogo I (1545–1561), expanded the faith beyond this limit, first through encouraging the Jesuits to extend education and then when political differences alienated him from the priests (who left in 1555) on his own.[55] Certainly Kongo became a missionary center,

---

[50] Thornton, "Perspectives," pp. 173–83.

[51] Rui d'Aguiar to Manuel I, 25 May 1516, in Goís, *Chronica, MMA* 1: 361–3.

[52] Saccardo, *Congo e Angola* 1: 76–7, see also do Amaral, *Reino do Congo*, pp. 75–82.

[53] Afonso to João III, 18 March 1526, *MMA* 1: 460–1. This plan would have had a self-sustaining priesthood of hundreds as the bishops and schools would soon be ordaining Kongolese in large numbers. The Portuguese Crown balked at allowing this sort of self-sustaining church; see do Amaral, *Congo*, pp. 123–6; 129–33 for a good assessment.

[54] Jorge Vaz to Simão Rodrigues, 1 August 1548, *MMA* 15: 151–2; Jacome Dias letter, 1 August 1548, *MMA* 15: 153–4.

[55] On the politics of the Jesuits and their mission, see Thornton, "Early Kongo–Portuguese Relations, 1483–1575: A New Interpretation," *History in Africa* 8 (1981): 183–204.

sending out priests and "chapel boys" (lay ministers of noble Kongo origin) as missionaries of its own to convert neighboring kingdoms.[56]

In 1595, after long diplomacy, the papacy named Kongo an Episcopal See, and its principal church, São Salvador, became a cathedral.[57] A report of 1600 noted some 13 parishes in Kongo, each with a vicar and a parish church in provincial capitals.[58] Another report of 1607 showed that the church in Kongo was well supported, with teachers, episcopal offices, and the like being financed by both Kongo, from tithes, and by the king of Portugal.[59] There were never many priests, generally one for a vast province with several thousand inhabitants, according to Dominican visitors in 1610. At best the vicar visited his parish once a year during Lent.[60]

By the end of the sixteenth century, people in Kongo followed regular Christian ways in areas near the parish churches and in the capital of São Salvador with its cathedral, five other churches, as well as many private oratories. People from all walks of life residing in this area attended mass routinely and usually knew the principal elements of the faith, and many of the wealthier classes received regular education. Frequently, services were so well attended that they were held on the public square to accommodate the thousands. This level of religious life was not confined to São Salvador but could also be found in other towns.[61]

Kongolese villagers shared in this religious culture, although they received little in the way of regular church services as did the townspeople. By the end of the sixteenth century, however, they did recognize and accept the principal rituals and symbols of Christianity. They identified the cross, religious paintings, priestly garb and paraphernalia, and other blessed objects (perhaps religious medals or the rosary) as a part of their own religious lives. They became Catholics formally through baptism and sought to have their own children baptized when the opportunity

---

[56] "Apontamentos que fez o Padre Sebastião de Souto..." (c. 1561) *MMA* 2: 478–80.
[57] This complicated task is detailed in Teobaldo Filesi, *Le Relazioni tra il Regno del Congo et la Sede Apostolica nel XVI Secolo* (Como, 1968).
[58] Royal order, 18 January 1600 *MMA* 5: 4.
[59] "Relação da Costa de Guiné, 1607" in *MMA* 5: 387.
[60] Luis de Cácegas and Luis de Sousa, *Historia de S. Domingos* (Lisbon, 1662), part 2, book 4, chapter 12, in *MMA* 5: 611, which recounts a visit done in 1610.
[61] Testimony of Kongolese ambassador, Antonio Vieira, 1595, "Interrogatoria de Statu Regni Congensis," *MMA* 3: 502; testimony of Martinho de Ulhoa, Bishop of São Tomé, "De Statu Regni Congi," 1595 *MMA* 3: 511–12; testimony of Bishop Simão Rodrigues Rangel, 16 January 1604, *MMA* 5: 71.

arose. In all likelihood the custom of taking a Saint's name in Portuguese form was also widespread among the common people as it was among the elite.

Christian education was not restricted to ordained priests, for Kongo had a core of educated laity who carried the faith to every corner of the kingdom even when priests were lacking. When Carmelite missionaries crossed rural Mbamba in southwest Kongo in 1584 they reported that lay preachers, whom the people called teachers, were found in many villages. There were also lay ministers, like Dom João, a member of the royal family who had a license to perform baptisms, the only Catholic rite that was universally observed in Kongo. João, and no doubt others like him, had lived in Portugal during his youth and was thus bilingual. For their part the country people flocked to the priests to hear mass, confess, marry, and baptize their children. Some simply came to get a blessing or to have something blessed for them to carry away. The priests arrived in Mbamba to the sound of a mixture of African and European musical instruments, whereas Dom João for his part, knew how to sing "to the organ." Mass was like a great public festival with music and dancing as well as religious activities. In 1584 Mbanza Mbamba, a modest country town and parish seat, had a spotless church with a well-painted retable behind it, and some 3,000 came to hear mass. People were particularly devoted to the cult of Virgin Mary, for the priests carried her image, and droves of people came to them, expecting miracles in her name.[62]

Kongolese, however, retained many of their older beliefs within their Atlantic Creole form of Christianity. Marriage rules that allowed polygamy, for example, continued, and many did not partake in the Christian sacrament of marriage, especially in rural areas, and across class and education lines.[63] Most people also continued to revere local deities in their traditional locations by identifying them as Catholic saints or as angels. Local religious practitioners (known as *ngangas*, though Catholic priests were also called by this term) made charms in traditional ways and their products were accepted as valid throughout the area, even though clergy, and sometimes the Kongolese educated elite, usually denounced

---

[62] Diego de Santissimo Sacramento, 2 December 1584, *MMA* 3; 296; *idem*, "Relaçion del viage que hiçe[n] . . . fols. 117–18v, *MMA* 4: 361–5. These testimonies are possibly the only ones that give direct evidence of rural life at the time.

[63] Santissimo Sacramento, "Relaçion," fol. 126, *MMA* 4: 386; De Cácegas and de Sousa, *Historia, MMA* 5: 611–12.

this as "fetishism" and sought to end it.[64] Nevertheless, many local customs connected to older religious beliefs remained.

The Atlantic Creole version of Christianity that gave Kongo its appearance of a Christian country, with churches, crowds of parishioners, and general good will toward the faith, was not fully accepted by the regular clergy from Europe who visited. This local Christianity, however, was widely supported and encouraged by the secular clergy, attached to the Episcopal See, who ran the parishes and the daily life of education. Jesuits who came in 1575 thought Kongo's Christianity to be "very weak" because the people had been baptized by "idiot priests" and their customs were "heathen." But Jesuits were convinced that the store of good will in Kongo was such that they could easily eliminate the defective elements by teaching.[65]

The religious transformation of Kongo was the best-documented part of a larger process of the growth of Atlantic Creole culture in the region. The new culture was best represented by the profession of Christianity but also by knowledge of European languages (and some literacy) and political ideas, adopting mixed European and African names, some changes in dress with the adaptation of imported cloth and clothing items from both Europe and West Africa, some mixing of musical styles, and the absorption of American food crops and preparation techniques, among other things. These changes did not affect all regions within Kongo equally, nor all social ranks and classes. They were most pronounced at São Salvador and the provincial capitals, as well as commercial centers that served as residences for the Portuguese traders and their African servants and partners. Although all Kongolese had some contact with this emerging African Creole culture, the poor and rural people were the least exposed and the high born and urban the most involved.

Kongo and Portugal, 1483–1607: Economic and Political Dimensions

The Origins of the Slave Trade

If the leaders of Kongo were able to shape and organize their adaptation of European and Portuguese culture and religion, they had a harder time

---

[64] Santissimo Sacramento, "Relaçion," fols. 120v–121v, *MMA* 4: 369–71; "Relatione di quello che occorse, et videro nel Regno di Congo...fatta d'un di loro," (1584) *MMA* 4: 412–13. See also John Thornton, "The Development of an African Catholic Church in the Kingdom of Kongo, 1491–1750," *Journal of African History* 25 (1984): 147–67.

[65] Diogo da Costa to Jesuit General, 20 March 1592, *MMA* 15: 317.

controlling their military and economic relations with Portugal.[66] This was because commercial and political objectives informed Portuguese interaction with Central Africa as much as a desire to spread the faith. Sometimes the agenda could be advanced through colonization, beginning in 1485 with a charter to settle the formerly uninhabited island of São Tomé. Other times the objectives could be achieved by supplying military assistance in Africa. The first mission to Kongo in 1491 assisted the king in suppressing rebels,[67] and two other missions in 1509 and 1512 included provisions for military assistance.[68]

Military assistance provided the first step in the creation of the Central African slave trade, directed to the newly developing colony of São Tomé, which used slaves to grow sugar cane and as reexports to West Africa. As early as 1502, Kongo was mentioned as a chief supplier of slaves to São Tomé,[69] although another report of 1506 suggests that their initial numbers were small.[70] Portuguese soldiers fighting for Kongo received war captives as part of their pay, and they exported them as slaves or used their pay to buy slaves on Kongolese markets.[71] The instructions issued to the mission of 1509 envisioned slaves as one mode of payment,[72] and in 1514 Afonso complained that the Portuguese had allowed slaves he had given them after a battle to escape.[73]

In addition, any Portuguese who took service in Kongo for pay could convert his salary into slaves. The institution of slavery, including the right to buy and sell slaves and even a slave market existed in Kongo when Europeans arrived. Certainly Kongo had strong class divisions with rights of superiors to order inferiors to work. In 1491, nobles ordered a thousand of their subordinates to build the first church in Kongo, a reflection that

---

[66] Thornton, "Early Kongo-Portuguese." This article contains full documentation supporting the thesis that Afonso's reign was not that of a dupe of the Portuguese or a traitor to his country, views that prevailed in the historiography of the 1960s and that are often still repeated in textbooks.

[67] De Pina, Untitled Chronicle, 1492 (ed. Radulet), fols. 98rb-98vb, pp. 128–31.

[68] "Despacho de Gonçalo Roiz..." (1509), *MMA* 4: 61; Regimento to Simão de Silva, 1512, *MMA* 1: 228, 232, 236, 241.

[69] Legend on Cantino Atlas, 1502, published in Armando Cortesão and Avelina Teixeira da Mota (eds.), *Portvglliae Monvmenta Cartographica* (6 vols., Lisbon, 1960), pl. 4–5, p. 12.

[70] Duarte Pacheco Pereira, *Esmeraldo De Situ Orbis* (ed. Epiphânio da Silva Dias, Lisbon, 1905, reprinted 1975), book 3, chapter. 2, p. 134.

[71] Thornton, "Early Kongo-Portuguese Relations," pp. 191–2.

[72] "Despacho de Gonçalo Roiz..."(1509), *MMA* 4: 61.

[73] Afonso I to Manuel I, 5 October 1514, *MMA* 1: 312–15.

Kongo had a strongly hierarchical society, as other eyewitnesses of the time observed.[74] The earliest documents that shed light on social conditions in Kongo around 1510 describe a situation in which people could buy slaves on markets for money: for example, in 1508 some priests bought "some pieces which are slaves,"[75] masons who came in 1509 bought slaves with their wages, each one obtaining "15 or 20 pieces,"[76] and around 1510 or 1511 Christovão d'Aguir received sufficient money to buy 27 slaves. Moreover, officers sent with the mission of 1512 to Kongo were able to "buy pieces."[77] All these purchases had to be on existing local markets where one could obtain slaves for money.

The kings of Kongo also traded in slaves. King Afonso regularly participated in the actual trading himself. He sent slaves to Lisbon to pay for purchases of cloth in 1510,[78] for example, and in 1517 he asked to "be able to load a certain number of pieces without paying customs" at São Tomé if he could not obtain a ship of his own to deliver his cargos.[79] Some Kongolese nobles also settled on the island and owned estates where they used slave labor.[80]

Developing military and commercial relations with the Portuguese and allowing them to settle in Kongo's territories offered challenges to the Kongolese authority. The Portuguese community that had emerged in São Tomé created one set of problems, and even the Portuguese Crown found them notoriously difficult to govern, royal governors complaining that they fought private wars and avoided taxation through smuggling and dealing with unapproved foreigners. Afonso found the Tomistas (as they were called) troublesome as well. He complained that São Tomé traders violated his own tax and access restrictions, dealing with his enemies, like Mpanzulumbu (a territory around the mouth of the Kongo River) in the early sixteenth century and Ndongo later. Diogo, his successor, found other grounds to complain about Portuguese dealings with "Chamgalla"

---

[74] Rui de Pina, Untitled Chronicle, 1492 (ed. Radulet), fols. 94va-95ra, *Cronista*, pp. 120–21; Letter of Milanese Ambassador, 7 October 1491, Capelli, 416.

[75] Afonso to Manuel, 5 October 1514, *MMA* 1: 300–1. "Pieces," *peças* in Portuguese, was a term used to indicate the value of a healthy adult slave; for a full discussion see Beatrix Heintze, "'Stücke' handel in Angola. Zur Skaverei in den ersten hundert Jahren portugiesischer Okkupation," in *idem, Studien*, pp. 212–31.

[76] Afonso to Manuel, 5 October 1514, *MMA* 1: 304–5, 306.

[77] Afonso to Manuel, 5 October 1514, *MMA* 1: 317.

[78] Afonso to Manuel, 5 October 1514, *MMA* 1: 303, 305, 312.

[79] Afonso to João III, 26 May 1517, *MMA* 1: 404.

[80] Thornton, "Early Kongo-Portuguese Relations," pp. 191–2.

on the south coast north of Luanda, as well as the continuing problems with the Portuguese in Ndongo.[81]

Despite these problems, which were an irritation to the Kongolese authorities, Kongo kings always retained control over the Portuguese residents in the country. Afonso's attempts to exercise this control by monopolizing the whole slave trade of the Central African coast both in his own country and in those over which he claimed lordship illustrate the success of this strategy. From the beginning of his reign he supplied the Portuguese himself or gave them salaries to buy slaves. He also zealously guarded his rights to exclusive control of exports from Kongo against Portuguese interlopers and smugglers, including those in his jurisdiction from north of the Congo River to well south of the Kwanza. In 1514 and 1516, he objected to ships visiting Mpanzalumbu, as they were his enemies.[82] Although Afonso was a participant in the trade, he was cognizant of the place of slavery in Kongolese law in that there were legal bounds on who could or could not be a slave. When, in 1526, he felt that some Portuguese merchants were dealing with people of "bad conscience" who had enslaved others illegally, he decided it was necessary to establish a board to oversee the trade so as to ensure that only those legally enslaved could be exported.[83]

Kongo and the Development of a Luso-African Community

Portuguese who settled in Central Africa also helped to shape Atlantic Creole culture. Some of these Luso-Africans, as we designate them, their African slaves and dependents, and their mixed-race descendants, were merchants, others were priests, and still others were granted administrative office holding and military positions in the African states. An inquest of 1548 reveals how well the highly placed Luso-Africans in Kongo were doing and attests to the growth of the slave trade, now involving thousands of exports. The same inquest identified a significant Luso-African community in "Angola," lands then under the control of Ndongo.[84]

---

[81] Thornton, "Early Kongo-Portuguese Relations."

[82] Afonso to Manuel I, 5 October 1514, *MMA* 1: 311, 319; Afonso to Antonio Carneiro, 5 March 1516, *MMA* 1: 359–60.

[83] Afonso to João III, 6 July 1526 and 18 October 1526, *MMA* 1: 468–71; 490.

[84] "Auto de Inquirição," 12 November 1548, *MMA* 2: 197–205. For a quantitative estimate of the growth of trade in this period, see Joseph C. Miller, "The Slave Trade of Congo and Angola," in Martin Kilson and Robert Rotberg (eds.), *The African Diaspora* (Cambridge, MA, 1976), pp. 79–88.

FIGURE 2. The Kings of Kongo and Angola, ca. 1680. Photograph by authors from original at the archive of the Academia das Ciências, Lisbon.

The conflicting policies of Kongo and Portugal led to a situation where Kongolese monarchs sided with their Luso-African clients against aggressive agents of the Portuguese Crown. Diogo's power over the Luso-African community was eventually recognized in Portugal in an act of 1553 conceding to Diogo the right to "elect a person from among my vassals and natives [of my kingdom] who would serve as ouividor and who would have jurisdiction up to natural death," taking them out of Portuguese control altogether, although these problems would reemerge later.[85]

Because employment in Kongo (and Angola) offered protection to Portuguese New Christians who were subject to persecution in Portuguese, they figured prominently in the Atlantic Creole community, perhaps introducing some Jewish customs to the Atlantic Creole mix, as they were often accused of doing. A royal order of 1569, for example, renewing an earlier order forbade New Christians to go to São Tomé or hold office there.[86] But orders of this sort did not keep them from Kongo. Belchior de Sousa Chicorro, who visited Kongo in 1553, denounced the role of the New Christians in Diogo's government who came "without the king sending them," which he thought a bad influence.[87]

Ndongo: Political and Social Structure, Origins to 1600

The kingdom of Ndongo, located south of Kongo, was another powerful center that became part of the Atlantic Creole world. At the beginning of the sixteenth century the region that stretched inland from Luanda to the Kwango River, south of the Dande River and including the south bank of the Kwanza River, was, according to later tradition, known as Mbundu, from which the language name Kimbundu was derived.[88] This region was under less centralized leadership and thus rulers were less able to shape religious and cultural interactions as was the case of the kingdom of Kongo.[89] Mbundu was divided, according to the sixteenth-century

---

[85] Alvará to King João III to King Diogo I, 1553, *MMA* 2: 321–2.

[86] Alvará of 21 November 1569 in *Collecção da Legislação Antiga e Moderna* ... (Lisbon, 1816), pp. 13–14, reprinted in *MMA* 2: 570.

[87] Belchior de Sousa Chicorro to King, 18 July 1553, *MMA* 2: 285–6.

[88] From his first extant letter of 1512, Afonso referred to himself as "King of Manicongo and Lord of the Ambundos"; see Afonso to his lords, *MMA* 1: 260 (a letter that may have been composed on his behalf based on an earlier letter of 1509); for the first undoubtedly first-hand letter, see Afonso I to Manuel I, 5 October 1514, *MMA* 1: 294, "King of Conguo and lord of the Ambundos, etc." These are also the first references to the Mbundu area. When Afonso provided a full list of titles in a letter to the Pope, 21 February 1535, *MMA* 2: 38, it included under "Lord of the Ambundos, and of Angola, of Quisyma, and Musuru, of Matamba, and Muyllu, and of Musucu." Because these areas are all Kimbundu speaking, it is reasonable to suppose that they formed constituent parts of a larger entity called "Mbundu"; see also do Amaral, *Reino do Congo*, pp. 176–7.

[89] For this chronology and a good overview of Ndongo's early history, see Beatrix Heintze, "Der Staat Ndongo im 16. Jahrhunderts," in Heintze, *Studien zur Geschichte Angolas im 16. und 17. Jahrhundert. Ein Lesebuch* (Cologne, 1996), pp. 68–74. Readers seeking

accounts, among 736 independent territories, called *murindas*,[90] whose rulers were known as *sobas* (often called *fidalgos* in Portuguese or "lesser nobles").[91] Given the size of this region this would mean that each *murinda* was little more than a few villages.

Disputes among *sobas* over territory and jurisdiction led sometimes to wars and often these wars or alliances resulted in the formation of larger groupings of *sobas* known in Kimbundu as *kandas* or even larger units frequently described in the traditions as provinces.[92] It is unclear from the sources how many provinces there were, although there seem to have been between 4 and 12 dominant ones, with some irregular and shifting subdivisions among them.[93] Some provinces that are frequently mentioned include Ilamba, Lumbo, Hari, Kisama, Haku, and Museke.[94]

annotation should also consult an earlier version entitled "Unbekanntes Angola: Der Staat Ndongo im 16. Jahrhundert," *Anthropos* 72 (1977): 749–805, which contains fuller annotation. Other accounts include Joseph C. Miller, *Kings and Kinsmen*, especially for earlier history, and Birmingham, *Trade and Conflictt*; recent work includes Virgílio Coelho, "A sociedade túmúndongò antiga," Paper presented at the conference, "Bantu into Black," Washington, DC, September 1999, and do Amaral, *Reino do Congo*, pp. 175–192.

90 We have pluralized words in Kimbundu in the same way as with Kikongo, according to the rules of English, adding a final "–s" to the stem without its class marker.

91 This account is based on correlating information in several independent texts of Jesuit authorship or inspiration written or published between 1582 and 1610 but probably based on an early description compiled by the Jesuits who came to Angola with Paulo Dias de Novais in 1575. Because Jesuits had connections with the court of Ndongo before 1579, they may have collected their traditions there. All these texts have a generally similar structure and often virtually identical language, suggesting at least a common original source from which each either took slightly different parts or to which each added additional details known to its author. The original text may have been written by Baltasar Barreira, author of the earliest recension. See Barreira, c. 1582–3, *MMA* 3: 227; Pero Rodrigues, "Historia da residência dos Padres da Companhia de Jesus em Angola, e cousas tocantes ao reino, e conquista" (1 May 1594)," *MMA* 4: 561; Pierre du Jarric, *Histoire des choses plus memorables*...(3 vols., Bordeaux, 1608–1612), 2 [1610]: 76–80; "Informação do Reino de Angola" (undated, c. 1590), *MMA* 15: 364–7.

92 The term *kanda* in this usage is very clear in the account of the *sobas* under Portuguese jurisdiction found in António de Oliveira de Cadornega, *História geral das guerras angolanas (1680)* (ed. José Matias Delgado, 3 vols., Lisbon, 1940–1942, reprint 1972) 3: 234–48, based on the tribute books maintained since the early seventeenth century. For more direct earlier evidence, see Garcia Simões to Luis Perpinhão, 7 November 1576, *MMA* 3: 146, refers to a rebellion of "the principal people of this Mocanda."

93 This wide divergence is based on observer perspective as well as administrative reality. Some counted all territories as provinces whether they were a part of Ndongo or not. Others only counted as provinces those territories under Ndongo. Even Ndongo's jurisdiction varied according to how firmly it administered a territory that it claimed.

94 Provincial structure is discussed fully in Hentize, "Staat Ndongo," pp. 68–74; see also Coelho, "Sociedade túmúndongò."

There may have been a number of consolidations in the period before 1500, as some historians suggest, led by one or another of the *sobas*.[95] The kingdom that the Portuguese knew as the kingdom of "Angola" (Ngola, probably a dynastic name) since 1518 was the largest of these consolidations.

Ngola included Ndongo and its neighbors in the highlands as well as conquests located as far west as the border with Kongo's possessions around Luanda, south across the Kwanza River into regions like Kisama, Libolo, and Tunda, and east to the lands of Matamba, and less well known areas like Songo. To the north the Ngola dynasty's sovereignty reached into lands claimed more directly by Kongo. In this mountainous area, both Kongo and the Ngola variously claimed some regions, like Mbwila.[96]

Ngola emerged sometime before 1518, when its core province, Ndongo, led by Ngola Kiluanje (c. 1515–1556), known as "Angola Inene" or "Angola the Great," managed to dominate a number of the others.[97] He founded a dynasty named after him, and it was from this dynastic name that the "kingdom of Angola" derived. The earliest kings, however, were not particularly demanding; eyewitness descriptions from 1560 to 1564 suggest that they left the *sobas* to govern their own territories, more or less independently, in exchange for payment of a tribute and service in war.[98]

Ngola's ruling class was composed, on the one hand, of the king, along with members of his immediate family and his officials and, on the other,

---

[95] This idea was first suggested by Joseph C. Miller, *Kings and Kinsmen: Early Mbundu States in Angola* (Oxford, 1976), pp. 55–106; recently it has been taken up with new data and reinterpreations of older traditions by Virgílio Coelho, see especially, "A data da fundação do 'Reino de Ndòngò," in *Actas do II Seminário Internacional sobre a História de Angola. Construindo o Passado Angolano: As fontes e a sua interpretação* (Lisbon: 2000), pp. 479–554.

[96] For borders, see the detailed investigation of Heintze, "Staat Ndongo," in *Studien*, pp. 68–74.

[97] For a thorough study of the various traditions and contemporary documents as well as a variety of proposed chronologies, see Beatrix Heintze's fundamental work, "Written Sources, Oral Traditions and Oral Traditions as Written Sources: The Steep and Thorny Way to Early Angolan History," *Paideuma* 33 (1987): 263–87. There are two complete lists, by Gaeta and Cavazzi, that are more or less completely compatable except for one king (found in MSS Araldi, Cavazzi, "Missione Evangelica," book 2, cap. 1, p. 12), "Nginga Angola quilombo quiacasenda," who is found in Cavazzi's lists with this name but in Gaeta as "Angola Chiluangi." Some thoughts on the reasons for the divergence are found in John Thornton, "Legitimacy and Political Power: The Case of Queen Njinga, 1624–1663," *Journal of African History* 32 (1991): 36–7. Other lists with different chronologies are found in do Amaral, *Reino do Congo*, pp. 180–92, and Saccardo, *Congo e Angola* 3: 17.

[98] *Apontamentos*, Antonio Mendes, Francisco de Gouveia letters.

of two classes of nobles whose members had authority over land and people in the central district and the provinces.[99] The first of these two classes of nobles were powerful *sobas* descended from the founder of the dynasty but not in direct line to rule, and the second were *sobas* who ruled their own jurisdictions as tributaries of Ndongo.

The king and his extended family exercised their authority from a central base, called a *kabasa* (capital), in one or another of several large towns, such as Ngoleme, Muanga Luamba, or Vunga, in the core of the highlands south of the present-day town of Ambaca (Kwanza Norte).[100] The population of the district of the central court, Kabasa and nearby settlements was extremely large, for when one of the towns, Ngoleme, burned in 1564, there were tens of thousands of displaced persons.[101] Members of the ruling family carried out important political and military functions. For example, among the casualties in a battle in 1585 was "Sanguiandali who went as captain of all the noble kinsmen [*fidalgos familiars*] of Angola who reside within his walls."[102]

Beyond his family, the king relied on officials to manage the kingdom and carry out his orders. The most important official was the *tendala*, drawn from a servile class called *kijikos* (see below). The *tendala* was a sort of viceroy with authority to rule in the king's absence and to handle day-to-day business. He was paired with a second official, the *ngolambole*, possibly also drawn from the *kijikos*, who served as a military commander in charge of mobilization.[103] In addition, the king had a group of other officials, collectively called *makotas*,[104] who were "the gentlemen of the land, and by consequence of a free condition."[105] But their functions were those of a household staff, acting as a bureaucracy directly under royal authority. There was the *mwene lumbo*, who as head steward

[99] For two detailed studies of the institutions of Ndongo, see Heintze, "Staat Ndongo," in *Studien*, pp. 80–8, and Virgílio Coelho, "*Os de dentro, os de fora*: análise sucinta de um modelo estrutural de organização administrative e urbana do 'Reino de Ndòngò' desde a sua fundação até fins do século XVI," *Fontes & Estudos* 4 (1998–1999): 163–228.

[100] Heintze, "Staat Ndongo," p. 88; see especially Virgilio Coelho, "Em busca de *Kábàsà*: uma tentativa de explicação de estrutura político-admistrativo do Reino de Ndòngò," in Maria Améila Madeira Santos (ed.), *Encontro de Povos e Culturas. Actas do Seminário* (Lisbon, 1995), pp. 443–77.

[101] Francisco Gouveia to Mirão, 1 November 1564, MMA 15: 232–3.

[102] Baltasar Barreira to Provincial do Brazil, 27 August 1585, MMA 3: 323.

[103] Rodrigues, "História," MMA 4: 559.

[104] In Kimbundu this term is *dikota* in the singular and *makota* as a plural. We have followed the widespread convention of pluralizing the plural form instead of using the Kimbundu form, or as our usual custom, pluralizing the singular form without a class marker.

[105] Du Jarric, *Histoire* 1: 79.

was in charge of managing the palace, or the *mwene kudya*, who gathered royal food and thus managed procurement and taxation, the *mwene misete*, who handled the royal reliquaries and hence religious affairs, and so on.[106]

This bureaucracy exercised control and authority over the subordinates in the territories. Each *soba* had a direct liaison with an official at court who collected tribute from him.[107] In the 1560s these officials went on missions to carry out the king's directives and collected tribute, one observer noting that the king would dispatch an emissary on a mission to enrich him with tribute.[108]

The first of the two classes of nobles was composed of families who claimed descent from an early king. The Italian Capuchin missionaries Giovanni Antonio Cavazzi and Antonio da Gaeta, whose records of oral traditions collected in the late 1650s provide their heritage, disagreed on exactly how remote their ancestry was.[109] They were hereditary lords of large *kandas* or small provinces in Ndongo near the royal capital. Like the kings, they also had officials, headed by a *tendala* and *ngolambole*.[110] Among these nobles of royal blood were the Ngola Hari family, who ruled the formidable rocks of Pungo Andongo; the Ngola Kanini Kiluanji lineage's leaders ruled the lands of the present-day Ambaca, whereas the Mubanga Kiluanji was close by, and the Mwenge Kiluanje ruled Lembo, which was some two days' journey from Ambaca.[111]

The second noble class was the formerly independent rulers of territories of various sizes, which had submitted to Ndongo's rule either voluntarily or by conquest. They governed their own territories as long as they paid tribute and supplied men at Ndongo's request to fight or serve. The *sobas*, according to Garcia Simões's 1575 account were "like Dukes or

---

[106] Cadornega, *História* 1: 38.
[107] Jesuit Annual Letter, 1602–1603, in Fernão Guerreiro, *Relação Annual das Coisas que fizeram os Padres da Companhia de Jesus... MMA* 5: 51, relating to what was an "ancient custom."
[108] Garcia Simões, 20 October 1575, *MMA* 3: 138.
[109] This is easily seen on Heintze's chart, "Written Sources," pp. 280–1.
[110] Rodrigues, "História," *MMA* 4: 559; Cadornega, *História* 1: 38.
[111] These names and their place in the genealogy come from MSS Araldi, Cavazzi, "Missione Evangelica," vol. A, book 2, chapter 1, p. 10, and modified and expanded from Cavazzi, *Istorica Descrizione*, book 2, no. 129. Other details are found in Antonio da Gaeta, *La maravigliosa conversione... della Regina Singa...* (Naples, 1668), p. 144. However, Cavazzi has them descended from the semimythical founder, Ngola Kiluanji kia Samba, and Gaeta has them descended from Ngola Kiluanji, son of this founder.

Great Lords, and each one has in his land authority to sell and kill their vassals, when the nature of the crime in which they are fallen requires it."[112] A seventeenth-century witness, António de Oliviera de Cadornega, wrote that within their owns lands they were as if "lords of the rope and axe," meaning they had jurisdiction even over life and death, "without any dependence on their king."[113] When summoned, as they were in 1563, for example, *sobas* appeared with thousands of soldiers, prepared to fight under their king's command.[114] The most powerful of the *sobas* had their own military forces, as did Kakulu ka Kabasa, who served more as an ally than a subject. In 1586 Kakulu ka Kabasa mobilized soldiers and fought as a separate army (*lukanzo*) from that of Ndongo.[115]

These different categories of rulers were connected to the kingdom by more than administrative ties. Kinship links were critical to hold the structure of the kingdom in place. Many *sobas* sent their daughters to marry the king, and the children of these children would marry with the great men of the country.[116] These marriages were a means of uniting the country and keeping the king and the more powerful *sobas* in obedience and alliance "in their wars and pretensions."[117] Because the state was still in evolution, there was likely to be a conflict between the greater *sobas* and the kings over such matters as succession. Disputes over succession – which was at least partially hereditary in the context of these marriages – would also lend itself to disruptive conflicts.

Both the *sobas* and the kings drew income from taxation of their free subjects who lived in each territory and who were called *ana murinda* or "children of the murinda." In addition both could count on the labor of bond subjects called *kijikos*, the "serfs and slaves of the murinda," whose condition originated in capture but who could not be sold. They were "annexed to the patrimony of the lord" of the *murinda* and were passed on as part of the *murinda* from ruler to ruler.[118] The Ngolas, however, controlled directly much larger numbers of *kijikos* than any of the *sobas*

---

[112] Garcia Simões to Provincial, 20 October 1575, *MMA* 3: 129.

[113] Cadornega, *História* 1: 38.

[114] Letter of Antonio Mendes, 9 May 1563, *MMA* 3: 509.

[115] Diogo da Costa, 31 May 1586, *MMA* 3: 336–7.

[116] Cadornega, *História* 1: 29–30. Although Cadornega did not come to Angola until 1639, he wrote some of these earlier passages based on local documentation found in the archives in Masangano and other sites of the country.

[117] Rodrigues, "História," *MMA* 4: 559.

[118] Du Jarric, *Histoire* 2: 79–80. See on this category Coelho, "*Os do dentro,*" pp. 210–215.

and thus enjoyed a secure income beyond the tribute of the *sobas*. *Kijikos* belonging to the king were found in other areas in addition to the capital region of Ndongo and thus helped to solidify royal influence even in *sobas'* lands; for example, in 1584, in the district of Talandongo, just north of the confluence of the Kwanza and Lukala, all the "libatas [villages] are quejiquos of the person of the King."[119] Kings usually drew their *tendala*, and perhaps the *ngolambole*, from among these *kijikos*.

Ndongo also had a class of slaves, *mubikas*, who were war captives, people enslaved judicially or people who were purchased. Although free people or *kijikos* were enslaved on slight pretexts, and often the families of the condemned could be sold as well, most *mubikas* were war captives.[120] In 1563, the king of Ndongo captured many slaves in his campaign against "twelve lords" who had risen against him.[121] Most of the 14,000 people whom Garcia Simões believed were "bought and sold" in Angola in 1575 were "slaves of the king [of Ndongo]" captured in war from rebels or reduced to slavery judicially.[122] These slaves could be bought and sold or inherited and employed in any labor their master deemed fit. Slaves were often used as a sort of money for high-value items, insofar as the value of a slave was equal to that of a bull.[123]

Although the *mubika* status is not described until the 1580s, the fact that there was an extensive slave trade from at least 1520, and certainly at least some trading even before that, points to a history of exporting people of this category.[124] There was a substantial trade in slaves at markets, a custom that later Portuguese said was very ancient, and by the 1590s slave traders obtained more slaves on the market than from wars.[125] The rulers of Ndongo, like the kings of Kongo, had strict rules about enslavement and export. This included close regulation of the slaves for export, including questioning them to determine the legality of their enslavement and that no free people or *kijikos* were wrongly taken. Baltasar Barreira,

---

[119] Paulo Dias de Novais noted this of the lands he selected to be a personal estate at a place he called "new Gaza"; see Paulo Dias de Novais to his Father, 2 January 1584, *MMA* 4: 418. On the location of "New Gaza," in Talandongo, see Rodrigues, "História," *MMA* 4: 568.

[120] Du Jarric, *Histoire* 2: 79–80.

[121] Letter of Pedro Mendes, 9 May 1563, *MMA* 2: 509.

[122] Garcia Simões to Luis Peripinhão, 7 November 1576, *MMA* 3: 146.

[123] Baltasar Barreira, 1582–1583, *MMA* 3: 227.

[124] Regimento to Baltasar de Castro and Manuel Pacheco, 16 February 1520; Regimento to Factor of São Tomé, 2 August 1532, *MMA* 2: 14–15; see Inquest into the slave trade of Angola, 12 November 1548, *MMA* 2: 197–205.

[125] Pero Rodrigues, "Historia," *MMA* 4: 560–1.

commenting on this system in 1582, remarked, "in no other part of Guinea can you buy pieces more securely than in Angola."[126]

Religious officials were important in the political fabric of Ndongo. There were many priests, both male and female,[127] who had substantial influence over people's beliefs. As a Jesuit priest noted ruefully, this influence was "because they believe that they give and prevent the rains for the plantings and give them health in their infirmities."[128] Their places of worship were shrines to "idols" (*kitekes*), sculpted figures carefully represented local deities (*kilundas*).[129] One, *mwene ndongo* ("grande sacerdote" or great priest), was held to be the kingdom's religious leader, and he probably presided over the cult of the local deities of the core region of Ndongo. However, the king himself claimed tremendous personal religious power, and in 1575 Garcia Simões reported that he "holds and says openly that he is the lord of the Sun and rain, and he orders it to rain, or not to rain as it seems fit to him."[130] This power explains why the Ngola had ultimate power over priests and could kill them at will.[131]

Ndongo-Portuguese Relations, 1518–1600

As the emerging kingdom of Ngola came into contact with the Portuguese, the domestic rivalries within the kingdom played as important a part in how the two countries' interacted as Portugal's initiatives. Initially Ngola was seeking to expand and break free from Kongo's claims to rule "the Ambundos" and looked to the free-spirited "Tomistas" (Luso-Africans from São Tomé) as helpful allies. Later Jesuit accounts credited Portuguese mercenaries with helping Ngola Kiluanje establish his kingdom and subjugate neighboring provinces.[132] Perhaps encouraged by these informal mercenaries, and as a show of its independence from Kongo, in 1518 Ngola Kiluanje sent his own ambassadors to Portugal asking to become a Christian and in this way to develop his own independent relationship with Portugal and join more directly in the developing Atlantic Creole

---

[126] Baltasar Barreira, "Informação acerca dos escravos de Angola," 1582–1583, *MMA* 3: 228–9.

[127] Diogo da Costa to Jesuit Provincial of Portugal, 31 May 1586, *MMA* 3: 339, "feiticeiros e feiticeiras."

[128] A Jesuit to Provincial of Portugal, 15 December 1587, *MMA* 3: 348.

[129] Pedro Mendes, 9 May 1563, *MMA* 3: 509–10; Rodrigues, "História," 4: 559; see Thornton, "Religious and Ceremonial Life" pp. 76–7.

[130] Garcia Simões to Provincial, 20 October 1575, *MMA* 3: 134.

[131] Pedro Mendes, 9 May 1563, *MMA* 2: 509–10.

[132] Du Jarric, *Histoire* 2: 81–2.

community. Portugal's response was to send a mission, which arrived in Ndongo in 1520 under Manuel Pacheco and Baltasar de Castro.

The Portuguese vision of conversion coincided with that of Ngola Kiluanje, for the ambassadors were told to "meet with the King of Angola and that you make him and his people Christian, as has been done with the King of Congo."[133] When the embassy arrived, however, Ngola Kiluanje, perhaps convinced by the denunciations of the Luso-Africans already established in his court, arrested the members of the mission. In response, King Afonso dispatched his own ambassador and Afonso Anes, a priest, to baptize Ngola Kiluanje, but when this mission also ran into trouble with the Portuguese and Luso-Africans, who engaged in swordplay in the newly constructed chapel, he extracted the mission in 1526. Father Anes, however, remained to continue his missionary work, but Ngola Kiluanje never converted to Christianity and returned to his older religious belief.[134]

Despite the problems with the Portuguese alliance, Ndongo's power continued to grow and expand, still attracting many Portuguese and Luso-African slave traders, especially those violating the Portuguese and Kongolese Crown's control from São Tomé. An inquest conducted in Kongo in 1548 revealed widespread diversion of the trade to the south of Kongo because of the expanding commerce of Ndongo with São Tomé merchants.[135] When Afonso died in 1542, Kongo went through a prolonged succession crisis, which was only gradually resolved by Diogo I after about 1550. Perhaps because of Kongo's preoccupation with its own problems, Ngola Kiluanje decided to send another mission to Portugal in 1549 to seek an alliance, again stressing religious conversion as his goal. This mission was retained on São Tomé for nine years. When Ngola Kiluanji died in 1556 the issue of whether the new king was or would be a Christian was considered a crucial element in Portugal's reestablishing relations with Ndongo.[136]

This new king, Ndambi a Ngola (1556–c.1562) the son of Ngola Kiluanji,[137] was not much interested in the church but rather in a military and commercial arrangement. However, the Portuguese mission headed

[133] Regimento to Manuel Pacheco and Baltasar de Castro, 16 February 1520, *MMA* 1: 431–2.
[134] Baltasar de Castro to João III, 15 October 1526, *MMA* 1: 485–7; João III to Afonso, c. 1529, *MMA* 1: 532; Saccardo, *Congo e Angola* 1: 76–7, see also do Amaral, *Reino do Congo*, pp. 75–82.
[135] Inquest into trade of Angola, 7 May 1548, *MMA* 2: 197–205.
[136] "Noticiaz muitos antigos," summarizing provision of 22 November 1557, *MMA* 2: 466.
[137] According to Jesuit materials, probably Baltasar Barreira's account, the king who greeted Dias de Novais was named Dambe Angola, the son of Angola Inene; Rodrigues,

by Paulo Dias de Novais, which arrived at the mouth of the Kwanza River in 1560 had no military capacity. De Novais's instructions called for nothing other than missionary work, which was left to the four Jesuit priests who accompanied him.[138] It was probably for this reason that Ndambi a Ngola sent a religious official from the "house of the chief fetisher" to meet him.[139] Initially, the relationship went smoothly but changed soon afterward. Ndambi a Ngola died not long after Dias de Novais's arrival, the Jesuit Francisco de Gouveia, who wrote in 1564 about knowing both him and his successor, his son Ngola Kiluanje kia Ndambi, also noted that he had "just begun to reign a little time."[140] Pedro Mendes, who left Angola in 1562 recorded that "Angola Quiloange" was "very tall, one of the tallest people in the land, seeming to be a giant and very strong" and "feared by his subjects because he does great justice on them, and there is no day that he does not order justice."[141] Ngola Kiluanje, responding to letters from the new king of Kongo, Bernardo I, that the Portuguese were coming "to see if we had silver or gold in order for the King of Portugal to take the land" and moreover that the king of Kongo "would not suffer that we were in Angola and that he alone would send presents of things which he got from Portugal before they came there."[142] In response, Ngola Kiluanje stopped missionary work for a time and imprisoned Dias de Novais as well as the Jesuits, allowing only Dias de Novais to return to Portugal in 1565, possibly in search of military assistance against a rebel, according to later accounts.[143]

Although the priests who came with the Dias de Novais mission soon discovered that the people had preserved the ornaments of Father Anes,

"História," *MMA* 4: 552. The fact that this information is found in both du Jarric and Rodrigues suggests a common source in Barreria, probably written around 1582.

[138] Miguel Torres to Jesuit General, 11 January 1560, *MMA* 15: 223.

[139] Pedro Mendes to Jesuit General, 9 May 1563, *MMA* 2: 499.

[140] "Apontamentos das Cousas d'Angola tiradas duas cartas que o padre Francisco de Gouuea..." in Ruelo Pombo, *Angola Menina* (Lisbon, 1944), p. 9. Gouvea "says that the past king lived 200 years and the present one says he is 80 years old and held to be a boy." Francisco de Gouveia to Diogo Mirão, 1 November 1564, *MMA* 2: 527. Both the comprehensive king lists of the seventeenth century, by Cavazzi and Gaeta, agree on this order of names as well.

[141] Pedro Mendes to Jesuit General, 9 May 1563, *MMA* 2: 509 and 511 (his name). The original text, in the Biblioteca Nacional de Rio de Janeiro, I, 5, 2, 38, fol. 223v, is corrupt at the point of his name; this is Brásio's restoration. There is no doubt that the first three letters are *qui* and the last one *e*. The pattern of the smeared other letters, though illegible, is consistent with *quiloange*. The idea that a new ruler was responsible for the change was proposed by do Amaral, *Reino de Congo*, p. 210.

[142] Pedro Mendes to Jesuit General, 9 May 1563, *MMA* 2: 502.

[143] Saccardo, *Congo e Angola* 1: 79–82; do Amaral, *Reino do Congo*, pp. 208–10.

the priest sent from Kongo in the mid-1520's,[144] they failed to convert the king and did little work save occasional education of noble children. The one priest who remained, Francisco de Gouveia, was told that because the king was new, he was not paying attention to the priest, but "the time would come in which he would call me to teach him."[145] Indeed, the new king eventually accepted Gouveia's teaching, for when Gouveia died, on 19 June 1575, he was buried in the church he had built in Ndongo's capital city to serve the needs of the Portuguese and Luso-African merchants and their African converts. Out of respect for the priest "who had raised and trained him since he was small," Ngola Kiluanji kia Ndambi sent his own musicians to play as the priest lay dying and gave him a lavish funeral.[146] Although this is hardly evidence that he had become a fully engaged member of the Atlantic Creole community, it does reveal the first steps in that direction.

Dias de Novais and the Creation of the Portuguese Colony of Angola

The colony of Angola (Reino de Angola) came to be a second great center of Atlantic Creole culture. The origins of the colony date from Dias de Novais's return to Ndongo in 1575. He arrived a few months before de Gouveia's death and found Ngola Kiluanji kia Ndambi, thanks to Gouveia's teaching, somewhat more favorable to the Portuguese. Ngola Kiluanji kia Ndambi was prepared to welcome Dias de Novais to his kingdom and to create a military–religious alliance. Alas for Ndongo, however, Dias de Novais had other plans.

Dias de Novais bore a charter, given to him in 1571 by King Sebastião I, which initiated a new era in Portuguese relationships with the leaders of Central Africa. The opening clause of the charter is revealing. It informed Dias de Novais that it would be "in the service of Our Lord and to me, to order to subjugate and to conquer the Kingdom of Angola."[147] This charter marked a major change in the way Atlantic Creole culture would develop in Ndongo. Although the Portuguese Crown had sometimes taken an interest in trying to control Portuguese subjects living on the

[144] "Noticiaz muitos antigos" (copies of old documents, summarizing document of 17 July 1560), *MMA* 2: 466–7; Rodrigues, "História," *MMA* 4: 553.

[145] Francisco de Gouveia to Jesuit General Mirão, 1 November 1564, *MMA* 15: 232, and same to Mirão, same date, *MMA* 2: 527.

[146] Rodrigues, "Historia," *MMA* 4: 555–6; also Garcia Simões to Provincial, 20 October 1575, *MMA* 3: 141.

[147] Carta da doação a Paulo Dias de Novais, 19 September 1571, *MMA* 3: 36.

Central African mainland, it had never before thought to "conquer and subjugate" African kingdoms in the region. The charter's other clauses, modeled largely on similar donations given earlier in Brazil, clearly envisioned a new government under the control of Dias de Novais and the king of Portugal. Large stretches of territory south of the Kwanza River were designated for the exclusive hereditary rule of Dias de Novais; other lands lying north of the river up to the border of Kongo were to be "conquests" for the Crown and governed by Dias de Novais for his lifetime only. Dias de Novais was expected to establish an administration, collect taxes, build fortresses, and bring in settlers. Because this conquest was to be for the good of the Church and to further missionary work, he was ordered to bring in at least three priests who would build a church dedicated to St Sebastian.[148] Indeed, the charter given to Dias de Novais in 1571 had as its principal goal "to celebrate divine cult and offices and the increase of Our Holy Faith and Holy Evangelization," for which the support of various learned theologians was provided.[149]

This dramatic shift in policy was probably the result of the new thinking of Portugal's Sebastião, one of its most aggressive monarchs, who was more interested in conquest than the earlier monarchs. Second, the military alliance that Dias de Novais made with Ndongo in the 1560s made it easier for him to bring armed forces to Ndongo under the cover of an alliance. Yet another factor facilitating the new thinking was that Kongo had been transformed from an opponent of Portuguese presence in Ndongo to a supporter, thanks to the support that Álvaro I received from Portugal in expelling the Jagas, a mysterious group that invaded Kongo from the east around 1570.[150] Even as Dias de Novias arrived, the governor of São Tomé, Francisco de Gouveia Sottomaior, with some 600 soldiers, was still in Kongo helping Álvaro expel the Jagas. Álvaro was forced to make some concessions to Portugal to pay for their help by ceding certain mining rights for the shell money from Luanda Island for some period of time. Indeed, Dias de Novais's decision to land first at Luanda in Kongo territory and not at the mouth of the Kwanza River,

---

[148] The best study of this charter and its background is in do Amaral, *Consulado*, pp. 49–72. The whole charter's text is found in *MMA* 3: 36–51.

[149] Donation to Paulo Dias de Novais, 19 September 1571, *MMA* 3: 36–7; for a comparative discussion of the religious element in this charter, see do Amaral, *Consulado*, p. 54.

[150] The Jaga invasion has been the subject of a long and contentious literature. For a good summary and convincing synthesis, see the long footnote by Michel Chandeigne in his new translation of Pigafetta (Paris, 2002), pp. 291–95.

as he had in 1560, probably reflected Kongo's new relationship to the project.

Even though the Portuguese Crown planned the conquest and colonization of Angola, it was not clear that this could actually be carried out, because the king lacked the necessary forces. To augment his 700 troops, Dias de Novais summoned the Luso-Africans of Kongo to come and help him. Many did, bringing Kongo Christian troops with them, with their "bows and arrows, swords and shields," as well as the private forces of some Kongo nobles.[151]

Because of his military weakness, Dias de Novais's behavior in Angola for the first few years appeared fully in line with the older tradition of Portuguese military missions and perhaps with Ngola Kiluanji's expectations of military alliance rather than the conquest envisioned in Dias de Novias's instructions. Initially, he joined with Kongo's forces in attacking rebels in Kasanze, near Luanda, though this attack failed.[152] Not long after, Dias de Novais's army was in Ndongo, aiding Ngola Kiluanji against rebels, and until 1579 the military relationship seemed to proceed as normal.[153]

Dias de Novais's ultimate success was made possible by the crisis that surfaced in Ndongo, the reverberations of which would undermine Ndongo for the next 75 years. Shortly before Dias de Novais arrived in Ndongo, Ngola Kiluanji kia Ndambi had died and Ndongo was going through a major constitutional crisis. Traditions recorded 80 years later recall that Ngola Kiluanji kia Ndambi was a king who had used the Portuguese to fight rebels and expand the kingdom in the region of the Dande, Zenza, and Lukala Rivers, exactly where Dias de Novais had assisted in the 1560s.[154] One version of the traditions maintained that he died without issue, requiring an election to choose his successor, as previously all the rulers up to this point had succeeded their fathers by

---

[151] Garcia Simões to Provncial, 20 October 1575, *MMA* 3: 140–41.
[152] Rodrigues, "Historia," *MMA* 4: 571.
[153] Rodrigues, "Historia," *MMA* 4: 556, 577; Garcia Simões to Luis Perpinhão (7 November 1576) *MMA* 3: 146 (an action in 1576); Baltasar Afonso letter (9 October 1577) *MMA* 3: 157.
[154] The two traditions, set down by Gaeta and Cavazzi, differ in some crucial details, probably a feature of the way in which they were collected. Gaeta's, collected in Njinga's court, focused on her legitimacy and essentially denied the whole tradition that followed by omitting Njinga Ngola Kilombo kia Kasenda and replacing him with another king, Ngola Kiluanje. Cavazzi traveled more widely and his tradition, which we follow here, reflected a consensus of various rival lines. For a full exposition of this background, see Thornton, "Legitimacy and Political Power."

straightforward father-to-son succession.[155] The royal officials, including the *tendala* and *makotas* and clearly in this case also the *kilunda*, a quartermaster general who emerged as the kingmaker, apparently conducted the election.[156] According to Garcia Simões, writing in 1575, power was temporarily held by a "tyrant who governed the Kingdom" as an "administrator [regidor]" named Kilundu, but he was killed by the new king, who received Dias de Novais's emissaries.[157]

This new king that the electors chose, Njinga Ngola Kilombo kia Kasenda (1575–1592), claimed to be a great-grandson of the founder from a different line than that of Ngola Kiluanje kia Ndambi. Baltasar Barreira, writing in about 1582, noted that Angola "began with the grandfather of he who presently reigns."[158] In 1575, when he had just become king, Njinga Ngola was so greatly feared that when the king was in his city "they will not even kill a rat in it, they are all his rabbits" but "at least a rat does not order heads cut off continuously ordering people killed both in public and in secret."[159] The crisis and election caused lasting dissention, for Njinga Ngola Kilombo kia Kasenda was remembered later as being very cruel to his *sobas* and for having fought many rebellions, especially against the *soba* of Hari. The rulers of Hari could claim the throne as one of the *sobas* of royal blood, descendants of the first king, whereas Njinga Ngola's contention of descent from Ngola Kiluanji kia Samba, who had ruled earlier than their ancestor, made him a stronger candidate.[160] Njinga Ngola Kilombo kia Kasenda's dealings with the *sobas*, perhaps a product of these uncertainties, dissentions, and rivalries, made him fearful and violent. "He cuts off their heads for nothing, and for this is very feared" and as a result, according to Diogo da Costa in 1586, "many of his lords go to the Governor [Paulo Dias de Novais]."[161] The rivalry among Hari, other ancient lines, and Njinga Ngola Kilombo kia Kasenda's line would

---

[155] In fact, Ngola Kiluanji had many descendants. Pedro Mendes mentioned that he already had 70 children by various wives in 1563, *MMA* 2: 511. This suggests that the tradition masks the real origins of the struggle through legitimizing language.

[156] *Quilundo* probably corresponds to *Ilunda* in Cavazzi's list of such titles, MSS Araldi, Cavazzi, "Missione evangelica," book 1, chapter 4, p. 46. In Kimbundu *ilunda* is the plural of *kilunda*; see also Coelho, "Sociedade antiga."

[157] Garcia Simões to Provincial, 20 October 1575, *MMA* 3: 134.

[158] Barreira, "Informação," *MMA* 3: 227.

[159] Garcia Simões to Provincial, 20 October 1575, *MMA* 3: 134–5.

[160] MSS Araldi, Cavazzi, "Missione Evangelica," vol. A, book 2, chapter 1, p. 12; also *Istorica Descrizione*, book 2, no. 132.

[161] Diogo da Costa to Provincial, 31 May 1586, *MMA* 3: 339.

dominate Ndongo's politics for many years and gave the political opening the Portuguese needed to advance their vision.

Dias de Novais's alliance with Ndongo upset the Luso-Africans of Ndongo and their related branch in Kongo, who relied on African patronage and resented Portuguese Crown control. This was especially because Gouveia Sottomaior had as one of his tasks the control over the Luso-African community, which was to pass to Dias de Novais when he arrived. The Luso-Africans, who had developed their own informal leadership, looked for ways to undermine the initiatives from Portugal. One of them, Francisco Barbuda d'Aguiar, who had lived in Central Africa for more than 25 years and had served Álvaro I as confessor, had already persuaded Álvaro not to trust de Gouveia Sottomaior's mission.[162] Barbuda then went to Ndongo, and in 1579 he met with Pero da Fonseca, Dias de Novais's representative. Barbuda took the opportunity to denounce the king of Portugal, Dias de Novais, and da Fonseca, in "Portuguese and in the language of the country," finally asserting that "he did not recognize any other king except the King of Angola that gave him income [*rendas*]." Da Fonseca scolded him for his intemperate and disloyal language, "Portuguese that you are," and had him imprisoned. But da Fonseca could not hold him long, and Barbuda, once free, went directly to the king and told him he knew a "great secret" – that Dias de Novais's men, then in Ndongo, and those who were soon to arrive had come to take over his lands and seize his mines, suggesting that he knew the contents of Dias de Novais's charter. The king thought this was cause for war, called his council, and decided to eliminate the small Portuguese force at the capital of Kabasa.[163]

Acting on the pretense of sending his Portuguese allies out to fight against a rebel, Njinga Ngola ordered the Ndongo forces who were fighting alongside Portuguese soldiers to massacre the 40 Portuguese. Njinga Ngola then confiscated or destroyed their goods, said to be worth some "200 thousand lefucos [*lifuku*, an African monetary measure of 10,000 *nzimbu* shells], which equals to 60,000 cruzados," and in the process more than 1,000 Christian slaves were killed.[164] He then sent orders to his vassals to kill all the other Portuguese and Luso-Africans in the country, 60 Portuguese and 200 "black Christians," including those of Dias de Novais, then at a small stockade on the Kwanza at Nzele. Dias de Novais

[162] Pigafetta, *Relatione*, p. 61.
[163] Auto de Pero da Fonseca, 18 April 1579, *MMA* 4: 308–9.
[164] Rodrigues, "Historia," *MMA* 4: 572.

and his men barely beat off the attack, and a war between the Portuguese and Ndongo that would last a decade began.[165]

To extricate himself Dias de Novais needed allies. First, he asked Kongo for assistance and Álvaro I agreed to send an army to his aid. Second, he worked hard to exploit Ndongo's factionalism and the unpopularity of Njinga Ngola with many of his subjects and to recruit dissident nobles into his forces. Moreover, many Luso-Africans from Kongo and Kongolese nobles joined the army with their soldiers, and by 1588 some 4,000 soldiers from Kongo (referred to as Christian Africans in the sources) had joined Dias de Novais's ranks and would participate in all the campaigns against Ndongo.[166]

The campaign against Ndongo began sometime after May 1580, when Dias de Novais's troops and those of his Kongo ally were supposed to join somewhere along the Bengo River. Kongo's army (reputedly 60,000 Kongolese and 120 Luso-African mercenaries) failed to cross the Bengo to get to the Kwanza where De Novais's troops were located because of a shortage of boats and sustained Ndongo resistance.[167] By September 1580 Dias de Novais had to abandon his vulnerable fort at Nzele, and, loading his soldiers and Christian Africans into several ships, he set off up the Kwanza River toward Ndongo. His aim was to gain more local support by capitalizing on the independent strivings of many *sobas* who hoped to free themselves from Ndongo rule.[168]

As the political dissention set off by Njinga Ngola Kilombo kia Kasenda's actions had disturbed the core of Ndongo, its tenuous hold on the subjected *sobas* whose lands lay between the highlands and the coast faltered. As a result Dias de Novais succeeded in allying with Muxima Kitangonge, a powerful *soba* on the Kwanza who swore vassalage to Portugal and supplied both food and troops, agreeing to "help the governor against the said King of Angola."[169] Dias de Novais formed several more alliances, mostly with *sobas* like the Mocumbe, who "was the lord of other nobles and lands who did not obey the King of Angola and who offered his friendship."[170] Using these tactics, and managing to defeat armies led by *sobas* loyal to Ndongo, Dias de Novais was able to establish

---

[165] Frutuoso Ribeiro to Francisco Martins, 4 March 1580, *MMA* 3: 190.
[166] Memorias de Diogo de Ferreira, 1588, *MMA* 4: 491.
[167] Pigafetta, *Relatione*, pp. 19–20, 22.
[168] Do Amaral, *Consulado*, pp. 132–7.
[169] Baltasar Afonso to Miguel de Sousa, 4 July 1581, *MMA* 3: 200.
[170] Baltasar Afonso to Miguel de Sousa, 4 July 1581, *MMA* 3: 203; Do Amaral, *Consulado*, pp. 132–6; 142–3.

a base at Massangano on the Kwanza at its strategic confluence with the Lukala River in 1582.[171] From this base Dias de Novais was able to build up a creditable military force that allowed him to make wars in 1583 against Talandongo in Musseque province near the silver mines and found a community that he called New Gaza.[172]

Meanwhile, Novais's subordinates near the base in Luanda were also consolidating Portuguese alliances in the region of Ilamba, between the Kwanza and the Bengo Rivers. These lands, lying farther from Ndongo's capital were harder for Njinga Ngola to defend, and defections were more general. In 1581 Dias de Novais gained his first ally, *soba* Songa, who controlled the mouth of the Kwanza River, and sent forces into Ilamba, defeating several *sobas* in areas where they believed the king of Ndongo had not been able to control. Nevertheless, Njinga Ngola sought to bring the region back under his control by sending detachments into Kisama (the territory lying south of the Kwanza) in 1581 and to Ilamba (the area inland of Luanda and north of the Kwanza) in 1582. However, the combined forces of Dias de Novais's men and the rebel *sobas* managed to defeat these detachments. After these successes the Portuguese boasted that they controlled the whole of Ilamba, including 34 *sobas* who became Portuguese vassals for the first time, in addition to replacing some of the *sobas* loyal to Ndongo with men loyal to Dias de Novais.[173] These victories allowed Portugal to become a real power and pose a significant threat to Ndongo, which now moved to isolate Masangano. In 1585, Njinga Ngola sent the largest army the Portuguese had ever encountered to Ilamba, which met the Portuguese forces, now consisting of 120 Portuguese soldiers in addition to 8,000 local archers supplied by some 40 vassal *sobas* who scored a "miraculous" victory at Kasikola on the eastern border of Ilamba. The losses included "the flower of the Angolan nobility," a number of recently armed musketeers, and other *sobas* whom the Portuguese tried as traitors because they failed to stay in the alliance.[174] Not discouraged by his defeat, Njinga Ngola sent a second large army against Masangano in 1586, but the Portuguese again defeated it when it was divided crossing the Lucala, frustrating his designs.[175] Having failed to regain Ilamba or to dislodge the Portuguese from Masangano, Njinga

---

[171] For a careful overview of the period, see do Amaral, *Consulado*, pp. 132–58.
[172] Rodrigues, "Historia," *MMA* 4: 567–8.
[173] Rodrigues, "Historia," *MMA* 4: 566–7.
[174] Rodrigues, "Historia," *MMA* 4: 568–70.
[175] Diogo da Costa, 31 May 1586, *MMA* 3: 336–7.

Ngola did not support a powerful anti-Portuguese rebellion in Ilamba in 1589 and thought of new ways to regain lost ground.[176]

Dias de Novais also sought an alliance with the king of Benguela not only because the king there was a major enemy of Ndongo but also because Kisama, which lay between Benguela and Ndongo, had been given to him as a perpetual grant in his charter, and he was anxious to establish himself there. It would be valuable because of its salt mines, but it proved much harder to take over than Ilamba.[177] In 1586 the king of Benguela contacted Dias de Novais seeking "friendship" and asked to "be subject to the king of Portugal."[178] However, it was only in 1587 that Dias de Novias acted to make this alliance good by sending forces to the Longa River in an attempt to contact the kingdom of Benguela, "with whom he was at peace." No contact was established because local rulers in the area destroyed the fort and killed most of the soldiers who were sent.[179]

By 1589 it was clear that Njinga Ngola Kilombo kia Kasenda failed to regain lost lands in Ilamba following his defeat in 1586, and indeed, he had to concentrate on defending his capital against the threat that the combination of dissident *sobas* and Portuguese forces presented. At the time Jesuits boasted that Portugal had conquered half of Angola, or rather the territory that Ndongo claimed when they arrived. Njinga Ngola was so desperate that he sought an alliance with Matamba, the kingdom on his northeastern border.

Dias de Novais, however, was now confident that he had garnered resources in Ilamba sufficient to take the war into the heart of Ndongo, but his death on 9 May 1589 left this task to his second-in-command, Luis Serrão. To continue the advance into Ndongo, Serrão sent troops up the Lucala River to Angolomene a Kitambo, a point north of Kabasa, Ndongo's capital. From there he dispatched the most powerful force that Portugal had assembled in Angola, some 15,000 African archers supported by 128 Portuguese musketeers, to the capital, which they found deserted. But then they met the combined army of Ndongo and Matamba, which enveloped and totally destroyed them on 29 December 1590. Only a determined rearguard operation allowed the survivors and unengaged elements to withdraw to Massangano. The defeat was followed by the

---

[176] Rodrigues, "História," *MMA* 4: 570.
[177] Pedro Mendes to Jesuit General, 9 May 1563, *MMA* 2: 509.
[178] Diogo da Costa to Provincial, 31 May 1586, *MMA* 3: 339.
[179] Rodrigues, "Historia," *MMA* 4: 571–2. The text says 1578, but other documentation suggests that these two numbers were transposed from 1587; see also Regimento to Manuel Pereira Forjaz, 26 March 1607, *MMA* 5: 278.

massive desertion of *sobas* throughout the conquest, so that even ships sailing on the Kwanza from Luanda were harassed by archers.[180]

As a result of this major defeat, the Portuguese Crown decided to revoke the Dias de Novais's charter and take over its administration, replacing the donatary captain with a royally appointed governor.[181] A royal inspector, Domingos Abreu e Brito, sent in 1591 to determine what policies the Crown should follow after taking the colony over, reported that there were areas that could still be conquered and important resources like salt and silver that could be obtained if royal agents led a serious effort with larger forces.[182]

By then, the area that remained under Portuguese control following the defeat in Ndongo was hardly a colony, however, for it was held together by vassalage agreements that various *sobas* had accepted, generally to assert themselves against Ndongo. They might easily reverse these alliances, as many did in the aftermath of Serrão's defeat, though some still remained loyal, and the Portuguese were able to cow many of the rebels in Ilamba, like Muje a Zemba, attacked in 1591.[183] However, the Portuguese had lost the power for effective aggression in areas still held by Ndongo, as they learned by their disastrous second defeat in Kisama in 1594–1595.

Having been thwarted in their attempts to expand beyond their bases on the Kwanza southward, the Portuguese looked to increase their hold in the areas to the north of Luanda. In 1596–1598, directly after the debacle in Kisama, Governor João Furtado de Mendonça launched a bloody and successful campaign along the Bengo, the river from which Luanda drew its water supply and that served as the unofficial boundary between Portuguese Angola and Kongo. The campaign was aimed at rebels loyal to Ndongo but also forced Kongolese vassals such as Ngombe a Mukiama to accept Portuguese vassalage.[184] In the short run, Furtado de Mendonça's

---

[180] Rodrigues, "Historia," *MMA* 4: 574–6; Letter to Gaspar Dias de Beja, March 1591, *MMA* 3: 423–4; Domingos de Abreu de Brito, "Svmario e Descripção do Reyno de Angola," 1591, fols. 33–35v, in Alfredo de Albuquerque Felner (ed.), *Um Inquérito à vida administrativa e económica de Angola e do Brasil* (Coimbra, 1931), pp. 41–2 (this section is also reproduced in in *MMA* 4: 533–5 and can be followed by folio numbers), Abreu de Brito's argument that Ndongo was helped by Kongo, "Guindes" and "Jaguas" is not found in other sources, and appears exaggerated. His hostility to Kongo (revealed on fols. 36v–37v, pp. 44–6) goes well beyond truth and hence his claim that Kongo helped Ndongo may be false.

[181] For reasoning and debates of the time, see do Amaral, *Consulado*, pp. 249–55.

[182] De Abreu e Brito, "Svmmario," fols. 4–14, in Felner, *Inquerito*, pp. 6–18.

[183] "Catalogo dos Governadores," in Silva Corrêa, *História* 1: 209.

[184] "Catalogo dos Governadores," in Silva Corrêa, *História* 1: 216; better geographical details and contemporary eyewitness accounts are found Andrew Battell, *The Strange*

campaigns captured thousands of slaves, a substantial number of whom were Atlantic Creoles, but in the longer run, they would start to unravel the political alliance between Kongo and the Portuguese and initiate a period of increasing hostility between the two countries.[185]

Despite the military setbacks, the Crown did not give in on extending its conquests and especially in capturing mines. Between 1591 and 1607 authorities in Portugal gave orders to the governors, Franscico de Almeida (1592–1593, whose term was continued by his brother-in-law Jerónimo de Almeida following his death, 1593–1594), João Furtado de Mendonça (1594–1601), and João Rodrigues Coutinho (1601–1603, continued after his death by his subordinate, Manuel Cerveira Pereira, 1603–1607) to build forts and take lands, either silver mines at Cambambe or salt mines in Kisama.[186] For example, Rodrigues Coutinho's instructions were to build forts at Demba to control salt, Cambambe to gain the silver mines, and to explore further trading links to the south by reestablishing the post at Benguela.[187]

Although Portuguese troops would not make direct attacks against Ndongo for many years, and eventually the two made a peace agreement in 1599, Portuguese military actions had long-term consequences for Ndongo domestic politics by making dissident factions more willing to seek Portuguese assistance.[188] Around 1592 Njinga Ngola Kilombo kia Kasenda died and was replaced by his son Mbandi Ngola Kiluanji. Although initially there was little direct dissention at his ascension, political factionalism soon became strong. Marriage patterns defined two factions, as the Italian missionary Giovanni Antonio Cavazzi described hearing of it 40 years later. One faction formed around Mbandi a Ngola Kiluanji's wife, a daughter of the *soba* of Hango a Kikaito "whom he

---

Adventures of Andrew Battell in Angola and Adjourning Lands (ed. E. G. Ravenstein, London, 1901), p. 84. This edition draws together material from Samuel Purchas, *Purchas, His Pilgrimmes* (London, 1625), and Purchas's notes on his interviews with Battell published in an earlier work, *Purchas, His Pilgrimage* (London, 1613), pp. 13–16.

[185] The events are alluded to in a contemporary document, Letter of Gaspar Dias de Beja, March, 1591, *MMA* 3: 424; other episodes of war in the early 1590s can be reconstructed from later sources, such as a biography of Alvaro III, born about 1593, who had a mother who was seized by his father in putting down a revolt by the Marquis of Wembo and the same account mentions a revolt at the time by Nsundi, [Mateus Cardoso] "Relação da morte de D. Alvaro rei do Congo e eleição de D. Pedro II Afonso" (1622) *MMA* 15: 493.

[186] For overviews of this period see Birmingham, *Trade and Conquest*, pp. 56–63 and Saccardo, *Congo e Angola* 1: 149–53.

[187] Battell, *Strange Adventures* (ed. Ravenstein), pp. 36–7.

[188] Du Jarric, *Histoire.*

loved so much that he seemed bewitched by her Love" and whose brothers he greatly favored. Its partisans were located primarily in the northern
and eastern parts of the country along the Lucala River. The second faction was aligned around his second wife, Kingela Kagombe, whose father
was the *soba* of Dumbo a Pebo and dominated the southern part of the
country, on both sides of the Kwanza.[189] Another important *soba* of the
region, Axila Mbanza, also gave his sister as another of Mbandi a Ngola's
wives.[190] The southern faction was boosted by Kafuxe ka Mbare, the most
powerful *soba* of Kisama after his stunning victory over the Portuguese in
1596. His fame was such that "even the very king of Angola feared him,
because he was the one who according to their laws, would succeed him
in the kingdom." The other *sobas*, according to Jesuit sources, "would
attempt to make him king immediately, for he being so valiant that he
could defend them against the Portuguese."[191]

In 1600 Governor João Rodrigues Coutinho decided to move against
the faction whose representatives occupied the southern region of Ndongo
on both sides of the Kwanza. The two rulers, Kafuxe and Axila Mbanza,
had suffered major losses at the hands of raiders from the south and
Coutinho saw an opportunity to strengthen his ties with Mbandi a
Ngola.[192] Although Rodrigues Coutinho died in the midst of the campaign, his successor, Manuel Cerveira Pereira, defeated Kafuxe, pillaged
and humiliated Axila Mbanza, and constructed the *presidio* (fort) of
Cambambe on the site which the Portuguese believed contained silver
mines.[193] The war on Axila Mbanza advanced Mbandi a Ngola's favored
northern faction, led at this point by Kabonda.[194] Mbandi a Ngola,
pleased to see this threat from his competitors reduced, sent an embassy
to Cerveira Pereira around 1603 to assure himself that the news of the
defeat was real and to put himself in the favor of the Portuguese, including suggestions that he might become a Christian and even a vassal.[195]
The real impact of these alliances and wars was that they provided the
Portuguese the opportunities to acquire slaves who might be taken and
sold even if campaigns failed to yield permanent conquests.

[189] MSS Araldi, Cavazzi, "Missione evangelica," book 2, chapter 1, p. 14.
[190] Regimento to Manuel Forjaz Pereira, 1607, *MMA* 5: 269.
[191] Guerreiro, *Relaçam* in *MMA* 5: 53.
[192] Battell, *Strange Adventures* (ed. Ravenstein), pp. 26–8.
[193] "Catalogo dos Governadores," in Silva Corrêa, *História* 1: 219.
[194] Regimento to Manuel Forjaz Pereira, 1607, *MMA* 5: 269.
[195] "Relaçion del Gouernador d'Angola sobre el Estado en que tem Aquella Conquista...
28 September 1603," *MMA* 5: 61 see also Guerrerio, "Relaçam," *MMA* 5: 55.

Warfare, Trade, Slaves, and the Asiento, 1579–1607

At the same time that the Portuguese governors were making political alliances with the various factions in Ndongo, building the fort at Cambambe, and acquiring captives through their own direct military activity, they also purchased captives as a result of the commercial and military alliances they made with local Africans. For the next 50 years the history of Angola would reflect a tension among purchasing slaves, direct capture of Africans by Portuguese-led forces, and obtaining captives through military and commercial cooperation with Africans. Although these strategies sometimes overlapped, frequently commerce in slaves gave way to capture of slaves through warfare.

Portuguese relations with the Imbangala before 1615 highlighted the commercial route and military routes to acquiring slaves. The Imbangala were independent armies that lived in fortified camps in well-integrated and well-disciplined military units numbering several thousand or more. Andrew Battell, a ship-wrecked Englishman who eventually spent 16 months living as a hostage with the band of Imbe Kalandula in 1600–1601, noted they were not part of an integrated local political system. They had a religious ideology based on Central African concepts of witchcraft best symbolized by acts of cannibalism, a feature that brought fear and dread to all who met them. Unlike the civil authorities that the Portuguese had dealt with so far, the Imbangala lived by rapine with no local loyalties other than their own leaders. To obtain new recruits, Battell noted that "when they take any town they keep the boys and girls of thirteen and fourteen years of age as their own children."[196]

The Imbangala's reliance on captive children and their methods of training them to build their forces using alcohol and brainwashing, especially the practice of forcing the captive children to wear a collar until they killed an enemy had them "hemmed in by hope and fear they grow very resolute and adventurous." Their employment of their youthful captives is perhaps the earliest documented use of child soldiers in Africa. Their use of children gave them the callous ruthlessness and mobility for which they would become infamous.[197]

Because they were not attached to any stable community they did not participate in the agricultural activities of the societies they invaded, and their method of subsistence resulted in the destruction of the communities

[196] Battell, *Strange Adventures* (ed. Ravenstein), pp. 84–5 (1613) (which extends the age range of captives from 10 to 20 years) and pp. 32–3 (1625).
[197] Battell, *Strange Adventures* (ed. Ravenstein, 1625), pp. 32–33

they attacked. According to Battell's testimony, "they stay no longer in a place than it will afford them maintenance ... for they will not sow, nor plant, nor bring up any cattle, more than they take by wars."[198] Their desire for alcohol intensified their tendency to live by general pillage and magnified their mobility. They met their needs for alcohol by massive consumption of palm wine, the principal source of alcohol in Angola at the time, and procuring it required them to move frequently. Battell wrote that they "delight in no country, but where there is great store of Palmares, or groves of palms." Instead of tapping palm trees over years, the Imbangala simply cut them down and drained them of them of their fermented sap over a period of 26 days. Five months of such destruction in one place was enough to ruin the country; after that they simply abandoned it and moved on to fresh palm groves.[199] Their relentless pillaging resulted in the deliberate destruction of large areas, the removal of captives, and the flight of refugees whose subsistence base was destroyed and who also feared the Imbangala aggressors. These refugees sometimes traveled over long distances to escape, all the while remaining vulnerable to enslavement.

The Portuguese connections to the Imbangala provided one of the major sources of captives. Around 1600 merchants from Luanda trading for cattle and copper along the barren coast near to the modern port of Benguela established relations with the Imbangala, whom the Portuguese called "Jagas."[200] The Imbangala were ravaging the country and had taken many captives; as a result the traders were immediately able to load

---

[198] Battell, *Strange Adventures* (ed. Ravenstein), p. 30.
[199] Battell, *Strange Adventures* (ed. Ravenstein), p. 84 (1613), pp. 30–1 (1625).
[200] Historians disagree about the ultimate origins of the Imbangala, but the band that Battell and his Portuguese associates met in 1600 had originated in the central highlands of Angola, home of the present-day Ovimbundu people. There is a lengthy debate, started by David Birmingham and Jan Vansina and going back to the mid-1960s, on the origins of the Imbangala and their connection to the "Jagas" that invaded Kongo in 1568. Much of the earlier argument, and a theory connecting them to migrations from the Lunda Empire, is summarized and cited in Joseph C. Miller, "Requiem"; and *Kings and Kinsmen*. For a position that makes their origin local in the central highlands of Angola, see John Thornton, "The Chronology and Causes of Lunda Expansion to the West, ca. 1700–1852," *Zambia Journal of History* 1 (1981): 1–13. For a recent comprehensive summary, see Paulo Jorge de Sousa Pinto, "Em torno de um problema de identidade. Os "Jaga" na História de Congo e Angola," *Mare Liberum* 18–19 (1999–2000): 193–246. Recently Jan Vansina has used linguisitc and archaeological evidence to place their origins in the southern end of the central highlands and adjacent coastal regions. *How Societies Are Born: Governance in West Central Africa Before 1600* (Charlottesville and London, 2004), pp. 196–201.

their ships.[201] In addition to buying slaves, the merchants also provided covering fire and ships to help the Imbangala cross the Kuvo into the kingdom of Benguela and then joined them in the war and shared in the spoils. The merchants obtained "a great store" of slaves in this alliance, so that in just five months three more ships hauled away the Portuguese share of the captives.[202]

By 1607 the Imbangala had effectively destroyed the kingdom of Benguela and had pillaged the lands of Kafuxe and provided the Portuguese the openings to found the presidio of Cambambe. More important, however, was that even without an official connection to the Portuguese government the devastation they caused allowed the Portuguese to purchase thousands of refugees and captives. The opportunities that the Imbangala presence gave the Portuguese to acquire slaves were a continuation of the links between warfare and enslavement that went back to Dias de Novais's first war with Ndongo. The factor's book in 1592 revealed that some 52,000 slaves had been legally exported through Luanda since war began in 1579. Dias de Novais had the right to collect one third of the duties on slaves, and this helped finance the conquest up to the time of his death.[203] Indeed, in 1579, the House of Mina in Portugal paid 15,000 cruzados to Dias de Novais's father from the rights that he obtained on the Angola-Brazil slave trade.[204] Many slaves had been captured in war; for example, the spoils of one operation in 1581 "would fill two India ships" with slaves.[205] When Luis de Serrão's force advanced into Kabasa in 1590, he was followed by a chain of merchants bearing goods worth "a million in gold," enough to fill 24 ships, for it "was the custom of that kingdom that merchants and conquistadors going along with the army with their goods so that they could make their trade with them." In fact, Serrão saved the army after the rout of 1589 by leaving this vast store of goods for their opponents to loot, delaying their pursuit and allowing the remnants to escape.[206]

Even without making a military alliance with local Africans or alliance with groups such as the Imbangala, Portuguese merchants could tap into

---

[201] Battell (ed. Ravenstein), *Strange Adventures*?] 1613), from which this note is drawn.
[202] All this material is gathered together in the Ravenstein edition, whose chronology we follow (see pp. xii–xiii). Battell, *Strange Adventures* (ed. Ravenstein), pp. 16–21.
[203] Provanças feitas ao Embargo de Paulo Dias de Novais, 1579, *MMA* 3: 319–22.
[204] Alvara of the treasurer of the Casa da Mina, 19 October 1579, *MMA* 4: 317.
[205] Baltsar Afonso to Miguel de Sousa, 4 July 1581, to *MMA* 3: 202.
[206] Abreu e Brito, "Svmario," fol. 34.

many local slave markets throughout West Central Africa. In the 1580s the Jesuits wrote that more captives were obtained by purchase than by war,[207] and a vast slave-trading network extended from Okanga on the northeast of Kongo to south of the Kwanza on the south. Kongo's ambassador to Rome, Duarte Lopes, describing the situation in Kongo as he witnessed it in the first half of the 1580s, "there is [in Mbamba] the major traffic of slaves conducted from Angola in which the Portuguese buy each year more than 5,000 heads of Negroes and thus lead them to various places to sell."[208] Many of the buyers were Portuguese and Luso-Africans who had come from Kongo to join Dias de Novais, and those in the more remote areas were quite frequently New Christians. An Inquisition enquiry in 1596 reported that slave markets were found in several places in Kongo, such as Mbumbi in the south, the capital, São Salvador, Ngongo Mbata in the east, and Mpinda at the mouth of the Kongo River; others were found at places such as Cabonda, Casangongo, and Mutemo in the unconquered regions between Kongo and Ndongo, as well as the posts at Bengo, Luanda, the "market of the Ambundos" at Pinganá, Cafecuta between the Dande and Bengo Rivers, and Massangano.[209] In many of these *resgates* (markets), there was a community of Luso-Africans as well as a slave market.

Many of these Portuguese and Luso-African traders continued to be outside the control of Angola and spread their business between areas. The New Christian Ayres Fernandes, who "was waiting for the Messiah to come," divided his business interests between "the markets of Congo and Angola." Another slave trader Pedro das Neves was involved in "both kingdoms."[210] The New Christian presence only increased when Philip II decreed in 1601 that New Christians, formerly forbidden to travel to the empire without special license, were now permitted to go anywhere in the Portuguese empire with "their families and their goods."[211]

Dias de Novais tried to bring all the merchants together under his control. In 1582, he complained that they posed a threat to his grant and

---

[207] Rodrigues, "História," *MMA* 4: 561.

[208] Pigafetta, *Descritione*, p. 26. This may have included slaves transported from beyond Mbamba as well as Mbamba itself; also it probably included people taken in the Dembos, which were under Mbamba's control.

[209] ANTT, Inquisição de Lisboa, Livro 877, "Visitições a Angola," 1596–1597, fols. 26v, 62v, 64, 84v, 89.

[210] ANTT, Inquisição de Lisboa, Livro 877, "Visitições a Angola," 1596–1597, fols. 37, 37v, 64.

[211] Alvará of Felipe II, 31 July 1601, *MMA* 5: 34–5.

they questioned him spitefully about it.[212] But there was no resolution to the impasse, for in a report of 1599, Jeromino Castanho noted that only 200 of the 2,000 Portuguese who had come to Angola still resided there. Aside from those who had died, the rest had "fled" to Congo or elsewhere in the interior to become Luso-Africans.[213]

João Rodrigues Coutinho, conqueror of Cambambe, accepted the value of the slave trade and its link to war as well as commerce. His instructions were to conquer the salt and silver mines, which would require him to wage relentless war. Whether he conquered any mines or not, his wars would surely yield abundant slaves, as he had been "given [probably bought] seven years' custom of all slaves and goods that were carried thence to the West Indies, Brazil, or whithersoever."[214] In addition to the fiscal privileges he obtained as part of his governorship of Angola, he also held the Asiento to deliver 4,250 slaves to the Spanish Indies from the Philip II.[215] These privileges gave him a direct interest in linking the conquest to wars to obtain slaves.

Even before he left Madrid, Coutinho sold 400 slave licenses to the dealer Jorge Rodrigues Solis for the Spanish Indies.[216] Although Rodrigues Coutinho died not long after his arrival in Angola, his brother managed to sell 15,768 slave licenses to a certain Melchior de Teves.[217] A later inquest revealed that when he died in the Cambambe campaign, the inventory of his goods revealed that he had the cargos of 14 ships and that "no other merchants had half the goods" that he had. Moreover, he had kept *kijikos* taken in the campaign for himself and failed to pay royal taxes on much of the spoils.[218] Even though Rodrigues Coutinho sent the army to fight for mines and slaves in Kisama, Jesuits at the time still grumbled that he did "nothing more than trade, bargain for slaves without going forward in a such a conquest that would have brought so many millions of souls to God, and so much wealth in mines to His Majesty."[219] He did, however,

---

[212] Alvará proibindo o commercio para a Africa de Paulo Dias de Novais, 13 March 1582, *MMA* 3: 344.

[213] Memorial of Jeronimo Castanho, 1599, *MMA* 4: 600, see also p. 607 for a repetition of the plan to concentrate them.

[214] Battell, *Strange Adventures* (ed. Ravenstein), p. 36.

[215] Alfredo de Albuquerque Felner, *Angola. Apontamentos sôbre a occupação e início do estabelecimento dos Portugueses no Congo, Angola e Benguela* (Lisbon, 1933), p. 186 and documentation cited.

[216] Contracto dos escravos de Angola, 2 May 1601, *MMA* 5: 29–31.

[217] "Avenças dos escravos de Angola," 9 December 1608, *MMA* 5: 487–8.

[218] Arquivo Histórico Ultramarino (AHU) Caixa (Cx) 1, doc. 18, Andre Velho da Fonseca, 4 March 1612.

[219] Guerreiro, *Relação Anual* in *MMA* 5: 52–3.

fulfill the slave quotas for the Americas.[220] According to an anonymous account of 1607, when the king ordered governors to conquer the mines of Cambambe, "on which he placed a lot of hope," he noted that the wars would also yield "a fruitful trade in slaves."[221]

Atlantic Creole Culture in Angola and Ndongo

The establishment of the Portuguese colony of Angola, the founding of forts in Ndongo's territory, and the alliances the Portuguese made with discontented elements of Ndongo's ruling groups set the stage for a second center where Atlantic Creole culture emerged. Long before Dias de Novais's arrival the Mbundu had been in contact with Atlantic Creole culture, especially Christianity, through Kongo. By 1518 these interactions had spread, until about 1526, when missionaries from Kongo built a chapel in Kabasa, the Ndongo capital. By 1520 the Luso-African community in the capital was another source of Atlantic Creole culture that influenced the Mbundu. More Mbundu may have converted as a result of the work of the Jesuit mission that came to Ndongo with Dias de Novais in 1560, even though the missionaries were partially prisoners. By the time the last missionary, Francisco de Gouveia, died in 1575, he had a substantial following from his 15 years of teaching. As he lay sick and dying, the religious mixing that had been going on for some years revealed itself clearly. The king called his "holy men and fetishers" to minister to de Gouveia, for whom he "had a lot of affection" and regarded as "his ganga [*nganga* – religious teacher]."[222]

The religious penetration that had taken place at Kabasa was also evident in other parts of Mbundu. The island of Luanda and nearby mainland, though Kimbundu speaking, were under Kongo sovereignty, and were "ancient Christians of the land" governed by delegates sent from Kongo. Jesuits had also made conversions around the mouth of the Kwanza, in the same region, when they landed there in 1560.[223] But in 1575 it was the Jesuits who arrived from Portugal in Dias de Novais's second mission with royal financial support and who began to augment and extend the Christianity in the region. They began their work in Corimba,

[220] Battell, *Strange Adventures* (ed. Ravenstein), p. 38.
[221] "Relação da Costa da Guiné," 1607, *MMA* 5: 388.
[222] Garcia Simões to Provincial, 20 October 1575, *MMA* 3: 141.
[223] "Residençia de Angola," 1588, *MMA* 3: 378.

a province located north of the mouth of the Kwanza River, as well as on the island of Luanda.[224]

Christian practices in the Luanda region exhibited the same Atlantic Creole tendencies seen in Kongo, tolerating, for example, a great deal of local religious mixture. But even here, however, not all places were equally influenced. Beringó, located at the border of Corimba's authority, for example, had never had a priest or a Portuguese when Baltasar Afonso arrived there in 1582, though the people were anxious to burn idols and accept instruction.[225] Jesuits, after 1575, welcomed the Christian identity of the Luandans but were hesitant to credit what they regarded as an imperfect understanding of the faith, saying they were "Christians in name only," and insisted on treating them as newly converted.[226] At Christmas Mass in 1577, they heard many confessions by Portuguese, but denied the sacrament to the many of the Africans deeming them insufficiently instructed.[227]

This reflected Jesuit hostility to the Atlantic Creole form of Christianity, which, as in Kongo, they blamed on the secular priests. Nevertheless, Jesuits contributed to making the Atlantic Creole form of Christianity for Mbundu as other Portuguese priests had earlier in Kongo. When they were working in the Luanda area, the Jesuits relied heavily on a bilingual Portuguese native of São Tomé to interpret for them in Kimbundu. His translations of Christian prayers would form the basis for the kind on linguistic melding of traditions that took place earlier in Kongo and that would form the touchstone for Jesuit teaching. Thanks to his teaching, a newly baptized *soba* could greet a Jesuit priest with the opening line of the Lord's Payer, *Tatétu oé cála que úlo* ("Our Father which art in Heaven"), marking him as ready for baptism.[228]

Moreover, as Luso-African and Kongolese merchants outside of Luanda and Kabasa increased steadily following Dias de Novais's arrival, their presence also affected the spread of Christianity and Atlantic Creole

---

[224] Jesuit Annual Letter, 1579, *MMA* 3: 185.

[225] Baltasar Barreira to General, 31 January 1582, *MMA* 15: 277.

[226] Jesuit Annual Letter, 1 January 1578, *MMA* 3: 164–5.

[227] Carta annua da residencia de Angola, 1577, *MMA* 3: 162.

[228] Baltasar Barreira to General, 31 January 1581, *MMA* 15: 271, 274. This short text confirms that the language of Luanda and its vicinity was Kimbundu, even though it was under Kongo's authority, and that Kongo influence in religion did not extend to language, because the form of the first line of the prayer is substantially different from the Kikongo one.

culture. This was especially so as fairly large private military contingents came from Kongo under Luso-African and Kongolese leadership to assist Dias de Novais and brought with them the Atlantic Creole culture of their homeland. In 1577, a group of some 100 Portuguese with "many Christian Macicongos [Mwisikongos]" in "Angola" were surrounded by 4,000 hostile soldiers, which King Álvaro II proposed to relieve.[229] Furthermore, a Jesuit visit to a community of Luso-African merchants and Kongolese Christians located in the "interior of Angola" revealed that both groups followed many unacceptable practices, as they were "far from the rigors of ecclesiastical and secular law," which required correction.[230] The Jesuits' displeasure reinforces the notion that they were practicing an Atlantic Creole form of Christianity.

A good illustration of the way in which Christianity and, more importantly, Atlantic Creole cultural practices were spreading in this period is revealed in the baptism of *soba* Songa in 1581. When Dias de Novais initiated the process of getting *sobas* to submit formally to vassalage in 1581 after his initial campaigns, he required them to be baptized. *Soba* Songa, an "in-law of the King of Angola [Ndongo]" whose lands lay south of the Kwanza's mouth across from Kongo territory, was the first of them, baptized on a feast day, Epiphany (6 January) 1581. Songa's ceremony formed the pattern of conversion that would accompany the treaties of vassalage that became the basis for emerging Portuguese authority in Angola. Baptism was a combination of feast (usually held on a feast day) and public celebration. Songa, and his most powerful and influential family members, accepted baptism and took Christian names, in his case Constantino, in honor of Constantine who converted Rome. Songa, wearing an outfit of Portuguese clothing, then traveled through his lands with the priest, Baltasar Afonso, planting crosses in key locations and identifying and burning "houses of idols" or the shrines dedicated to *kilundas*. Here they erected a cross, and local people carried their "idols" to be destroyed. As the secular aspects of this Atlantic Creole culture included obedience to the Portuguese, Songa was granted the title of "Captain Major of the local people." The historical precedent from Kongo's conversion was reinforced by Songa's feast held at his house, to which the Kongolese governor of Luanda, other Kongolese nobles and his Portuguese godparents were

---

[229] Report on a letter of Baltasar Afonso, reporting events before Easter 1577, 9 October 1577, *MMA* 3: 157.
[230] Jesuit Annual Letter, 1 January 1578, *MMA* 3: 165.

invited. Songa was then given the right to sit on a carpet, a local custom. The Jesuit report of the ceremony also noted a practice that would
become commonplace in the Atlantic Creole world that was emerging: he
replaced "the idols of this land and instruments of their idolatries, which
are still found in some cubatas [villages] of the Christians," with Christian
religious objects.[231]

No sooner had Songa been baptized than the *soba* Quicunguela, who
controlled Mucombe where Dias de Novais had his camp upcountry,
sought to be baptized and to learn Christian teaching as well.[232] Quin-
cunguela was baptized on 2 February (the Feast of the Birth of the Most
Holy Virgin), 1583. In addition to the elements already noted in the baptism of Songa, the public rituals, burning of idols, and richly dressed cate-
chumens, the ceremony also included a celebration of the recapture of an
image of the Virgin taken by Ndongo in the 1579 war. The incident reveals
a positive Mbundu attitude toward Atlantic Creole culture, because they
did not burn this religious object of their enemies, unlike the Portuguese,
who regularly burned Mbundu "idols." Instead, they installed it in one
of their own shrines as an object of devotion.[233]

The structure of subordination that Dias de Novais established would
help to shape the form of Atlantic Creole culture as well. The presence of
thousands of Kongolese and Luso-Africans in Dias de Novais's army and
their settling in various areas of the conquest was another avenue for the
spread of the Atlantic Creole culture of Kongo. The Englishman Battell
noted how important Kongo soldiers were to the conquest and how Luso-
Africans cooperated with them. He wrote that a Kongolese nobleman
"known to be a good Christian" would come to Angola with some 100
of his own followers and would then be appointed military commander
(*tendala*) with considerable political power. He in turn would bring *sobas*
to the Portuguese to submit and pay tribute.[234]

Each *soba* was given an *amo*, a protector, which Dias de Novais argued
was already present in Ndongo. This protector was a Portuguese, drawn
from "captains, principal persons ... and [Jesuit] priests." Frequently,
sobas accepting vassalage would ask for Jesuits because they expected
better treatment from the fathers, thus helping the priests to extend their

[231] Baltasar Barreira to General of the Jesuits, 31 January 1582, *MMA* 15: 269–78; same to
Sebastião de Morais, 31 January 1582, *MMA* 3: 209–10.
[232] Baltasar Barreira to General, 31 January 1582, *MMA* 15: 276.
[233] Anonymous Jesuit letter to Provincial, 20 November 1583, *MMA* 15: 283–4.
[234] Battell (ed. Ravenstein), *Strange Adventures*, pp. 64–5 (1625).

influence.[235] In this way, a stable African Creole Christian community emerged.

But conversion of rulers was not sufficient for Atlantic Creole culture to spread, and in 1582 Dias de Novais recognized that to advance Christianity fully he would need at least 10 new priests to deal with the Christians who had been baptized by then, not counting the others who were asking for the doctrine.[236] The Jesuits, for their part, were already sending "chapel boys" whom they had trained out to other places to teach and prepare the way for them in areas that were, in their opinion, barely Christian, such as Kasanze or Bengo.[237] Some of these chapel boys were trained in European musical instruments and other skills that would contribute to an Mbundu manifestation of Atlantic Creole culture.[238] Mass baptism of the subjects followed; Dias de Novais announced he had 5,000 to 6,000 of "our Mbundus" baptized when they allied with him in 1582.[239]

The same political forces that made *sobas* ally with Portugal also made them seek baptism, a gateway to Atlantic Creole culture, and that would set the pattern that would allow Atlantic Creole culture to spread on its own beyond the priests and formal membership in the church. The formal spread was initially fairly rapid, as Diogo de Costa wrote in 1586, "because of the cruelty of the king [of Ndongo], many of his vassals come to the Governor, this year I baptized a few more than 100."[240] Dias de Novais gave the right of patronage over some of these *sobas* to the Jesuits, in order that they might set an example by their fair dealing to other *sobas* who would then be inclined to seek out priests.[241] At the same time, political decisions to renounce Portuguese alliance had an adverse effect, at least the Jesuits believed, on the status of conversion, but not necessarily Atlantic Creole culture, which might continue unabated. In 1594, the head of the Jesuit mission ordered that "in no way should Holy Baptism be given to any fidalgo in Angola . . . until the land is conquered and secure," so as to avoid having him "rise up and turn against everything," as "too many heathens have been baptized without instruction."[242] The pattern

[235] Guerreiro, *Relaçam annual* (1602–1603), *MMA* 5: 51; Battell, *Strange Adventures* (ed. Ravenstein), p. 65.
[236] Paulo Dias de Novais to King, 12 January 1582, *MMA* 4: 337.
[237] Baltasar Barreira to General, 31 January 1582, *MMA* 15: 278.
[238] Baltasar Barreira to General, 15 May 1593, *MMA* 15: 332.
[239] Paulo Dias de Novais to King, 3 July 1582, *MMA* 4: 342.
[240] Diogo da Costa, 31 May 1586, *MMA* 3: 339.
[241] Guerreiro, *Relação*, in *MMA* 5: 51.
[242] Pero Rodrigues, "Visita da Residencia de Angola, 1594," *MMA* 3: 477.

of asking for priests and baptism when Portugal was strong, and rejecting it in revolt, would continue; for example, Jesuits noted that the same had taken place when Portuguese forces penetrated Kisama. Even Ndongo had responded this way after the notable Portuguese victory over Kafuche in 1601, as did a host of other neighboring rulers.[243]

Religious conversion and ministering to the converted was not solely the work of Jesuits or the Portuguese military and political authorities. There was a secular establishment whose orientation was more toward Atlantic Creole culture and religion and who also worked with the people, often through the Kongo church. Some lay Kongolese teachers served in this secular establishment, not just in Mbamba but also as far afield as the eastern province of Mbata, where João Milão (Lau) was teaching in 1593. A visit of the Inquisition to Angola, which heard testimony in 1596–1598, reveals the presence of numerous secular priests in Kongo and Mbundu.[244] Many of these priests were Luso-Africans who had stayed for many years in Kongo, making them familiar with the Atlantic Creole ways of that church. A good number were deeply involved in the slave trade – Father Miguel da Silveira, known also by his Kikongo name of Quitingo, was accused of being too busy counting *nzimbos* and dealing with slaves to say Mass for the Mwene Mbamba, D. António.[245]

The subordination of the Angolan church to the Kongolese one was critical to the development of an Atlantic Creole form of Christianity in Mbundu. This subordination was evident by the fact that the Jesuits had to obtain a license from King Álvaro II of Kongo to work near Luanda in 1586.[246] The next year, Álvaro also granted them license to teach and "raise crosses and churches in all parts of my kingdom, without anyone stopping them."[247] In 1590, in fact, both Luanda and Masangano were made parishes under the authority of the bishop and financed under royal instructions.[248] In 1596 the situation was further complicated by the selection by Rome of São Salvador, capital of Kongo, as an Episcopal See. By placing the secular establishment firmly under the control of the Kongo

[243] Guerreiro, *Relação* in MMA 5: 55–6.
[244] ANTT, Inquisição de Lisboa, Livro 877, "Visitições a Angola," 1596–1597, fols. 65, 67v, 70–70v, 72, 79v–80, 82v.
[245] ANTT, Inquisição de Lisboa, Livro 877, "Visitições a Angola," 1596–1597, fols. 80–82v.
[246] "Residençia de Angola," 1588, MMA 3: 378.
[247] Provisão of King Álvaro II, 7 July 1587, MMA 3: 344–5.
[248] Alvará of Bishop Martinho de Ulhoa, 15 November 1590, MMA 3: 407–8; Alvará on Treasury of Angola, 12 February 1592, MMA 3: 437.

church, they continued the spread of Kongo's Atlantic Creole form of Christianity to other regions of West Central Africa, including territory controlled by Portugal. A report on parishes in 1600 reveals the distribution of religious centers under São Salvador: in addition to parishes in each of the principal Kongo provinces, or in borderland provinces such as Mbumbi and Mutemo that had Luso-African populations, both Luanda and Masangano were also a part of the See.[249] The parish of Masangano was responsible for all the Portuguese-controlled communities along the Kwanza, from Muxima to lands somewhat beyond Masangano. Many Africans in the area practiced an Atlantic Creole form of Christianity, which visiting Jesuits in 1606 regarded as sufficiently Christian that the only thing they had to do was to hear confession from Portuguese "and their negroes."[250]

Regular priests like the Jesuits were not always happy with the spread of this Atlantic Creole religious form, as Baltasar Barreira's comments that the secular clergy in Kongo were "idiots" reveals. The Jesuits established a college in Luanda in 1593 to teach interpreters, the Portuguese in Angola, and the "sons of nobles of Congo" in hope that they would move Atlantic Creole Christianity closer to their ideal model from Europe.[251] Jesuits were anxious to learn to speak Kimbundu to reduce their dependence on interpreters and to present the doctrine more effectively. But the Jesuits were few, their mortality was high, and they were restricted to the areas where there was either a strong Portuguese conquest or where they had been granted control over *sobas* who were near Luanda, along the lower Bengo, and on the lower Kwanza.[252] The Jesuit Diogo Ferreira, who "knew the language and had a great facility with the blacks and never stopped teaching them doctrine," had converted 20,000 Mbundu in addition to those in the towns of Luanda and Massangano before his untimely death in May 1602.[253] In addition to the Jesuits, the Third Order Franciscans established a house in Luanda in 1606; although they were regarded as zealous and were prepared to work in Kongo as well as Angola.[254] Unfortunately, their work is poorly documented, but what

---

[249] Royal order for payment to churches, 18 January 1600 *MMA* 5: 4.
[250] Guerreiro, *Relação*, in *MMA* 5: 242.
[251] Fundação de Colégio em Angola dos Padres da Companhia, 15 June 1593, *MMA* 15: 333.
[252] Guerreiro, *Relação*, in *MMA* 5: 51; Jesuit Annual Letter, 1603, *MMA* 5: 82.
[253] Guerriero, *Relação*, *MMA* 5: 57.
[254] Saccardo, *Congo e Angola* 1: 164–5. Virtually all the material about their activity concerns various grants of income and land to them.

survives shows that they were active outside the city, establishing mission posts in Kongo, Massangano, and Cambambe that year.[255]

Neither group of regular priests traveled as widely as the Church was spread. Outside of their jurisdiction, a new Mbundu version of Atlantic Creole Christianity was taking shape, largely influenced by the presence of the secular clergy and the Atlantic Creole model of how to integrate Central African religions and Christianity, which had developed first in Kongo.

This situation was reflected in a somber report of 1606, in which a Jesuit and his lay assistant came to an unidentified district of 2,000 and later another district called Casanha, both of which were already deemed Christian, all having received baptism "some years ago by certain [secular] priests" but which, in their opinion, "had nothing more than the name of Christians" because they had "never been cultivated in the faith."[256] Despite this opinion, the older people considered their adherence firm and told the priests that they could instruct the youth in the doctrine but that "they already had nothing to learn of it." Their ignorance took several forms: not being able to make the sign of the cross, having a plurality of wives (the ruler of Casanha had over 300 wives), disinterest in Christian forms of marriage (only two people had been married in a church), and the continued existence of an active cult of non-Christian religious observances (there were functioning "houses of idols" and other elements of the original Mbundu religion, which the people sought to conceal). The *soba* of Casanha had long discussions with his council of *macotas* over whether to allow the Jesuits to build a church, and in general there was debate over exactly which elements of the new religion they should adopt and which of the old one they should abandon. For all their supposed irregularity, Casanha's people were clearly already integrated into Atlantic Creole religion if not the Jesuits' model of Christianity as they eagerly brought their children to be baptized.[257]

---

[255] Academica das Ciências, Lisbon. MS Vermelho 804 "Memorias para a historia de congregação da Terceira Ordem de Penitencia" fols, 5v–6v. This early nineteenth century history cites, in footnotes, unpublished archival materials from the convent in Lisbon as well as from Angolan sources. Our thanks to Cecile Fromont for advising us of this source.

[256] Guerreiro, *Relação*, MMA 5: 238. In 1607, King Philip II noted that he had been informed that many people had been baptized by priests without much catechism and they went back to their lands and were not heard from again; Regimento to Manuel Pereira Forjaz, 26 March 1607, MMA 5: 266.

[257] Guerreiro, *Relação* in MMA 5: 238–9.

Loango, the North Coast, and Atlantic Creole Culture

The lands lying north of the Congo River, especially the kingdom of Loango, came into the Atlantic Creole orbit during the 1580s and would ultimately become a trading conduit for slaves. The lands north of the Congo formed a family of states related to Kongo. These included Ngoyo at the mouth of the Congo River, Kakongo, whose subordinate state of Nzari was said to be the root of Loango, and Vungu, supposedly the root of Kongo.[258] Loango's founding king, like his counterpart in Ndongo further south, managed to subject a group of feuding, independent petty states to his rule.[259] Initially, Loango had been a vassal of Kongo, but by the end of the sixteenth century the rulers of the two states simply regarded each other as friends.[260]

Later, as Loango consolidated its power, it also created the institutions that are described in detail only in the early seventeenth century. By that time, the ruler's court at Mbanza Loango was a large city, which Dutch observers compared with Amsterdam, and was also an administrative and religious–judicial hub. An administrative staff, headed by four principal nobles, also had a number of functional titles below it, whereas the larger rural provinces were each ruled by close relatives of the king, specifically the children of his sister.

In addition to the political offices, the kingdom had a large and complex series of shrines, presided over by various religious authorities. Chief among these officers was the *mwene nkisi*, who administered a poison ordeal and served as an important advisor to the king. The shrines were judicial centers, where guilt was determined and law proclaimed. At the same time, the king had an important religious role, being described as a "great magician" and a rainmaker. In this way he dominated ultimately the entire chain of shrines and religious offices.[261]

---

[258] These three states are cited in Afonso's royal titles in 1535 in the lands over which he ruled as "king"; see Afonso to Paulo III, 21 February 1535, *MMA* 2: 38.

[259] Olfert Dapper, *Naukeurige Beschrijvinge der Afrikaensche gewesten* (Amsterdam, 1676), pp. 143–4.

[260] Lopes in Pigafetta, *Relatione*, p. 14.

[261] The early government of Loango is described by three observers who all lived in Loango in the first part of the 1610s, Andrew Battell, *Strange Adventures* (ed. Ravenstein), pp. 42–62 (1625), 77–83 (1613); Pieter van den Broecke, *Reizen naar West-Afrika van Pieter van den Broecke, 1605–1614* (ed. K. Ratelband, The Hague, 1950), English translation and edition, J. D. La Fleur, *Pieter van den Broecke's Journal of Voyages to Cape Verde, Guinea and Angola, 1605–1612* (London, 2000); and Samuel Brun, *Schiffarten* (Basel, 1624), *Samuel Bruns's Schiffarten (1624)* (ed. S. L. P. L'Honoré Naber, Hague, 1913), English translation in Adam Jones (ed. and trans.) *German Sources for West African History, 1599–1669* (Wiesbaden, 1983). Our account is a synthesis drawn from

Loango and the smaller kingdoms north of the Congo River entered the Atlantic Creole complex when Portuguese merchants began visiting them in the early sixteenth century. When Battell visited on a trading voyage in the mid-1590s trade was already well established.[262] English and French corsairs raided the coast in the 1580s, and the Dutch followed them soon after with more commercial interests.[263] The first recorded Dutch trading voyage was in 1593, when a small private commercial venture joined the older trade of the Portuguese, but that had little known follow up, though trading voyages in 1598–1599 to Kongo and also to Loango are also known.[264] Commercial motivations joined the larger political operations of the Dutch war with Spain, and in 1598 Dutch naval vessels attacked São Tomé, followed by a full-scale invasion in 1599.[265] Trading with Loango and Kongo became more regular after 1600, especially by Gerard Reinst, who formed a company with his colleague, Pieter Brandt, that was acknowledged by the Dutch States General as the first to trade in the Central African region.[266]

Once Loango became a part of this commercial network, it joined the Atlantic Creole religious world when the king asked Kongo for missionaries during the reign of Diogo I (1545–1561).[267] In 1584, Carmelite missionaries mentioned that the people of Loango "had knowledge of our Holy Faith for many years," and the king asked again for a priest to baptize him.[268] In 1603 Jesuits in Luanda reported that the Portuguese factor in Loango was teaching nobles of that country the elements of Christian

---

all three, for the best secondary account see Phyllis Martin, *The External Trade of the Loango Coast, 1576–1870* (Oxford, 1972).

[262] Battell, *Strange Adventures* (ed. Ravenstein), p. 9.

[263] Louis Jadin, "Rivaltés luso-néerlandaises au Sohio, Congo, 1600–1675: Tentatives missionaires des récollets flamands et tribulations des capucins intaliens, 1670–75," *Bulletin de l'Institut Historique Belge de Rome* 37 (1966): 137–9; Martin, *Loango Coast*, pp. 43–4.

[264] Martin, *Loango Coast*, p. 43, citing Gerard Brandt, *Histoire der vermaerde zwee-en koopstadt Enkhuisen* (Enkhuisen, 1666), p. 195. See also Ratelband, *Nederlanders*, pp. 32–3. For the later voyages, see Staten-Generaal, resolution of 13 November 1598, Japiske, *Resolutiën*, 10, 356, and Johann von Lübelfing, *Ein schön lustig Reissbuch* (Ulm, 1612), no pagination, p. 31 in Jones, *German Sources*, p. 12; possibly the same voyage, as the ship they met at Cape Lopo Gonçalves had been at sea for 11 months.

[265] Ratelband, *Nederlanders*, pp. 35–8.

[266] ARA St. Gen. Resol. re OWIC, 6 August 1610; see also Ratelband, *Nederlanders*, pp. 39–42.

[267] Apontamentos que fez o Padre Sebastião de Souto, ca. 1561, *MMA* 2: 478.

[268] "Relatione di quello che côcorse, et videro nel Regno di Congo...," 1584, *MMA* 4: 400; also Letter of Fr. Diogo da Encarnaçaõ, in Belchior de Santa Anna, *Crónica dos Carmelitas Descalços Particular do Reyno de Portugal e Provincia de Sam Felippe* (Lisboa, 1657), 1: 113–18 quoted in *MMA* 3: 279.

doctrine.[269] In 1605 the king of Kakongo joined his counterpart in Loango in seeking to enter the Atlantic Creole world, when he sent a present to the bishop "asking for fathers who would baptize everyone in his kingdom."[270]

On the whole, by 1607 the Atlantic Creole culture had attained a distinctive form, particularly in Kongo, Luanda, and around the Portuguese settlements along the Kwanza. It had also touched but had not yet fundamentally altered the larger zone commercially integrated into the Atlantic world. But the next half century would witness a more intense penetration of Atlantic Creole culture as commerce, wars, and colonization extended northward and eastward.

[269] Jesuit Annual Letter, 1603, *MMA* 5: 82.
[270] Guerreiro, *Relação*, *MMA* 5: 241.

3

Wars, Civil Unrest, and the Dynamics of Enslavement in West Central Africa, 1607–1660

Almost all the captives that English and Dutch privateers would carry to their emerging colonies in the Americas between 1607 and 1660 came from West Central Africa, where dynastic crises in the kingdom of Kongo and Portuguese/Ndongo wars created the theatre in which enslavement took place. Analyzing the exact location of the wars, who was enslaved, and who did the enslaving is essential to determining the cultural background of the captives. Throughout this period, West Central Africa possessed a cultural geography that distinguished places where Atlantic Creole culture had penetrated deeply from areas where there had been very limited contact with Atlantic Creole culture. Such a situation places great significance on determining the distribution of enslavement. This chapter outlines the precise geography of warfare over the course of the whole period, which can be understood only by reconstructing the underlying politics. The following chapter explores the geographic spread and characteristics of Atlantic Creole culture.

Although violent and disruptive, the wars fought in the different localities that led to enslavement were not wars of ethnic hatred. The Portuguese/Ndongo wars were dominated largely by the insatiable thirst of the Portuguese for slaves to fulfill their *asiento* contracts and to supply the expanding market for slaves in Brazil. Conversely, the wars of resistance of Ndongo against Portugal that led to the enslavement of thousands of Mbundu pitted factions supporting the Portuguese against others intent on retaining Ndongo's independence. The wars were also not based on ethnic differences between the various Central African societies, as the major differences that separated peoples in the region were divisions between Kongolese and Portuguese, on the one hand, and

Mbundus and Portuguese, on the other. This frequently led to collaboration between Kongolese and Mbundus against the Portuguese. If the Portuguese/Ndongo wars were based on conquest and enslavement for profit, in Kongo they were civil wars driven by dynastic ambitions in which followers of different claimants to the throne joined armies and engaged in shifting alliances. In the process, thousands of Christian Kongolese were enslaved and were sold into the Atlantic slave trade.

The Failure of the Commercial Model in Angola, 1607–1615

Although the Portuguese Crown's model for the kind of colony they envisioned for Angola focused on maintaining the colony as a commercial outpost, the realities of governance and revenue forced Portugal to adopt a policy of unrelenting military aggression against Central Africans. The Crown's resorting to war was evident especially after officials in Lisbon attempted and eventually failed to eschew the colony's previous penchant for conquest (which resulted in acquisition of slaves) to trading for slaves between 1607 and 1615. During this period, most of the enslaved Africans purchased by Portuguese merchants came from the fairly distant interior. These distant markets included Mpumbu northeast of Kongo, or Songo to the southeast of Ndongo, and the Benguela highlands to the south.

In 1607 King Philip III of Spain (Philip II of Portugal), concerned that the wars waged by previous governors of Angola had been detrimental to commerce and had not located workable mines, decided that his governors in Angola should focus more on the trade. He believed that control of trade, especially the slave trade, rather than war would be the means to make the colony payable. His new policies, though intended to make the colony peaceful and payable, ultimately failed to yield the expected revenues and opened the way for a return to war as the means to acquire slaves.

Governor Manuel Pereira Forjaz, who came to Angola in 1607, received instructions requiring him to implement a program of "peace and justice" through diplomacy, words that were more or less repeated in subsequent instructions (*regimentos*) drawn up for other governors in 1611 and 1616.[1] These instructions set great importance on making and keeping peace with Africans to repair damaged relations caused by Rodrigues

---

[1] Regimento to Manuel Pereria Forjaz, 26 March 1607, *MMA* 5: 270. Regimento of 22 September 1611, supposed to be for Francisco Correia da Silva, who actually never went to Angola, *MMA* 6: 21–39; and also for João Correia da Silva, 3 September 1616, who also did not go at the time, *MMA* 6: 257–9.

FIGURE 3. Mbundu Cloth Merchant. Source: Ezio Bassani, "Un Cappuccino nell'Africa nera del seicento. I disegni de Manoscritti Araldi del Padre Givanni Antonio Cavazzi da Montecuccolo," *Quaderni Poro* 4 (1987).

Coutinho's building of the fort of Cambambe in 1602 and his war on Axila Mbande.[2] To compensate for lost revenue from war captives, the king envisioned commercial agriculture like sugar growing or fishing *nzimbu* shells.[3] In addition, royal officials believed that more efficient collection of tribute slaves through taxation of the subordinate *sobas* could offset the loss of war-generated slaves.[4]

Additionally, the Crown sought to channel, control, and monopolize commerce from West Central Africa. One part of the strategy was to

[2] Regimento to Manuel Pereira Forjaz, 26 March 1607, *MMA* 5: 269–70.
[3] Regimento to Manuel Pereria Forjaz, 26 March 1607, *MMA* 5: 264–79; 1611. Regimento, *MMA* 6: 30. Pedro Sardinha proposed taxing the coast as well; Alvitre de Pedro Sardinha, c. 1611, *MMA* 6: 54–5.
[4] Regimento to Manuel Pereira Forjaz, 26 March 1607, *MMA* 5: 267–70; Jesuits protested his order, maintaining that they kept their *sobas* loyal; Guerreiro, *Relação*, in *MMA* 5: 52; see, 1611, Regimento, *MMA* 6: 25.

concentrate the Portuguese in a few, easily supervised locations, ostensibly to prevent them from waging private war to capture slaves.[5] The king was particularly concerned about the Luso-African community in Kongo whose members lay outside government control and taxation and who necessarily promoted Kongo's interest in the colony.[6] A second part of the strategy was to prevent the Dutch trading in a region whose commerce the Crown sought to control. The Dutch began trading on the coast of Kongo and Loango around 1605 and had entered into diplomatic relations with the Count of Soyo, and the Crown was concerned that they might drain off trade that would otherwise go to Angola and reduce royal revenues.[7] Luso-Africans in Kongo were drawn to this new outlet for trade, and to prevent this, the Crown decided to build a fort at Mpinda, Soyo's port on the Congo River, to concentrate Luso-African merchants operating in Kongo there and drive off the Dutch.[8]

From the perspective of governors and settlers, it was possible to obtain substantial profits through peaceful slave trading only if a large region was tapped. To obtain the slaves (and the ivory which was also a major export) merchants needed to operate over a vast region, purchasing locally produced cloths throughout West Central Africa and exchanging these, along with Spanish and Portuguese products like Canary wines, wheat, horses, and luxury goods, for slaves.[9] However, this practice made it easy for merchants to avoid taxes and thus effectively reduce Crown profits, as Pereira Forjaz's years as governor illustrate.

Pereira Forjaz, who served as governor from 1607 to 1611, profited from his activities as a merchant. The governor developed an extensive commercial network during his years in Angola, in conjunction with a Lisbon-based commercial society headed by João de Argomedo that forwarded him capital and had agents in various parts of the Atlantic – Brazil,

---

[5] Regimento to Manuel Pereira Forjaz, 26 March 1607, *MMA* 5: 274, also repeated in 1611 *MMA* 6: 31.

[6] Regimento to Manuel Pereira Forjaz, 26 March 1607, *MMA* 5: 276. He would then allow only a very few to go there with a special license from the governor. These penalties would be extended even to those Portuguese in Luanda who acted as correspondents of Kongo-based merchants who brought goods to them without the knowledge of the government.

[7] An exchange of letters between Soyo and the States General is noted in the resolution of 24 August 1607, Japikse, *Resolutiën* 14: 159; van Wassenaer, *Historisch Verhael*, 13te Deel, June 1627, fol. 27; Ratelband, *Nederlanders*, pp. 39–42.

[8] Plan of João Salgado da Araújo, 1615, *MMA* 6: 246–7, on the failure up to 1615 and attempts to explore possibilities by a priest, Antóino Gonçalves Pita, in 1614.

[9] AHU, Cx 1, doc. 17, Petition of Maria Tavora, widow of Manuel Pereira Forjaz, 26 January 1612. The report includes a long inquest into the alleged chicanery of Manuel da Costa, her husband's agent.

the Spanish Indies, and Buenos Aires.[10] Pereira Forjaz bought slaves and ivory on the Mpumbu markets in northeastern Kongo, at the port of Mpinda, at Loango, and in Benguela to the south. He had many agents and servants – *negros pombeiros* – to carry his goods and manage his local business. All of this trade was ultimately to acquire slaves, which remained Angola's most important export. In 1606 Manuel Cerveria Pereira estimated that in that year 10,000–13,000 slaves were exported annually.[11]

Slaves had become so essential to the local economy that the Crown demanded that all financial transactions be handled in slaves and not in silver money, as had been the case before.[12] Pereira Forjaz's trading factor was supposed to have cheated him of cloth goods prepared for the purchase of some 300 slaves in northeastern Kongo.[13] Even the Church's income in Kongo and Angola, often collected in cloth or local money (*nzimbu*), had to be "reduced" to slaves, who were shipped to markets in Brazil and the Spanish Indies and whose sale prices were returned to Europe in letters of credit.[14]

Remembering his years as governor, later Angolan historians credited Pereira Forjaz with strengthening the fort of Cambambe as a commercial center and seeking to explore trade routes to deep in the east, even dreaming of reaching as far as Mozambique, on the other coast.[15] His commercial interests in Benguela helped to increase Portuguese trade to the south as well.[16] The captives generated by this type of trade, however, came largely from regions that were at the outer perimeter of the Atlantic Creole world or even beyond it.

If the Crown's views about Angola were in general to promote peaceful slave trading and thus increase state revenue, this strategy did not yield much revenue primarily because merchants had so many ways of evading taxes. An inquest in 1612 revealed the myriad ways that merchants,

[10] Fuller documentation of the society in Felner, *Angola*, pp. 193–6.
[11] Caderno de Manuel Ceveira Pereira, 14 October 1606, *MMA* 5: 224; see also Birmingham, *Trade and Conquest*, pp. 79–80. These numbers were either estimates by contemporaries or indirect calculations based on tax revenues.
[12] Regimento to Manuel Pereira Forjaz, 26 March 1607, *MMA* 5: 274.
[13] AHU, Cx 1, doc. 17, Petition of Maria Tavora, widow of Manuel Pereira Forjaz, 26 January 1612.
[14] Bras Correia to Juan Baptista Vives, 20 October 1619, *MMA* 6: 405 (this situation applied from the time of the Bishop's arrival at least, in 1609).
[15] "Catalogo dos Governodores," in da Silva Corrêa, *História* 1: 221–2.
[16] AHU, Cx 1, doc. 17, Petition of Maria Tavora, widow of Manuel Pereira Forjaz, 26 January 1612. The regimento of 1607 that guided him asked him to explore and develop trade with Benguela.

including even the commercially minded governor, could evade fiscal oversight and commercial control. The failure of commerce to yield the kind of revenues the state was expecting encouraged the belief that in fact the best and easiest way to insure Crown revenue was to tax and oversee the capture of slaves in war rather than their purchase by merchants.[17] Therefore by 1610 Phillip and his counselors were again seriously thinking of resorting to war by opening up a new conquest in Benguela. The king dispatched Manuel Cerveira Pereira (the founder of Cambambe) with the charge of conquering the copper mines in the interior. Instructions prepared for Francisco Correia da Silva (who was supposed to be dispatched to Angola in 1611 but never took up office), reasoned that copper and slaves from this new conquest could be used to found artillery to take to Brazil. Phillip believed that such a war could generate a slave trade through Benguela that might exceed the Luanda trade, because the interior had a high population density and because the local people "are a warlike and treacherous people of evil nature."[18]

War, Chaos, and Enslavement: Portuguese-Imbangala Alliance 1611–1641

The transition from trade to war as a means of procuring slaves was dramatically illustrated by the alliance that the Portuguese made with the Imbangala, the mercenary bands who had earlier sold the Portuguese slaves in the Benguela. Bento Banha Cardoso was a maimed veteran soldier who had been in Angola since 1592, and in 1611, when he took over as interim governor of Angola following the unexpected death of his predecessor, Forjaz Pereira, he made the first official alliance with the Imbangala to pursue his war policy.[19] Banha Cardoso thus circumvented royal instructions that still required governors to keep the peace with their African neighbors and argued that he was undertaking large-scale wars to bring disobedient vassals back under Portuguese control and open up the route for peaceful trade. Although he also mobilized all the traditional armed forces that previous governors had used, the Imbangala alliance proved to be the key to the sudden and dramatic success of Portuguese arms against formerly difficult opponents. In the words of his own report

---

[17] AHU, Cx. 1, doc. 18, da Fonseca, 4 March 1612.
[18] Regimento to Francisco Correia de Silva, *MMA* 6: 33.
[19] Processo de Justificação dos Actos de Bento Banha Cardoso, 31 October 1616, Felner, *Angola*, p. 438.

filed in 1615 he referred to "the war which I ordered made by the Jagas [Imbangalas] and the Portuguese black army."[20]

Exploiting the rivalry between northern and southern factions in Ndongo, his army and its Imbangala allies operated along both the Lukala and Kwanza Rivers. Claiming that the former Portuguese vassal *soba* Xilonga, who lived along the Lukala, had become disobedient and blocked trade, he attacked the *soba* and also built a fort nearby in the lands of Hango a Kikaito, who was a leader of the northern faction in Ndongo.[21] The governor also undertook another campaign along the Kwanza east of the fort of Cambambe, attacking the lands of the southern faction, which included Dumbo a Pebo and Pungo Andongo in the province of Hari.[22]

Defending his actions to the royal government, Banha Cardoso highlighted his success. He wrote that he had taken more than 80 *sobas* from the surrounding kingdoms and brought them under Portuguese control, guaranteeing tribute in slaves and thus the continued functioning of the slave markets.[23] He pointed out that not only did he acquire slaves by war, but he had also imposed tribute in slaves on the newly annexed lands, and he dutifully drew up a detailed list of their obligations.[24]

In light of Banha Cardoso's success the Crown overlooked the violations of his instructions and decided to support a two-pronged war in Angola. They chose Manuel Cerveira Pereira to undertake the new strategy, directing him first to take over the war that Banha Cardoso had initiated in Angola to gain additional resources. He was then to go south and establish a new "kingdom" in Benguela to take over the copper mines, which the Crown was confident would also yield abundant slaves.[25]

---

[20] AHU, Cx 1, doc. 40, Devassa of 21 August 1615.

[21] AHU, Cx 1, doc. 40, Devassa de Bento Banha Cardoso, 21 August 1615. Letters of Bento Banha Cardoso, 28 June 1614, *MMA* 6: 178, and 31 October 1616 in Felner, *Angola*, 438. Cadornega's account places the rebels in Ilamba province claiming for support old papers that he had seen before they were destroyed by the Dutch in 1641. However, Cadornega is often hazy on dates (he placed these events in 1615), suggesting that he was working from memory of the documents, and no longer had them before him in 1680 when he wrote, *História* 1: 77. The rebel's name is given in the sketcher account in the "Catalogo," Silva Corrêa. *História* 1: 223–4.

[22] Bento Banha Cardoso, 31 October 1616, Felner, *Angola*, p. 439. Details in Cadornega, *História* 1: 78–9.

[23] Bento Banha Cardoso, 31 October 1616, Felner, *Angola*, p. 438.

[24] AHU Cx. 1, doc. 40, Devassa of Banha Cardoso, 21 August 1615. The list itself is no longer extant. True to the local settler constituency that elected him, Banha Cardoso proposed reintroducing the system of granting settlers the right to collect tribute and draw income from the *sobas*.

[25] Manuel Cerveira Pereira to King, 11 March 1612 *MMA* 6: 77–81; the anticipation of slaves was expressed in the instructions for Francisco Correia da Silva, chosen as governor

Following this plan Cerveira Pereira went to Banha Cardoso's fort at Hango and launched a campaign against Kakulu ka Hango in alliance with Imbangala forces. After this war his forces penetrated northeast into the upper Zenza valley, where they pillaged the independent rulers in the Dembos region between Ndongo and Kongo.[26] Profits from the sale of captives taken in this war augmented his coffers for the conquest of Benguela. Cerveira Pereira subsequently established himself at Benguela and, after failing to make an alliance with the Imbangala there, fought a minor war that resulted in the export of two boatloads of slaves and 1,000 head of cattle and other livestock to Luanda, but he failed to create a second Angola, as the Crown had hoped.[27] In the wake of this debacle, the post at Benguela became a minor outpost engaged in local commerce in foodstuffs.

After Cerveira Pereira's departure for Benguela in 1617, the Crown chose Luis Mendes de Vasconcelos Mendes to succeed him as governor of Angola. Mendes de Vasconcelos's subsequent war was to carry chaos and destruction to the heart of Ndongo that would engulf ally and enemy alike.[28] It was Mendes de Vasconcelos's campaigns that would flood the Spanish Indies with captives. Even before his arrival in Angola Mendes de Vasconcelos believed that slaves could be generated by military action and had written in an earlier memorial that "the trade in slaves, which is so important to your Majesty's treasury, could scarcely be maintained, because in order for the trade to be satisfactory, it is necessary to have an army in the field."[29] A veteran solider from Portugal's

of Angola but never sent, 22 September 1611, *MMA* 6: 32–3, which surely was factored into their reception of Cerveira Pereira's plan.

[26] "Catalogo," in Silva Corrêa. *História* 1: 224–5. On the Imbangala in this campaign see Luis Mendes de Vasconçelos to King, 28 August 1617, *MMA* 6: 283, 285.

[27] Representation of Manuel Cerveira Pereira, 2 July 1618, *MMA* 6: 315–19. Cerveira Pereira originally intended to go to the post founded and abandoned in the time of Paulo Novais de Dias, at the modern port of Porto Amboim, but finding the area deserted by the Imbangala wars, moved southward to the location of modern Benguela; Ralph Delgado, *História de Angola* (4 vols., Luanda, 1946; reprinted 1977), 2: 41–4; Saccardo, *Congo e Angola* 1: 158. For the course of events to the 1630s, see Saccardo, *Congo e Angola* 1: 158–60.

[28] An essential study of the Portuguese activities in Angola from Mendes de Vasconcelos's reign to the 1630s is found in Beatrix Heintze, "Das Ende des Unabhängigen Staates Ndongo (Angola). Neue Chronologie und Reinterpretation 1617–1630," *Paideuma* 27 (1981): 199–273; revised but without annotation in *idem, Studien zur Geschichte Angolas im 16. und 17. Jahrhundert. Ein Lesebuch* (Cologne, 1996), pp. 111–68.

[29] Memorial of Luis Mendes de Vasconcelos, 1616, *MMA* 6: 264.

Asian empire, he proposed a grandiose plan of conquest that could be underwritten by his wealthy relatives, especially his wife, Beatriz Caldeira, daughter of the New Christian merchant Manuel Caldeira, an important founder of the Portuguese slave trade to the Spanish Indies and closely connected to the highest circles at court in Lisbon and Madrid.[30] At the same time another New Christian, António Fernades de Elvas, had just gained the contract for Angola and the *asiento* to supply 5,000 slaves per year.[31]

In his initial plans Mendes de Vasconcelos proposed using traditional European tactics to win these wars and denounced the use of Imbangala, which he said was "very much against the service of God and Your Majesty," to have used them, especially because they had been used as "hunting dogs to unjustly bring them slaves." He predicted that if the strategy of using Imbangala continued, "in a short time they would consume the natives of this kingdom, in a way that would lead to depopulation."[32]

Building on the lead of his earlier counterparts, Mendes de Vasconcelos undertook a massive war of conquest to take over Ndongo, an enterprise that had failed a quarter century earlier. Mendes de Vasconcelos demonstrated that with Imbangala assistance, he could do what his predecessors could not. Beginning in the dry season of 1618, he provoked the *soba* Kaita ka Balanga, "who had been favored by the king of Angola," to attack him in order to move the Portuguese army to a newly built fort at Ambaca, dangerously near to Kabasa, Ndongo's capital. The governor did not attack Kaita ka Balanga, however, but launched an all-out war against the *soba's* benefactor, Ngola Mbandi, king of Ndongo.[33] Mendes de Vasconcelos received support from within Ndongo from *soba* Mubanga, "relative of

---

[30] For his plan of conquest see Memorial of Luis Mendes de Vasconcelos, 1616, *MMA* 6: 263–70. On his family see Salgado de Aruja, *Svmmario*, fol. 43; for more on his background, see Luis Felipe de Alencastro, *O Trato dos viventes. Formação do Brasil no Atlântico Sul. Séculos XVI e XVII* (São Paulo, 2000), p. 357; Salvador, *Cristãos-Novos*, p. 311; Heintze, "Ende" pp. 205–7; on Caldeira and his fortune and connections, see Mateus Ventura, *Negreiros portugueses*, pp. 75–119, especially 115–117 (for Beatriz' and her marriage to Mendes de Vasconcelos).

[31] Heintze, *Ende*, pp. 118–19.

[32] Luis Mendes de Vasconcelos to King, 28 August 1617, *MMA* 6: 283–4.

[33] Manuel Severim da Faria, "História portugueza e de outras provincias do occidente desde o anno de 1610 até o de 1640...," Cadornega, *História* (ed. Delgado), 1: 88, n. 1; Fernão de Sousa, "Lembrança do estado em que achej a ElRey de Angola... c. October 1624, in Beatrix Heintze, ed. *Fontes Para a História de Angola* (2 vols, Wiesbaden, 1985–88) (*FHA*) 1: 195.

the kings of Angola [who] gave a gate and entrance to his lands for the said conquest."[34]

In the remaining three years of his governorship, until 1621, Mendes de Vasconcelos and his son, João, who served as his lieutenant, were almost constantly at war, while strengthening alliances with the ancient noble families in Ndongo who wanted to change the status quo. The allied forces twice sacked Kabasa, the capital of Ndongo, and drove Ngola Mbandi to take refuge on the Kindonga Islands in the Kwanza River. Mendes de Vasconcelos used the opportunity to place his own candidate on the throne of Ndongo, "Antonio Corrêa by country name of Samba Antumba," who was perhaps a member of the rival faction, but "it had no effect, because he was not obeyed." Ngola Mbandi was still alive and considered more legitimate as the people did "not obey anyone who is not a child or descendant of a king."[35] In addition, João Mendes de Vasconcelos demanded oaths of vassalage from other ancient families of the southern faction, including Hari a Kiluanji, who ruled a part of Hari province called Dambi a Ngola, and his brother, Ngola Hari, ruler of Pungo Andongo. These nobles had at first resisted the Portuguese, following a tradition that went back to Banha Cardoso's governorship, but would eventually rely on Portuguese help to claim the throne.[36]

This prodigious military advance was also facilitated by the continued large-scale participation of Imbangala forces, despite Mendes de Vasconcelos's disparaging view of the use of non-European tactics and forces and his fervent denunciation of the Imbangala when he arrived. Manuel Bautista Soares, the bishop of Kongo and an enemy of the governor, disdainfully noted in 1619 that although Mendes de Vasconcelos condemned the use of Imbangala as it was "a great sin" for anyone "to have dealings with them, and those who do so risk great punishments from God," when he began his campaigns "since he did not wish to lose in profiting from it ... he embraced them and took them with him to war."

Mendes de Vasconcelos's campaigns into Ndongo and beyond were more than simply campaigns to achieve strategic objectives, although he

---

[34] This detail only from Cadornega, *História* 1: 86. Although Cadornega wrote much later, he stated in this section that he based his account on papers of both Luis and João Mendes de Vasconcelos; see p. 83, author's marginal note.

[35] Fernão de Sousa, "Lembrança," *FHA* 1: 195.

[36] Cadornega, *História* 1: 141–2. For the earlier campaigns, see *História* 1: 79, for the one in 1621, see *História* 1: 93–4, based on service papers of veterans and the documents left by Mendes de Vasconcelos. Fernão de Sousa placed their vassalage in the time of João Correia de Sousa, but this was probably the more formal submission.

did manage to get some 110 *sobas*, including several from ancient families, as tribute-paying subjects of the king of Portugal.[37] His military action was directly linked to the desire to obtain a maximum number of slaves in any way possible, and the participation of a lawless element like the Imbangala heightened the extent of the devastation on the people of Ndongo. During the initial campaigns the governor and Imbangala succeeded in "capturing innumerable innocent people, not only against the law of God and nature, but even against the expressed instructions of Your Majesty."[38] Traders, both black and white, accompanied the Imbangala bands and Portuguese forces, quickly buying up any captives for trade abroad.[39]

The Portuguese–Imbangala invasion meant immediate disaster to the population of Ndongo. In 1619 two of the principal Imbangala bands rebelled against the Portuguese or may have simply begun pillaging on their own. To complicate matters, one of them, commanded by Donga, ended up joining the forces of the defeated king Ngola Mbandi and thus defied the Portuguese.[40] Other rebel Imbangala bands, most notably that of Kasanje, raided extensively in the lands of Ndongo and even further east, but they were active closer to the Portuguese territories as well, for the bishop complained in 1619 that "more than four thousand baptized Christians have been made Jagas [Imbangala], being totally lost to their masters,"[41] and presumably they sold many thousands more. It was probably from among this group that Angela and her companions, who crossed the Atlantic on the *São João Bautista*, were enslaved.

The peculiar practices of the Imbangala, such as cutting down palm trees and seizing food crops, as well as widespread killing and cannibalism, added to the chaos and helped to erode civil order beyond the effects of

---

[37] Secret Instructions to Fernão de Sousa, 29 March 1624, *FHA* 1: 138; for details on accounting see Beatrix Heintze, "The Angolan Vassal Tributes of the XVI Century," *Revista de história económica e social* 6 (1980): 57–78.

[38] Bishop Manuel Baptista Soares "Copia dos excessos que se cometem no gouerno de Angola que o bispo deu a V. Magestade pedindo remedio delles de presente, e de futuro," 7 September 1619, *MMA* 6: 367–8.

[39] Manuel Vogado Sottomaior, "Papel sobre as cousas de Angola," c. 20 April 1620, *MMA* 6: 476.

[40] Cadornega, *História*, 1: 91 and 93. This is the most detailed account, but it was written only in 1680. Cadornega says he learned the details of this campaign from written accounts left by the governor and his son, as well as reports of service of Portuguese who served in the campaigns. The rebellion is reported in a contemporary source by Vogado Sottomaior, "Cousas de Angola," c. 20 April 1620, *MMA* 6: 476. The date is established largely by speculation from Vogado Sottomaior's report, as he was in Madrid in early 1620, before the campaign season of that year, but reported the rebellion as recent.

[41] Soares, "Excessos," *MMA* 6: 370.

war alone. In their sack of Kabasa, the Imbangala were able, according to
Manuel Vogado Sottomaior, a top Portuguese judicial official in Angola,
to "capture, eat, and kill thousands of souls, cutting down the palm trees
from which these people collect wine and oil, in such a way that today
there is a great lack of everything that they had before."[42] In spite of
misgivings about Imbangala atrocities, the Portuguese felt hamstrung by
their need to rely on them. "I believe," wrote Baltasar Rebelo de Aragão,
a long-time resident, "that it is bad to make them our friends because
of what a corrupt company we make of them when they are under our
patronage, but they can acquire others as friends and treat them well."[43]

Destruction and the resulting refugee situation were not limited to
Imbangala attacks, or even to Ndongo, as disorder spread to African communities that had been subject to the Portuguese since the 1580s. Some
Portuguese settlers used their own armed slaves to assist in the war and
also to engage in raiding and pillage on their own, often within the area
of Portuguese control. When he left, Mendes de Vasconcelos arranged for
his own private force of 2,000 archers under the command of Manuel
Antunes da Silva and supervised by Esperança, his female African slave
overseer (*maculunta*), to remain in this region and Ilamba, to the east
of Luanda. For the next six years they harassed and raided the population and demanded slaves from the *sobas*, whose sale by Mendes de Vasconcelos' confidant and procurador, the New Christian Luis Gonçalves
Bravo, ultimately benefited the ex-governor in Lisbon.[44] They joined other
groups of raiders in Ilamba and made this province a place of constant turmoil and slave raiding.[45] The chaos in the region would not subside until
the early 1630s, as Pedro Tavares, a Jesuit active in the area after 1632,
was often told about their atrocities and was even shown a field with 200
skulls of unburied victims of one such raid.[46] Vogado Sottomaior complained that "some of the residents are in war and they do not respect the
damage that they have done to the land either present or future."[47] Older
residents bewailed this new destruction that harmed their larger interests.
Rebelo de Aragão protested that existing practices caused raiders to wage

[42] Vogado Sottomaior, "Cousas de Angola," *MMA* 6: 476.
[43] Baltasar Rebelo de Aragão, c. 1618, *MMA* 6: 342.
[44] Complaints of sobas of Ilamba, c. mid-March, 1627 summarized in Fernão de Sousa to sons, 1630, *FHA* 1: 286.
[45] Fernão de Sousa to Governo, 6 September 1625, *FHA* 2: 144.
[46] Biblioteca Pública de Évora (BPE) Códice (Cod) XVI/2-4, fol. 4, Pedro Tavares to Jeronimo Vogado, 29 June 1635.
[47] Vogado Sottomaior, "Cousas de Angola," *MMA* 6: 476, 477.

"war in the same province where we have our cities and presidios, and so instead of destroying our enemies we destroy ourselves." The profit of this was largely for Mendes de Vasconcelos and his ministers, and the "residents and merchants are lost."[48]

Because chaos favored the governor's plans to enrich himself through the capture and export of slaves, Mendes de Vasconcelos pursued wars and adopted policies that kept the area in conflict. He refused to make an agreement of peace with Ngola Mbandi, and so a state of war remained in much of the area of the core of Ndongo, including its once densely settled capital region.[49] In this region, roving Imbangala bands, private armies, and the Portuguese army raided at will. It is likely that local *sobas* who had recently agreed to be Portuguese vassals, and even those who still supported Ngola Mbandi, used their own armed forces to defend themselves or attack others, thus ensuring the flow of slaves from Ndongo. Because so many free people were enslaved during this period, Governor Fernão de Sousa, a later governor, decided to mark all slaves in 1624 so as to avoid the wrongful trading in free people, hoping this would allow the "sobas would return from the woods to their banzas [capital towns] secure from the evils that they get from the whites."[50] In 1625, Bento Banha Cardoso wrote from the presidio of Ambaca that it was "consumed by the Portuguese who pass by it with their slaves, destroying the land . . . and the heathens are unquiet and cannot make their markets."[51]

The Imbangala alliance also gave the Portuguese the ability to move against Kongo to acquire slaves. In 1615 Banha Cardoso and the Imbangala invaded Nambu a Ngongo, an outer district of the kingdom of Kongo, giving as an explanation that the Kongolese official was harassing friendly allies near Luanda and threatening its food supply. Nambu a Ngongo was "almost reduced to a captive" in the conflict and Banha Cardoso was able to annex or attack Kongo territories north of Luanda, including Kasanze, Sonsa, and the Bengo River crossings.[52] When Álvaro III took his throne

---

[48] Rebelo de Aragão, *MMA* 6: 336.
[49] Severim de Faria, "História Portuguesa," in Cadornega, *História* 1: 89n, on early and indecisive efforts to reach a peace.
[50] De Sousa to sons, *FHA* 1: 221–2.
[51] Bento Banha Cardoso to King, 6 October 1625, *FHA* 2: 348; AHU Cx. 2, doc. 83, Bento Banha Cardoso to Fernão de Sousa, 6 October 1625.
[52] Bento Banha Cardoso, 31 October 1616, Felner, *Angola*, p. 439; other details supplied by later sources, Cadornega, *História* 1: 78–9, and "Catalogo" in Silva Corrêa, *História* 1: 223–4.

in 1615, he wrote to Phillip III complaining that Banha Cardoso was a rogue governor who took lands that "pertain to me and contribute to the royal rights, as their ancestors have always done, having memory of no other thing."[53]

Banha Cardoso's campaign was followed in 1618 by an attack from the forces of Mendes Vasconcelos, who redeployed some forces from the Ndongo operations to besiege Kongo's vassal Kasanze, located near Luanda.[54] The war on Kasanze was especially important because it lay so close to the city and because it was a rich agricultural territory that could help in the city's provisioning and security. The activities of this army would be particularly disastrous for a large zone stretching beyond Kasanze to include the whole territory some 50 kilometers inland from Luanda. Álvaro III wrote to Pope Paul V in 1617, complaining that the governors of Angola "united with a nation of people called Giagas or Iagas, who are so barbarous that they live on the flesh and bodies of humans."[55] His letter resulted in a papal inquest that eventually led Phillip III to denounce the use of Imbangala formally in 1618.[56]

In addition to the campaign against Kasanze, in 1619, João Mendes de Vasconcelos took an army with Imbangala northward into Kongo's lands of Kabonda and Mbwila.[57] The next year, hoping to repeat the strategy of exploiting the factionalism and civil strife that he had used so successfully in Ndongo, Mendes de Vasconcelas took advantage of a civil war between Álvaro III and his one-time benefactor, António da Silva, the Duke of Mbamba, to push deeper into Kongo. Álvaro had spent much of his seven-year reign forcing or cajoling these recalcitrant senior relatives to accept him, crowned by his violent overthrow of his erstwhile patron, António da Silva, from Mbamba in 1620. [58] Mendes de Vasconcelas's campaign disrupted the still-existing Luso-African trade, "destroying friends and enemies... with the death and captivity of many people" to the great "perturbation and scandalization of the king of Congo." Anti-Portuguese

---

[53] Álvaro III to Felipe III, 24 October 1615, *MMA* 6: 236.
[54] Severim de Faria, "História," fol. 163v in Cadornega, *História* 1: 88–9, n. 1.
[55] Álvaro III to Pope Paulo V, 25 October 1617, *MMA* 6: 290.
[56] Royal Letter to the Carindal de Borja e Velasco, 28 August 1618, *MMA* 6: 323.
[57] The details of his campaigns are found in Heintze, "Ende," pp. 202–9; also see Thornton, "African Experience," pp. 428–32, and Birmingham, *Trade and Conquest*, pp. 86–8.
[58] "Da alcuni Provisioni di Don Alvaro Terzo," *MMA* 6: 252–3; Da Silva led a revolt in 1619 that encompassed much of the kingdom, which was calmed with much difficulty, then when he died in February 1620 he left his son as Duke of Mbamba, a sign that he hoped his own province would become hereditary, provoking Álvaro III's invasion that killed the son and returned Mbamba to royal power.

rioting broke out in Kongo in response, and some Portuguese possessions were looted and destroyed.[59]

The wars and associated chaos shifted the source of slaves from the very large zone that had been served by the merchants of the earlier period to a much narrower area around which the armies operated. Mendes de Vasconcelos and his friends and associates, with little stake in the long-term stability of the colony, were unconcerned that the wars had virtually stopped trading at markets that had been functioning during Pereira Forjaz's administration. Bishop Soares wrote, "with these extortions the *ferias* [markets] stop, even up to many places in the Kingdom of Congo where the wars reach and close to the roads where there is not trade in *peças* [slaves]."[60] Not only did the violence prevent free travel of merchants, but Mendes de Vasconcelos undermined the existing slave markets that the older settlers had established by imposing special taxes and monopolies that favored them and limited competition. Rebelo de Aragão described the process in commenting on why the traditional markets had stopped, placing blame squarely on the governor, who placed "a tribute tyranny on the said markets" such that the for every 10 slaves sold, the governor got 1, one of his officials got a second, a third went to an official buyer, and so on, for most of them, and furthermore, "they choose the best slaves and leave the few miserable ones, the rebels and the refugees who are old negros or children; they are sold for one quarter less [and] no one gains on these." Beyond this, they sent other agents into "remote parts" outside normal jurisdiction, and particularly the war zone, where the chaos allowed them "never [to] have markets because they want them only for their servants, doing nothing for the common good."[61]

The Triumph of War and Civil Unrest: The Portuguese, Ndongo, Kongo, and the Slave Trade, 1621–1641

Four interrelated issues defined and complicated the history of West Central Africa in the two decades following Mendes de Vasconcelos's departure from Angola. First, the interconnection between Portuguese military aggressions to acquire mines, lands, and slaves and succession disputes within Ndongo led to near-constant war in a shifting zone starting in

---

[59] Bishop Manuel Soares, "Excessos que se cometem no gouerno de Angola . . . ," 7 September 1619, *MMA* 6: 368; Mateus Cardoso letter, 16 March 1621, *MMA* 6: 568.
[60] Soares, "Execessos," *MMA* 6: 370.
[61] Rebelo de Aragão, *MMA*: 337.

the highlands of Ndongo and moving east to the Kwango Valley. Second, the expansion of a settler economy with a regular administrative presence from the Kwanza Valley northward gradually slowed the pattern of chaos and lawlessness set off by Mendes de Vasconcelos's campaigns. Third, the kingdom of Kongo gradually slid into an increasingly protracted and devastating civil war that was ended only with the accession of Garcia II in 1641. Fourth, the impact of the Dutch presence, as the renewal of the Spanish–Dutch war in 1621 caused them to move beyond commerce to a much more aggressive naval and diplomatic position. This new Dutch posture partially restrained Portuguese aggression in Ndongo and Kongo and offered the African powers an alliance against Portuguese Angola.

The Portuguese/Ndongo War

Mendes de Vasconselos's overwhelming success in Ndongo and his forays into Kongo confirmed the viability of war as a means to acquire slaves and guarantee royal revenue. Even if it was devastating to Luso-African interests and the diplomatic agreements of the sixteenth century, in Ndongo, the African victims of Portuguese aggression hoped for peace. King Ngola Mbandi, who had taken refuge on the islands of Kindonga in the wake of the last of Mendes de Vasconcelos's wars against Ndongo, was anxious to see peace and order restored to his lands, now "without markets or commerce" and being ravaged by undisciplined Imbangala bands, especially the one commanded by Kasanje.[62] He saw an opening for peaceful coexistence with the Portuguese in 1621 when João Correia de Sousa arrived to relieve Luis Mendes de Vasconcelos as governor of the colony. Ngola Mbandi sent his three sisters, led by the eldest, Njinga Mbandi, to Luanda with a present of slaves to negotiate. Njinga's involvement in the negotiations and the relationship she developed with officials there provide another lens through which to assess the links between the wars and enslavement. When Njinga's party arrived in the city with great pomp and ceremony for the audience with the governor and officers of state, Correia de Sousa prepared a "cushion on the ground according to the custom of black people," expecting Njinga to sit upon it while he was seated on a chair. In Central African etiquette such actions implied subordination, and Njinga insisted on equality in the negotiations. Thirty years later Njinga related to the missionary Cavazzi that "when she saw she was not given a magnificent & showy chair she called one of her waiting-women, &

---

[62] Fernão de Sousa, "Lembrança," *FHA* 1: 196.

FIGURE 4. Njinga's Baptism. Source: Ezio Bassani, "Um Cappuccino nell'Africa nera del seicento. I disegni de Manoscritti Araldi del Padre Givanni Antonio Cavazzi da Montecuccolo," Quaderni Poro 4 (1987).

sat on her as if she had been a chair, rising & sitting down as necessary, & explained her embassy with much acuteness and intelligence of mind."[63]

[63] MSS Araldi, Cavazzi, "Missione Evangelica," vol. A, book 2, p. 24–5. Cavazzi collected this information at Njinga's court around 1662, from Njinga herself and others in her court, including her sister Barbara Kambu, as he wrote in the margin at this point, "The following case has been told me by several people, and having known and frequented Queen Ginga I have no difficulty in believing it, or even making others believe it ... [Ginga] does not lack great powers of observation and curiosity and what follows from them." Heintze, who favors a different reconstruction of events, has pointed out that the reports of Fernão de Sousa written in 1624–5, closer in time to the events, has a different chain of events, with the Portuguese initiating negotiations through the mission of Dionisio de Faria Baretto and Manuel Dias, and with the Njinga and her two sisters coming to Luanda as "hostages" at the same time; Heintze, "Ende," pp. 210–17. She discounts Cavazzi's version as reflecting legendary elements of Njinga's life through the passage of time. We have favored Cavazzi's account, however, which even though written later, was certainly that of eyewitnesses (including Njinga) on the strength of its logic: the "hostages" would not negotiate a treaty and be allowed to return without some immediate exchange; de Sousa was not an eyewitness (unlike Njinga and Cavazzi's other

FIGURE 5. Chapel Boys at Njinga's Funeral, 1663. Source: Ezio Bassani, "Um Cappuccino nell'Africa nera del seicento. I disegni de Manoscritti Araldi del Padre Givanni Antonio Cavazzi da Montecuccolo," Quaderni Poro 4 (1987).

Njinga's mission was to all appearances successful as Correia de Sousa agreed to withdraw the fortress of Ambaca from Ngola Mbandi's lands, to assist in the rounding up and expulsion of the Imbangala, and to return the many *kijikos* and *sobas* that Mendes de Vasconcelos had illegally taken in his wars. In exchange, Njinga agreed on behalf of Ngola Mbandi that he would become a Christian and Njinga herself was baptized immediately, taking the name Ana de Sousa. She also agreed that Mbandi and his court would return to the mainland, restore the kingdom, and restart trade with the Portuguese.[64] On her return to Kindonga, Ngola Mbandi asked

informants) but received his information from the confused and charged atmosphere of Luanda after the expulsion of Correia de Sousa (in 1622). De Sousa, moreover, frequently put the Portuguese in the best light and had the upper hand in their dealings with Africans, as witnessed by his accounts of Kongo and elsewhere where independent witnesses are available.

[64] "Relação de Dongo," *FHA* 1: 198; other details in Fernão de Sousa to Governo, 15 August 1624, *FHA* 2: 86; *idem*, "Lembrança," *FHA* 1: 196. Also see Heintze, "Ende," pp. 210–17.

for more formal diplomatic relations and agreed to accept Christianity. Correia de Sousa sent two mixed-race, Kimbundu-speaking emissaries, a Catholic priest named Dionisio de Faria Baretto to baptize him, and the soldier Manuel Dias to make peace.[65]

Correia de Sousa's conciliatory meeting with Njinga came to nothing, however, because he never dispatched troops to remove the Imbangala from Ndongo. As a result, Ngola Mbandi, still exiled in the Kindonga Islands, sent Njinga a second time to Luanda to attempt to fulfill the agreements she had negotiated earlier. Although the Portuguese continued to accept the conditions, even going so far as to raise an army to attack the Imbangala, the troops were never sent because internal disputes in Luanda prevented any action. Ngola Mbandi, "seeing these delays, supposed that they were deceits and died from depression and they said that it was poison that he himself took in desperation."[66]

Although Mendes de Vasconcelos had shown that wars could yield slaves, they also created levels of chaos that were damaging to Portuguese's interests as well as to those of their enemies. His successor, João Correia de Sousa, attempted to replicate in Kongo what Mendes de Vasconcelos had done in Ndongo, but Correia de Sousa's invasion of Kongo in 1622–1623 was a humiliating disaster and the governor was expelled by angry residents of Angola, as we shall see later. In 1624 the Crown sent Fernão de Sousa to replace the humiliated Correia de Sousa. His instructions were to stabilize the country and see to it that the profits from the colony went to the Crown and that they come from trade rather than war. His plans also called for more systematic taxation from all taxpayers, including *sobas*. To ensure this program's success, he had to put an end to the chaos that had overtaken Ndongo since Mendes de Vasconcelos's time. Although de Sousa diligently pursued the Crown's plans for taxation and commerce, he completely ignored the provisions that called for an end to warfare and peaceful relations with African rulers. The situation meant that Ndongo would continue to be a major source of slaves for the American markets.

His first step was to establish *feiras*, or government markets, at strategic locations in the southern boundaries of Kongo and improve relations with the rulers who still wanted to trade with the Portuguese. The *ferias* were located in Bumba a Kizanzo, near Ambaca, at Kakulu ka Kabasa on the upper Zenza, and at Mbwila so that Luso-Africans would concentrate their trade there and tap the slave and cloth trade coming down from

---

[65] MSS Araldi, Cavazzi, "Missione Evangelica," vol. A, book 2, pp. 25–8.
[66] Fernão de Sousa, "Lembrança," *FHA* 1: 196. Further details worked out in Heintze, "Ende," pp. 218–19.

Kongo and points east as it passed between mountain ranges that bordered Mbwila.[67] Once again, slaves arrived in Luanda from the far eastern region, although the cost was great because they "do not come to the warehouses because they are Anzicos [from Maleba Pool region] and many die."[68] Nevertheless for a time this chain of markets functioned smoothly.[69]

In spite of his instructions and initial intentions, de Sousa found the situation in Ndongo made peaceful trade less attractive than outright war. Ndongo was still reeling from Mendes de Vasconcelos's campaigns, Ngola Mbandi's suicide, the issue of the treaty with the Portuguese, and an unsettled question of succession. Njinga, now serving as the regent of Ndongo, was eager to reopen negotiations with de Sousa, who wanted to regularize Portuguese relations with Ndongo by establishing the market at Kisala. She wrote to him as "lord" (or "lady") of Ndongo and, giving primacy to executing the treaty that she had twice negotiated with the Portuguese on behalf of her deceased brother, asserted that "if the presidio [of Ambaca] is moved, she will come out from the islands where she is and cross to the mainland." She also promised to renew the slave market at Kisala, where "she will order her [subjects] who go to them and to take pieces [slaves], as this was agreed by her macotas." She asked for Jesuits to come and baptize those of her subjects who wished to become Christians, noting that her "tendala who is her principal person wishes to be baptized right away." She also wanted the bishop to erect churches and send someone "who is respected" to handle church affairs.[70]

Although initially responsive to completing the treaty as negotiated, de Sousa rapidly changed his mind after a few months. De Sousa's correspondence after the end of 1624 no longer referred to removing the presidio of Ambaca, a critical element of the treaty that he was now violating. De Sousa was now openly refusing to turn over the *kijikos* ("free people"), who all had agreed had been illegally seized by Mendes de Vasconcelos and his followers who had now settled at Ambaca. On the one hand, many *kijikos* joined Njinga's ranks as she encouraged them to be "lords in their own lands rather than our [Portuguese] captives." On the other hand, de Sousa argued on behalf of the Ambaca settlers that the slaves were "fleeing" them and demanded that Njinga return them as runaways. De Sousa

---

[67] Fernão de Sousa to sons, *FHA* 1: 223, relating events of 1624.
[68] De Sousa, "Relação de Dongo," *FHA* 1: 197.
[69] Fernão de Sousa to sons, *FHA* 1: 232, relating events of 1625.
[70] Fernão de Sousa to Governo, 15 August 1624, *FHA* 2: 85–6.

was also intent on undertaking war against Ndongo and referred to the *kijikos* as "our slaves" who are accustomed to "fight in the shadow of our arcabusses." He believed that surrendering them weakened the Portuguese position and strengthened Njinga's military resources.[71] De Sousa's concern about Portuguese military strength and Njinga's intransigence explains his unwillingness to follow royal instructions on diplomacy.

De Sousa's temptation to make war against Njinga was strengthened because the succession in Ndongo was still unresoved. Ngola Mbandi had left a minor son as his heir, whom he had entrusted to an Imbangala ally, Kaza, with Njinga as the child's regent.[72] The Portuguese had themselves tried to secure the nephew, so that they could install him as a puppet king, but without success.[73] Sometime between March and September 1625 Njinga asked Kaza to hand over her nephew to her "by presents which she gave him" and offered to marry him. As witnesses later recalled, the Imbangala leader, lovestruck by her beauty, was blinded to her larger plans.[74] Once the child was in her power "she killed him so she could retain government" and then abandoned Kaza. De Sousa used the murder of Ngola Mbandi's son as a pretext for war and sent reinforcements and munitions to the settlers in Ambaca and ordered all the vassal *sobas* to have no relations with Njinga. He then "persuaded" Hari a Kiluanji, lord of Dambi a Hari, in the province of Hari, to visit Ambaca to declare him king of Ndongo.[75]

His choice of Hari a Kiluanji was no accident. Hari a Kiluanji was descended from the great nobility of Ndongo and claimed origins from

---

[71] Fernão de Sousa to Governo, 19 March 1625, *FHA* 2: 129–30, see also "Relação de Dongo," *FHA* 1: 199. De Sousa had even earlier thought that he could obtain a tribute from Njinga as a price for carrying out the treaty, see same to Governo, 15 August 1624, *FHA* 2: 86.

[72] De Sousa, "Relação de Dongo," *FHA* 1: 199.

[73] Cadornega, *História* 1: 141–2, taken from evidence of Lopo de Carvalhal Fogaça who had been entrusted with the task of dissuading Kaza from sending the royal child to Njinga. De Sousa appears to have alluded to this in "Relação de Dongo," *FHA* 1: 199.

[74] The traditions were related by both Cavazzi (MSS Araldi, "Missione Evangelica," book 2, pp. 33–4) and Gaeta (*Maravigliosa Conversione*, p. 205). Although de Sousa's original report did not mention a marriage, the fact that four years later Kasanje refered to it suggests that Njinga had indeed manipulated Kaza through a marriage offer; Report of Alexandre Ladino and Manoel de Nobrega to Sargento Mor Antonio Bruto, c. September 1629, summarized in de Sousa to Sons, *FHA* 1: 345.

[75] Fernão de Sousa to his sons, c. 1630, *FHA* 1: 230. His name and origin are given in Cadornega, *História* 1: 141, taken from Cadornega's interviews with a number of people, including a niece of the king, named Dona Angola; and from papers of Antonio Abreu de Miranda, who had either witnessed Hari a Kiluanji's will, or that of Hari a Kilunaji's son in law.

the children of the first king.[76] During earlier episodes of factional struggle and Portuguese intrusions, he had promised vassalage to João Mendes
de Vasconcelos and confirmed it with Correa de Sousa and was thus an
excellent tool for Fernão de Sousa's plan to make war on Njinga and
bring Ndongo under Portuguese control. Success here would allow him
to establish a government where Portugal could exploit trading opportunities, extract revenue, spread Christianity under their guidance, and
gain more military support.[77] For Hari a Kiluanji, however, the alliance
with Portugal represented an opportunity to rid Ndongo of the rival line
of Njinga Ngola Kilombo kia Kasenda (c. 1575–1592) from which both
Ngola Mbandi and Njinga descended.

War, which lasted from February to October 1626, pitted the Portuguese and the two great Ndongo factions against each other. The war
matched several ancient but traditionally nonreigning families against the
royal family descended from Njinga Ngola Kilombo kia Kasenda, who
they had always regarded as a tyrant and usurper and from whom Njinga
was descended. Since 1592, the factions created behind Mbandi Ngola's
several wives had divided the kingdom and had given the Portuguese
opportunities to manipulate them. Added to these long-term divisions was
the question of a woman's right to rule. Those who fought against Njinga
supported Fernão de Sousa's assertion that "she did not have power to be
the successor, because a woman cannot govern this kingdom."[78] Njinga
herself must have been bothered by this charge, for she gave the title of
king to her husband, Kia Tuxi, "much loved by her," and then after his
death to another man named Ngola Tombo.[79] Apparently this did win
wide acceptance, for subsequently, she took yet another husband, but

---

[76] Cavazzi and Gaeta disagreed on the exact origins of the line, though the foundations
were the same, MSS Araldi, Cavazzi, "Missione evangelica," vol. A, book 2, p. 10;
Gaeta, *Maravigliosa conversione*, p. 144.

[77] Much of this plan is spelled out in the instructions given to Bento Banha Cardoso, sent
to Ambaca with troops in January 1626, "Regimento a Bento Banha Cardoso, around
January 1626, *FHA* 1: 204–5; a *Junta* of officials in Luanda had decided much the same
thing, meeting in midsummer of 1625; see de Sousa, "Relação de Dongo," *FHA* 1: 199–
200; Heintze, "Ende," p. 226–7 and sources cited therein.

[78] Fernão de Sousa to King, 21 February 1626 *MMA* 7: 417. The question of Njinga's
legitimacy has long been a contested issue among historians; for example, Joseph C.
Miller, "Nzinga of Matamba in a New Perspective," *Journal of African History* 16 (1975):
201–16; John Thornton, "Queen Njinga, 1624–63: Legitimacy and Political Power,"
Journal of African History (1991), pp. 25–40; Adriano Parreira, *Economia e sociedade*,
pp. 177–83.

[79] MSS Araldi, Cavazzi, "Missione Evangelica," book 2, pp. 33 and 40.

instead of naming him king, she "wished to be called by the name of King herself, not Queen." To stress her role as king, she forced her new husband to dress in women's clothing.[80]

Allied with the Portuguese were Hari a Kiluanji, whose lands were in Dambi a Hari, and his brother, Ngola Hari, who held the fortress district of Pungo Andongo (also in Hari), and Mubango, who had also been a staunch Portuguese ally since 1617. The Portuguese, commanded by Bento Banha Cardoso, brought their own troops, their Imbangala allies, and Mbundu forces raised from the vassal *sobas* in Ilamba and Lembo. Njinga counted on the Kwanza valley *sobas* around Kindonga, Tunda and Kisama, south of the Kwanza, and parts of Museque, whose lands lay on the west of Pungo Andongo, north of the river.[81] She could also rely on the thousands of refugees from central Ndongo who had fled from Ambaca and the Portuguese, including a good many soldiers, and her own Imbangala allies, Kaza and Kaeta. Njinga had gained widespread popular support as the legitimate ruler; she was greatly admired and her islands of Kindonga were "the pride of the River Cuanza" and were widely regarded as the real capital of Ndongo.[82]

The civil war in Ndongo that followed lasted until 1631 and moved the theater of operations from the lands around the capital at Kabasa to about 100 kilometers east. As the war progressed each of the parties gradually established more settled rule as they partitioned the area and created firmer alliances and overlordship. As a result of this, the chaos and disorder that had characterized the region since the invasion of Mendes de Vasconcelos was brought to bay in some areas. De Sousa's actions in the Luanda area are illustrative. He had been attempting to bring some order to the areas around Luanda since he took office, and in 1625 began to punish residents for illegal taxation with temporary exile to Benguela and their slaves with permanent transportation to Brazil.[83] De Sousa took another decisive step in this direction in 1627 by ordering gangs of ex-soldiers, armed slaves of resident Portuguese, and other vagabonds to be rounded up and either sent to war in the east or punished by having their

[80] MSS Araldi, Cavazzi, "Missione Evangelica," book 2, p. 40.
[81] On Portuguese allies in Ndongo, see Regimento a Bento Banha Cardoso, *FHA* 1: 204; on Njinga's allies, see Fernão de Sousa to Governo, 9 July 1626, *FHA* 2: 166; Cadornega, *História* 1: 130.
[82] Cadornega, *História* 1: 128; 131. Cadornega interviewed participants in this battle later, at least one of whom, Rodrigo Serrão, an Angolan born soldier, he named.
[83] Bando of 16 September 1626, *FHA* 2: 279–80.

ears cut off, and as a result peace was restored to the area of Ilamba, east of Luanda and along the Kwanza to Masangano.[84] The process was slow; in 1629, de Sousa was still seeking to stop abuses in which private citizens collected tributes, including slaves from the population around Luanda and the presidios.[85]

In the old centers of war the Portuguese and Hari a Kiluanji continued their efforts at establishing Hari a Kiluanji's claim to be ruler of Ndongo. However, when they attacked Njinga's capital in the Kindonga Islands in 1626, they faced a formidable defense, directed and led by Njinga in person. Only after heavy fighting did they manage to drive her out. The expulsion of Njinga was only temporary as she resumed her positions in Kindonga the next year. When a smallpox epidemic at the height of the campaign claimed Hari a Kiluanji among its victims, the Portuguese attempted to transfer his claim to the throne to his brother, Ngola Hari, both of whom headed major military contingents, in an election by pro-Portuguese *sobas* and *macotas* on 12 October 1626.[86] The Portuguese believed that this would result in the opening up of the markets for slave trading and ease the flow of tribute.[87]

Njinga soon made it clear that she did not regard the Portuguese selection of Ngola Hari as valid when she sent her Mwene Lumbo (her court spokesman) to them in 1627, "saying that she had come for her lands of which she was the lord in which she had no enemy and that Angola Aire was her slave and seeing that he was a relative, he could not be king."[88] Njinga sought to undermine Ngola Hari by opening the slave market and sending 400 slaves (added to another 400 sent by her Imbangala ally Kaza) to the Portuguese.[89] She also harassed the new *feira*, established at Ndala Kisuva, by attacking Portuguese merchants and their agents, thus cutting off trade from outside the immediate area.[90] As a result, de Sousa resumed the war in support of Ngola Hari, and in 1629 the combined forces of Ngola Hari and Portugal assaulted the islands for a second

---

[84] Fernão de Sousa to sons, 1630, *FHA* 1: 286.

[85] Orders of Fernão de Sousa to Paio de Araújo de Azevedo, 14 September 1629, *FHA* 2: 308.

[86] Fernão de Sousa to sons, 1630, *FHA* 1: 256–7, summarizing a report from Bento Banha Cardoso.

[87] Fernão de Sousa to Government, 6 July 1626, *FHA* 2: 166.

[88] Fernão de Sousa to Sons, 1630, *FHA* 1: 299, summarizing testimony of Njinga's Mwene Lumbo as reported in letter of the commander of Ambaca, 20 December 1627.

[89] Fernão de Sousa to Government, 10 July 1628, *FHA* 2: 197.

[90] Álvaro Rodrigues to de Sousa, 20 December 1627, summarized in de Sousa to sons, *FHA* 1: 299.

time.[91] Njinga again fled eastward, hotly pursued by her enemies, while much of her family, including both of her sisters, were captured. Njinga made her daring escape with a few hundred of her remaining followers after a harrowing descent on ropes down the cliffs of the Baixa de Cassange.[92] Even though she had lost on the battlefield, many local Mbundu leaders still regarded Njinga, or at least her royal line, as more legitimate than Ngola Hari. For this reason de Sousa and his advisors considered, but ultimately rejected, a scheme to install Njinga's sister Maria Kambu as ruler of Ndongo, instead of Ngola Hari, "for reasons of state."[93]

But the insecurity and chaos caused by the war continued, even though Njinga, her army scattered, cut her losses by accepting a humiliating position as wife of Kasanje, leader of a large Imbangala band that had deserted Portuguese service and had just returned from raiding Wandu in Kongo.[94] He demanded that Njinga throw away her *lunga*, a symbol of political and military authority, as "he did not want to have two lords in his quilombo nor did he care for her to do with him what she did with the jaga Caza, and that she had to remain as his wife." Still believing in Njinga's right to rule, her followers retrieved the *lunga* and retained it. While she was with Kasanje, their combined armies marched northward along the eastern border of Kongo, perhaps in an extended raid like the one made by Kasanje the previous year.[95] As the wife of Kasanje, Njinga became an Imbangala by engaging in the stipulated rituals typical of that band while at the same time reestablishing a power base within the Imbangala organization.[96] She used the Imbangala forces that Kasanje gave her to take back the islands in 1630, once again making them her capital.[97]

---

[91] These events, documented in detail in the voluminous papers of Fernão de Sousa, have been outlined in Heintze, "Ende," pp. 229–64.

[92] Described in the report of Araújo de Azevedo, 4 June 1629, summarized in de Sousa to sons, 1630, *FHA* 1: 333–4.

[93] Fernão de Sousa to Governo, 25 August 1629, *FHA* 2: 230–1; where the two sisters were regarded as "goddesses on earth" by most Mbundu. On Ngola Hari's legitimacy see especially Fernão de Sousa's own thinking about it in "Lembrança das rezones que ha pera Angolla Are não ser rey" (c. 20 July to 14 September 1629), *FHA* 1: 209–10.

[94] Report of Captain Mor, 16 February 1629, summarized in de Sousa to sons, *FHA* 1: 327.

[95] Report of Alexandre Ladino and Manoel de Nobrega to Sargento Mor Antonio Bruto, c. September 1629, summarized in de Sousa to Sons, *FHA* 1: 345.

[96] Our only source is Cavazzi, whose account is based on Njinga's testimony but is not secure chronologically. The ritual, called *maji ma samba*, involved pounding up a baby in a grain mortar and smearing its bloody remains on herself and her followers, MSS Araldi, Cavazzi, "Missione Evangelica," book 2, pp. 35–6 and 40–2.

[97] Information obtained from "a Negro who accompanied Dona Ana when she fled the last time from the islands" shortly after March 1630, in de Sousa to sons, 1630, *FHA* 1: 347; see also Fernão de Sousa to King, 2 March 1632, *MMA* 8: 162–3.

But the war continued to move eastward and between 1630 and 1635, Njinga was continuously at war "with victory one day & defeat the next; here she was destroyed & there she was in the field with more people, to whom she made gifts & promises, & she was everyone's enemy; when one foe fled there were ten more coming."[98] During this period Njinga broke off her relationship with Kasanje but retained a large Imbangala unit under the command of Njinga Mona. Using these forces that she commanded more directly, she conquered Matamba, helped, no doubt, by many of her loyal subjects who had fled there since 1629.[99] By 1635 Njinga, following the conquest, established her own capital, which was an armed and protected camp that she always called *quilombo* (*kilombo*, a Kimbundu word meaning military camp or army).[100] She did not abandon her claim to rule a larger kingdom of Ndongo, including the lands she had negotiated for in 1622 and kept a number of her supporters on the islands of Kindonga, where her brother and predecessor was buried and which she regarded as a symbolic center of the kingdom of Ndongo. From 1635 to 1641 Njinga harassed Ngola Hari, testing Portuguese resolve to defend him, and her propaganda encouraged the population to leave the areas controlled by Ngola Hari and the Portuguese and to settle in Matamba.

Njinga's relationship with the Portuguese continued to be based on her desire to get them to return her sisters, whom they had captured, and establish her own authority in the areas of Ndongo where the Portuguese had made inroads. On the other hand, the two governors – Manuel Pereira Coutinho and Francisco de Vasconcelos da Cunha – who succeeded de Sousa as governor from 1630 to 1639 focused on Mbwila, which offered greater potential for conquest and slaves. The war in 1634–1635 forced the Dembo ruler to submit after the Luso-African troops devastated the countryside and took "numerous prisoners."[101]

In spite of her military successes, Njinga did not abandon diplomacy, and with the encouragement of some of her Luso-African allies, in 1630, at the same time Coutinho had arrived to take up the governorship, she stopped the trade in slaves and the passage of traders in the lands that Ngola Hari claimed. She hoped that her actions would force the governor

---

[98] MSS Araldi, Cavazzi, "Missione Evangelica," book 2, p. 41.

[99] Fernao de Sousa to sons, 1630, *FHA* 1: 346, based on testimony of Ladino and de Nobrega, on the conquest of Matamba, see Cadornega, *Historia* 1: 194; MSS Araldi, Cavazzi, "Missione Evangelica," book 2, pp. 42–3.

[100] Cadornega, *História* 1: 193. For the usage of kilombo, see Queen Njinga to Governor General of Angola, 13 December 1655, *MMA* 11: 524–28.

[101] Cardonega, *História*, vol. 1, p. 190.

into negotiations in which she was prepared to give up her claims to the throne and proposed that the governor nominate one of her sisters, become a vassal, and pay a yearly tribute of 100 *peças*.[102] Although nothing resulted from the negotiations, Njinga did not abandon her desire to make peace with the Portuguese, and as part of her strategy, in 1637 she sought to develop independent contacts with the Jesuits in Luanda and went so far as to send them a gift of ivory and slaves. Here also her initiative was rebuffed by the fathers, who argued that she had ulterior motives and observed that she had "the most corrupt morals."[103]

In 1637 the possibility of peace through negotiations opened up again when governor Pedro Cezar de Menezes, who took over the governorship in 1635, wrote to her demanding the return of the *kijokos* who he regarded as runaways, and she in turn invited him to send her an embassy to deal with these matters. The mission, sent out in 1640, had some success with both Kasanje and Njinga, though the details are unclear. It did not succeed in getting Njinga to rejoin the Church, one of the conditions set by the Portuguese for a peace. She refused the entreaties of Father António Coelho, arguing that "consenting would have detracted from her fame as a true female Giaga [Imbangala], & contravened her laws."[104]

Toward Civil War in Kongo

While the war over Ndongo was raging, events in Kongo, although following a radically different pattern from those in Ndongo, would also play an important role in the enslavement and export of people in this period. In Kongo, unlike Ndongo, Portuguese attempts to undermine its sovereignty and expand the slave trade failed, thanks to Kongo's military strength and diplomatic acumen. Portugal did, however, manage to attack border regions like Mbwila and Nambu a Ngongo, where Kongo's authority was weak. Instead, Kongo's internal conflicts generated political instability and civil war that, although not replicating the chaos in Ndongo, led to the enslavement of thousands of people.

The crisis began with the death of Álvaro II in 1614 as a power struggle to replace him sapped the kingdom's ability to defend its frontiers as contenders for the Crown jockeyed for position. The Duke of Mbamba,

[102] Fernão de Sousa to King, *MMA* 8, 23 February 1632, p. 140.
[103] Franco, *Synopsis Annalium* 1637, no. 19, p. 273.
[104] Cadornega, *História* 1: 209–10; MSS Araldi, Cavazzi, "Missione Evangelica," book 2, pp. 44–6.

António da Silva, acting as a king maker who claimed to be executor of Álvaro's will, marched on the capital and "gave and took as he saw fit." Over the next year, however, da Silva was unable to stabilize Kongo. After failing in his first attempt at a creating a puppet ruler, he hit upon Álvaro's teenaged son and had him crowned as Álvaro III.[105] This was not acceptable to other members of the royal family, especially Álvaro's "uncles,"[106] who refused to obey him or relinquish their provinces. Álvaro spent much of his seven-year reign forcing or cajoling these recalcitrant senior relatives to accept him, and ordering the overthrow of his erstwhile patron, António da Silva from Mbamba, in 1620.[107]

In 1621, when Correia de Sousa arrived, these conflicts might have appeared to offer Portugal the same opportunities for obtaining slaves and political advances as Ndongo's political crisis did. The new governor turned his attention toward Kongo, perhaps hoping that he could use private Portuguese armies, forces of the loyal *sobas*, and his Imbangala allies to invade and generate the kind of chaos that had produced thousands of slaves for export in Ndongo during Mendes de Vasconcelos's term.

The unfinished war against Kasanze, a loyal vassal of Kongo who lived in the immediate hinterland of Luanda, which he inherited from Mendes de Vasconcelos, served as an excellent stepping off point for de Sousa's larger campaigns into Kongo. His army first won a particularly violent and duplicitous war against Kasanze, whose people were "all Christians."[108] After his military success on 25 May 1622, according to his report to Lisbon, he ordered the field commander, Pero de Sousa Coelho, to bring "all the souas, macotas who are counselors, tendalas and maculuntos, ministers of his wars," 26 in all, to coastal settlement in order that they *undar*, or swear formal vassalage, so that he could "confirm them in their lands." When they came "all in good faith," he then sent for the "four gingos who are heirs and pretenders of Casange," in order that they might chose from among themselves who would be the next ruler.

[105] Álvaro III to Juan Bautista Vives, 19 October 1619, *MMA* 6: 390; Soares, "Relação," *MMA* 6: 379.

[106] In the text, these men are often uncles, but they were probably any men of his father's generation that were related to him in any way. Kikongo kinship terminology does not distinguish from a father's brothers and what might otherwise be called cousins.

[107] "Da alcune Provisioni de Don Alvaro il Terzo Rè di Congo, passate se a Biagio Correa..." (covers period 1616–1619), *MMA* 6: 252.

[108] Mateus Cardoso, "Relação do que se passou em Angola no anno de 623," *MMA* 7: 177. The governor could claim that he was still staying within his instructions from the Crown that forbade offensive war.

Finally he sent people to "look for morindas, which are most of the people of each soua, both of war and women and children," who appeared "also in good faith." But instead of holding an election, he put the whole lot, nobles and commoners, "in ships, with all their people, and sent them to the governor of Brazil," so that he could "give them land where they would be together or separate." To justify this bit of treachery, Correia de Sousa maintained that their rebellion had rendered them captives and that without this deception he would have had to "enter their woods, and in order not to kill them," as it would be a waste to kill so many "pieces." He also noted that the people of Kasanze occupied the best land within a radius of eight leagues (40 kilometers) of Luanda, and he did not want to have "so suspicious neighbors near our door."[109]

Of the 1,211 Kongolese captives who had been sent on five ships to Brazil, almost half (583) died during the Middle Passage and another 68 died shortly after arrival from the "work of navigation and lack of necessities."[110] Having emptied the region of its population, Correia de Sousa then distributed the lands among the veteran soldiers for 12 leagues around.[111]

While his army was still in the field in Kasanze, Correia de Sousa learned of the death, on 4 May 1622, of Álvaro III of Kongo.[112] Given the difficulties that Álvaro had had in containing the ambitions of his relatives, the fact that he left a young son as heir and the general belief among the Portuguese "that in [Kongo], at the death of the king," there were "numerous great revolts" by nobles "to make a king who conforms to their partisanship and to take revenge on one another,"[113] De Sousa was confident that he could create a situation of chaos similar to what Mendes de Vasconcelos had created in Ndongo. Often Portuguese merchants capitalized on the interregnum to profit from the "cruelties and robberies" of the time by buying slaves.[114]

---

[109] João Correia de Sousa to D. Duarte, Marques de Frecilha, 3 June 1622, *MMA* 7: 17–24; Severim de Faria, "História," fol. 182, in *MMA* 7: 79.

[110] Apostolic Collector to Cardinal Pavilicino, 20 October 1623, *MMA* 15: 510. The statistics come from a document cited in Heintze, "Ende," p. 210, n. 76. Her reference, a report of 17 July 1622 transcribed in C. Coelho da Cruz, "O Trafico Negreiro da 'Costa de Angola.'" (unpublished licenciate thesis, Lisbon, 1966), pp. xvii–xix. We were unable to locate the original of this document in AHU, Cx 2.

[111] Severim de Faria, "História," fol. 182, in *MMA* 7: 79.

[112] Correia de Sousa to Marquis of Frechilha, pp. 22–3.

[113] [Mateus Cardoso], "Morte de D Alvaro III, Rei de Congo e eleição que se fez em Pedro Afonso, Duque de Bamba," 1622, *MMA* 15: 484–5.

[114] [Cardoso], "Relação da morte," *MMA* 15: 485.

It seemed that a Portuguese invading army could almost certainly prolong the instability and create the chaotic conditions that would allow a huge export of slaves. Using the pretext of recovering runaway slaves, Correia de Sousa ordered Sousa Coelho to move his forces of over 20,000 Mbundu and Portuguese, in addition to Imbangala contingents, into Nambu a Ngongo, well within Kongo's province of Mbamba. Ignoring various conciliatory gestures by its ruler, Paulo Afonso, Sousa Coelho devastated the territory and forced Paulo Afonso to flee to the nearby commercial town of Mbumbi.

While Sousa Coelho's forces were ravaging Nambu a Ngongo, the Kongolese electors surprised everyone by immediately choosing the Duke of Mbamba to be King Pedro II Nkanga Mvika on 26 May 1622.[115] His supporters, led by the Spanish priest Bras Correa, the president of the royal council, "through his vigilance, zeal and rudence," as Pedro noted in his report of the events to Rome, made it so that "all was quieted without there being any collapse in a time when the destruction of the kingdom was feared."[116]

The closing of ranks allowed Pedro to address the Portuguese threat unhindered. Immediately upon taking office, he sent an embassy to Luanda demanding an explanation for the Portuguese invasion of Nambu a Ngongo, his vassal. Correia de Sousa countered by claiming outrageously that he had the right to choose the king of Kongo and that Pedro, when he was Duke of Mbamba, had harbored and aided Kasanze. Threatening to bring the king of Kongo "back to Luanda in chains," he made absurd demands on Pedro – that he turn over the copper mines, cede lands, including the whole Duchy of Mpemba and the island of Luanda, allow Portuguese exemption from customs duties, and the like, demands that the new king summarily dismissed. [117]

Ignoring these diplomatic overtures, the Portuguese army approached Mbumbi, a small commercial town in southern Mbamba, in pursuit of Paulo Afonso, and faced a hastily gathered force of 3,000 under the duke. Though badly outnumbered, the duke gave battle on 18 December 1622. Although he routed 30,000 Mbundu archers of Sousa Coelho's army, he was defeated by an Imbangala counterattack. The duke fell, along with the Marquis of Mpemba and 90 lesser nobles and thousands of common soldiers.[118] This first victory proved to be illusory, for shortly thereafter Pedro

---

[115] [Cardoso], "Relação da morte," *MMA* 15: 483–4; 488.
[116] Pedro II to Juan Baptista Vives, 20 July 1622, *MMA* 7: 40–1.
[117] Apostolic Collector to Cardinal Pavilicino, *MMA* 15: 517.
[118] Apostolic Collector to Cardinal Pavilicino, *MMA* 15: 517.

II mobilized his forces (300,000 men, according to the Portuguese) and drove "all the Portuguese from the conquered duchy with great losses."[119] As a result, Correia de Sousa had to abandon his plans to advance further into Kongo[120] and to capitalize on political discord in order to "overpower the duchy of Pemba [and] enslave the inhabitants."[121]

Beyond his military response to this violation of Kongo's sovereignty, Pedro also undertook a vigorous writing campaign to Pope Gregory XV and the new king of Spain, Philip IV. He complained that Correia de Sousa, with his army "of 200,000 Jagas, barbarous heathens who sustain themselves on human flesh," had "desolated and destroyed many provinces, where there are infinite Christians."[122] Widespread anti-Portuguese rioting broke out all over Kongo and many of the Luso-Africans in Soyo and those in the port of Pinda "were stripped of their clothes right down to their bread-knives and their hat and shoes," and all their property was "taken into custody."[123] Pedro, in detailing the dangers to the larger Portuguese interest that this rioting presented, noted that there were over 1,000 Portuguese in Kongo who had some 800,000 *cruzados* in slaves and property in his lands and that he had to intervene to prevent their total loss.[124] Luanda merchants who had interests in Kongo complained that "to make war on Congo was to make war on Luanda" and forced the governor to flee the city for Brazil on 2 May 1623. Correia was able, however, to take with him a huge quantity of money and 300 slaves, only to be arrested later in Portugal.[125]

Phillip IV responded to Pedro's denunciations by promising an investigation and expressing displeasure that Pedro was discontented.[126] Writing to officials in Brazil, he ordered over 1,000 of the Christians taken from Kasanze to be returned to Angola from Brazil, though the long process that this entailed did not ultimately lead to the return of many

---

[119] ARA: St. Gen., 5751, Meeting of 27 October 1623. The Dutch account of the battle was brought to the Netherlands, along with letters from Soyo and Kongo by Joris Pietersen shortly after the battle. Our thanks to Andrea Mosterman for locating this document.

[120] Apostolic Collector to Cardinal Pavilicino, *MMA* 15: 517, 522.

[121] ARA: St. Gen., 5751, Meeting of 27 October 1623.

[122] Pedro II to Juan Baptista Vives, 28 November 1623, *MMA* 7: 161. His letter to Spain is not extant, but Felipe IV's reply indicates its contents, Felipe IV to Pedro II, 17 June 1623, *MMA* 7: 116–17.

[123] ARA: St. Gen., 5751, Meeting of 27 October 1623.

[124] Mateus Cardoso to Manuel Rodrigues, 1624, *MMA* 7: 294.

[125] Apostolic Collector to Cardinal Pavilicino, *MMA* 15: 518–24; Mateus Cardoso, "Relação...1623," *MMA* 7: 188. His goods were seized, and he died penniless in Limeiro prison, Saccardo, *Congo e Angola* 1: 179–81.

[126] Felipe IV to Pedro II, 17 June 1623.

people.[127] Bishop Simão Mascarenhas, the interim governor who took over after Correia de Sousa's precipitous departure, repatriated a cousin of the Duke of Mbamba and some 53 high-ranking Kongolese taken at Mbumbi.[128] The new governor, Fernão de Sousa, who arrived in 1624, also returned additional captives in response to a royal order.[129]

Perhaps the most important consequence of the Portuguese invasion of Kongo was that it led Pedro to decide to make an alliance with the Dutch to drive the Portuguese from Central Africa. In 1623 he wrote to the newly formed Dutch West India Company and proposed that "if the prince of Orange would send some four or five warships along with five or six hundred soldiers to secure the water and the land to get rid of the Portuguese on the coast" he would "pay for the cost of the ships and the soldiers pay in gold, silver and ivory." He also promised to "hand the fort and the city of Luanda" over to the Dutch.[130] This opening to the West India Company with its military as well as commercial aims would redirect the patterns of political alliances that had governed Afro-European relationships in Central Africa. It would eventually shift enslavement from the interior to areas closer to the coast and thus ensure that people with the deepest involvement in the Afro-Portuguese world would continue to be enslaved.

In 1624, the West India Company responded to Pedro's letter by sending a fleet under Piet Heyn to carry out the joint attack on Luanda, though when it arrived in Kongo at the end of the year, the improved Luso Kongolese relationship caused Count António of Soyo to put him off. Feigning ignorance, he contended that Kongo was interested only in trade, making

---

[127] This long correspondence and activities are summarized in Saccardo, *Congo e Angola* 1: 187–8.

[128] Simão de Mascarenhas to Phillip IV, 3 February 1624, *MMA* 7: 200; Fernão de Sousa to Felipe IV, 22 August 1624, *MMA* 7: 363.

[129] Fernão de Sousa to Felipe IV, 22 August 1625, p. 363.

[130] ARA: St. Gen., 5751, Meeting of 27 October 1623. This letter is not extant, but was summarized in the States General Archives and also in the diary carried on board Piet Heyn's expedition that came to Kongo in 1624. The letter mentions specifically the killing of two Kongolese "counts," Piet Heyn, "Journael van de Brasiliese Reyse, gehouden opt Schip De Neptunus...15 January 1624 tot den 16 July 1625," fols. 24v–25, published with original pagination marked in L. M. Akveld, "Journaal van de Reis van Piet Heyn naar Brazilië en West-Afrika 1624–25," *Bijdragen en Medelingen van het Historisch Genootschap* 76 (1962): 85–174, at pp. 144–5. This account is fuller and more immediate than two other accounts of the expedition that lack some of these details, de Laet, *Iaerlijck verhael*, pp. 66–7, and "Tguint den Admirael Pieter Heyn Beiegent often weervaeren is seeded den.5. Agustes Anno 1624 tot den 12 Julij Anno 1625" (ed. Karl Ratelband), *De Westafrikanse Reis van Piet Heyn, 1624–25* (Hague: Nijhoff, 1959), pp. 7–8.

as an excuse that Pedro II had died and his son and successor, Garcia I, wanted only "peace and friendship" with the Portuguese, with whom they shared a Catholic faith.[131]

Despite Pedro's success in effecting the humiliating expulsion and arrest of the governor, and his ability to garner effective support from European allies, Kongo kings could not contain the factionalism that would set Kongolese against each other. Pedro's uncontested election and that of his son, Garcia I, in 1624 gave an appearance of stability that proved to be an illusion. Within two years of his election, Garcia had been overthrown by a coalition of disgruntled nobles led by the Duke of Nsundi Manuel Jordão. Jordão put one of his allies, Ambrósio, on the throne but within two years Jordão and his allies fell out with the king. Once again Jordão bought an army to São Salvador, allegedly to protect Ambrósio from his enemies, but the king soon turned on his benefactor, accusing him of having his eyes on the throne, and exiled him to an island in the Congo River, where he soon died "in great penury and misery."[132] Ambrósio's unsteady rule continued, beset by rumors, war mobilizations,[133] and eventually massive revolts that led to his overthrow and death on 7 March 1631.[134]

Kongo's instability during Ambrósio's rule also gave the Portuguese opportunities to attack frontier regions, particularly Mbwila, a strategic area for trade between Portuguese Angola and eastern areas like Kundi and Okango and the gateway to copper mines in the Kongo province of Wembo province.[135] Between 1627 and 1630 the Mwene Mbwila defied both Portugal and Kongo, refusing to acknowledge Governor Fernão de Sousa (claiming he was a Kongo vassal) but making no obeisance to Ambrósio either. When de Sousa demanded he renew vassalage following the first war against Njinga (1626–1627), Mbwila stalled by prolonging diplomatic negotiations between the Portuguese and Kongo.[136] This led de

---

[131] Heyn, "Brasiliense Reyse" (ed. Arkveld), fol. 25, p. 145.

[132] Franco, *Synopsis Annalium* 1628, no. 22–23, pp. 253–4; de Sousa to sons, *FHA* 1: 304.

[133] Including a threat from Daniel da Silva in Mbamba, and his flight to Soyo, see Fernão de Sousa to Ambrósio, 5 January 1629, *MMA* 7: 579–80, referring to a lost letter of Ambrósio to de Sousa, 12 November 1628, in which he unsuccessfully sought Portuguese help against Soyo. See also de Sousa to Sons, *FHA* 1: 304, where he also notes Soyo as agreeing to Jordão's attack on São Salvador. For another plot problem, in 1629, see Franco, *Synopsis Annalium* 1629, no. 15–16, pp. 256–7.

[134] Biblioteca Nacional de Madrid (BN Madrid), MS 3533, "Descripcion Narrativa," p. ix (Antonio de Teruel, writing in 1664, may also have relied on João de Pavia's chronicle).

[135] De Sousa to sons, *FHA* 1: 340–41. De Sousa claimed that Portugal had the right to work these mines based on past concessions and an alleged Kongo vassalage.

[136] On these negotiations, see de Sousa to sons, *FHA* 1: 258–9; 269–70.

Sousa to send a military expedition to Mbwila, provoking anti-Portuguese riots in Kongo.[137] As de Sousa told Jesuit critics, "time and experience with this heathen shows that he obeys harquebuses and not messages...and it pays to castigate him when he deserves it."[138] Unable to continue the campaign because of a Dutch threat to Luanda, he withdrew the troops.[139] In the aftermath of the Mbwila wars the flow of slaves from Kundi, Okango, and other eastern markets came to a halt and remained closed for many years, as de Sousa was still attempting to reopen them after the Mwene Mbwila's death in 1630.[140]

The unstable situation in Kongo itself that affected trade was hardly altered when the 11-year-old son of Álvaro III was crowned Álvaro IV on 8 March 1631, the day after Ambrósio's death.[141] Such a youthful king was bound to be manipulated by powerful men around him, including Daniel da Silva, to whom he gave the title Duke of Mbamba and Paulo, Count of Soyo. But in 1633, da Silva, claiming that he wished to "free his nephew from nobles who were considering overthrowing him," marched an army said to be 20,000 strong to São Salvador. The young king fled to Soyo to seek Count Paulo's protection, taking with him loyal followers from the Brotherhood of St. Ignatius, including his staunchest defenders, two brothers named Álvaro Nimi and Garcia Nkanga. Da Silva's army, now said to number 50,000, followed the king to Soyo, where he pinned the smaller force of the king's supporters in the marshy and forested land south of the Congo River. The two brothers erected a cross and invoked St. Ignatius to intercede for them, noting that they had "only our faith in God, our right hand, and the justice of our cause" as their defense. Garcia then heroically attacked da Silva's army by wading through the swamp, felling da Silva himself with an arrow. Another noble from the Brotherhood, who witnessed da Silva's fall, ran to salute the young king in the wood where he was hiding. The victors carried Álvaro back to São Salvador in triumph.[142] This civil war again provided the opportunity for Portuguese slave traders to purchase thousands of Kongolese Christians from Mbamba, São Salvador, Nsundi, and Soyo.

---

[137] Franco, *Synopsis Annalium* 1627, no. 14, p. 250.

[138] De Sousa to Governo, 2 August 1627, *FHA* 2: 184.

[139] This seems likely from the testimony of a very damaged page and marginal notes in de Sousa to sons, *FHA* 1: 275.

[140] De Sousa to Sons, *FHA* 1: 341–2; 348, hoping that the death of the *soba* would bring about an opening of markets.

[141] Dates for the death of Ambrósio and accession of Álvaro IV come from BN Madrid, MS 3533, "Descripcion Narrativa," p. ix.

[142] Franco, *Synopsis Annalium* 1633, nos. 6–8, pp. 262–3.

Álvaro's restoration did not stop the intrigue and civil war, for two years later one of his enemies poisoned the young king.[143] His half-brother, Álvaro Mpanzu a Nimi, was crowned Álvaro V[144] three days later in the midst of the continuing civil war. The war matched forces from the eastern part of Kongo led by Gregorio against the forces of the Count of Soyo and the two brothers Álvaro Nimi and Garcia, who had been supporters of Álvaro IV. Álvaro Nimi overthrew the youthful king and was crowned Álvaro VI on 14 August 1636.[145] Álvaro's election did not end the conflict and intrigue, for in 1637 he had to defend his capital, São Salvador, against the forces of Gregorio.[146] Álvaro's reign brought a period of stability but came to an end when he died suddenly in 1641, rumored to have succumbed to poison, and was succeeded by his brother, Garcia, on 22 February 1641.[147] His death coincided with that of Count Paulo of Soyo, which would begin a new round of warfare between Kongolese over the place of Soyo.

Beyond Ndongo and Kongo: Wars and Trade in the Periphery

Military and commercial developments in regions outside of Ndongo and Kongo also led to the capture of slaves for the American markets. These areas included the Portuguese colony of Benguela to the south, and some slaves were exported from the distant lands of Kakongo and Loango in the north during this period. Benguela was not primarily a slave-exporting region, for following the military operations in 1617 that led to its

[143] Jesuit work flourished under Álvaro IV; see Miguel Afonso to Jesuit General, 22 August 1634, *MMA* 8: 301–2. This was particularly true of the brotherhoods, same to same, 3 January 1636, *MMA* 8: 342–3.

[144] Dates and names come from BN Madrid, MS 3533, de Teruel, "Descripcion Narrativa," unnumbered front matter.

[145] This reconstruction is an attempt to reconcile several different accounts; we have favored in most places Franco, *Synopsis Annalium* 1636, nos. 10–12, p. 269, as it is based, we believe, on João de Pavia's chronicle and thus on immediate eyewitness accounts. A second detailed account, based on post facto testimony of Garcia, is found in BN Madrid, MS 3533, de Teruel, "Descripcion Narrativa," pp. 124–5; Daniel da Silva, who was also involved in Soyo gave his version in a letter to the Pope, 25 March 1648, *MMA* 10: 124–5; finally there is the account of Dapper, based on Dutch testimony from Soyo, *Naukeurige Beschrijvinge*, pp. 211–2. We have also given some attention to Parecer de Francisco Leitão, 4 December 1643, *MMA* 9: 88–9. For other, somewhat different attempts, see Saccardo, *Congo* 1: 260–1, 271–2; Hilton, *Kingdom of Kongo*, pp. 151, 171, which is not entirely reliable.

[146] Franco, *Synopsis Annalium*, 1637, nos. 15–17, pp. 272–3. It is difficult to reconcile this with Dapper, *Naukeurige Beschrijvinge*, p. 211, which has the 1637 involve an invasion of Soyo from Kongo, because Franco's account makes it clear the fight was at São Salvador, unless somehow there were two wars that year.

[147] BN Madrid, MS 3533, de Teruel, "Descripcion Narrativa," p. ix.

foundation, it was largely known for the export of cattle products and some copper. However, there was one major exception. In 1627–1628 Governor Lopo Soares Lasso made a major invasion of Sumbi shortly after he arrived with a primary objective of capturing mines of copper. Although no mines were captured, the war did result in the capture of "many pieces and 5,000 head of cattle," and more than 1,500 captives in another action in 1628.[148] The campaign's success was not further followed up, however, for in 1632 and 1633, de Sousa described Benguela as a place that sold just "a few slaves."[149] When Soares attempted another big raid into the interior in 1638 directed against the great king Njimbo Ngola, he and all his soldiers were slaughtered.[150]

Northern outlets such as Kakongo and Loango were not centers of slave exports, though they were famous for exporting copper and cloth. A report of 1611 explicitly stated that slaves "never leave from these markets," and even in 1620, they were not among a list of exports from the region.[151] Wars in Loango, which began with a royal campaign against the Mani Benso in 1624 started the slave trade, which continued with the destruction of Vungu by "Jagas" in the pay of Loango the same year.[152] Slaves from these campaigns may have provided the exports that Portuguese took from the region. In 1626 Governor de Sousa sent Manuel Barbosa to Kakongo to engage in the slave trade.[153] A fiscal accounting of August 1626 noted duties paid on only a dozen slaves by then, suggesting an annual rate of something like 50 to 100 slaves per year.[154] The trade continued for a number of years, albeit at a fairly low level, as de Sousa noted that a ship with "many slaves" as well as copper departed from Loango in 1627, and slaves continued to be exported along with copper, cloth, and ivory in 1632.[155]

---

[148] Auto of Providor da Fazenda do Benguela, 23 July 1629, *FHA* 2: 302–5.

[149] Fernão de Sousa to King, 1632, and 13 June 1633, *MMA* 8: 129, and 13 June 1633, 129 and 231–3.

[150] Factor of Angola to king, 16 March 1638, *MMA* 8: 393; more fully described in Cadornega, *História* 1: 201–2.

[151] Bento Banha Cardoso, reply to João Salgado de Araújo, 10 August 1611, *MMA* 6: 18; "Relação tocante ao Reyno de Loango," 1620, *MMA* 6: 479–81.

[152] van Wassenaer, *Historisch verhael*, 8ᵗᵉ Deel, 20 May 1625, fols. 26v, 28v (reflecting reports of October 1624); Cardoso letter, 1624, *MMA* 6: 295.

[153] De Sousa to sons, *FHA* 1: 257.

[154] Certidão da escrivão da Fazenda de Angola, 15 August and 18 October 1626, *FHA* 2: 356. The certificate indicates payment of 34$490 reis and, using the rate for the Brazil trade indicated in the same text, converted to 12 slaves.

[155] de Sousa to Manuel Barbosa, 9 March 1627, *MMA* 7: 503; De Sousa to Governo, 2 August 1627, *FHA* 2: 181–2; Fernão de Sousa, "Relação da Costa de Angola de Angola e Congo," 21 February 1632, *MMA* 8: 123; and, "Relação," 1632, *MMA* 8: 135.

War, Chaos, and Enslavement: Later Years, 1641–1660

The Dutch conquest of Luanda, their alliance with Kongo, and their attempts to enlist Njinga to make a common front against the Portuguese led to a shift that altered the geographic scope of the wars, intrigues, violence, and unstable alliances that had fed the slave trade in the earlier period. Njinga took the opportunity to capitalize on the Dutch presence to make her own alliance with the Dutch and Kongo, and to attempt once again to assert her right to lead Ndongo by making wars on the Portuguese and their African allies. The period began with the Dutch conquest of Luanda (1641–1648) and heralded a time of political realignment that altered the geographic scope of enslavement as the theatre of war shifted from the eastern interior of Ndongo to the Luanda hinterland and intensified in the coastal province of Soyo in the Kongo kingdom.

After the Portuguese restoration of Angola in 1648, the pattern shifted again, moving to the interior. Although some slaves still came from Portuguese pressure on Kongo's southern vassals, and their war in Kisama, the shift was eastward and southward. After the defeat of the Njinga/Dutch alliance, Njinga withdrew her forces to Matamba, and both she and Kasanje concluded peace agreements with Portugal that established their capitals as major slave-trading emporia, thus moving the focus of the slave trade to the Kwango valley. In Kongo, the civil wars that had contributed to the export of large numbers of Kongo slaves slowed as Garcia consolidated his rule and passed power peacefully to his son in 1661.

The Coastal Phase: Portuguese Angola and Ndongo, 1641–1650

The Dutch decision to invade Angola was a result of the long series of correspondence that Kongo had developed with the Dutch West India Company, which had provided intelligence to its factor Cornelis Ouman in Soyo that the Portuguese forces were weak and that Kongo was ready to renew the anti-Portuguese alliance it had proposed in 1622. The Dutch officials also believed that the African vassals and slaves of Portugal were ready rise up against their colonial master.[156] Acting on this information, Admiral Cornelis Corneliszoon Jol landed 2,145 soldiers from the Dutch Brazilian conquests in Luanda on 25 August 1641. Some "800 whites, both soldiers and townsmen with about thirty thousand negroes, without wives and children" fled on the approach of the Dutch but regrouped and

---

[156] ARA OWIC 56, Jan Maurits van Nassau and Council to XIX, 31 May 1641.

made a stand at Kilunda, just outside the city.[157] The Dutch forces drove them from there on 19 September and forced them to retreat to positions among the Portuguese plantations along the Bengo River.[158] The Dutch then built a fortified trading post at the mouth of the Bengo and began assessing the political realities in the country.[159]

The Dutch had three major strategies that they hoped would consolidate their position in central Africa and advance their larger Atlantic designs. The first was "to tie up an alliance with the King of Congo and with the Count of Sonho [Soyo] and the other neighboring kings and princes [*Conings et Vorsten*]," which would include Njinga, and the second was to insure their continued dominance of Angola by co-opting the Portuguese settlers into their rule. Finally, they wanted to control the slave trade from Brazil to the Americas.

For African rulers, the arrival of Dutch armed forces signaled a major change in the status quo that they believed would work to their advantage. For those under Portuguese control, the Dutch presence provided grounds for an immediate uprising, especially in Dembos, where Kakulu ka Kahenda promptly pillaged and tortured Portuguese residents, including the priest.[160] To exploit this sentiment, the Dutch sent an expedition in October and November to the African leaders along the Bengo and the Kwanza Rivers with instructions to convince the local people that "we can come to help them drive out the Portuguese."[161] This tactic worked; fearing imminent Dutch advances up the river, the Portuguese commander at Muxima abandoned the fort, though his superiors in Massangano stood firm and organized a fleet to harass Dutch on the Kwanza.[162]

In Kongo, Garcia understood the Dutch attack in light of the longstanding Kongo–Dutch alliance for a joint attack on Luanda, first broached by Pedro II in 1622. He responded to the Dutch attack by turning

---

[157] *A Little True Forraine Newes: Better than a great deale of Domestick Spurious false News*... (London, 1641), p. 5; Another estimate given in the same publication lists "1000 white men and 25,000 blackamores," p. 6. Charles Boxer points out that the pamplet was probably published in 1642, see Charles Boxer, "Salvador Corriea de Sa e Benevidas and the Reconquest of Angola in 1648," *Hispanic American Historical Review* 28 (1948): 491.

[158] AHU Cx. 4, doc. 8, Sworn Statements of Portuguese officers, 20 October 1641; Minutes of Luanda Council, 20 September 1641, *ACA* 1: 252; Cadornega, *História* 1: 245–61. For a full account, see Ratelband, *Nederlanders*, pp. 102–15.

[159] ARA St. Gen. 5773, 11 November 1641; OWIC 56, Directors of Luanda to Captain Waldeck at Bengo, 22 September 1641.

[160] Cadornega, *História* 1: 279.

[161] ARA OWIC 57, Nieulant and Mortamer to Brazil Council, February–March 1642 (Bengo); Minutes of Luanda Council, entry of 9 November 1641, *ACA* 1: 256 (Kwanza).

[162] Cadornega, *História* 1: 275.

against the Luso-African merchants in Kongo, rousting them from their villages and seizing their goods and slaves. His brother, the Duke of Mbamba, took "a powerful army, declaring himself openly an enemy of the Portuguese and drove them out of his territory." He held back, however, from advancing against the Bengo.[163]

Garcia welcomed the embassy from the Dutch under their former factor in Soyo, Cornelis Ouman, led by Dom Agostinho, the Kongolese governor of Luanda Island. Ouman's instructions were to convince Garcia that they would be "friends of his friends and enemies of his enemies" and to remind him that they were also Christians whose mission was "to deliver all the blacks of Congo from the frightful tyranny that they had long endured from the Spanish and Portuguese."[164] Garcia responded by sending two emissaries of his own, Diogo Fernandes de Santa Maria and Domingos Fernandes, with Ouman back to Luanda.[165] Shortly after arriving in Luanda, the two Kongo ambassadors claimed to have found, by chance, on the street in Luanda, a document showing that the governor was planning a war on Kongo, signed by council and bishop, which persuaded them that the Dutch help had been important.[166] On 28 March 1642 Diogo Fernandes signed an offensive–defensive alliance on behalf of Garcia between Kongo and the West India Company.[167] The Dutch were confident the alliance with Kongo would "reestablish the slave trade."[168] Garcia, however, was more interested in seeing Dutch fortifications at Soyo, Dande, and other places.[169]

Njinga's response to the Dutch was linked to her long-standing attempts to push the Portuguese out of Ndongo. Although she had no prior history of dealing with them, she had been following developments closely because of the unsettled state of her relations with the Portuguese. She was aware that earlier Dutch threats had affected Portuguese operations against her and hoped that their success would benefit her. Indeed,

[163] ARA OWIC 56, Director of Luanda to Pieter Segers, 22 September 1641; ARA OWIC 57, Nieulant and Mortamer to Brazil Council, February–March 1642; ARA OWIC 58, Report of Pieter Mortamer, 14 September 1642. This duke was brother of king of Kongo and next in line for the throne; he was "like a sun which rises and upon whom all the vassals fixed their eyes." This might be the relationship between Garcia and Álvaro but by this time Garcia was already king. Apparently this was another of Garcia's brothers.
[164] Meeting minutes of Luanda Council, 1641–1642, Louis Jadin, ed and trans. *L'ancien Congo et l' Angola* (3 vols, Brussels 1975) (*ACA*) 1: 252–4, entry of 12 October 1641.
[165] ARA OWIC 58, Mortamer Report, 14 September 1642.
[166] ARA OWIC 58, Brazil Council to Nieulant 13 February 1643.
[167] Minutes of Luanda Council, entry of 28 March 1642, *ACA* 1: 260.
[168] ARA OWIC 57 Cornelis Nieulant and Pieter Mortamer to Count van Nassau, 19 April 1642.
[169] ARA OWIC 57, Nieulant and Mortamer to Count van Nassau, 19 April 1642.

the Dutch intercepted a letter of King João IV of Portugal ordering the governor to work on getting a new alliance with Njinga and Kongo.[170] João's hopes were in vain, however, for trust was long finished, as the embassy that Njinga had dispatched to the Dutch in Luanda arrived on 7 November 1641, a few months after the invasion.[171] From their negotiations, the Dutch saw an opportunity to work "with a certain woman called Nzinga [with whom] the Portuguese have never had peace or friendship, as they have with other inhabitants."[172] Undoubtedly encouraged by the positive response the Dutch gave her embassy to Luanda, Njinga moved her army into the upper Dande region at Sengas de Cavanga by mid-1642, bringing it under her control.[173] This alliance would take on greater significance in the coming years.

Whereas Garcia and Njinga sought to advance their political objectives with Dutch assistance, the Portuguese turned to their African allies to regain lost ground. Early in 1642, António Bruto and the Imbangala band of Jaga Kabuku ka Ndongo counterattacked in the rebel Dembos area, mercilessly pillaging Kitexi ka Ndambi and Ndambi a Ndonga.[174] This campaign culminated with the brutal slaughter of 8,000 people at Nambe a Kalombe on 20 January 1642, on Bruto's order that "no one be left alive." Bruto then built a *xalo* or a monument out of the heads of the slain to serve "as a reminder to traitors."[175] As Bruto rampaged in the west, in the east his compatriot Antonio Miranda attacked Ngolome a Keta, Kakulu ka Kahenda, Kakulu ka Kabasa, Kapele, Kakulu ka Njimbo, and Mutemo a Kingenga, killing many people and capturing others, before moving to join Bruto in a joint attack on Nambu a Ngongo. Nambu a Ngongo, however, reinforced with Dutch troops, destroyed Bruto's force on 24 September 1642.[176]

---

[170] ARA OWIC 57, João IV to Pedro Cezar de Meneses, 26 October 1641 letter intercepted by the Dutch, *ACA* 1: 123–5.

[171] Minutes of Luanda Council, entry of 7 November 1641, *ACA* 1: 255.

[172] ARA OWIC 69, Deliberations of High Council of Brazil, 31 December 1641, *ACA* 1: 153–4.

[173] Noted in the Registro de Camara de Ambaca, p. 127, Certificão de Francisco de Saraiva, 29 November 1642, Biblioteca da Universidade de Coimbra (BUC) MS 1505, unpaginated (notes on archives made in the mid-eighteenth century) noting her threat was felt at Ambaca by 7 July; Cadornega, *História* 1: 292. Most of the local powers welcomed her and declared their loyalty, but she had to attack an insubmissive Kitexi ka Ndambi.

[174] Cadornega, *História* 1: 278–80, 286.

[175] Cadornega, *História* 1: 261–2; ARA OWIC 57, Relation of late 1641–early 1642.

[176] Cadornega, *História* 1: 287–91.

Although the Portuguese were rampaging in the Dembos, strains began to appear in Kongo–Dutch relations. The Dutch, concerned about the cost and risk of extensive military operations, were content to control trade through possession of a few strategic coastal points and to that end signed a treaty with the Portuguese on 30 January 1643. Garcia, however, wanted total expulsion of the Portuguese and wrote emphatically that "I do not consent that in any of my lands or ports that any Portuguese have his house or his commerce and if their ships come to these places, do not deal with them and let them go back."[177] Acting on Garcia's directives, on 17 May 1643 a joint Kongo–Dutch army sacked the Portuguese post at Gango on the Bengo. Many Portuguese and their African allies were killed or captured, including governor Pedro Cesar de Meneses, and some were sent as prisoners to Brazil, leading the remaining Portuguese forces to withdraw to Massangano.[178] In addition, the Dutch agreed to send 50 soldiers to assist Garcia to suppress a rebellion in Nsala, a rebel area just north of the Dembos.[179]

The Dutch, however, had no long-range plan to drive the Portuguese out of Angola and signed a new Dutch–Portuguese treaty on 1 July 1643 that established two zones of authority and regulated commerce between the two powers.[180] With this treaty, the Portuguese capitalized on Dutch reluctance to fight to reassert their authority in the area around Masangano and Ambaca, fighting in Mbwila and along the Zenza, as well as harshly pacifying the *sobas* of Musseque who were suspected of cooperating with Njinga or the Dutch.[181] The daring escape that Governor de Meneses made from the Dutch allowed him to reassume the governorship

---

[177] ARA OWIC 59, Garcia II to Dutch Governor of Brazil, 20 February 1643, read in conjunction with the Portuguese translation in *MMA* 9: 13–16 (see pp. 15–16) as a clue to the original language. He proposed sending the Portuguese to Benguela if it were too hard to send them to Brazil.

[178] Treaty details are reviewed in Saccardo, *Congo e Angola* 1: 288–90; OWIC 57, Nieulant and Mortamer to Count van Nassau and Brazil Council, 16 September 1642; OWIC 58, Nieuland to Brazil Council, 31 October 1642 (complaints of Garcia); for details of the attack on Gango see Livro de Camara de Ambaca, p. 130, Certidão of Pedro Cezar de Menezes, 8 October 1645, extract in BUC MS 1505; for details see Cadornega, *História* 1: 462–8, see also Diogo Lopes de Faria, 17 May 1643, *ACA* 1: 467 (Jadin cites this document in AHU, but it is not presently in Cx 4 as it should be).

[179] Dapper, *Naukeurige Beschrijvinge*, pp. 186–7.

[180] Cadornega, *História* 1: 319.

[181] Livro de Registro de Camara de Ambaca, p. 129, Certifacão de Antonio Teixeira de Mᵃ extract in BUC MS 1505 (Mbwila and Zenza); AHU Cx 4, doc. 25 Devassa of Antonio de Abreu de Miranda, 8 August 1643.

at Masangano in early 1644, and the Portuguese pressed the war against Imbangala bands in Libolo, south of the Kwanza.[182]

Without further Dutch support, the African authorities pushed their own strategies. Garcia invited Njinga to assist him in suppressing a revolt in Wandu, and Ninga promptly dispatched her general Njinga Mona to pillage the rebel province for three days.[183] More importantly, Njinga turned to defend her ally Ngolome a Keta near Ambaca, who had appealed to her for help against the newly revived Portuguese army. Early in 1644 Njinga routed the Portuguese force, inflicting heavy casualties on them and capturing prominent Portuguese and Imbangala captains and many slaves.[184] Following this crushing defeat the Portuguese could do no more than encourage *sobas* who had joined the Dutch to return to them, as they anxiously awaited reinforcements from Brazil.[185]

Although Imbangala bands destroyed the first reinforcement contingent that came from Brazil, on 26 October 1645 the long-expected reinforcement under Francisco de Sotomaior arrived safely in Massangano.[186] Included among de Sotomaior's forces was a company of soldiers of Angolan descent from the Afro-Brazilian Henrique Dias Regiment, already famous for fighting the Dutch in Brazil.[187] With these reinforcements, the Portuguese were able to make a minor offensive against Kongo and capture slaves,[188] but Njinga remained a major threat, and they turned to attack her. Njinga's lieutenant, Gaspar Aquibata, in a daring raid, pillaged the village of a rich African freeman and Portuguese ally living near the fort at Ambaca.[189] In late January 1646 the full Portuguese army invaded Njinga's temporary capital at Cavanga and handed her a crushing defeat. In the aftermath of the defeat they captured her sister Barbara Mukambu, sacked the capital, and released a number of

---

[182] Cadornega, *História* 1 344.

[183] Cadornega, *História* 1: 325–8 (the editor's note placing this battle in 1648, pp. 328–9, no. 3 is in error; see Sousa Coutinho letter, 6 September 1643, *MMA* 9: 64). There was indeed another attack in 1648.

[184] Cadornega, *História* 1: 346–55; see also Francisco Sotomaior to João IV, 13 September 1645, *MMA* 9: 355.

[185] ARA OWIC 9, XIX to Directors of Luanda, 6 July 1645.

[186] "Relação da viagem que fizerão o Capitão Mor Antonio Teixeira de Mendonça ... April-June 1645," *MMA* 9: 332–44 (first expedition), the second one is carefully reconstructed in Saccardo, *Congo e Angola* 1: 306–309.

[187] Cadornega, *História* 1: 380; for the significance of this company, see Alencastro, *Trato dos viventes*, pp. 228, 259.

[188] ARA OWIC 61, J. V. Rasenberg to XIX, 10 December 1645.

[189] Cadornega, *História* 1: 389–90.

Portuguese whom Njinga had captured at Ngolomene a Keta.[190] When they looted Cavanga, they discovered a number of letters that Njinga's other sister, Graça Kifunji, had written regularly to her from Luanda, where she had been a prisoner of the Portuguese since 1629. In the letters Graça had detailed Portuguese military plans against Njinga. When the Portuguese realized the duplicitous role Graça had played they drowned her in a whirlpool in the Kwanza River. Barbara, the other sister, escaped the same fate only because the Portuguese captain believed that she was partial to their cause.[191] Cesar de Menezes, however, continued the war against Njinga as he encouraged the Imbangala of Kasanje to attack her, and Kasanje obliged by occupying and pillaging Kituxila, an ancient capital of Ndongo.[192] Although temporarily weakened and forced to escape from the Portuguese occupied areas, Njinga nevertheless went north and attacked Wandu again and took "many slaves."[193]

The Dutch directors in Luanda, concerned with Njinga's defeat and the Portuguese resurgence, decided to adopt a much more aggressive strategy, not only to assist their ally but also to use this occasion to attempt to conquer and subject all the Portuguese in Angola.[194] In September, they began raiding all along the Kwanza almost up to Masangano and then in February 1647 made an unsuccessful attempt to storm Muxima with a river fleet.[195]

Finally the grand alliance that the Dutch had envisioned finally materialized as 400 Dutch soldiers, soldiers from Kongo, other African soldiers from *sobas* loyal to the Dutch, and 8,000 battle-hardened archers from Njinga's army moved against a Portuguese army consisting of 30,000 African archers, 600 Portuguese and Luso-Africans, and a force of Imbangala. The armies met at Kombi north of Masangano on 29 October 1647 and the Portuguese were routed: over 3,000 of the Portuguese-led army were "cut in pieces and beaten to death without counting the wounded or those captured by our [Dutch] black soldiers or those captured by us." The victorious army ruined 200 villages and the Portuguese rural properties right up to the presidios of Masangano, Muxima, and Cambambe.

[190] Cadornega, *História* 1: 394–406; 421–7. The Portuguese captured no less than 500 firearms from her camp; António Teles da Silva to João IV, 18 December 1646, *MMA* 9: 471.
[191] Cadornega, *História* 1: 418.
[192] Cadornega, *História* 1: 429.
[193] Dapper, *Naukeurige Beschrijvinge*, p. 186.
[194] ARA OWIC 10, XIX to Luanda Directors, 1 August 1646.
[195] Cadornega, *História* 1: 437–41, 462. The date is given in statement of Francisco Pinheiro, 10 March 1649, *MMA* 10: 329.

Njinga laid siege to Muxima, supported by three Dutch artillery pieces,[196] though she lost 900 soldiers in an attempt to storm Ambaca.[197] Sure of success, she called a general gathering at Kwanga, near Masangano, and demanded that all the *sobas* of the region recognize her as their queen "and natural lord."[198] An attempted Portuguese counterattack in Ilamba in June 1648 was also defeated, costing them that region as well.[199]

Njinga realized no long-term benefit from her greatest victory over the Portuguese, however. On 12 August 1648, another large relief expedition from Brazil under Salvador de Sá landed on the coast south of the Kwanza and found Luanda weakly defended, as the bulk of the Dutch army was fighting at Masangano. Faced with the Portuguese counterattack, the Dutch command in Luanda capitulated, and their army surrendered on 25 August.[200] Njinga, lacking Dutch support, had to raise the siege of Massangano and was forced once again to withdraw to the north and, as earlier, pillaged Wandu before she finally returned to her old base in Matamba.[201] The following year, Salvador de Sá gained back the submission of many of the *sobas* around Luanda, retook the Bengo area in a harsh campaign, relieved Masangano and Muxima, and established a force to patrol the Kwanza.[202] Moreover, Salvador de Sá and Kongo's king Garcia came to a tacit agreement not to meddle in each other's affairs, though they would wrangle over treaty terms for three more years.[203]

The Coastal Phase: The Kongo–Soyo Civil War, 1641–1650

As much as Garcia wanted to expel the Portuguese with Dutch help, his efforts were hampered by the continuing civil war and dissentions in

[196] "Extract van seeckeren brief, gheschreven uyt Loando... "(The Hague, 1648) [in collection Pamflet Knuttel 5780] published as appendix in S. P. L'Honoré Naber, "Nota van Pieter Moortamer over het gewest Angola...," *Bijdragen en mededeelingen van het Historisch Genootschap* 54 (1933): 41–2 (the Dutch version). Portuguese versions are in Cadornega, *História* 1: 498–500 and testimony taken 30 August 1648 from Portuguese survivors, published in *Arquivos de Angola*, 2nd series, 2 (1945): 149–64; see also Testimony of Pilot Manuel Soares, 11 November 1647, *MMA* 10: 69–70, which put the Portuguese force at 30,000. There were many popular stories about the siege of Muxima and the miraculous actions of their statue of the Virgin Mary, see MSS Araldi, Cavazzi, "Missione Evangelica," book 2, pp. 55–8.
[197] MSS Araldi, Cavazzi, "Missione Evangelica," book 2, p. 54.
[198] MSS Araldi, Cavazzi, "Missione Evangelica," book 2, p. 75.
[199] Cadornega, *História*, 1: 521–3.
[200] Based on testimony of Antonio do Couto, 31 August 1648, *MMA* 10: 228–42.
[201] BN Madrid, MS 3533, de Teruel, "Descripcion Narrativa," pp. 88–90.
[202] Cadornega, *História* 2: 24–6; 62–3 (this last part involves the Kwanza force).
[203] On the vagaries of the treaty, see the best treatment in Saccardo, *Congo e Angola* 1: 397–401, in English, see Hilton, *Kingdom of Kongo*, pp. 165–6.

Kongo. This insecurity at the beginning of his reign manifested itself in lawlessness in Mbamba and Mpemba, where he attempted to consolidate his control. Dutch traveling from Luanda to São Salvador in 1642 commented on the situation, noting that the region was infested with noblemen "or king's children" who had "fallen into the king's disfavor" and who maintained troops of bandit soldiers, plundering travelers "until they are back in the king's grace."[204] A Capuchin visitor, Giovanni Francesco da Roma, who lived in Kongo from 1645 to 1646 noted the depopulation war in Mbamba had caused and commented that "the elders of that nation, remembering happier times, usually say customarily: Congo is no longer Congo."[205]

The trouble in Mbamba and Mpemba was minor compared with the formidable resistance Garcia faced in Soyo, which became a focus of intrigues and conflicts. Upon the death of Count Paulo in 1641, Daniel da Silva, with his allies in court, claimed the office. However, Garcia disputed the election and refused to confirm him, claiming that this right was a royal prerogative. For his part da Silva contended that "election by his subordinates was enough to invest him in his new rule, and he needed no other."[206] By 1648 da Silva continued to assert this claim, writing in 1648 that "I am a vassal of the King of Conguo, but of all his vassals, only those of this county make their own Count when one dies."[207]

This dispute over rights of succession led to open warfare when Garcia invaded Soyo in 1641 at the same time that the Dutch invasion of Luanda was under way.[208] Soyo repelled this attack, and Garcia made another attempt in 1645. Da Silva's men again defeated the invaders and captured Garcia's son, Afonso, on 10 April. The Duke of Mbamba's attempt to rescue Afonso was also repelled on 25 July.[209] Although Garcia failed to recover his rights in Soyo, he succeeded in stamping out dissention in other areas of the kingdom by the mid-1640s. All of these disturbances created a climate favorable to the enslavement of ordinary Kongolese.

---

[204] Dapper, *Naukeurige Beschrijvinge*, p. 199.
[205] Da Roma, *Breve Relatione*, p. 54. The expression is best stated in Kikongo: *Kongo ke Kongo ko*.
[206] Dapper, *Naukeurige Beschrivinge*, p. 211. His patron in Mbamba was likely Daniel da Silva, who was defeated by Garcia and his brother Álvaro in 1633. Paulo's spirited defense of their patron, King Álvaro IV, was perhaps connected to Daniel's patronage and claims on his office.
[207] Daniel da Silva, Count of Soyo to Pope Innocenzio X, 25 March 1648 *MMA* 10: 123–4.
[208] Dapper, *Naukeurige Beschrijvinge* p. 211–12.
[209] Giovanni Bernardo Falconi to Propagande Fide, 26 August 1646, *MMA* 15: 607; Da Roma, *Breve Relatione*, pp. 47–9.

The Interior Phase: Kisama, the Dembos, Matamba, and Kasanje, 1650–1660

Having reestablished themselves in Luanda and the immediate interior, the Portuguese moved against rulers they deemed disloyal during the Dutch period. Salvador de Sá made two such campaigns, the first in 1650 south of the Kwanza into Libolo with the specific instructions to avenge the defeat and destruction of the relief forces sent to Angola in 1645. On this campaign they brought back slaves and cattle taken in the "lands of the Quimbundu [Ovimbundu]" in the central highlands.[210] To recover their prestige in the Dembos area that had backed Njinga during the war, as well as to retrieve runaway slaves, Captain General Antonio Teixeira de Mendonça mustered the army of Hari a Ngola, loyal Imbangala, settlers and their slaves and paid soldiers and *soba's* levies. With this force he attacked northward to Mbwila, besieging its capital, and forced its ruler to renew his vassalage to Portugal while also capturing thousands of slaves.[211] Portuguese forces followed this up the next year with a campaign to build a fort at Mangombe in the southern part of Mbwila's domain, again capturing many slaves.[212]

With the Portuguese reestablished in their former domains, the question of how aggressive Angolan governors should be in conducting wars to capture slaves versus how much they should devote resources to creating the right commercial environment for the trade in slaves again came to dominate discussions. Salvador de Sá had fought his wars in the name of revenge and, having achieved his goals, left Angola in March 1652.[213] His successor, Rodrigo de Miranda Henriques, now faced the problem of justifying further fighting to obtain slaves in the face of the still longstanding royal prohibition against offensive wars. The Ouividor of the kingdom, Bento Teixeira de Saldanha, relaying discussions held in Angola, wrote to Portugal in July 1652 contending that the slave trade was "the only resource of this Conquest, which in former times they had by trading in the markets or by capture in war." He asked permission to fight against "the King of Congo, Ginga, and the Province of Quissama" because they impeded the trading option. In his opinion war was the only way to obtain slaves and to clear the routes.[214]

---

[210] Cadornega, *História* 2: 43–6.
[211] Cadornega, *História* 2: 53–61.
[212] Cadornega, *História* 2: 67.
[213] See Salvador de Sá's boastful letter to João IV, 6 October 1650, MMA 10: 571–2.
[214] Consulta of Conselho Ultramarino, 14 December 1652, MMA 11: 245.

The Crown was reluctant to support another round of wars, and royal response was first to deny past actions by African rulers as grounds for war but to allow it if present or future actions blocked commerce or prevented evangelization or if Africans allied with enemies of the Crown to attack Portuguese vassals.[215] These instructions explain why governor Miranda Henriques did not fight any wars during his term and even dismantled the fort built by Salvador de Sá near Mbwila.[216]

If the Portuguese in Angola were not making war, the neighboring African states were – and capturing thousands of slaves. In the east, Njinga and Kasanje, who had fought each other during the Dutch occupation, were now redefining their zones of influence through fighting against each other. Although there are no records of their activities from 1649 to 1655, it seems certain that they fought both their neighbors and each other, as they would continue doing in the following period. In 1655, in fact, Njinga's army attacked Pombo Samba, a land lying just east of Mbwila.[217] Njinga's correspondence from this period is telling, dated from her *quilombo* or "army," and complaining of having been forced "to stay all the time in the country with my army ready to defend myself."[218] Her army was in a perpetual state of mobilization and was located in the central part of Matamba to protect her from enemies within and without, so she could be recognized as "queen of all." Her army enforced this order and provided defense. In her speech to her army on 31 January 1657, Njinga thanked them for capturing slaves that she used to ransom her sister, Barbara, from the Portuguese.[219] This situation put her in possession of a ready and constant supply of captives for trade.

Kasanje, who, like Njinga, had established a permanent armed camp (*kilombo*) in a strategically located area in the Ngangela region along the Kwango, also became a source of slaves. His constant wars supplied slaves to the Luso-African slave-trading community in his capital. When the Italian Capuchin Antonio da Serravezza came to Kasanje's lands in 1655 to minister to the religious needs of the Luso-African Christians, he

---

[215] Crown to Luis Martins de Sousa Chichorro, 16 September 1653, *MMA* 11: 328–9.
[216] Cadornega, *História* 2: 71, 80.
[217] Gaeta, *Maravigliosa Conversione*, p. 107–112 (the place is listed as Embulla = Mbwila); MSS Araldi, Cavazzi, "Missione Evangelica," book 2, p. 115 (giving the exact place as Pombo Samba, but placing it in Wandu).
[218] Gaeta, *Maravigliosa Conversione*, pp. 88, 100.
[219] Serafino da Cortona to Governor General, 21 March 1657 (Italian version), *MMA* 12: 108.

noted that Kasanje had no other aim in life than to "spill human blood" in "making unjust war against all his neighbors," including the lands of "Queen Zinga of Matamba, the Provinces of Lubolo, Bembe, Oacco [Haku], Songhe [Songo] and others."[220] Kasanje's military adventures had extended further, to the kingdom of Yaka, for he had captured a son of the king "who reigns in a kingdom situated at the frontiers of Casangi and Queen Singha, on the far eastern border of the Kingdom of Congo." These wars had created such a diversity of people in his camp that Pasqual Fernandes Quemba, a Luso-African resident there, spoke Kikongo, Kimbundu, the Yaka language, and Umbundu.[221] In 1656, Cavazzi learned that an army from Kasanje had penetrated as far east as Libolo.[222] The next year, a raiding party was repelled and destroyed by Hari a Ngola's forces in Ndongo on 6 May 1657.[223]

Undeterred, in October 1657 a great Kasanje army bridged the Kwanza and crossed to Bembe, which it despoiled mercilessly before turning north and pillaging the lands of Gunza Mbambe, "Lord of Oacco and Tamba." Gunza Mbambe, cowed by Kasanje's threat to return "and kill them all," met his council and decided to become Christian and seek Portuguese protection and vassalage. As they reasoned in the debate, Portuguese vassalage was the lesser of two evils, because it was "tyranny of robbery and not of blood."[224] Ninga's people continued to remain vigilant about attacks by Kasanje's forces, and in 1659 they had to interrupt Mass when a warning sounded of an attack by Kasanje. They immediately sent out scouts and called up a general mobilization though the attack proved to be only a rumor.[225] Like Njinga's violence, the wars of Kasanje supplied a steady stream of captives to the Luanda market.

Although Portuguese warfare slackened after 1652, Luis Martins de Sousa Chichorro, who arrived in Luanda in 7 October 1654, renewed the militant traditions of governors of the 1620s. In a memorandum written in 1653 before his embarkation for Luanda, Sousa Chicorro, noted that slaves, which were few at that time, were the "only resource of the residents" of Angola, and to have them he "had to order wars against the King

---

[220] Archivio Provinciale de' Cappuccini da Toscana, Florence, Filippo Bernardi da Firenze, "Ragguagli del Congo..." MS of c. 1720, p. 383.
[221] Archivio Provinciale de' Cappuccini da Toscana, MS, Antonio da Serravezza, "Ragguaglio del Frutto delle Missioni del Congo," 1658, fol. 8.
[222] MSS Araldi, Cavazzi, "Missione Evangelica," vol. B, p. 448.
[223] MSS Araldi, Cavazzi, "Missione Evangelica, vol. B, p. 587.
[224] MSS Araldi, Cavazzi, "Missione Evangelica," vol. B, pp. 475–81.
[225] MSS Araldi, Cavazzi, "Missione Evangelica," book 2, pp. 151–2.

of Congo, Queen Ginga and the Province of Quissama."[226] Njinga recognized the role of the Sousas in shaping Portuguese policy concerning her, as she was accustomed to say, that "the Sousa House had killed her and brought her back to life," meaning that João Correa de Sousa had "given her a soul" by baptizing her in 1622 and that Fernão de Sousa had "killed her by throwing her out of the Kingdom, for which reason she became a Jaga," in 1626–1629. Luis Martins de Sousa Chichorro saved her "by giving her her sister and Priest [he] brought back her soul and body to being Christian."[227] His negotiation of a peace treaty with Njinga, which he began as soon as he arrived and finalized on 12 October 1656, caused her to renounce the Imbangala elements of her lifestyle and reembrace Christianity. The treaty guaranteed her borders and independence as well as Portuguese recognition of her choice of successors while establishing Portuguese claims to much of the lands formerly under Ndongo. The most important outcome for the Portuguese was that it guaranteed access to the slave markets of Matamba.[228] As with João Correa de Sousa's negotiation with Njinga in 1622, it left the Portuguese free to focus their military forces on other areas, notably Kisama and Kongo.

Kisama, the vast province south of the Kwanza once claimed by Ndongo, was as much a thorn in de Sousa Chichorro's side as Kasanze had been in the days of Correa de Sousa – a refuge for runaway slaves and a threat to the navigation of the Kwanza. In 1655, Sousa Chirchorro mounted a major and very expensive campaign into Kisama. His move was more like a great slave raid than an attempt to bring the area into submission, however. The army built a large armed camp in the area and conducted raids in all directions from it, making surprise attacks to gather supplies and capture people. These raids were not without casualties for the Portuguese, which led Cadornega, their chronicler, to compare them with glorious wars fought in India and not simply as wars of "Cuata, cuata" or slave raiding wars.[229] This type of raiding continued, for no sooner had the army returned to Ambaca than some of the soldiers were sent on a raid to Gemgembo in the north.[230]

---

[226] AHU Cx 6, doc. 92, Sousa Chicorro letter, 16 September 1653.
[227] MSS Araldi, Cavazzi, "Missione Evangelica," book 2, p. 108.
[228] For a detailed treatment, see Saccardo, *Congo e Angola* 1: 514–16; the treaty itself is in *MMA* 12: 57–60.
[229] Detailed description in Cadornega, *História* 2: 88–127. Chronological details in Consultas of Conselho Ultramarino, 13 July 1655, 4 September 1655, *MMA* 11: 498–501, 514–17; King to Governor of Angola, 6 December 1656, *MMA* 12: 87.
[230] Cadornega, *História* 2: 135.

In Kongo, meanwhile, the continuing intrigue and political in-fighting gave Sousa Chichorro another opportunity to invade the country in hopes of encouraging chaos. Garcia had been unable to resolve the opposition to his succession from his rivals. He was still troubled by what he considered the illegal usurpation of Daniel da Silva in Soyo, and in 1655 he made one more unsuccessful attempt to unseat him. Garcia tried to rebuild his army by encouraging Portuguese-held slaves in the border regions to join his forces.[231]

Soyo's defiance led Garcia's rivals for the throne, especially the resident Marquis of Mpemba, Álvaro, son of King Pedro II and Álvaro's two brothers, who lived in São Salvador, to plot against him. On 29 March 1657, Garcia discovered the plot and arrested and executed the two brothers in São Salvador, but Álvaro escaped by fleeing from Mpemba with his armed forces and seeking refuge in Soyo.[232] Álvaro became the rallying point for all who opposed Garcia, and in a short time he had a growing army of 5,000 archers and 100 musketeers as others implicated in the plot joined him.[233]

Meanwhile, the complaints of the Portuguese slaveholders in Luanda that Garcia had lured their slaves to Kongo gave Sousa Chichorro the legal opening to start another campaign against Kongo, even though the Portuguese king had explicitly forbidden it.[234] After first presenting an ultimatum for the return of slaves, to which Garcia half-heartedly responded,[235] Sousa Chichorro sent an army into Kongo in mid-1657 to assist Álvaro, who, he argued, had more rights to the throne than Garcia. However, the troops did not go far into Kongo; the captain of the forces stopped them from crossing the Loze River, because he had heard that Álvaro had already been killed by Garcia.[236]

In 1659 the new governor, João Fernandes Vieira, who had come from Brazil, where he owned plantations, was all too ready to move against Kongo, as such a campaign would allow him to acquire slaves. For his first

---

[231] AHU Cx 6, doc. 61, Consulta of 3 Aug 1656, attached document; summary of Consulta of Conselho Ultramarino, 3 August 1656, *MMA* 12: 42, see also João IV to Sousa Chichorro, 27 September 1656, *MMA* 12: 56 based on information in a letter of 25 February 1656.

[232] BN Madrid, MS 3533, de Teruel, "Descripcion Narrativa," pp. 125–6.

[233] Biblioteca Estense, Modena, Monari, pp. 554–6 (copy of a chronicle, probably by Giacinto Brugiotti da Vetralla, c. 1659).

[234] Royal Letter to Sousa Chichorro, 27 September 1656, *MMA* 12: 56.

[235] King to Cabido of See, Congo, 19 April 1657, *MMA* 12: 113–14; Junta of Declaration of War, 9 June 1657, *MMA* 12: 124–5.

[236] Cadornega, *História* 2: 131–5.

two years as governor, Fernandes Viera made two lengthy wars into southern Kongo, the first against Ngoleme a Kaita, just north of Ambaca,[237]
and the second, a much longer one, against Dandi a Ngonga and Kitexi
ka Ndambi.[238] During the second campaign, Álvaro, the former Marquis of Mpemba, sought to join the Portuguese forces but was caught
in ambush by the forces of the Duke of Mbamba and slaughtered.[239]
Unable to make the joint action, the Portuguese army in the field deserted
en masse, angered at being made to pay the expenses of the governor's
war in the two grueling campaigns.[240] The Camara of Massangano registered a complaint that the district had been reduced to a "miserable
state" by the war and that the vassal *sobas* had suffered serious losses
"to their morindas."[241] Thwarted in his Kongo campaign, he then turned
south, hoping to capitalize on the alliance with Gunza Mbambe in Libolo.
A Portuguese-led army marched deep into the central highlands in 1660
but met a powerful force at Kilembi Lembi and was annihilated.[242] All
throughout these campaigns, traders followed the armies, acquiring captives whom they fed into the slave trade.

War, Chaos, Rivalries, Trade, and Enslavement, 1607–1660

The Volume of the Slave Trade, 1607–1641

During the early period of the seventeenth century, the wars and resulting
chaos saw the numbers of slaves exported from Central Africa to Brazil
and the Spanish Indies double from the 5,000 annual exports of the latter
part of the sixteenth century. Over the entire period from 1607 to 1660,
regardless of the strategy employed, the annual legal exports from the
region ran around 9,000 captives and could be as high as 12,000, if estimates for smuggling are included.[243] This increase explains why Fernão

---

[237] Cadornega *História* 2: 141–9; AHU Cx 8, doc. 8, Report of Bartholemeu Paes Bulhão,
16 May 1664.

[238] Cadornega, *História* 2: 150–6. For the demands of the Luanda merchants, Petition of
Camara of Luanda, 29 April 1659, *MMA* 12: 231–32; and his response, Declaration of
War, 11 March 1659, *MMA* 12: 223–30.

[239] BN Madrid, MS 3533, de Teruel, "Descripcion Narrativa," p. 155.

[240] Cadornega, *História* 2: 153–7.

[241] BUC 1505, Livro da Camara de Massangano, p. 17, Assento da Camara de Massangano
de 1 de Agosto de 1659, referring to wars of 1658.

[242] Cadornega, *História* 2: 157–60; Cavazzi accompanied this army as chaplain and left his
own long account, MSS Araldi, Cavazzi, "Missione Evangelica," vol. B, pp. 516–37.

[243] These figures are drawn from Heintze, "Ende," pp. 112–15 and 139–42, for the period
1611–26; The 1606 estimate, based on custom revenues, see Caderno de Manuel Ceveira

de Elvas and the later holder of the *asiento* were able to deliver so many slaves to the Indies from the Angola contract alone. This also explains why Central Africa came to replace the Upper Guinea Coast as the main supplier of slaves and why British and Dutch privateers and traders acquired so many central Africans for their emerging colonies.

There is no continuous record of slave exports from Central Africa for most of the seventeenth century, though the Portuguese government did keep detailed tax books that have not survived. Some estimates of the trade were based on a direct study of the records at the time, whereas extracts have survived. The total volume of the trade was greater than the tax records indicate, because smuggling and tax evasion on the part of shippers and government officials were widespread. A modern historian, Beatrix Heintze, has estimated that Mendes de Vasconcelos's campaigns (waged in 1618–1621) resulted in the export of as many as 50,000 people as slaves, taking account of the fact that taxes on many slaves were never recorded. This would put the yearly export at about 12,500 slaves, probably the largest three-year run of slave exports in the history of West Central Africa up to that time.[244] Heintze's estimate is supported by evidence from a 1623 petition that quoted fiscal records showing that the Crown collected 232,000 milreis on the slave trade from 1616 to 1622, which would have represented a legal export of about 55,000 slaves, not including those smuggled.[245]

Governor Fernão de Sousa regime revealed a similar pattern of export to Mendes de Vasconcelas. Another run of statistics shows that taxes were paid on 18,507 slaves before leaving Angola on 79 ships between 2 December 1624 and 18 October 1626, also suggesting an average of just under 9,000 per year.[246] These statistics cover the years when de Sousa, fearing a Dutch attack, reduced the fierce military campaigns against Njinga, and a period of calm in Kongo, but it would include the first of the captives taken in the war against Njinga in 1626. Exact statistics are not

---

Pereira, 14 October 1606, *MMA* 5: 224; see also Birmingham, *Trade and Conquest*, pp. 79–80.

[244] Heintze, "Ende," pp. 208–9. Heintze's calculation is indirect, using both estimates of the time and extrapolating from customs revenue figures.

[245] AHU, Cx. 2, doc. 22, Petition of Helena Rodrigues, 4 November 1623. This petition was a lawsuit concerning the accounts of her husband in which official records are quoted. We have converted the number of slaves based on the ratio of slaves to total customs duties in a more detailed report (AHU Cx. 2, docs. 103 and 108) covering the period 2 December 1624–26 June 1626, as summarized in Heintze, "Ende," p. 235. The actual calculation yields 54,635 slaves.

[246] Studied in detail in Heintze, "Ende," pp. 235–7.

available for the following period, but in 1643 Francisco Leitão, a fiscal official in a position to examine the tax registers, contended that in the last years before the Dutch conquest "they only carried 10,000 slaves a year, and before that they carried more."[247] John Coulombel reported from Pernambuco, two months after the Dutch conquered Luanda, that "it is certain, that within the space of 6 years, the King of Spain hath had from that Country 76,000 Negros."[248] This would have put annual exports for the mid-1630s to around 15,000 before the numbers fell to 10,000 annually. These captives would certainly have included the thousands of people captured in the wars and chaos that led to the expulsion of Njinga, the wars between Njinga and Kasanje, and the Portuguese campaigns against Mbwila.

The impact of these exports is revealed in the documentation from the American side. Between 1620 and 1623, according to customs books that the Dutch captured, 15,430 slaves were imported from Angola to Pernambuco, Brazil, which averages to just under 4,000 per year.[249] Similarly, no less than 32 ships bearing 6,886 registered slaves from Angola arrived in the port of Vera Cruz alone during Mendes de Vasconcelos's term.[250] One of the many ships leaving Luanda was the *São João Bautista*, part of whose cargo was seized by the *White Lion* and *Treasurer* and which brought the first Africans to Virginia. The battle of Mbumbi also led to a very large haul. Four ships were dispatched to Bahia between 6 January and the 4 February 1623, including the behemoth *Nossa Senhora do Rosário*, burdened with no less that 1,041 people.[251] Many more victims of Mbumbi were certainly shipped out in the following months bound for Brazil and the Spanish Indies. In the following period, between 1624 and 1640, 35,000 slaves from Angola (94 percent of the total) were registered for import into the Spanish possessions in America, roughly 2,100 per year.[252] Nevertheless, tax evasion makes these figures substantially too low; the number was probably closer to 5,000 per annum.[253]

---

[247] Francsico Leitão Memorial, 4 December 1643, *MMA* 9: 86.
[248] John Coulombel's to Philip Bishop, 14 October, 1641, in *A Little True Forraine Newes*, pp. 9–10.
[249] De Laet, *Iaerlijck Verhael*, 2: 139.
[250] Vila Vilar, *Hispanoamerica*, Cuadro 3.
[251] AHU Cx. 2, doc. 98, Fernão de Sousa to King, 12 June 1626, based on certified readings of the factor's book.
[252] Calculated from Vila Vilar, *Hispanicoamerica*, cuadro 1, based on licenses issued for imports.
[253] For example, in the 18-month period cited by Fernão de Soua, some 9,070 slaves were exported and taxed from Angola bound for the Spanish Indies, an annual export rate of

The period from 1641 to 1660 was another in which West Central
Africa continued to feed slaves into the Americas, but afterward the area
would lose its primacy as the exclusive source for Africans carried to
Dutch and English colonies. The period began with the Dutch conquest of
Luanda, with hopes that Dutch Angola would become a part of "Brazil's
conquest" and that they would "feed Brazil from the lands from which
Negroes come."[254] They also planned to use Angola to carry on their eco-
nomic war against the king of Spain, for without "the Negroes of Angola,
the ruin of the Indies is inevitable."[255] Representatives of the Dutch West
India Company based their predictions of massive slave exports from
Angola on statistics that they compiled in Luanda, perhaps also hoping
to restore the annual rate of the early 1630s, when Brazil and the Spanish
Indies had received 15,000 slaves annually., Some optimistically thought
the total Angolan trade could reach 50,000–60,000 per year.[256] Queen
Njinga's lands alone, according to one of these estimates, were "over-
flowing with slaves" and 12,000–13,000 were said to be obtained from
her lands each year.[257]

The Dutch believed that they could reach the high numbers of slaves
through renewing Portuguese long-distance trading contacts, through
exploiting the existing Portuguese tribute system, or, finally, by warfare.
Despite their plans and their optimistic assessments, the Dutch failed to
realize that Portuguese exports were almost entirely the result of the

6,046 per year, yet the official license registers for those years suggests an annual import
of 2,695.
[254] ARA OWIC 56, doc. 24, "Instructie van Wegis Sijn Excie Johan Maurits grave van
nassau...voorde Heer Admirael Cornelis Cornelisz Jol De Haeren pieter Morthamer
ende Cornelis Nieulant politique Raden ende de h.Overste Lieutenant James Hinderson...van de Stadt Loanda de St. Paulo ende desse Lffs omleggen de forten"; ARA
OWIC 56, J. Maurits and Council to XIX, 20 December 1641.
[255] ARA Koninklijk Huisarchief, Johan Maurits Papers. Anonymous French report, 26
August 1641.
[256] ARA St. Gen., 5773, 11 November 1641 (15,000 to Spanish Indies); OWIC 56 Hoogen
Raad van Brazilie, 3 December 1641, Appendix A; OWIC 56 (15,000 to Brazil, based
on testimony of Portuguese merchants) Commis Elias Moet to Count of Nassau and
Council of Recife, 1641 "Eenige aen merckinghen aen gaende van stadt van St. Paulo de
Loanda voor onse Comste," Luanda 11 September 1641 (50,000–60,000 total slaves).
[257] "Schriftelijck Raport van Pr. Mortamer gewesen vaedt van Justitie de Directeur in
Loanda..." 29 June 1643, fol. 8, published S. P. L'Honoré Naber, "Nota van Pieter
Mortamer over het Gewest Angola. Een verzuimd hoofstuk onzr Koloniale Geschiedenis,
1641–48," in *Bijdragen en mededeelingen van het Historisch Genootschap* 54 (1933):
1–42 (at 30); another longer version (but identical here) is ARA OWIC 58, Report of
Pieter Moortamer to Council of Brazil, 14 October 1642 (French translation, very free,
in *ACA* 1: 334–354 at 347).

massive wars in Ndongo and factionalism and civil wars in Ndongo and Kongo. In fact, for the first months of their conquest they actually exported few Africans.[258] By the end of 1642, West India Company records showed that somewhat more than 1,500 slaves had been exported from Central Africa to their positions in Brazil, far lower than the 15,000 per annum that they had estimated.[259] These slaves, many from their older trading posts in Kongo, were bought in small lots, one report noting that "the merchants come with 20 or 30 slaves at a time to exchange a little for wine, oil, brandy and items of clothing."[260]

Apparently the English were also hoping to capitalize on the Dutch advances in Angola by anticipating a boom in exports of Angolan captives. In 1642, two English merchants, Burchett and Phillips, approached the Spanish Crown through the governor of Flanders and offered to carry "2,000 negros taken from Dutch factories in Angola" and threatened that if "Spain did not take them up they would offer it to Duke of Braganza (Portugal)." Spanish officials rejected this offer as they did a similar one made by another English merchant, Ferdinand Franklin.[261]

The hopes of exporting thousands of slaves from Angola were partly realized in 1643 when the West India Company exported a total of 4,354 slaves. More than a third of these captives, however, were "gifts" from the king of Kongo and his nobles in exchange for the Dutch military service in Kongo wars. Between the Dutch capture of Luanda and the end of 1643, Garcia II sent the Company 1,200 slaves, along with a personal gift of 170 slaves to the director, Cornelis Nieulant.[262] In addition, there were gifts from other Kongolese nobles, including smaller gifts from the Count

---

[258] ARA OWIC 57, Baltasar van de Voorde to Council of Holland, 14 January 1642.

[259] This data is culled from letters of the officials of the West India Company, especially ARA OWIC 68 and 57. It is drawn from the revised version of the DuBois Database, and our thanks to David Eltis for sharing this data with us. His list shows 10 ships during this period carrying 1,393 slaves. One additional voyage did not have statistical information. We located one additional ship, a Portuguese prize, that carried 150 slaves, ARA OWIC 57, Nieulant and Mortamer, May 1642, not found among these data.

[260] ARA OWIC 57, Nieulant and Mortamer, end May 1642; ARA OWIC 58, Nieulant to Brazil Council, 17 December 1642. Some ship movements given in ARA OWIC 57, Mortamer and Nieulant, 24 January 1642 (voyage of Diemen); ARA OWIC 57, Ouman to Recife Council, 27 February 1642; ARA OWIC 57, Cornelis Hendrikz Ouman to Brazil Council, 16 January 1642 (voyage of Leiden).

[261] Georges Scelle, *L'traite negrere aux indes de castile* (Paris, 1906), 1: 484.

[262] ARA OWIC 60, Hans Mols to XIX, 19 September 1643. The total size of the gift and the impact of mortality was eventually considered in ARA OWIC 60, Report of Council of Recife, 13 February 1645.

of Soyo.[263] These included, for example, a gift of 150 slaves to a captain sent to Kongo to assist in the suppression of the rebellion of Nsala. All the gifts were explicitly framed in the old terms, first laid down by Pedro II, of Kongo financing Dutch attacks on the Portuguese.[264] Between 1644 and 1645 the Company exported a total of 4,502 slaves.[265]

While the Company struggled to export a few thousand slaves a year, the Portuguese continued to export slaves to the unconquered regions of Brazil and through the port of Buenos Aires. From their base at Gango on the Bengo River, Governor Pedro Cezar de Menezes, led Portuguese campaigns against various "rebels" and Kongo in 1642–1643 capturing many slaves. In one encounter in 1642 the Portuguese commander António Bruto "carried many Libambos and malungas, which are prizones [restraining devices] of iron in which they keep them," some of whom ended up being purchased by the Company.[266]

Problems with payment delays from Brazil ultimately caused the European Chambers of the Company to stop dispatching ships to Angola for slaves early in 1646, and the Company, responding to this, eventually threw the trade open to private traders and taxed only the merchants.[267] Although through January 1646 the Company shipped 1,101 slaves to Brazil, slave trading by the Company to Brazil effectively ceased, and therefore Company records provide no information on the thousands of slaves who undoubtedly left Angola as a result of the Dutch/Kongo/Njinga victory against the Portuguese and their African allies. It was this situation that allowed the English to penetrate the Central African market, for between 1648 and 1649 "at least 20 English ships were engaged in the Brazil trade."[268]

The Portuguese never lost control over the slave trade from the Mbundu areas. For example, when Francisco de Sottomaior's relief expedition arrived in Masangano in August 1645 and the Portuguese took the

---

[263] ARA OWIC 9, XIX to Governor and Brazil Council, 10 October 1642.
[264] ARA OWIC 9, XIX to Governor and Council of Recife, 29 October 1643.
[265] Ratelband, *Nederlanders*, pp. 228–30; 248.
[266] Cadornega, *História* 1: 287–91.
[267] Advice of the Chamber of Accounts of the West India Company, 27 May 1647, ARA Register of West Indian Affairs, 1633–1651, in O'Callaghan, *Documents* 1: 243–4.
[268] C. R. Boxer, "English Shipping in the Brazil Trade, 1640–65," *Mariner's Mirror* 37/3 (July 1951), p. 204. Van den Boogaart and Emmer, "Dutch Participation," p. 363 contend that the lack of records following 1646 is a sign that no slaves were exported from Angola, and attribute this to a lack of supplies being sent to Brazil, but slaves taken in war did not need to be purchased with goods. A simple change in administration of the trade better explains the change in records keeping.

opportunity to invade Kongo because Garcia refused to sell them slaves, they netted 600 slaves. Garcia's retaliation, which led to the killing of more than 100 Portuguese residents in Kongo, completely stopped the slave trade, which further hurt the Dutch by depriving them of their best African trading partner.[269] Continued Portuguese ability to export slaves was demonstrated in 1645 when Pedro Cezar de Menezes left Angola by way of the Kwanza bearing more than 2,000 slaves, as the Dutch watched helplessly.[270] When the Portuguese routed Njinga's army at Cavanga in 1646 and "seized and captured many of her people," they exported many of the captives by way of the Kwanza River to Pernambuco.[271]

The period from 1648 to 1660 saw a reconfiguration of the business of slave trading, both in Angola and those areas that had been supplied with Angolan slaves. In Angola itself, when the Portuguese forces finally dislodged the Dutch following Salvador de Sá's relief expedition in 1648, the governor moved quickly to reestablish the trading conditions that had existed before the capture.[272] The Dutch, on the other hand, having lost the commerce of Luanda, were forced to fall back to their trading positions at Loango and Soyo, trading in "libongos...a lot of tacula wood, pieces of slaves, and other finely woven cloth."[273] They also continued their attacks on Portuguese slave ships leaving Luanda. Angola slaves thus continued to leave Africa on Dutch and Portuguese carriers. New carriers also joined the trade, including ships from Spain or its territories and Genoa. English and French shipping undoubtedly continued to visit ports in Central Africa as well, now with an eye to buying slaves.

From the very beginning of the reconquest of Angola, Portuguese merchants had continued to deliver slaves to Brazil, commencing with the return voyage of the ships that brought Salvador de Sá.[274] In his four years in Angola (1648–1652), the governor had sought to reestablish the trade

---

[269] ARA OWIC 61, J. van Rasenberg to XIX, 10 December 1645.

[270] ARA OWIC 10, XIX to Luanda Directors, 1 August 1646; ARA OWIC 4, Report of c. August 1646; Francisco de Sotomaior to João IV, 4 December 1645, *MMA* 9: 405. The Kwanza route had been opened by Sotomaior against Dutch helplessness, Cadornega, *História* 1: 381.

[271] Cadornega, *História* 1: 424; Mestre de Campo de Pernambuco, 27 November 1646, *ACA* 2: 866.

[272] The Dutch continued to entertain notions that they could retain some part of the Angola slave trade by cooperation with Portugal, but their trade would be confined to the Kongo and Loango ARA OWIC 64, High Council of Brazil to XIX, September–October 1648, *ACA* 3: 1078.

[273] Cadornega, *História* 2: 47.

[274] Consulta of Conselho Ultramarino, 8 July 1649, *MMA* 10: 359–60.

with the Spanish possessions that Portuguese merchants had controlled during the time of the *asiento* trade. He was particularly interested in the trade with Buenos Aires (and through it the Spanish in Peru) because these could be bought with silver, and he possessed interests in the Buenos Aires region.[275] Portuguese interest must have been successful in establishing the trade through Buenos Aires, for Tardieu, studying one notary in Cusco from 1655 to 1683 (227 slaves), found origins of 52 slaves, 38 of whom, or 73 percent were from Angola.[276] A late-seventeenth-century Jesuit plantation in Mexico showed that 78 percent of its slaves were Angolan, demonstrating the continuing dominance of Angolans in the slave trade to Spanish territories.[277]

The level of slave trading in Angola must have quickly reapproached the volume of the period before the Dutch conquest, for after the restoration Baltesar Vandunem was prepared to pay the same 30 *contos* for the slave contract that previous contractors had paid in the 1630s.[278] Although there are few quantifiable data for this period, Governor Sousa Chichorro reported that according to the books of the factor in Luanda, 13,945 slaves were exported for the first 16 months of his term (October 1654 to January 1656), a rate of nearly 10,500 per year, which he boasted was "something which had never happened in this kingdom, nor had it experienced so much opulence as it experiences today."[279] The Capuchin prefect, Giacinto da Vetralla, noted that during his time in Angola (1652–1657) an average of 5,000–6,000 slaves embarked annually for Brazil alone.[280] Although Sousa Chichorro credited the "opulence" on the reopening of trade routes, his own lengthy war in Kisama surely netted a large number. This volume doubtless continued into the term of Fernandes Vieira, who claimed in a report of 1659 that his war in Libolo

---

[275] Boxer, *Salvador de Sá*, pp. 279–82; for more detail, see Esteves, "Estudo das relações comercias."

[276] Jean-Pierre Tardieu, *El Negro en el Cusco. Los camínos de la alienación en la segunda mitad del siglo XVII* (Lima, 1998), p. 20.

[277] Created by Aguirre Beltran from their records, p. 241.

[278] Maria Luísa Esteves, "Para o estudo do tráfico de escravos de Angola (1640–1668," *Stvdia* 50 (1991): 83. Curiously, the government lowered the price in subsequent years even though the volume was as high or higher.

[279] Luis Mendes de Sousa Chichorro to King, 3 February 1656, in Maria Luísa Esteves, "Para o estudo das relações comercias de Angola com as Índias de Castela e Génova no periodo da Restauração," *Stvdia* 51 (1992): 41.

[280] Archivio "De Propaganda Fide" (APF) Scritture Originali refirite nelli Congressi Generali (SOCG) 250, fol. 197, Giacinto da Vetralla, "Nelli Schiavi che si comprono e vendero nell' Congo," cited in Saccardo, *Congo e Angola* 1: 502.

had "opened up a great commerce and *resgate* (slave trade) which is very useful to the residents of this Kingdom."[281]

Despite the Dutch transfer to Loango, they continued to participate in the Central African trade, especially to the Spanish Indies and Caribbean. Only a year after their expulsion from Angola, Amsterdam merchants approached the Spanish Crown with a proposal to sell slaves for the Indies, though the Council of the Indies rejected the idea.[282] No doubt some of these slaves were to come from both privateering and the continuing commercial links with with Soyo and Luango. In 1649 one of their privateering attacks on a Spanish vessel netted 500 slaves, and the following year, another "big haul" was brought in by Dutch warships.[283] In 1651 the Portuguese sent a fleet to Mpinda to drive off the Dutch, fearing that they would buy slaves brought in from areas that the Portuguese considered their own markets, like Matamba.[284] Their attack had no long-term effect, for in 1659 Governor Vieira was boasting of sending another Portuguese fleet against the Dutch.[285]

Between 1648 and 1657 Dutch shippers supplied some 3,800 slaves from Curaçao to the Spanish Caribbean colonies, some of whom would certainly have had Central African origins.[286] Dutch merchants, of course, also furnished slaves to the English colonies in America, as Thomas Lynch, living in Jamaica, noted in 1660, "supplied by the curtesye and trade of the Dutch, who still furnishes them at reasonable rates: Slaves Servants coppers or such things."[287]

The English merchants stayed in the Luanda market, which they had entered in the early 1640s. For example, in 1658, an English ship with a Dutch captain carried 1,200 slaves and 22,000 pounds of ivory from Angola to Brazil, and "all of the officers and some of the ordinary seamen bought Negro slaves at Luanda to adventure for their own account."[288] Moreover, in that same year the English ship the *Hopewell*, captained

---

[281] João Fernandes Vieira to Afonso IV, 10 May 1659, *MMA* 10: 238–9.
[282] Wim Klooster, *Illicit Riches*, p. 106, citing AGI, Indifferent 1668, Antonio Brun to king, 27 August 1649.
[283] Ratelband, *Nederlanders*, pp. 297–8; Boxer, *Salvador de Sá*, pp. 281–2.
[284] Cadornega, *História* 2: 63–5.
[285] João Fernandes Vieira to Afonso VI, 10 May 1659, *MMA* 10: 239.
[286] Klooster, *Illicit Riches*, p. 106.
[287] Thomas Lynch, "Consideracons about the peopling and settling of Jamaica," November 1660, quoted in Claudia Schnurmann, *Atlantishce Welten: Engländer und Niederländer im amerikanisch-atlantischen Raum, 1648–1713* (Cologne, 1998), p. 167.
[288] C. R. Boxer, "English Shipping in the Brazil Trade, 1640–65," *Mariner's Mirror* 37/3 (July 1951), p. 214.

by John Cobbs, was confiscated in Luanda and was not released until 1661.[289] This incident, however, did not discourage other English vessels from venturing into the Angolan market, for in 1659 another English ship visited Angola to load slaves.[290]

Even the Spanish took an interest in slave trading during this time, sending ships to Angola. Though the Portuguese government was moderately hostile to this, demanding bonds and insisting that they pay only in gold, silver, and jewels and carry no less than 400 slaves each, there was a trade. From 1653 to 1654 four Spanish ships came with silver and wine to get slaves for the Indies. Though the Portuguese insisted that payment be only in silver, the Spanish ships also brought wines that were in great demand in the interior, especially Kasanje and Matamba, where they "would even sell their domestics to get this wine.[291]

[289] PRO HCA 13/73, 27 June 1659.
[290] PRO HCA 13/73, 27 June 1659.
[291] Cadornega, *História* 2: 79–80; for a detailed study see Esteves, "Estudo das relações."

4

Atlantic Creole Culture

Patterns of Transformation and Adaptations,
1607–1660

The wars of conquest, factionalism, commerce, and colonization that led to the enslavement of hundreds of thousands of Central Africans drew a considerable number of their victims from regions where Atlantic Creole cultures flourished or at least had made significant inroads. In any given year this might produce captives with various degrees of exposure to Atlantic Creole culture. If defeated armies whose members became enslaved were recruited from core Atlantic Creole areas like Kongo or Massangano, then slave ships would be filled with Atlantic Creoles. However, when slave traders purchased their captives on the banks of the Kwango River there might be no Atlantic Creoles in their *libambos* (coffles). Alternatively, the civil wars that Kongo experienced might produce victims with manners and bearing similar to those of higher class status in Europe.

In addition to the political and military events that caused people who lived in the core Atlantic Creole areas to be enslaved, Atlantic Creole culture itself was expanding into new areas and incorporating more European elements in others. This expansion and Europeanization had been already visible in the first decade of the seventeenth century but would accelerate over the next half-century. Evangelization by European missionaries and local Kongo lay teachers, Portuguese efforts to regularize its administrative presence in conquered areas, and the push by the elites of Kongo and Ndongo to become major players in the Atlantic Creole complex all contributed to expansion of Atlantic Creole culture. Moreover, the mobilization of soldiers for service in the various armies in the Atlantic Creole zone, related movements of refugees to and from the colony of Angola, and the enlargement and intensification of the commercial zone centered on the Atlantic economy incorporated ordinary Central Africans into the Atlantic Creole culture as well.

We can arrange the degree of Atlantic Creole culture in Central Africa during the period along a continuum based on how much Africans had accepted European elements into their culture. By 1607, two regions formed the cores of Atlantic Creole culture: Kongo, which had chosen to mix various European cultural norms into their culture over more than a century, and Portuguese Angola, where European settlers had established an outpost that in turn had been influenced by the African culture of the local population. These two cores spread their variant of Atlantic Creole culture to intermediate and adjacent areas: Ndongo and Matamba were influenced by the Atlantic Creole of Portuguese Angola and, to a certain extent, by Kongo. Beyond this intermediate region stretched areas where there was some Atlantic Creole impact: the states north of the Congo River, such as Loango and its neighbors, and the northern Kwango valley kingdoms of Okango and Kundi, which looked to Kongo and Angola, whereas Kisama and the Libolo region looked more to Angola, often through Ndongo. All these regions supplied slaves to the Atlantic trade, and the Central Africans in the early Dutch and English colonies might have been exposed to Atlantic Creole culture from any one of these regions.

Core Atlantic Creole Regions

Kongo

Between 1607 and 1660 Christianity continued to be the most visible element of Atlantic Creole culture in Kongo and was respected grudgingly by the Portuguese, even as their expansion in Angola soured relations between the two countries. Both local Portuguese officials and the Dutch and English interlopers who began appearing in the region openly acknowledged Kongo's status as a Christian country. When the Portuguese fiscal officer Antonio Bezerra Fajardo advised the Crown on selling guns in 1612 he made a distinction between "heathens" and "Congo," even though he noted that neither should get guns.[1] The Dutch traveler Pieter van den Broecke, visiting the coastal province of Soyo in 1608, was immediately struck by the visibility of Christianity: "They are mostly Christian and go to mass every day and twice a day when it rains. They

---

[1] António Bezerra Fajardo, "Lembrança das couzas que se haõde declarar a S. Magestade tocantes ao Reyno de Angolla," 24 February 1624, *MMA* 7: 210.

maintain five or six churches" in the capital of Mbanza Soyo, "and every-one goes the whole day with a book in hand and with a rosary."[2]

Indeed, an Angolan official, João Salgado de Araújo, believed that Soyo had "70,000 souls for mass" in 1615.[3] Ferdinand van Capelle, another Dutch visitor who lived in Kongo from 1638 to 1642, noted that Chris-tianity was visible not only in Soyo and the capital of São Salvador, where there were "many churches, where Portuguese priests say mass every day and perform other ceremonies," but even in remote rural areas. "All the country is full of wooden crosses which they salute very devoutly and which they kneel down before." He noted that "every noble in his village has his own particular church and crosses," and like Van den Broecke before him, the Dutch trading factor was also impressed by the frequency with which people wore rosaries, which "most have in their hand as they pray."[4] This phenomenon was not restricted to coastal areas or the capi-tal, as even in Wandu, an eastern province visited by the Dutch in 1643, they noted that "all hold themselves as Christians" and that "one finds churches and schools there, and schools with black schoolmasters and some priests who conduct church services in the Roman fashion and in that way baptize and give communion."[5]

When Italian Capuchin missionaries first arrived in Soyo in 1645 they immediately saw the prominent cross of a small church, which was deco-rated with "ancient" statues of the Virgin Mary and Saint Anthony, and a painting of Saint Francis. The country people "threw themselves on the ground" before the priests, kissing the crucifixes and saying *Amen Mene y mene*, or "amen for ever and ever," continuing the tradition of trans-lating Christian concepts into Kikongo. Thus the crowds lined the road chanted, *Enganga augussti Zambi allassi* [*E nganga a ukisi Nzambi alazi*] ("Holy priests of God who wander about") as the priests passed to the count's palace. There, Count Daniel da Silva had a "well chosen" painting of Saint Francis in the habit of a Capuchin monk.[6]

---

[2] Pieter van den Broecke (English translation J. D. La Fleur), *Pieter van den Broecke's Journal of Voyages to Cape Verde, Guinea and Angola 1605–1612* (London, 2000), entry of September 1608, p. 59.

[3] Plan of João Salgado de Araújo, 1615, *MMA* 6: 247.

[4] ARA OWIC 46, fols. 4–5, Ferdinand van Capelle to Count Jan Maurits van Nassau and Directors, "Corte beschrijvinge van de principaelste plaetsen gelegen in Angola te weten Commo, Goby, Maiomba, Loango, Cacongo, Molemboe, Zarry, Sonho, Congo, en aderen omleggende plaetsen..." March 1642.

[5] Dapper, *Naukerige Beschrijvinge*, p. 215? (German 569).

[6] Bonaventura da Alessano to Propaganda Fide, 4 June 1645, *MMA* 9: 258–9; Gio-vanni Francesco da Roma, *Breve Relatione del svccesso della missione de Frati Min.*

Christian devotion in Kongo had intensified years before as a result of the fervent campaign launched by Álvaro I (1568–1587) following his deliverance from the Jagas in 1574. According to Duarte Lopes, his ambassador to Rome, Álvaro felt that the Jaga attack had been a divine punishment for his previous sins, and to make this right, he sought to strengthen Christianity by asking for more priests and "teachers of Holy Scripture, so that he could maintain the Catholic faith."[7] In addition, Álvaro I and his seventeenth-century successors sought to have the Vatican recognize Kongo as a fully Christian kingdom of the first rank, with all the rights and benefits that European kings enjoyed.[8] As a sign of this new fervor, Álvaro changed the name of his capital from Mbanza Kongo (or "City of Congo") to São Salvador, and soon after, the officials of the kingdom were given European titles such as Duke, Count, and Marquis.[9] Álvaro I began the process of petitioning the Vatican to have São Salvador made into an Episcopal See, a request that was granted to his son, Álvaro II, (1587–1614) in 1596. Conscious of the appropriate etiquette shown to Christian kings, in 1613 Álvaro II demanded that "priests observe the Roman ceremonial around his person."[10]

Continuing in the tradition of their predecessors, seventeenth-century Kongo kings established a wide range of Christian institutions and organizations, including the Order of Christ (established by 1607) and the Holy House of Mercy (Santa Casa de Miseracordia) founded in 1617. Between 1618 and 1619 the Vatican granted Kongo specially blessed religious medals, crosses, relics of saints, and other paraphernalia of Christian devotion.[11] In the case of the military order, Álvaro II did not wait

---

Capuccini...al Regno del Congo (Rome, 1649), pp. 19–20; Juan de Santiago to Capuchins of Castille, 11 June 1645, *MMA* 9: 286–8.

[7] Pigafetta, Chandeign, p. 179.

[8] For fuller treatment of the complicated diplomatic maneuvers for this period see Saccardo, *Congo e Angola* 1: 112–25, 131–6.

[9] In the signatures of their letters, the sixteenth-century kings of Kongo gave the name of their city as "City of Congo," a translation of the Kikongo Mbanza Kongo. Álvaro I, however, in his first extant letter, Álvaro I to Garcia Simões, 27 August 1575, *MMA* 3: 127–8, signs it "Written in this city of Salvador, 27 of August of 15." The use of European titles began later; Duarte Lopes, who left Kongo in 1583, still used the old title "Mani" for provincial rulers in his account, *Relatione*. The earliest use of such a title comes from Dom Miguel, count of Soyo, in a provision that he issued in 1593, Archivio Segreto Vaticano (ASV), Armadio (Arm) I, 91 (vol. II, Collettione di Scritture di Spagna, Tom II, fol. 125, Provision of Miguel, Count of Soyo, 4 February 1593.

[10] Álvaro II to Pope Paulo V, 27 February 1613, *MMA* 6: 129–31.

[11] Álvaro III to Juan Baptista Vives, 19 October 1619, *MMA* 6: 389, 392; Bras Correa to Juan Baptista Vives, Bras Correa to Juan Baptista Vives, 20 October 1619, *MMA* 6: 400, 405–6.

for approval and, indeed, defied demands from Spain that he desist from granting knighthoods and made the Order of Christ a central part of Kongo's military life. By 1645 both the king and even nobles "of middling sort" wore the symbol of the Order of Christ on their garments.[12] To strengthen Catholic education, in 1615 Álvaro III (1614–1622) pressed the Jesuits to establish a college in Kongo. Jesuits arrived in Kongo in 1620, and by 1625 had completed the college. To further their religious aims, the Jesuits organized lay brotherhoods for men in São Salvador in 1627, and the next year "the same zeal and piety that had seized the men" led noble women to demand and obtain one for themselves, which was then dedicated to the Blessed Virgin of the People.[13] As a further recognition of the special status of the kings of Kongo as "Expander of the faith of Jesus Christ and defender or it in these parts of Ethiopia," Álvaro III sought to establish relations with Ethiopia, the only other Christian kingdom in Africa.[14] Later rulers continued representing themselves as Christian kings and paragons of the faith, which led the first Capuchin missionaries, who arrived in Kongo in 1645, to declare that not only was the then-ruler Garcia II (1641–1661) "the most handsome man they had ever seen...with an aspect equal to that of one of the Magi kings" but also "the most ardent Catholic of all his ancestors, frequently making the profession of faith."[15]

The impact of these initiatives was soon evident in all layers of society, although it was most obvious at São Salvador and other large towns in

[12] Apparently, Álvaro I had granted these knighthoods with the permission of the King of Portugal, but in 1607 the Spanish Crown denied the right. See Considerations on Requests of Congo Ambassador, 31 March 1607, *MMA* 5: 291–292, Álvaro II asked to give habits to his nobles who had served well in the wars against his uncles and brothers, Notes on Embassy of Congo, 12 June 1607, *MMA* 5: 314. In 1617, Álvaro III asked Rome for the right to have his own order, describing its habits and devices, Instructions to Giovanni Baptista Vives, 25 October 1617, *MMA* 6: 292–3. We have not located documentary confirmation that it was granted, but the kings granted the titles for the rest of the kingdom's existence. For the use of the order's symbols in 1645, see da Roma, *Breve Relatione*, p. 99.

[13] Franco, *Synopsis Annalium*, 1627, no. 17, po. 250; and 1628, no. 20, p. 253.

[14] Juan Baptista Vives to Emperor of Ethiopia, 18 April 1617, *MMA* 6: 277–8; for a full development of the Vatican and European side of this discussion, going back to the foundations of the Jesuit mission in Ethiopia, see Richard Gray, "The African Origins of the *Missio Antiqua*," in Vicenzo Criscuolo (ed.), *Clavis Scientiae: Miscellanea de Studi offerti a Isidoro Agudo da Villapadierna in Occasione del suo 80° Compleanno* (Rome, 1999), pp. 405–23. For Álvaro III's titles, see his letter to Felipe II, 24 October 1615, *MMA* 6: 234.

[15] Giuseppe da Milano to Procuror General, 30 October 1647, *MMA* 10: 52; da Roma, *Breve Relatione*, p. 105.

Kongo, such as Soyo, and also Mpemba, whose capital "was the most Catholic in Congo" and whose schoolboys in 1652 were "well educated and already cultivated in the courts, who have a great disposition to learn."[16] Kongo's peculiar demographics, which led to one quarter of the people living within 15 kilometers of São Salvador or Mbanza Soyo, exposed this population to Kongolese Christianity.

Military service heightened the centrality of Christianity among even the rural population, especially because the people likely to be enslaved were associated with the army, including soldiers, their wives, and camp followers. Christian rituals were evident at the beginning of major battles. For example, in preparing to fight the Battle of Mbumbi in 1622, Pedro Afonso, the Duke of Mbamba, after "first confessing and receiving the Holy Sacraments, he armed himself with the relics of various saints."[17] At the high point of battle that followed, as Jeronimo do Soveral, a participant, recalled later, "our Portuguese . . . called on Santiago [Saint James Major], and the Muxicongos also, seeing this . . . said that if ours was white theirs was black. . . ."[18] When King Álvaro VI (1636–1641) faced an army of rebels from Mbata in 1637 whose numbers included non-Christians who had been inspired by a "witch" to carry poisoned animal horns, he ordered his troops to arm themselves with the crucifix and every solider attached one to his belt.[19]

In not only the army but also daily life the sense of religious identity seeped into the commoners' perceptions. Their lives came to mirror those of Christian nobility in some ways: in a marriage celebration, for example, in 1645, "even slaves dress up as if great lords, with a great escort they go to church where they hear Mass, take communion and contract marriage according to the form of the Roman Church, then go back with a great escort."[20]

European missionaries and church officials had differing assessments of the state of Christianity in Kongo. The source of these different assessments was due to the fact that Kongolese Christianity was grounded in an Atlantic Creole tradition that combined the African and Christian religious traditions. Jesuits and secular priests tended to ignore the African portion as harmless, whereas Capuchins, Dominicans, and priests like

---

[16] Cavazzi, *Istorica Descrizione* IV, no. 45.
[17] Mateus Cardoso, "Relação do que se passou em Angola no anno de 623 . . ." *MMA* 7: 178.
[18] Cadornega, *História* 1: 105.
[19] Franco, *Synopsis Annalium*, 1637, nos. 15–17, pp. 272–3.
[20] Da Roma, *Breve Relatione*, pp. 111–13.

the bishops connected to Angolan colonization (who wanted to paint a negative view of a hostile country) focused on the African portion as a major obstacle to the development of orthodox Christianity.

For example, Jesuits, who in the sixteenth century had been skeptical of Kongolese practices, changed their views radically when they returned to the country in 1619. By 1623, Jesuit Francesco Paccone could reflect the common opinion of fellow Jesuits that in Kongo "the Faith flourishes almost universally."[21] Mateus Cardoso, who helped to restore the Jesuit mission, wrote of Kongo that they "never had idols among them, nor temples where they were venerated, but only knew God who they called Zambiampungu." He shared the Kongolese view that God had "predestined them to be Christians," in which he believed they "live very constant." He was not as happy with their state of education, however. When he traveled to São Salvador in 1625, he found that in Dande there were few people who knew anything of Christian doctrine and "the most advanced only know the Our Father and the Creed in Latin, which is poorly pronounced and little understood." His solution to many of these problems was the newly published Kikongo catechism, which he distributed. He found the situation somewhat better in the small village of Mwala, whose ruler could read and had been teaching, and especially at Mbamba, where a native of the Island of Luanda was teaching prayers in Kikongo.[22]

The Jesuit Cardoso also recognized that in some places in Kongo, like the eastern provinces, there were non-Christians or people with very little regular Christian knowledge.[23] Cardoso persisted in his positive view of Christian Kongo even when he confronted evidence of a noble Christian Kongolese engaging in practices associated with indigenous religion, as did Afonso Mvemba a Mpanzu, a rebel whose base was in a remote eastern area where they were "quite given" to "superstitions, heathen rites, and fetishism" and where a royal embassy was greeted by rebel soldiers "full of fetishes."[24] He and other Jesuits in Kongo saw these practices as a part of the Kongolese environment without saying that Kongolese religion was not Christian.[25]

---

[21] Francesco Paccone to Giulio Cesare Recupito, SJ, 8 September 1623, *MMA* 7: 145.

[22] Mateus Cardoso, "Secunda ida," *MMA* 7: 371–6.

[23] [Mateus Cardoso], in António Brásio (ed.), *História do Reino do Congo (Ms 8080 da Biblioteca Nacional de Lisboa)* (Lisbon, 1969), chapter 3, fols. 3–3v, pp. 20–1.

[24] [Mateus Cardoso] "Relação do alevantamento de D. Afonso irmão do rei do Congo D. Alvaro III," 24 January 1624, *MMA* 15: 531, 535.

[25] For example, the way in which such customs are treated in Antonio Franco, *Synopsis Annalium*, probably based on the correspondence of João da Pavia, see, for example,

For all the adoption of European-style Catholicism, deportment, and education, not all clergy from Europe were as generous as the Jesuits. Arriving in Kongo in 1610, Dominican missionaries contended that after baptism Kongolese "fall in the heathen customs, augury and fetishism with the Devil who fools and blinds them."[26] Moreover, Manuel Bautista Soares, the bishop and head of the secular clergy, also did not approve of Kongo Christianity. He observed in 1619 that the king of Kongo "asks the sun and the rain from the prelates and the priests, as he asks of his fetishers, and complains when they do not give it to him, even if it is out of their hands."[27]

Capuchins who came to the region in the 1640s fired up by the ideas of the Counter-Reformation, which took aim at popular Christianity in Europe as well as in Kongo, left detailed reports of the continued existence of the older religious tradition, which they believed formed a separate and rival religion, which was as ubiquitous as were the public crosses or the saying of the rosary. Furthermore, some of them worked in the eastern regions like Mbata where there were some non-Christians, and indeed, they met people who laughed at them and dismissed their teaching, even turning their backs to preclude further discussion.[28] Their prefect, Serafino da Cortona, wrote in 1653, "There are so many superstitions and heathen rites among these people that one finds very few of their actions that do not have the poison of superstition and all of this while being baptized under the name of Christians." He went on to contend that the older religion was "as deeply in them, as Divine Law can be in the heart of a very good Christian."[29] Eventually Capuchins would conclude that some customs were not worth trying to root out as "impossible to reform these corruptions, which do not prejudice the essence of [Christian] Relgion."[30]

Their denunciations, which were much more specific than any former complaint by regular priests, included theologically significant elements such as the existence of a rival priesthood: the *nganga za ngombo,*

1637, no. 17, p. 273, where a rebel's men have taken the advice of a fisher [veneficus] and put a "deers horns drenched with poison" on their shields. The writer simply notes that the king's soldiers hung crosses on their belts.

[26] Luís de Cácegas and Luís de Sousa, *História de S. Domingos* (Lisbon, 1662), part II, Book IV, chapter XIII *MMA* 5: 611.

[27] Soares, "Relação dos costumes... *MMA* 6: 383.

[28] Cavazzi, *Istorica Descsrizione* IV, no. 13.

[29] Da Cortona, "Breve Relatione," p. 329.

[30] Cavazzi, *Istorica Desscrizione* I, no. 160.

for example, were, according to Father Serafino, the "plague, ruin and destruction of this poor Christian people," as well as "the root and origin of all superstition and greatly offend God."[31] They blamed the *ngangas* for teaching the people, "there is [not] any other life but this one, and therefore they say that what we preach about death, Judgement, Hell, and Heaven is a lie, and they ask how can a person after their death go to Heaven or Hell?" Missionaries noted that their rivals conducted public cults and rituals like the *kimpasi* ("a healing cult"), the ministrations of the *kitome* ("a priest dedicated to territorial deities"), or private divination, augury, and healing, like *nkisi* ("consecrating charms") and *kiteke* ("idols").[32] Capuchins were so aggressive in their efforts to root out these practices that they oftentimes met armed resistance, such as the confrontation at a *kimpasi* in Nkusu in 1649 where a missionary was saved only by the timely intervention of a good number of Kongolese "faithful who opposed the fetishers and allowed the Father to flee."[33] In 1652 the Belgian Capuchin priest Joris van Geel was actually killed in one of these encounters with local *ngangas*.[34]

The Calvinist Dutchman Olifert Dapper captured the spirit of this religious tradition well when he wrote, "Even though the people of Songen [Soyo] both of high and low status, consider themselves good Christians in that they cross themselves and they pray the rosary," he noted that "most of the time they have two arrows in their bows: namely the Roman Religion and their idols or the so-called fetishes. It happens that when they are in need, if one side does not give them help, then they seek it from the other."[35]

Other Dutch writers also commented on the juxtaposition of the two religious systems. In 1642 Pieter Mortamer wrote that "their religion consists of superstitions they have learned from the Portuguese; they wear a rosary around their neck and murmur the words especially where they go and where they are found." But, as a true Calvinist he contended that "among themselves they have no religious knowledge." Although he argued that the king of Kongo, Count of Soyo, and Duke of Mbamba all

[31] Da Cortona, "Breve Relatione," p. 327–8.

[32] Memorial of Bonaventura da Alessano, August 1649, *MMA* 10: 395–400.

[33] Cavazzi, *Istorica Descrizione* IV, no. 28 (confrontation in Nkusu).

[34] See Hildebrand de Hooglede, *Le martyr Georges de Gheel* (Antwerp, 1940).

[35] Dapper, *Naukeurige Beschrijvinge*, p. 215. His own, Calvinist, bias is perhaps revealed in the final part of the observation, "but they lack a great deal in their understanding and belief about the true maker of souls."

professed Christianity, none could see the sea "according to what their fetishers say, or else the beach of the island of Luanda will not longer yield great Simbes (*nzimbu* shells)."[36]

Father Serafino spoke to this intermixing of Christian and Kongo belief systems when describing oaths, "Their ordinary oaths are by the crown, the rosary, and by the souls of their dead, they do not customarily swear by God or the Saints."[37] He was put off by the attitude he met, "that it is enough to be baptized to be saved."[38] He, like his fellow Capuchins, believed that the practices could be purified by eliminating the rival priests like the *nganga ngombo*: "removing them, one would be able to reform Christianity totally."[39] Capuchins like Francisco de Veas also referred to the practices when he preached "against the idolaters, but principally against those who, even though declaring themselves Christians, follow the ministers of Satan and mix the True Faith with the adoration of idols."[40]

The efforts of the missionaries in Kongo increased the Europeanization of Kongo Christianity. With the support of the kings, the regulars tried to purify Kongo Christianity through founding the lay brotherhoods that promoted reform. When the Dominicans founded the Brotherhood of Our Lady of the Rosary in 1610, they obtained ample financial support from the king and the upper nobles who became its officers.[41] The Jesuits, in turn, founded their own brotherhoods in 1627 and 1628, and, not surprisingly, the Capuchins followed suit shortly after their arrival in the country, founding congregations of the Rosary, Saint Francis, and Saint Bonaventure, from which those who kept public concubines, panderers, and practitioners of superstitions were banned.[42]

---

[36] ARA OWIC 58, Report of Pieter Moortamer to Council of Brazil, 14 October 1642, *ACA* 1: 334–54; shorter version published by Naber in "Nota van Pieter Moortamer," found in ARA OWIC 46. "Schriftelijck Raport van Pr. Mortamer gewesen vaedt van Justitie de Directeur in Loanda ... " 29 June 1643, published S. P. L'Honoré Naber, "Nota van Pieter Mortamer over het Gewest Angola. Een verzuimd hoofstuk onzer Koloniale Geschiedenis, 1641–48," in *Bijdragen en mededeelingen van het Historisch Genootschap* 54 (1933): 1–42. This passage is on p. 30 of the Naber edition; neither report has folio numeration in original.

[37] Serafino da Cortona, "Breve Relatione dei riti gentilichi e ceremonie diaboliche e superstitioni del infelice Regno de Congo," in Calogero Piazza (ed.), *La prefettura apostolica del Congo alla metà del XVII secolo. La relazione inedita di Girolamo da Montesarchio* (Milan, 1976), p. 325.

[38] Da Cortona, "Breve Relatione," p. 328.

[39] Da Cortona, "Breve Relatione," p. 327–8.

[40] Cavazzi, *Istorica Descrizione* IV, no. 32.

[41] De Cácegas and de Sousa, *Historia, MMA* 5: 612–13.

[42] BN Madrid, MS 3533, de Teruel, "Descripcion Narrativa," pp. 38–41.

The mixed religious tradition continued in spite of the efforts of the missionaries, because the secular clergy and the lay teachers maintained a well-established approach that was tolerant of more ancient religious tradition. Interpreters also taught their local interpretation of Christianity as they translated, and the delays that translation required forced Capuchins to answer complaints from impatient people asking to be baptized and, angry that Capuchins wanted to teach them more thoroughly, others asked, "why so much caution and so much examination of the seriousness of our beliefs. Did we not come here spontaneously? We did not come just to eat all the salt that is approved to give us, as the whites do?"[43] The Jesuits, who taught both future ordained priests and the more numerous rural schoolmasters (*mestres*), had themselves tolerated it and shaped their theology to fit it, as Carodoso's historical commentary on Kongo religion demonstrated. Not surprisingly, the Capuchins saw the work of both groups as inimical to the development of the true faith.

Upper-class Kongolese were deeply tied to their vision of Christianity, which they saw as Catholic. Their resolve in this was tested by Dutch attempts to evangelize them to become Calvinist from the early seventeenth century. The Dutch did this by disseminating Calvinist literature such as "false Hours of our Lady, Bibles in popular language, and books that are formally articulated against the Roman Church and evangelical doctrine." Bishop Soares complained in 1619 that "they [the Dutch] teach their heresies to the Negros after selling them goods, eat and drink with them.... and they sought to teach pawns in their power Calvinist ideas."[44] Dutch efforts to convert Kongo increased when they captured Luanda. During their seven-year occupation, the Dutch made elaborate plans for a mission to Kongo, planning to send preachers to "win the heart of the King of Congo," with the idea that the preachers would learn Kikongo for "without this means it will be difficult to spread our religion to the blacks of the land."[45] In 1642 Peter Mortamer also thought that they should send preachers and the like to evangelize in Kongo where "the inhabitants are the most intelligent; it ought to turn their hearts towards us."[46] These actions were directly inspired by the fundamentalist zeal of

[43] Cavazzi, *Istorica Descrizione* IV, no. 6.
[44] Felipe II to Bishop, 22 February 1605, *MMA* 5: 139; [Manuel Baptista Soares] "Lembranças que fes, e deu a V. Magestade, o bispo de Congo..." 7 September 1619, *MMA* 6: 360–2.
[45] Report to XIX, 6 February 1642 (French translation) *ACA* 1: 201; ARA OWIC 9, XIX to Directors in Luanda, 14 June 1642.
[46] ARA OWIC 58, Mortamer Report, also "Schrijftlijk Raport," fol. 10 (translations from latter).

FIGURE 6. António Manuel, Kongo's Ambassador to Rome, 1618. Source: António Brásio, *Monumenta Missionaria Africana*, 1st series, volume 5 (Lisbon: Agência Geral do Ultramar, 1955), p. 401.

Calvinists and the Counter-Reformation ideas in the Catholic Church that sought the elimination and suppression of European folk beliefs and practices concerning the supernatural and in Kongo all evidence of religious practices and beliefs of local origin.[47]

Dutch efforts, however, proved futile because of the attachment that the Kongolese elite had to Catholicism. In 1624, Count António of Soyo opted against the plan to attack Luanda, citing among other reasons that "he and his subjects were Catholics or Christians."[48] Garcia II did as much in

---

[47] Keith Thomas, *Religion and the Decline of Magic* (London, 1971). The idea that European Christianity has to replace religious beliefs and practices of African origin is also found in recent scholarship on Central Africa. See, for example, Wyatt MacGaffey, *Religion and Society in Central Africa: The BaKongo of Lower Zaire* (Chicago, 1986), pp. 191–212, and James Sweet, *Recreating Africa: Culture, Kinship and Religion in the African-Portuguese World, 1441–1770* (Chapel Hill, 2003), pp. 87–102.

[48] L. M. Akveld, "Journaal van de Reis van Piet Heyn naar Brazilië en West-Afrika 1624–25," *Bijdragen en Medelingen van het Historisch Genootschap* 76 (1962): fol. 25, p. 145.

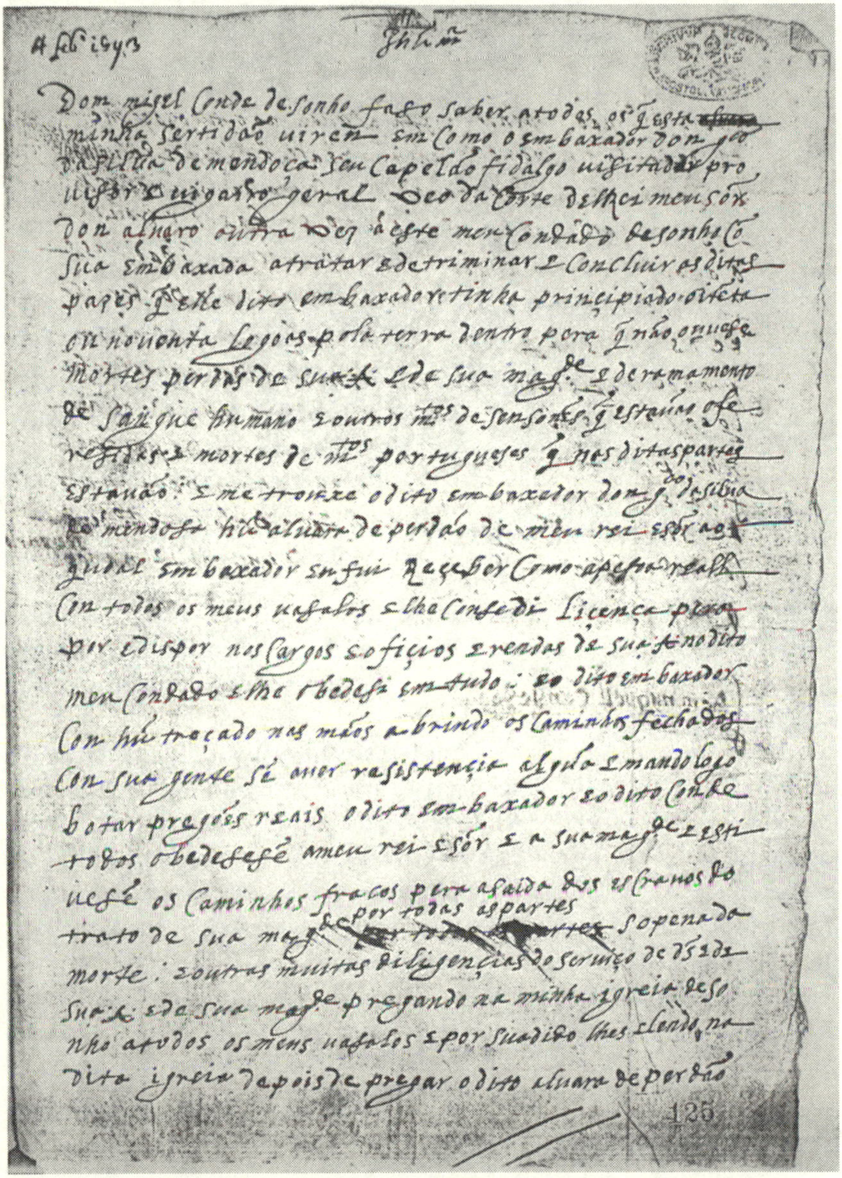

FIGURE 7. Appointment Letter of Miguel, Count of Soyo, 1593.

1642 when the Dutch attempted to send preachers to Kongo, stating, "there will not reside here any preacher or ambassador, as I believe in the True Catholic Faith and I obey the Holy Father, vicar of God; because the evil of the Portuguese, founded in ambition, is not sufficient for me

FIGURE 8. Miguel de Castro, Kongo's Ambassador to the Netherlands, 1641. Source: Paulo Herkenhoff, ed. *O Brasil e os Holandeses, 1630-1654* (Rio de Janeiro: GMT Editora/Sextante Artes, 1999).

to put aside the Catholic Faith."[49] A few years later, when the Dutch factor in Soyo tried to block the landing of Capuchin missionaries, the Count Daniel da Silva declared "that he and his people were ready to defend them with their lives."[50] During diplomatic negotiations to return a captive prince to Kongo, da Silva refused to turn him over to a Dutch middleman, saying, "He could not turn a prince and his nephew over to a heretic merchant."[51] Furthermore, in 1647 the directors in Luanda again tried to block the entrance of Catholic priests to Kongo, and Garcia wrote directly to the States General protesting that this blocked the terms of their alliance against the Portuguese.[52] However strongly the Kongolese felt about their Catholic faith, it did not prevent them from doing business with the Dutch, and this led Capuchin missionaries to complain that the Kongolese sold Christian slaves to the "heretics"[53] and to ban "those who

---

[49] Hessisches Hauptstaatsarchiv, 171 Z 4306, Garcia II to Jan Maurtis van Nassau, 12 May 1642, published in Elze M. H. Vonk Matias, "Reflexões sobre uma carta congolesa de 1642," *Stvdia* 46 (1987): 239–51 at pp. 247–8; a Dutch copy in ARA OWIC 58 was published in Portuguese translation in *MMA* 8: 584–7, we have supplied a few of the missing words created by lacerations on the text and corrected Vonk Matias's readings based on the original and the Dutch translation.

[50] Da Roma, *Breve Relatione*, pp. 23–5.

[51] Da Roma, *Breve Relatione*, p. 21.

[52] Remonstrance of Garcia II to States-General, 11 August 1647. Published as a footnote in François Bontinck, p. 71–2, no. 103 (see note 3 in *ACA* 2: 899–900, no. 3 on the provenance of the remonstrance; Da Roma, *Breve Relatione*, pp. 43–4.

[53] Bonaventura da Alessano to Secretary of Propaganda Fide, 4 June 1645, *MMA* 9: 266–7.

FIGURE 9. Servant of Miguel de Castro. Source: Paulo Herkenhoff, ed. *O Brasil e os Holandeses, 1630–1654* (Rio de Janeiro: GMT Editora/Sextante Artes, 1999).

sold free people as slaves or Catholic slaves to pagans or heretics" from joining their lay congregations.[54]

The permanent presence of the Portuguese and Luso-African community in various commercial (Mbumbi and Ngongo a Mbata) and political centers (Mpinda and São Salvador) in Kongo also helped to ease the incorporation of European elements into Kongo's Atlantic Creole culture. For example, a Jesuit report of 1623 put the number of Portuguese and Luso-Africans at 1,000, with property valued at 800,000 cruzados.[55] At São Salvador, according to a report of 1607, the Portuguese and Luso-African community resided in their own walled section of the country and had recourse to a judicial administrator appointed in Luanda.[56] They had such an easy coexistence with the African elite that both groups attended school together. When Mateus Cardoso passed Mbumbi in 1625, "famous" for its community of Portuguese and Luso-Africans, he heard their confessions, "Portuguese and natives," together – two years earlier both Portuguese and Africans served side by side against the invading army of

[54] BN Madrid, MS 3533, de Teruel, "Descripcion Narrativa," pp. 38–41.
[55] Jesuits to Lord Collector, 20 October 1623, *MMA* 15: 518.
[56] "Relação da Costa da Guiné, 1607," *MMA* 5: 385–6.

FIGURE 10. Servant of Miguel de Castro. Source: Paulo Herkenhoff, ed. *O Brasil e os Holandeses, 1630-1654* (Rio de Janeiro: GMT Editora/Sextante Artes, 1999).

João Correia de Sousa from Angola.[57] The relationship only strengthened after the Jesuits opened a Latin school (*gymnasium*) in São Salvador in 1626 "for the sons of the Portuguese and the Congolese boys who showed intelligence."[58] The contact between Portuguese and Luso-Africans and Kongos was more intimate than merely coresidence, as they frequently intermarried. A Dutch report in 1642 noted that the Portuguese had "deep roots" in Kongo, especially at São Salvador and Mbamba (Mbumbi), where most had "concubines" and many were married to local women so that "in all the country one finds black women married to them."[59]

This community was sometimes persecuted, especially when relations between Kongo and Angola soured. In 1622 Luso-Africans in Kongo

---

[57] Mateus Cardoso, "Relação da 2a ida..." 14 September 1625, *MMA* 7: 373; the Portuguese of Mbumbi signed a petition against the governor on 30 January 1623, as "we the Portuguese who are here in the army of the Catholic King Dom Pedro Afonso" [of Kongo], *MMA* 15: 522. Years later Cadornega claimed, wrongly, that they switched sides in the battle.

[58] Franco, *Synopsis Annalium*, 1626, no. 15, p. 245. A lower school taught literacy in Portuguese and was attended both by youths and some noble adults.

[59] OWIC 46, fol. 4, Capelle to Maurits, "Corte beschrijvinge."

were rescued from a general massacre by the king following the battle of Mbumbi, and in 1641 they suffered again when the Dutch invaded Angola. Even larger massacres all but drove them out of the country after the Battle of Mbwila in 1665.[60]

The Atlantic Creole culture that some Kongolese elite exhibited paralleled the bearing and outlook of educated Europeans at the time. António Manuel, the Marquis of Funta and Kongolese who headed a diplomatic mission to the Vatican (1604–1608) was an example of such an individual (see Figure 6). He was competent in Portuguese and Latin and arrived in Europe with a train of 50 servants, expecting to be treated as a "great personage."[61] He corresponded with high members of the European clergy, some of whom commented on his noble deportment and bearing. Manuel was not the only upper-class Kongolese who could move comfortably in the world of European nobles, for in 1642 when Soyo's three ambassadors to Brazil – Miguel de Castro, Bastião de Sonho, and António Fernandes – arrived in Recife, they knew Latin correctly and made several discourses in that language to Dutch officials.[62] Indeed, Kongo kings regularly received letters in Latin, Spanish, and Portuguese from Europe and from Portuguese officials in Angola, which they could translate into Kikongo for public announcements.[63] Literacy in Portuguese had become so widespread, at least among the higher classes, that observers in 1643 could write "many among them can read and write well, but only in Portuguese."[64]

Portuguese Angola

In contrast to Kongo, where there was a voluntary embrace of Christianity and Atlantic Creole culture, in the colony of Angola and the

---

[60] da Montesarchio, "Viaggio," ed. Piazza, fols. 68–68v.

[61] Teobaldo Filesi, *Roma e Congo all'inizio del 1600. Nuove testimonianze* (Rome, 1970). Antonio Manuel carried a file of letters, including many testimonials of his faith and noble deportment, with him to Rome, now in ASV Arm I, 91 (vol. II, Collett di Scritture di Spagna, Tom II, fol. 125–256v). Antonio Manuel is sometimes erroneously referred to as the Mani Vunda, from a misinterpretation of his title as Vunda and not Funta.

[62] Johann Nieuhof, *Gedenkweerdige Brasilianse Zee- en Lantreise* (Amsterdam, 1682), p. 56.

[63] Bras Correa to Juan Baptista Vives, 20 October 1619, *MMA* 6: 404; da Roma, *Breve Relatione*, p. 22.

[64] ARA OWIC 58, Mortamer Report, 14 October 1642, and "Schriftelijck Raport van Pr. Mortamer gewesen vaedt van Justitie de Directeur in Loanda...29 June 1643, fol. 9, published S. P. L'Honoré Naber, "Nota van Pieter Mortamer over het Gewest Angola. Een verzuimd hoofstuk onzr Koloniale Geschiedenis, 1641–48," in *Bijdragen en mededeelingen van het Historisch Genootschap* 54 (1933): 1–42. This report has no folio numeration in original.

Mbundu-speaking regions that bordered it, Portuguese colonial policy and interactions among the local population, settlers, and soldiers shaped the manifestations of Atlantic Creole culture. The areas of most intense interactions between Luso-Africans and Mbundu, and thus the most creolized, included the Island of Luanda and the capital Luanda and its immediate surroundings. The Luso-Africans owned estates that fed Luanda that stretched along the Bengo, Dande, and Kwanza Rivers from the coast some 50 kilometers inland and the vicinity of the Portuguese presidios of Massangano, Muxima, Ambaca, and Cambambe. A significant percentage of the African residents in these areas were slaves of the Portuguese, and, depending on the nature of their work and masters, they were pressured to convert and in turn helped to create elements of Atlantic Creole culture and religion among ordinary Mbundus. Indeed, the expansion of domestic slavery in these areas was so significant by the middle of the seventeenth century that Cavazzi estimated that one half of the Africans living among the Portuguese and Luso-Africans were slaves. One result of this situation was that Africans who would normally have lived outside the core Atlantic Creole zone were now concentrated inside it. The biggest holder of slaves in Portuguese Angola was probably the Jesuit Order, which by 1658 held 10,000 slaves on 50 plantations.[65] The threat of sale in the Atlantic tended to make these domestic slaves more receptive to their masters' cultural proclivities. "Slaves of Portuguese," wrote Cavazzi, "obey not only the word but even the signal of their masters, since they are afraid of being carried to New Spain."[66]

Those who were not slaves but comprised another significant portion of the population included African freedmen and subjects and slaves of independent *sobas* who had accepted Portuguese vassalage and interacted regularly with their Portuguese neighbors. Like the Portuguese, they worked their own plantations with slaves and were involved in the supplying food and other commodities to Luanda.

Outside of these areas of intense and often Portuguese directed interaction, the evidence of Atlantic Creole culture was more visible among the elite and less so among the common people. The elite's interest in being part of the Atlantic Creole world was shaped by political and social considerations, especially those who had sworn vassalage to the Portuguese. Portuguese officials required to them to participate in at least

[65] Sousa Chichorro to Afonso VI, 22 November 1658, *MMA* 12: 179–80.
[66] Cavazzi, *Istorica Descrizione*, book I, no. 329.

religious rituals. These Mbundu elite often found it advantageous to learn Portuguese or adopt other elements of Portuguese dress and culture. Those rulers whose lands were farther from Portuguese administration, such those of Ndongo and Matamba, or those whose lands were south of the Kwanza and the captains of Imbangala bands like Kasanje had even less direct interaction with Atlantic Creole culture. Some were outright hostile to Portugal, as Ndongo and Matamba were during most of Queen Njinga's reign, whereas others, like the Imbangala, were committed to un-Christian or even anti-Christian religious ideas, even when politically allied to Portugal.

As in Kongo, adherence to Christianity was the most visible indicator of the Mbundu participation in the Atlantic Creole world. By the early seventeenth century, the Church in Portuguese Angola had an established infrastructure that was on a firm financial basis only in Luanda and Massangano; a financial report of 1612 reveals fixed incomes for these but only proposals for churches at Muxima and Cambambe.[67] In 1607 Luanda had a population of some 300 Portuguese and Luso-African households, but because they were surrounded by the large Mbundu population, both slaves and free, the church did reach many Mbundu.[68] A shortage of funds and missionaries constrained missionary work and the formal spread of Christianity. In 1623 the Jesuit Francesco Paccone believed that although "the whole city [Luanda] in which the Portuguese live, [is] Catholic and professes religion... in the surrounding villages there is no lack of heathens, not so much because of their obstinacy, but because they have no missionaries to baptize and instruct them."[69]

The success in the city extended to a larger population as well, as Luanda grew in the following decades. In 1631 a parish was founded on the beach of Corpo Santo to serve "twenty thousand slave and free people" of the city, but even this effort was considered inadequate for regular sacrament.[70] A 1635 complaint of officials of the mother church in Luanda noted that they were "so many people both native and foreign" that they exceeded the capacity of the church to hold them. The mother church also

---

[67] Andre Velho da Fonseca to King, 28 February 1612, *MMA* 6: 69–70; see also two other documents of 1 March pp. 73–6, all from same source.

[68] "Relação da Costa da Guiné, 1607" *MMA* 5: 390.

[69] Francesco Paccone to Giulio Cesare Recupito, SJ, 8 September 1623, *MMA* 7: 145.

[70] Francisco do Soveral, "Relationem de Statu Cathedralis ecclesiae Sancti Saluatoris..." *MMA* 8: 22; on the founding of this church and disputes about it, see BPE CV/2–15, fols. 190–2.

served 600 households in addition to "others who go out to buy slaves."[71] When the Dutch captured the city, they hoped that they might be able to convert the Catholic core to Protestantism, as they hoped in Kongo. Pieter Mortamer argued that the one preacher that the Company stationed in Luanda could "give a good example and would turn them to our religion, state and government."[72] But this was never to happen, and the Catholic Church reestablished itself as soon as the city was recaptured in 1648.

Despite Jesuit complaints, from the early 1600s Luanda had become a center of Christian devotion for the Mbundu. The church hierarchy recognized this by charting the Brotherhood of Our Lady of the Rosary of the Blacks (*Nossa Senhora do Rosario dos Pretos*) before 1620. As in Portugal, Brazil, and Kongo, this brotherhood was especially dedicated to Africans. In Luanda, the church had to maintain a chapel where Africans would go to confession, learn the catechism "na lingua indigena [in the Mbundu language]," and oversee their burials. The church thus functioned as something of a parish church for the Africans in Luanda.[73]

The Mbundu had accepted the faith sufficiently as to put their mark on some of the religious celebrations held to honor the saints. They were particularly attached to St. Benedict of Palermo, whom the church regarded as being "a moor" and thus black skinned. Although the Portuguese in Luanda celebrated his day to commemorate the victories against the Turks at the battle of Lepanto, "the blacks of the land had their church and their day" dedicated to him and regarded him as black. In Cadornega's (1639–1681) day as many as 20,000 Mbundu would come into Luanda to celebrate St. Benedict's day, primarily the slaves and free people linked to the residents. By that time, a local legend maintained that Saint Benedict's mother "was born in the kingdom of Angola in Quisama Province who was captured as a child."[74]

Beyond these core settlements of Portuguese, Luso-Africans, their slaves, and freed people, there were many other communities integrated into the Atlantic Creole zone. These included Mbundu populations living around the Portuguese positions in Luanda and around the presidios along the Bengo, Dande, and Kwanza Rivers. Here, beginning in the

---

[71] Igreja da Conceição de Luanda, 4 December 1635, *MMA* 8: 337–8.
[72] ARA OWIC 58, Mortamer Report, also "Schrijftlijk Raport," fol. 10 (translations from the latter).
[73] The Brotherhood is first mentioned in "Relação das Festas que a Residência de Angolla fez na Beatificação do Beato Padre Fran^co de Xavier da Companhia de Jezus," Felner, *Angola*, pp. 531–41. See also, Cardornega, *História* 3, p. 28.
[74] Cadornega, *História* 3: 27–8.

early 1600s the Portuguese had encouraged missionary work in the early seventeenth century. In these interior areas Mbundu might be brought into Christianity by missionaries or through military service that concentrated them and made teaching easy.

Mass baptisms in the wake of the conquest of the region in the late sixteenth century had produced a nominally Christian population that numbered in the tens of thousands, these Mbundu had not received much beyond the act of baptism and little in the way of Christian education, though some did take sacraments and hear services. In 1611, for example, Portuguese authorities in Luanda reported that some people came without missionary persuasion from some distance to be baptized, even carrying presents for the priests. The diligent but, they believed, not particularly rigorous secular clergy baptized them without any catechism, thus creating a fairly large group of "Christians in name only."[75]

An anonymous Jesuit report of about 1615 described this religious situation in bleak terms. Dismissing the earlier spread of Christianity and its continuation, the author felt this type of Christianity had no benefit. A true Christian presence, he argued, was possible only in Luanda, the Island of Luanda, and the Presidios along the Kwanza Rivers, where in addition to the existing clergy and passing Jesuits, there were "ladino [creole] slaves" who might be able to assist in the effort, where they "can make heathens into Christians." Indeed, he believed the prospects for expanding Christianity beyond this narrow corridor was "committing a moral sin." His own efforts to spread the doctrine along the River Bengo (not yet fully occupied by Portugal) amounted to "nothing but losing time." The solution he proposed, along with that of the "captains and experienced men," required "cruel war" to destroy all and afterward "planting the faith" as they "would only come to the faith when they had fear of the Portuguese muskets."[76]

From a religious point of view, the Mbundu of this region were creating a mixed religion with the support of the secular clergy similar to that of Kongo, which the Jesuits and higher clergy condemned, and, when they could, sought to change. Bishop Manuel Bautista Soares, writing at the end of his term in 1619, believed that this state of affairs existed because the parish priests performed baptisms largely for the revenues that it brought and did no catechizing or teaching. The bishop tested this

---

[75] Regimento to Francisco Correia da Silva, 22 September 1611 *MMA* 6: 23.
[76] Arquivum Romanum Societatis Iesu (ARSI), Lusitania (LUS) 55, fols. 195, 195v, 198v, Anonymous, "Informação sobre as missões q[ue] se podem fazer em Angola e outros Reinos vizinhos," n. d. (post-1610 and pre-1617).

at Cambambe, where he publicly examined seven baptized people about the doctrine and found that "they did not know anything, not the sign of the cross, about confession, had never gone in a Church, and affirmed that they had not been told about these things." He was afraid that the spread of Christianity in this manner, which governors could then boast about as expansion of the faith, would be as meaningless as the mass baptisms of slaves embarking for America with no instruction.[77] The Jesuits were in no position to push a more European form of Christianity for in 1624 there were 23 Jesuits in Angola. Moreover, politics, especially their struggle against governors like João Correia de Sousa, who had nearly driven them out, had worked against them expanding to the missions outside of Luanda and Kongo.[78]

Fernão de Sousa, who observed the situation during his governorship from 1624–1632, laid the blame on the bishop, who he believed ordained too many "mestiços which is what they call filhos da terra [children of the land] or mulattos to fill these spots, as well as some negros of little sufficiency or age and in which one can have little confidence as they are inclined to their superstitions." People were certainly eager to receive baptism, but in the governor's view they were "poorly taught."[79]

As politics permitted, the Jesuits expanded their activities to include these mixed Christian areas where they intended to improve the faith by more intensive instructions and even baptizing. The best known of these missions was Pedro Tavares's in the Bengo River valley and adjacent areas from 1629 to 1635. Here Portuguese plantations dominated and enslaved and free Mbundu lived in close proximity with the Portuguese. Tavares believed that there were some 20,000 African Christians in this region, but even here there were many areas where Mbundu religious figures catered to the population, attracting blacks and whites, slaves and free alike. Tavares often expressed disappointment with the work of the secular priests who had preceded him, some of whom were scions of Portuguese settlers, New Christians, mestiços, or Mbundu who expected the local population to support them.

Tavares cited the case of one Eusebio Correa as an example of how the secular clergy had failed. Correa's father had constructed a church

---

77 [Manuel Baptista Soares] "Relação dos costumes, ritos, e abusos do Bispado de Congo, que o Bispo deu a V. Magestade, e pena dos que nelle se cometem," 7 September 1619, *MMA* 6: 381–2.
78 Pero de Novais to King, 20 April 1624, *MMA* 7: 226.
79 Fernão de Sousa to King, 29 July 1632, *MMA* 8: 176.

and received the authorization of the bishop to make it a parish, leaving his son to be its rector. However, when floods deprived him of the means to make an income because the population was unable to make payments, he abandoned his parishioners. Another case concerned a New Christian priest who, without sanction from the bishop, baptized people, encouraging them to come with "a live chicken" and after cursory questions concerning whether they wanted to be "a child of God ... takes salt, put it in the mouth of the Negro without teaching him anything of the faith."[80]

Tavares, who often did not have a license from the bishop to administer the sacraments – the bread and butter of the seculars – devoted his attention to teaching, though in the absence of curates he often did baptize and marry in some years thousands of Mbundu. His usual method was to give a sermon on basic Christian teaching ("the mysteries of the Faith"), for example, Heaven and Hell, and then to teach the people to memorize such matters as the Apostles Creed, how to make the sign of the cross, and the prayers like the Lord's Prayer and Hail Holy Queen. In Holy Week he might hold massive meetings, like the one he held in 1631 where the subjects of four *sobas* came to hear mass. "No one," he wrote, "either rich or poor, black or white dies without baptism or confession."[81] On another occasion at an estate in Ensaca he baptized and married 195 persons and "said mass to 2000 Christian blacks...." He regularly gave communion to white and blacks alike and would often send the dozen Mbundu linguists who accompanied him to teach the credo to the families of local *sobas*, including women and children.[82]

Tavares struggled against the continuing presence of local elements in the mixed religion, which was most visibly manifested in the public cult of *iteke* or religious shrines, and the ministrations of the *nganga* in the Bengo area.[83] He believed that the failure of the seculars to instruct the people, and their general tolerance for indigenous religious practice, much as was also taking place in Kongo, was operating in this region.[84] He tried

[80] ARSI, Lus 55, fols. 84–107, Pedro Tavares to Jeronimo Vogado, 29 June 1635. Material on the lives of the seculars cited here are found on fols. 86v, 91, 91v, 93v–94.
[81] ARSI, Lus 55, fol. 97v, Tavares to Vogado.
[82] ARSI, Lus 55, fol. 92v; fol. 95v–96, Tavares to Vogado.
[83] For a discussion of Mbundu religious beliefs during this period, see John K. Thornton, "Religious and Ceremonial Life in Kongo and Mbundu Areas, 1500–1700" in Heywood (ed.), *Central*, 71–90.
[84] ARSI Lus 55, fols. 91v, 98–98v.

to ridicule and dismiss the "idols," as he called the shrines, argued with their ministers, flogged those who attended the ministrations of traditional religion, and burned ritual objects. Some of the religious practitioners identified themselves, as they did in Kongo, as Christians who had probably been baptized. Francisco Cazola, a freed slave (*negro forro*) engaged in Mbundu religious practices to heal people, make rain, and perform miracles but identified himself as a "child of God" and, moreover, was "intelligent and...knew Portuguese" but "preached against the law of God and against what I taught."[85] When the Jesuit obtained an order from the bishop to arrest him, Cazola fled further inland, thus ensuring the informal spread of his version of Atlantic Creole religion and cultural practices in other Mbundu communities.

The combination of Jesuit teaching and military mobilization helped to bring Christianity to fairly remote Mbundu areas under Portuguese authority. For example, in 1622, Jesuits complained that the slaves who accompanied the Portuguese army in the war against Kazanze and Kongo were Christians but were being taught cannibalism by the Imbangala troops. This army also had other non-Christian elements "who come in peace with us."[86] Other Jesuits, such as Duarte Vaz, who preceded Tavares at Bengo, and those who came after tried to bring a deeper knowledge of the formal aspects of Christianity to the Mbundu population. They traveled to areas further in the interior like Massangano and Ambaca, where the Portuguese had both a military and commercial presence to do missionary work. This was in response to demands, such as the one made by settlers in Massangano in 1633 that there were 30,000 Africans in their area who were not being adequately served by their single parish priest and demanded that Jesuits join their evangelization.[87] The efforts of a vigorous bishop, Franscico do Soveral, and the Jesuits expanded the formal reach of the church considerably and probably also the degree to which the parishioners had some Christian instruction, as the Jesuits remained active. In 1640, on the eve of the Dutch invasion, bishop do Soveral reported that in addition to the establishment in Luanda, there were four parishes for the Portuguese settlers, their subjects, and slaves in the immediate vicinity of the city and the Bengo valley. Moreover, three Mbundu *sobas*, vassals of Portugal, also had parishes laying northeast

---

[85] ARSI, Lus, fol. 99v, Tavares to Vogado.
[86] Jesuits to Lord Collector, *MMA* 15: 517; Cadornega, *História* 1: 103.
[87] Mesa da Conscienca on Letter of Moradores of Massangano, 31 January 1633, *MMA* 8: 249.

of the city. Motemo, located in the Dembos region between Kongo and Portuguese Angola also claimed a parish, which served its Luso-African and Mbundu residents. The presidios of Massangano, Muxima, Ambaca, and Cambambe all had their own parishes as well.[88]

During the Dutch invasion the Jesuits abandoned their work outside of Luanda and Kongo, in part because the Dutch actively stopped the work of Catholic missionaries and tried to institute Calvinism among the Catholic population. Although this effort was mostly directed at Kongo, their net effect was to cause a halt to the sort of teaching that the Jesuits had done for some 10 years. However, Third Order Franciscans were still active in areas the Portuguese held in the interior of Angola, and served as chaplains in the army when not doing regular duties, using a Kimbundu catechism that they had composed.[89] Reports from Dutch officials suggest that the mixed religious practices that had become commonplace continued. Dapper's comments on the religious situation in Angola refer to the continuing presence of a Christian identity among the Kimbundu population, though coupled with resort to the local practice. Thus even the "Luso Africans of the country" resort to African ordeals, "though the Fathers of the Christian Religion would severely punish the same if it should come to their knowledge."[90] The French traveler de Massiac, visiting Angola in 1652, noted that the "blacks who live with the Portuguese . . . profess the appearance of the Catholic religion, the rest are idolaters," including the use of *iteke*, traditional oaths, and prohibitions (*ijila*).[91] Only in 1649, when Capuchins transferred some of their numbers from Kongo to Angola, did teaching on the level of the pre-Dutch period resume, augmented by the arrival of four new Third Order Franciscans in 1653.[92] Cavazzi, who came to Angola 1654 and labored there until 1667, after noting that the Portuguese ruled supreme in Bengo, observed that the "natives, at the same time that they cultivate the fields and palm groves, are cultivated in the Christian Faith."[93] However, in reference to the inhabitants of Ilamba, which lay between the Kwanza and

---

[88] Do Soveral, "De statu omnium ecclesium . . ." *MMA* 8: 447, 449. See for a somewhat earlier assessment, Fernão de Sousa, "Relação da Costa de Angola de Angola e Congo," 21 February 1632, *MMA* 8: 121–2.

[89] Academia das Cienças, MS Vermelho 804, "Memorias," fols. 8–9.

[90] Dapper, *Naukeurige Beschrijvinge*, Ogliby, p. 568.

[91] De Massiac, 1652, *MMA* 11: 262–3. He called the traditional taboo, "quigilo" the singluar form of *ijila*.

[92] Academia das Cienças, MS Vermelho 804, "Memorias" fol 9.

[93] Cavazzi, *Istorica Descrizione*, book 1, para. 36.

Bengo Rivers, he noted that the majority were Christians, "even though secretly there are many fetishers..." as the "abuse of superstition and other Diabolic rites has not yet dead...but survives hidden."[94]

By the time of Cadornega (1639–1680) the Bengo core was quite regularized through a number of churches and chapels, with most of the people baptized and attending Catholic services regularly, including taking communion and receiving the Holy Unction.[95] At Calombe, located at the eastern edge of the district there was a mixed population of "whites, mulattos [*pardos*] and blacks who dress as Portuguese with innumerable natives [*gentio*], free people as well as slaves of whites and others, all living together as Catholics in the customs and order of the Holy Mother Church of Rome."[96] In Dande, where some 80 Portuguese families had settled in Cadornega's day, the local population all served in church, along with chapels at the revenue collection point, and in the lands of one of the *sobas*.[97] Cavazzi wrote that "the major part of the natives are Christians" and that they were several churches and parish priests.[98]

Massangano also formed part of the Atlantic Creole core, though for the earlier period its position as a frontier made it more vulnerable and less well controlled than Bengo was. The Jesuit report of 1615 linked Christianity to the loyalty of *sobas*, as was the case of Domingo Chilunguela, who "was raised in Massangano with the old Fathers [Jesuits]" but who nevertheless revolted and in the aftermath was discovered to have had a house of idols. When asked why he could not spread Christianity in his lands, he answered "he could not leave them [his idols], since they were from his grandparents and ancestors, and that his vassals would rise up against him immediately."[99]

Although the Jesuits used the same intense methods as Tavares did in Bengo (though without the detailed letters to describe it) in Massangano, the recruitment of porters for trade and soldiers for the army in this frontier post also was a place where Christianity was promoted and accepted. As early as 1625 many of the Mbundu inhabitants who served in the Portuguese army were Christians, for Cadornega knew a number who served in campaign that year who were "already baptized, being in the granary of

[94] Cavazzi, *Istorica Descrizione*, book 1, para. 38.
[95] Cadornega, *História* 3: 48–9.
[96] Cadornega, *História* 3: 50.
[97] Cadornega, *História* 3: 54.
[98] Cavazzi, *Istorica Descrizione*, book 1, para. 35.
[99] ARSI, Lus 55, fol. 195v, "Informação."

the Catholic Church [and] not so mixed up in their idolatries."[100] Here also brotherhoods served Portuguese and Luso-Africans, as well as the numerous *kimbares* (freed slaves of the Portuguese) who lived in the fort and nearby villages where they owned small farms. One of the brotherhoods that served in this church was dedicated to St. Benedito, "black saint in color, but in works and sanctity very white."[101] The Christian community of Massangano was considerably strengthened when the Dutch expelled the Portuguese from the Bengo. The Jesuit priest João de Paiva led a column that included many of the Jesuit male slaves, distributed wherever whites were, so that the priests could say mass, collect taxes, and the like in those areas around Massangano and the lower Lukala River.[102] These Mbundu, in turn, came to serve oftentimes as porters in the armies during the war against Njinga and the Dutch.

After the reestablishment of Portuguese rule, the Capuchins built a hospice at Massangano in 1652 and engaged in constant teaching, traveling, and spreading "the customs of the Holy Faith" all throughout the eastern part of Angola. The Capuchin church also had a confraternity of the Holy Rosary for blacks, and the Jesuits had one as well.[103] Cavazzi recalled that when the Capuchin Father Serafino da Cortona arrived in Massangano in 1654 he had to spend a great deal of time rooting out "an incredible number of fetishers who had established themselves a short distance from his quarters and were doing great prejudice to the souls and bodies of the Africans." Most of these fetishers, along with others, were forced to convert, and those who still remained obstinate were gathered up and "sent to America to work in the mines." He also worked assiduously among the Catholic people to weed out abuses, showing no sympathy to any idolatry.[104]

The presence of Atlantic Creole religion and culture was also evident among the Mbundu who lived in the vicinity of the presidio of Ambaca, located about 100 kilometers from Massangano. As soon as the Portuguese occupied the area in 1617 they established a church and parish, along with a lay confraternity funded by tributes from the neighboring

---

[100] Cadornega, *História* 1: 140. Cadornega's informants recalled the terrible smallpox epidemic that ruined their army that year in the war against Njinga and swore oaths on the place using Christian forms.
[101] Cadornega, *História* 3: 121–4.
[102] Jesuit account of attack on Bengo, 17 May 1643, *MMA* 9: 48–9.
[103] Cadornega, *História* 3: 121–4.
[104] Cavazzi, *Istorica Descrizione*, book 1, para. 101–2.

Mbundu rulers.[105] Baptisms followed shortly after, and Ambaca became the Christian center for further evangelization, because Ngola Hari, whom the Portuguese confirmed as king, among others, was baptized at the presidio and not in his territory. The chaotic warfare that followed the founding of the presidio, especially Njinga's resistance in the 1620s, precluded any sort of regular parish organization, and it was only in the late 1620s that some sort of order prevailed. In 1630 Henrique de Magalhães, the Captião Mor of the fort issued orders excommunicating various "native sobas" for not paying the tithe, indicating that at least he considered them nominally Christian.[106]

Ambaca had a heavy Portuguese military presence, especially with the stationing of Imbangala bands, most notably that of Kabuku ka Ndonga, with thousands of his followers. There were also *kilambas* or military units of the African army under Portuguese command.[107] Evangelization of this region often took place through the military chaplains and the example of Portuguese soldiers with whom the Mbundu served, as well as the teaching of Jesuits, who were working in the region in the 1630s. Capuchins took up evangelization in 1652 when Serafino da Cortona traveled to the district, though it ceased to be a regular station after 1660.[108] Some measure of the success of the mission can be judged by the case of two *sobas*, condemned to death for political offenses. One was "old in faith but impenitent" and the other was 70 years old but "young in the faith." As the second was garroted he "called on Jesus and Mary," causing, Cavazzi believed, the cord to break twice; although it did not prevent death, the priest thought that his faith caused him to die "sweetly."[109]

Intermediate Atlantic Creole Regions: Ndongo and Matamba

Whereas Kongo and Portuguese Angola represented the core areas of the Atlantic Creole culture, the Mbundu in other areas such as the kingdoms of Ndongo and Matamba would integrate fewer Atlantic Creole elements into their preexisting religious practices. These areas, however, formed an

[105] Document of 1628, *MMA* 7: 530.
[106] Fernão de Sousa to Henrique de Magalhães, 7 Febraury 1630, *FHA* 2: 317. De Sousa, like other writers of the time, used the Portuguese term *gentio*, usually translated as "heathen," but clearly meaning non-Portuguese as much as non-Christian, at least in the nominal sense.
[107] Cadornega, *História* 3: 162–7. His account does not take into account the loss of many Imbangala loyal to Kalandula, whose troops were liquidated in 1657.
[108] For missionary work in Ambaca, see Saccardo, *Congo e Angola* 1: 502–3.
[109] MSS Araldi, Cavazzi, "Missione Evangelica," vol. B, pp. 473–4.

intermediate zone between the core and the more remote areas beyond them. The kingdom of Ndongo was first exposed to the Catholic religion during the 15-year residence of Francisco de Gouveia, who died in 1575, shortly after the arrival of Paulo Dias de Novias. Gouveia's impact did not go beyond the few members of the Ndongo elite who were responsible for keeping up the chapel that he had built, and there was little missionary contact for many years. Matamba had even less contact with Christianity in addition to what the elite had observed from the mission sent by king Diogo I of Kongo (1545–1561).

Some of the nobility of Ndongo, for political reasons, had accepted baptism during the period between Gouveia's death and the large-scale attacks on Ndongo initiated by Mendes de Vasconcelos in 1619. One such nobleman, a son of King Ngola a Kiluanji and rival of Mbandi a Ngola, had had his son baptized as Francisco Mwenga a Kiluanji, with a Portuguese resident named João Pereira Girão as a godfather.[110] However, this slow voluntary conversion of a few nobles halted with the campaigns following 1619, where war and destruction by the Portuguese armies ruled the day. To demonstrate his submission to Portuguese vassalage in the aftermath of the 1619 sacking of Kabasa and the flight of the Ndongo court, Ngola Mbandi sent his sister, Njinga, to Luanda in 1622 to negotiate a treaty of peace with the governor João Correa de Sousa and to submit to baptism. Cavazzi heard in the 1650s (perhaps from Njinga herself) that following her baptism, when she left Luanda in a Christian procession, that as soon as it had reached beyond the Portuguese limits she abandoned the "Christian weapons" she had been given and returned to her own rites.[111] In any event, Correa de Sousa sent an Mbundu priest, Dionisio da Faria Baretto, to the islands of Kwanza in 1622 to baptize the king, but he soon left and Ngola Mbandi was never baptized.[112]

Atlantic Creole culture made headway only after 1625, when the kingdom split over Ngola Mbandi's succession with Ngola Hari joining the Portuguese as the new leader of Ndongo and Njinga eventually losing her prolonged war and establishing herself in Matamba. Ngola Hari swore Portuguese vassalage and was baptized as Felipe, and a Jesuit mission headed by Francesco Pacconio and Jeronimo Vogado began in his fortress capital of Mpungu a Ndongo. Felipe's son traveled to Luanda

---

[110] Cadornega, *História* 1: 116.
[111] MSS Araldi, Cavazzi, "Missione Evangelica," vol. A, book 2, p. 27.
[112] De Sousa to sons, *FHA* 1: 227; Fernão de Sousa to Governo, 6 September 1625, *FHA* 2: 142.

to be baptized, as Francisco, in the Mother Church, in the presence of captains, regular and secular clergy, "and with this demonstration," the governor Fernão de Sousa wrote, "we obliged the heathens to ask for holy baptism."[113] Francisco remained in the city for many years, at least 10, studying in the Jesuit College.[114]

A succession of Jesuits worked at Mpungu a Ndongo at the court and with the army. Francesco Pacconio in particular did much of his service with Ngola Hari's army that fought alongside Portuguese troops and their allies from Massangano and Ambaca in the war against Njinga in 1626. In the aftermath of battle, Pacconio baptized the dying who were not Christians and confessed those who were. After the army disbanded the Jesuits followed the soldiers back to their own lands, catechizing them as they went. Ngola Hari built the priests a church and received lengthy instruction from the two Jesuits.[115] However, the Jesuit mission met longer-term resistance that kept it from progressing very far. Pacconio wrote in 1627 of the problems he faced, "they are material people and do not believe anything that they do not see with their eyes" and so resisted his teaching about heaven and hell.[116]

This resistance made the Christianity of Mpungu a Ndongo less European than those found in the lands around the presidios. Fewer people sought baptism willingly and they were even more resistant than elsewhere in parting with their traditional religious devices.[117] For example Ngola Hari was still very much a believer in the traditional religion, for when, in 1628, Njinga sent a "fetish" to remind him of her intentions he was reported to have been very frightened.[118] Moreover, Domingos Lourenço, writing in 1632, complained that in all the time they were in Mpungu a Ndongo the Jesuits had baptized only about 500 people, mostly children who lived around the church, and moreover there had been no mass baptisms by seculars, as there was no secular parish in the kingdom. Few people came to mass or to other religious training services. Father Domingos thought that the problem in Mpungu a Ndongo contrasted with the situation in the presidios, where the Portuguese could use force

---

[113] Fernão de Sousa to Governo, 2 August 1627, *FHA* 2: 183.
[114] Franco, *Synopsis Annalium*, 1637, no. 19, p. 273.
[115] Letter of Jeronimo Vogado, 21 January 1627, *MMA* 7: 494–5.
[116] Francisco Pacconio to Fernão de Sousa, 18 February 1627, summarized in de Sousa to sons, *FHA* 1: 282.
[117] Francisco Pacconio to Fernão de Sousa, 18 February 1627, summarized in de Sousa to sons, *FHA* 1: 282.
[118] Fernão de Sousa to Governo, 10 July 1628, *FHA* 2: 198.

to make the people accept baptism and training. Here also the elite were simply unwilling to push the program for their own subjects, and the king was reluctant to press them. The rulers in this area had accepted baptism only as a diplomatic ploy, the Jesuit believed; "they do not want the fathers to come except for reasons of state."[119]

Despite the reservations of the elite, Christianity and Atlantic Creole culture influenced the cultural and religious life of the populations surrounding Massangano, due in large part to deserting soldiers and runaway slaves from the Portuguese fort. For example, during the first period of the Portuguese war against Njinga, as the Portuguese army was camped across the Kwanza from her island in 1625, the sentries on both sides would call out to each other, and some could "see among them many of our runaway people who were in their power, slaves of Portuguese who were doing sentry duty in their guardhouses and lookouts." The former slaves would shout out jeeringly "asking if so-and-so was there, responding they were" and then the runaways would say "I told him to go to Loanda or to Massangano where he was married, [and] see his wife."[120]

The presence of Atlantic Creole runaway slaves and soldiers did not lead to large-scale Christianization, and when Capuchins took over the mission in 1655 they noted that little progress had been made. Cavazzi, who was one of the two founders of the Capuchin mission, described their tribulations in detail. His report echoes the complaints of the Jesuits. Cavazzi, however, had some more success in baptizing than the Jesuits did, for the king sent out an order that all the people must be baptized, and in one week he performed 547 baptisms, mostly of "tender age." But he still found the people to be "wolves in sheep's clothing," for the king did little to stop the robbery of the Capuchins personal goods, and women insisted on bathing naked within the missionaries' sight. When Cavazzi tried to burn the "idols" of two war priests that the king employed, the people came armed to prevent him doing so.[121]

However, Cavazzi received more support as time went on, and he was able, no doubt with royal support, to seize and destroy religious objects that he found "diabolic" and to have their priests flogged and made to confess their sins. In one case, the king's viceroy arrested a blacksmith who maintained that there were two gods, one in heaven and the other on Earth, who was him. Cavazzi had him beaten, at which point he shouted,

[119] Domingos Lourenço letter, 4 October 1632, *MMA* 8: 181–4.
[120] Cadornega, *História* 1: 132–3.
[121] MSS Araldi, Cavazzi, "Missone Evangelica," vol. B. pp. 445; 446–7.

Nganga Zambi imoxi kivi, meaning "Father, there is only one God."[122] In other cases, Cavazzi was allowed to impose a death penalty on a priest who was accused of bewitching people to death, which was commuted to "passing the salty sea" (enslavement and deportation to the Americas).[123]

The missionaries' most significant work was with the army, in which they served as chaplains and which conveniently gathered people from every corner of the kingdom to serve. In this work, they were assisted by the most Christian of the African population, such as Jerónimo, interpreter for the army and "a very good Christian," whose arrest Bernardo da Cutligiano managed to prevent. After learning to read and write, Jeronimo became an informant of the missionaries and wrote to complain of "witchcraft, idolatry, and concubinage" in the country.[124] Cavazzi's service with the army in 1658, whereby 2,000 soldiers of Mpungu a Ndongo served alongside 55 Portuguese soldiers in Libolo, provides a good illustration. Cavazzi performed a number of evangelical activities during the campaign, such as raising crosses, which the soldiers saluted. He often baptized the dying as well. He gave the army general absolution and confessed them before battle. He also worked with an Imbangala army from Rimba, a province south of Libolo that allied with the Portuguese for the campaign, baptizing their children and eventually even their commander, as Pedro.[125]

Matamba was another Mbundu area that had little early contact with Christianity before Njinga invaded the kingdom following her defeat at Kindonga in 1629. Even before Njinga and her army arrived, thousands of her subjects had moved eastward, where they had already founded villages and no doubt paved the way for her armies.[126] Njinga and her followers had been exposed to the early evangelization in Ndongo, and during the time she was ruling as queen of Ndongo, she welcomed thousands of slaves, many of whom came from the core Atlantic Creole communities established around the Portuguese forts in Ndongo.

Although Njinga may have counted a good number of Christians among her followers, her decision to ally with the Imbangala and take up some of their lifestyle prevented her from either openly encouraging

---

[122] MSS Araldi, Cavazzi, "Missione Evangelica," vol. B, p. 458. The original text has "Ganga Zambi imoxi quivi," which we have respelled in modern Kimbundu orthography (following Chatelein's rules).

[123] MSS Araldi, Cavazzi, "Missione Evangelica," vol. B, p. 471.

[124] MSS Araldi, Cavazzi, "Missione Evangelica," vol. B, p. 452–3.

[125] MSS Araldi, Cavazzi, "Missoine Evangelica," vol. B, pp. 516–31 *passim.*

[126] D'Azevedo to de Sousa, 29 March 1629, summarized in De Sousa to Sons, *FHA* 1: 328.

missionaries or practicing any element of Christianity herself. She did, however, have contact with Kongo and its Atlantic Creole connections, for in 1627 King Ambrósio sent her a chair and a fine carpet through an embassy led by the nobleman Dom Mateus.[127] Njinga also remained in regular contact with her sisters, captured in 1629, who were resident in Luanda, and one of whom, Barbara, was regarded by the Portuguese as a very pious Christian.[128]

In 1637, Njinga, who had been catechized by Jesuits while in Luanda, wrote to them suggesting that they correspond with her, and in fact sent silver, ivory, and slaves. The Jesuits had rejected many of her overtures because they did not wish to acknowledge the "benevolent signs of a person dedicated to such a corrupt customs."[129] It was not until 1640 that there was a firm new opening for a Christian impact in Matamba. When Pedro Cezar de Menezes arrived in 1639, he wrote Njinga to demand the return of the many former Portuguese slaves who had fled with her to Matamba. She in turn sent him a mission and returned some of the runaways, "who were so old they no longer knew their masters."[130] In 1640 Cezar de Menezes sent an ambassador with a secular priest, António Coelho, to Matamba. The priest hoped that he might be able win her back to the Church, as he noted that she "fortified herself by making the sign of the Holy Cross," but was reluctant to allow him to do any missionary work, even baptizing children taken from wars or of Portuguese living with her, which she believed "would have detracted from her fame as a true female Giaga, & contravened her laws." When she showed herself more favorable to his mission as a result of a serious illness, Coelho delayed his departure from her court for six months to minister to her, only to be disappointed when she recovered and refused to allow him to continue missionary work.[131]

Njinga later maintained that she had abandoned Christianity to ally with the Imbangala and that she always regarded herself as a Christian, which the alliance did not allow her to follow. She demonstrated this on several occasions during the years she was in Matamba or on campaign. For example, when the Portuguese priest Jerónimo de Sequeira fell into her hands as a prisoner of war in 1644, she showed him special reverence

---

[127] Fernão de Sousa to Governo, 2 August 1627, *FHA* 2: 184.
[128] Gaeta, *Meravigliosa conversione*, p. 78.
[129] Franco, *Synopsis Annalium*, 1637, no. 19, p. 273.
[130] Cadornega, *História* 1: 209–10.
[131] MSS Araldi, Cavazzi, "Missine Evangelica," vol. A, book 2, pp. 44–6. Cavazzi either interviewed this priest or read a report of his dated 1642.

and allowed him to keep his various "objects pertaining to Divine Worship," augmenting them with those she had captured in war and kept. She permitted him to build a church in her capital and she made "due salutations and reverence" when she passed it, and even attended the mass he conducted from time to time. She also gave the Portuguese prisoners "a quantity of Crowns & Rosaries, books & Crosses, all of them spoils of war."[132] When the Portuguese rescued Sequeira in 1646, Njinga continued to treat Christian priests reverently; she ordered that none be injured after her soldiers killed Agostinho Flores, a parish priest in Wandu, and when her captains captured two Capuchins, Father Buenaventura da Corrella and Father Francisco de Veas, and the Kongolese secular priest Calisto Zelotes dos Reis Magros on one of her campaigns in the Kongo Duchy of Wandu, she treated them with respect. Furthermore, Njinga had serious discussions with them and told them she wanted priests to come and work in her lands "for her people," and sent them safely back to Kongo in the company of some Kongolese who had come with an embassy to her camp.[133] Moreover, she rescued Father Calisto from her Imbangala allies and gave him the post of "Master of the House and major domo of her goods," later making him her personal confessor and councilor, a position he kept until her death.[134]

In choosing Kongo priests to evangelize and become her personal confessor and councilor, Njinga was able to have Christianity without the political overtones that came with missionaries sent out under Portuguese auspices. Nevertheless, Atlantic Creole Christians lived in Matamba, as over the years she captured Christians from the various Portuguese armies from Ambaca and Massangano against whom she fought. When Antonio da Gaeta entered her capital in 1657 he found among her people one of these Atlantic Creole Christians, who had become a *macota*. He had been baptized as a boy in Luanda, had been captured by Njinga, and had served with her 30 years, leading an Imbangala life along the way. Gaeta met him in Matamba, confessed his sins, and found him well inclined to Christian life.[135]

[132] MSS Araldi, Cavazzi, "Missione Evangelica," ms. A, book 2, p. 64–5. Cavazzi also related the story of a Calvinist who received a cross but tried to break it and subsequently was rendered unable to walk or use his arms, and when he died Njinga ordered him thrown to the dogs. Cadornega saw the church where Jeronimo de Sequeira said Mass for the queen when the Portuguese army captured Njinga's camp in 1646, *História* 1: 418.
[133] BN Madrid, MS 3533, de Teruel, "Descripcion Narrativa," pp. 89–90; MSS Araldi, Cavazzi, "Missione Evangelica," vol. A, book 2, pp. 77–8.
[134] Saccardo, *Congo e Angola* 1, pp. 405–7, 507, 514, 579.
[135] Gaeta, *Mervagliosa Conversione*, pp. 286–8.

Thus when Njinga made peace with the Portuguese in 1657, she had already decided in 1656 to welcome a formal Catholic presence in Matamba and to invite priests to come. Her decision was in part to satisfy Portuguese demands, in part to bring the Imbangala under her spiritual control, and also in part due to her long familiarity with Atlantic Creole Christianity.[136] Njinga explained her decision to establish Christianity as a result of a miraculous event, in which one of her Imbangala generals found a cross he desecrated during a raid on Wandu. However, he dreamed that the cross commanded him to bring it to his lady, which he did. She subsequently convened her *xingula* (possessed traditional mediums) of various of her ancestors who also enjoined her to rejoin the Christian fold.[137]

This background can explain the rapid expansion of Christianity in Matamba following the establishment of the Capuchin mission in 1656. In contrast with Pungo Andongo, where the local Mbundu were reluctant to be baptized, when Gaeta was in Matamba, after baptizing the principal lords, he baptized 8,000 people "as everyone follows their lords." The group included 1,000 babies born since the Capuchins came to Njinga's city, suggesting a preexisting baptized population up to 20,000 people. This rapid mass baptism resembled those in the Portuguese core areas in the earlier period, and Gaeta doubted their knowledge of the tenets of the faith.[138]

To assist in spreading the faith and its practices, the Capuchin called on the various merchants, black and white, who came to buy slaves to celebrate after they built the church. The group walked to Njinga's palace and put up a crucifix, while all sang hymns, psalms, and high spiritual canticles. Njinga and her sister Barbara carried torches in the procession. Barbara, who had been recently released after 13 years of Portuguese captivity as a result of the peace treaty, had come from Luanda, where she had become famous for her Christian piety, with a large group of Christian followers.[139] Other such ceremonies followed; at Easter the people participated in flagellations (a common part of Catholic devotion in Iberian lands, Kongo, and Portuguese Angola), processions, and other spiritual exercises, led especially by the Luso-African merchant community, which was encouraged to set an example. The Portuguese followed the local customs that had grown up around Massangano, which included Stations of the Cross, and the local people joined this to show that they, too, were

[136] On Njinga's motives, see Thornton, "Gender and Power."
[137] Gaeta, *Meravagliosa Conversione*, pp. 223–9.
[138] Gaeta, *Meravagliosa Conversione*, pp. 243–6. The estimate of potential baptized people is based on the assumption of a birthrate of 47 per 1000.
[139] Gaeta, *Mervagliosa Conversione*, pp. 116–7.

Christians. The queen followed with a great multitude of people.[140] Until her death in 1663, Njinga, along with many of her subjects, were regular participants in church services as well as maintaining many of the Catholic festivals and devotions.

Outer Atlantic Creole Culture Zones: Northeastern Kongo, Loango, and Southern Angola

The areas that had the least exposure to Atlantic Creole culture and Christianity and that also supplied an increasing number of captives to the Atlantic were either those that were remote, such as Okango, Kundi and others to the east of Kongo, Loango, and other smaller states north of the Congo River, or those that neither accepted Christianity voluntarily nor were actively hostile to Portugal, such as the lands of Kisama that lay south of the Kwanza River and Luanda.

Northeast of Kongo Luso-Africans and Atlantic Creoles who went to trade set up communities and attempted to keep the Catholic faith and perhaps spread it to their hosts with support from Kongo, which claimed to be the nominal overlord.[141] As early as 1604, for example, Álvaro II claimed to have had the eastern kings of Okango, Kundi, and Kala baptized,[142] and in 1619, Bishop Soares noted that Okango had a parish, but it must have been primarily for Luso-African residents.[143] A merchant from Okango wrote in 1620 that the king of Okanga or the king of the nearby Mococos wished to have a priest to be baptized. However, the Jesuits could not send missionaries to a place so far away.[144] In 1631 the bishop reported that the Duke of Mbata, in charge of these regions, had a parish in Okango and Kundi but he could not fill it.[145] The rulers in the region continued to express interest in a formal Christian presence, and in 1640 the bishop hoped that the Kundi's ruler, "always a queen," could bring many more to the church.[146] Although in 1650, at the request of the king of Makoko, whose lands bordered on Okango,

[140] Gaeta, *Mervagliosa Conversione*, p. 284.
[141] "Relação que faz o Capitão Garçia Mendes Castelobbranco do Reyno do Congo, 16 January 1620, *MMA* 6: 437.
[142] Instructions to Antonio Manuel, 1604, *MMA* 5: 114.
[143] Soares, *MMA* 6: 410.
[144] Matheus Cardoso to Jesuit General, 17 August 1620, *MMA* 6: 503–4.
[145] Francisco do Soveral, "Infra scriptam relationem de statu Cathedralis ecclesiae Sancti Saluatoris transmittit ad Sanctissimum D. N. Vrbanum Papam...Anno Domini de 1631," 1 April 1631, *MMA* 8: 16.
[146] [Francisco do Soveral], "De statu omnium ecclesiarum Episcopatus Congensis et Angolenesis..." 22 September 1640, *MMA* 8: 444.

the Capuchin Girolamo da Montesarchio traveled there and baptized the ruler and preached and taught, there was little follow up.[147]

Other regions like Kisama, Hako, and Libolo, which lay south of the Kwanza across from the Portuguese areas from Cambambe along the river to Luanda's southern hinterlands, had constant contact with the Atlantic Creole world and experienced frequent movements of Portuguese armies, traders, and escaped slaves back and forth across the river. From the late sixteenth century onward, Imbangala bands frequented the region as well, and a number of them took up permanent residence there. In 1618 some Imbangala captured "negros forros and escravos" who traded in the area. They also raided the communities scattered around the Portuguese presidios and carried away many resident slaves.[148] Again in 1622, the band of Zenza captured Portuguese slaves and free people from Cambambe and carried them to his base in Kisama, prompting a demand that the prisoners be returned.[149]

Even though Kisama was drawn into the politics of Portuguese expansion and was subject to regular raids and punitive expeditions by Portuguese forces, the Portuguese never had a presence there similar to that in Ndongo or Matamba. Nevertheless, they made occasional attempts to convert local rulers as was the case in 1607 when they converted the *soba* Agoaciaiongo.[150] For a variety of reasons people from Kisama moved across the river into the Portuguese territory and perhaps while there absorbed some of the religious practices. In 1629 as the Portuguese began claiming the rights over Kisama that Ndongo formerly exercised, the governor Fernão de Sousa ordered the expulsion of a Kisama community whose member had been living among other free groups of Africans who were Portuguese allies and who lived in the region of Lemba, near Massangano.[151] He also advised the *capitão-mor* (Portuguese government representative) of Massangano to require the heir of the Kisama-based *soba* Langere to become a vassal and pay a light tribute and forbade the *capitão-mor* from sending a "white or Creole or dressed person" to Kisama.[152]

---

[147] Da Montesarchio, "Viaggio del Gongho," fols. 30v–31v.

[148] Manuel Vogado Sotomaior, "Papel sobre as cousas de Angola," c. 1620, *MMA* 15: 475–6.

[149] Fernão de Sousa, 26 July 1624, *FHA* 2: 269.

[150] "Relação da Costa da Guiné, 1607," *MMA* 5: 391.

[151] Order to Captain Mor of Massangano, no date but in 1629 summarized in de Sousa to Sons, *FHA* 1: 345.

[152] Letter of King of Dongo to de Sousa, c. 1629, In de Sousa to Sons, *FHA* 1: 343–4.

Despite the intimate relations with Kisama, the Capuchin assessment in 1647 was that there were no Christians south of Kwanza (in Kisama), although when Bonaventura da Taggia came to Angola early in 1647 he landed at Quicombo in coastal Kisama and evangelized and baptized some people and *sobas*.[153] The two other major rulers in the region who agreed to baptism when Cavazzi went there in 1659–1660 did so for mostly political reasons.[154] Kisama thus became integrated into Atlantic Creole Christianity not so much because of the evangelization of missionaries or of Portuguese settlements but because of the frequent wars the Portuguese made against the region and the thousands of slaves from the Portuguese area who fled there. In Kisama many people renounced their loyalty to Portugal but not necessarily to what they had taken from Christianity.[155]

The rulers and people of the kingdom of Loango north of the mouth of the Congo River were also integrated into the Atlantic Creole world through Portuguese, English, and Dutch traders who operated in that area of the coast. From the sixteenth century onward the Portuguese had relations with the rulers here and received sporadic requests by them to be baptized, but they were never quite able to follow this up. The beginning of Dutch trading on the coast in the 1590s led the Portuguese to take steps to protect their own commerce and discourage the Dutch and eventually to found a factory.[156] In 1623 Fernão de Sousa, increasingly concerned about the Dutch following the alliance between them and Kongo, wrote to the king of Loango promising priests and a factory in exchange for throwing the Dutch out. However, the king was not interested in giving the Portuguese exclusive control of his external trade and maintained friendly relations with the Dutch, even as he asked "many times" for priests to come and baptize him.[157] In 1624, de Sousa insisted on the king's baptism, but the king deferred, saying he was "at present not disposed to eat salt [be baptized]." Even at that moment, however, the king of Kakongo,

---

[153] Report on Bonaventura da Taggia, 26 February 1647, *ACA* 2: 885. See the rather different account Pietro da Dolcedo, "Narratione de' successi accaduti alli 4 Padri Capuccini Genovesi … " fol. 133, published in Carlo Toso, ed. "La 'Missio antiqua' e la 'narratione' inedita del genovese Pietro da Dolcedo," *L'Italia Francescana* 54 (1979), pp. 179–214, 309–354, 437–498.

[154] João Fernandes Vieira to Álvaro VI of Portugal, 6 October 1660, *MMA* 12: 306.

[155] Beatrix Heintze, "Gefährdes asyl."

[156] Relação do Reino de Loango, *MMA* 6, 479.

[157] [Manuel Baptista Soares] "Lembranças que fes, e deu a V. Magestade, o bispo de Congo … 7 September 1619, *MMA* 6: 359–65 [AHU Cx. 1, doc. 105] Felner, 477–79.

Loango's small southern neighbor, was asking for Jesuits.[158] In 1628 the Jesuits did send a mission to Loango, which they believed resulted in significant results and the "conversion of many people," though in the longer run it seems to have had little effect on Loango's religious life.[159] In fact, the Jesuits had to forgo a renewal of the mission in 1637 because of a shortage of priests.[160] De Sousa was able to build a factory in Loango but felt it so ineffective that in 1632 he proposed removing it.[161] Even though at this time the English and Dutch did not buy slaves in Loango, the Portuguese did, though it is not clear where the people were enslaved, and some certainly came from Kongo.[162] After the failure of Portugal to make reglious change in Loango, the Dutch were not particularly willing to try. In 1642 Frans van Capelle, the Dutch factor, though interested in spreading Christianity, did not get far beyond a fruitless dialogue with the king. When asked to make it rain, van Capelle replied that only God could do this, and the king scornfully rejected his theological explanations.[163] Indeed, it was only in 1663, when the Capuchin Missionary Bernardo Ungaro managed to baptize the king and thousands of his followers, that Christianity seems to have made any progress, and even that was short lived, for the Christian king was overthrown by rivals who rejected the religion.

Loango's principal interest in its relations with the Dutch, Portuguese, and English was to maintain itself as an independent open trading port. The absence of large and long settled traders from abroad with their slaves and close African allies made the development of a sort of Christian community (as took place in Okanga) impossible, and politics made conversion of the rulers difficult to maintain. Loango was therefore the most religiously conservative region that had ongoing contacts with the Atlantic community and therefore outside the world of Atlantic Creole religion.

---

[158] de Sousa to Children, *FHA* 1, p. 227.

[159] Státní Ústrední Archív (Prague), Rádový archiv kapucinú, Spisy 2, kart. 1, B 8 ordo, "Collectio S^rum Missionum Aostolicarum ordinis Minorum S^ti Francisci Capuchinorum per quator mundi partes stabiitascum," (ca. 1650), Anno 1628, "Loango Regnum."

[160] Franco, *Synopsis Annalium* 1637, no. 19.

[161] Fernão de Sousa, "Relação da Costa de Angola de Angola e Congo," 21 February 1632, *MMA* 8: 121.

[162] BL, Add MSS 15183, "Historia de Congo e Angola, 1513–1749"; Anonymous, "Historia de Congo e Angola," comp. 1750. The account seems on internal evidence to be a copy of something written around 1624 or 1625 copied into historical notes of an Angolan author who began his work around 1730.

[163] ARA OWIC 46, F. Capelle to Count Jan Maurits van Nassau and Directors.

Beyond Religion: Atlantic Creole Cultural Dynamics

Naming Practices

Whatever the degree of formal practice of Christianity, Central Africans across the zones also adpoted a range of Iberian cultural elements, including naming patterns, burial customs, musical influences, and clothing stlyes, and consumed a range of food and drinks of Iberian origins. New patterns of naming came with the adoption of Christianity. Dapper noted that "men and women, both high and low, including the king himself, receive a name at Baptism."[164] In Kongo the custom was to add the honorific title "Dom" to all Christian names, even of the poorest, so that Giovanni Francesco da Roma, when baptizing a child of a very poor father, asked the godfather the child's name and was told it was to be Dom Julião, he was both amused and angered at the presumption of a poor man taking such a noble name.[165]

Central Africans had their own naming patterns, and they inserted the new baptismal names into these patterns. The prevailing one was to give a single name, but for people of higher status, the custom was to add the father's name as a second element. In Kongo, the people attached baptismal names to Kikongo personal names, for example, Antonio Nzinga. Nobles often attached a father's Kikongo name to the child's baptismal and Kongo names, as illustrated by the example of King João Nzinga Nkuwu's son, who was named Afonso Mvemba Nzinga. A variant of this was to do the same with Christian names, where the father's Christian name was added as a second element to the child's baptismal name.[166] This system created what appears to be double Christian names. Kongo's ambassador to the Vatican in 1608, "Antonio Manuel," is an example of a high-status person with two Christian names, perhaps because his father was named Manuel. Other examples of the Central African Atlantic Creole naming system include Manuel Jordão, who served as a general in Kongo's army and later obtained the position of Duke of Nsundi, António Manuel, half-brother of King Álvaro III, and Miguel Daniel, a member of Álvaro III's royal council.[167]

---

[164] Dapper, *Naukeurige Beschrijvinge*, p. 201.
[165] Da Roma, *Breve Relatione*, p. 78. Cavazzi confirmed the existence of this custom as well. *Istorica descrizione*, Book 1, no. 156.
[166] For an exploration of the naming patterns of the earlier periods, see John Thornton, "Central African Names and Naming Patterns," *William and Mary Quarterly* (1993).
[167] [Cardoso], "Morte," *MMA* 15: 483–4; Álvaro III, Provisions to Bras Correa, 1616–23, *MMA* 6: 252–4.

In addition to this pattern, some Kongo nobles also took Portuguese-style surnames, which they passed on from father to son. In the 1620s kings and other nobles adopted the surname "Afonso" to show their descent from the important sixteenth-century king.[168] Cadornega, describing the aftermath of the Kongolese defeat at Mbumbi in 1622, noted that some of the surviving Kongo nobles asked to bury their compatriots who lay on the field. They went about calling out the names of those who had fallen, "here is Dom Pedro Ponce de Leon, or here is Dom Calisto Andur-inha Zelotes dos Reis Magros, and thus many others were called out with names and surnames... in their fashion, and these surnames were very vain."[169] Some of these names were quite common, such as Anto-nio da Silva, Álvaro III's Duke of Mbamba, and two Daniel da Silvas, one the Duke of Mbamba in 1634 and the other the Count of Soyo in 1641.

The various patterns of naming are reflected in the register that the Capuchin father Joris van Gheel kept of marriages he performed at Sacamezo (probably in Matari) in April 1652. Among the list were Domin-gos Antonio, who married Maria [illegible Christian name], with the *nkuluntu* Antonio and Antonio José as witnesses; Antonio Sebastião, who married Graça Brigina before witnesses Antonio Feliciano and Antonio Paulo; and Antonio Luis, who married Manuela before witnesses Mateus Afonso and Antonio Afonso, both of whom also witnessed the marriage of Manuel José and Potencia Mbazi (from Mbamba).[170]

Ndongo naming patterns followed rules similar to those of Kongo, as can be seen in the names of the rulers of the sixteenth century, in which Ngola Kiluanji's son was named Ndambi a Ngola, whose own son was named Kiluanji kia Ndambi. Likewise Queen Njinga (Njinga a Mbandi) was the daughter of Mbandi a Ngola.[171] When João Correa de Sousa attempted to put a puppet king in Ndongo, the man was known as Antonio Correa Samba a Ntumba, so that he had baptismal name, a noble name (perhaps in honor of his benefactor), and a double local name.[172] Similarly, the baptism of new vassals was always accompanied by the giving of Christian names, such as Felipe Ngola Hari, king of Ndongo

---

[168] Cardoso, *Historia*, Chapter 16, fol. 16–16v, p. 48.
[169] Cadornega, *História* 1: 104.
[170] Biblioca Nazionale (BN) Fundo Minori 1896, MS Varia 274 Roma, van Gheel, "Vocab-ularium," last page of front matter.
[171] These names and successions are worked out in Chapter 2, based on Cavazzi and Gaeta.
[172] Fernão de Sousa, "Lembrança," *FHA* 1: 195.

in 1626, or the *soba* of Haku, whom Cavazzi baptized in 1655 with the name Dom Luis Antonio.[173]

Christian commoners and slaves of the Portuguese typically had a single Christian name, as did Antonio, the *mukuluntu* (an important leadership position among slaves), and his wife, Lucretia, who in 1623 were slaves of Pascal Antunes.[174] Antonio was probably the most common of these names. One of the most durable fruits of the mass baptism campaigns of the secular clergy in Angola was to ensure the dissemination of Christian names. The names carried prestige, so that even those Mbundu who had avoided or missed being baptized used them. On one occasion Cavazzi baptized a seriously wounded soldier, serving in the army of Ndongo in the Libolo campaign of 1658, who told him, "he was called Antonio but was not baptized,"[175] a custom he was told was common.

Atlantic Creole members who followed Christian burial customs such as the treatment of the dead and the sacrament of Last Rites, nevertheless maintained many elements of African customs. Cavazzi noted the changes that Christianity brought to Kongo, observing that although peasants and the unconverted of Matamba and other places outside the core regions of Angola were wrapped in cloth and buried in forests or other remote places away from settlements, Christians wanted to be buried in cemeteries, which, following Iberian custom, were often inside churches. In addition, the rural crosses, located throughout the countryside, were also found in places that served as burial grounds where holy images reminded travelers that this was hallowed ground. Priests said masses for the dead annually in place of the older system of sacrifices, a part of the veneration of ancestors common to Central African religious life, and if no priests were available, then the people left offerings and prayed for the dead.[176] In Luanda where the Brotherhood of Our Lady of the Rosary existed, members complained in 1657 that settlers prevented them from burying their dead in the European cemetery. They reminded the bishop that they were "the first founders of this confraternity in this city," and although "negroes and slaves," they were "all equal in the eyes of God." They requested permission "to inter our dead brothers," pointing out that they would then be able to collect offerings and "increase our fraternity for Misericodia."[177]

As in early modern Europe, women played a prominent role in the Afro-Christian rituals that Atlantic Creoles practiced. In both Kongo and

[173] MSS Araldi, "Missione Evangelica," vol. B, p. 490.
[174] Testimonio de Gaspar Alvares, 23 February 1623, *MMA* 7: 89.
[175] MSS Araldi, Cavazzi, "Missoine Evangelica," vol. B, pp. 516–31, *passim*.
[176] Cavazzi, *Istorica Descrizione*, Book 1, no. 260.
[177] Confraternity of Nosa Senhora do Rosario to Cardinals of Propaganda, 29 June 1658, *MMA* 12: 164–65.

FIGURE 11. Njinga's Court Musicians. Source: Ezio Bassani, "Un Cappuccino nell'Africa nera del seicento. I disegni de Manoscritti Araldi del Padre Givanni Antonio Cavazzi da Montecuccolo," Quaderni Poro 4 (1987).

Angola they remained for a up to a year in a special hut when a relative died and wore a black mantle, the strictness of this confinement being dependent on the closeness of the relation and the status of the people.[178] The custom of following such strict mourning was also found in the African culture, as indeed it was in Europe, though the specifics of the behavior were still creolized. Slaves of wealthy masters in both Luanda and São Salvador adopted a unique funeral dress, wearing long, hooded capes of black cloth, which gave them, in Cavazzi's opinion, "a majestic

[178] Cavazzi, *Istorica Descrizione*, Book 1, no. 271.

appearance."[179] Portuguese slave owners might suppress other customs, for example, the Mbundu practice of having a widow run down the road as if possessed (as there was a local belief that the soul of her dead husband would try to enter her body), which Cavazzi noted was done "with a stick if the woman is their slave."[180] Other customs, including having slaves appear at the deathbed of owners in exaggerated states of grief, continued in houses of both Portuguese and Atlantic Creole masters.[181]

As music is central to Christian rituals, Africans in both the core regions and elsewhere fostered the growth of Atlantic Creole musical traditions. Central Africa possessed a rich musical tradition that included a range of locally made and designed instruments such as horns, stringed instruments, and drums. At least some Europeans considered the locally produced music appealing, and the French traveler de Massiac noted that the people had "many diverse instruments that are very harmonious."[182] Dutchman van Capelle admired its natural composition, noting that seven or eight instruments formed a group that produced an "agreeable concert."[183] Visitors were also impressed with how commonplace music was in the everyday life of Central Africans, noting that the people used it in all their festivals, and especially at the birth and death of relatives, and when traveling. Cavazzi felt that some of the local dances were "totally obscene" but observed that even baptized people enjoyed participating in them.[184]

Music was also a major accompaniment for the armies going off to war, where drums figured prominently.[185] Dancing was also a common element of the music, and soldiers especially danced before combat.[186] This military dancing was called in Kikongo *nsanga*, which gave rise to the Portuguese word *sangamento*. Six hundred armed men performed this dance for Dominican priests "running, leaping and making warlike representations," as the fathers passed through Mbamba in 1610. Women and children followed, dancing and clapping their hands."[187] *Sangamentos* often included mock combat in which soldiers displayed their skill

---

[179] Cavazzi, *Istorica Descrizione*, Book 1, no. 271.
[180] Cavazzi, *Istorica Descrizione*, Book 1, no. 270.
[181] Cavazzi, *Istorica Descrizione*, Book 1, no. 274.
[182] De Massiac, 1652, *MMA* 11: 256.
[183] De Massiac, 1652, *MMA* 11: 256.
[184] Cavazzi, *Istorica Descrizione* I, no. 336.
[185] ARA OWIC 46, fol. 7, Capelle to Maurits, "Corte beschrijvinge."
[186] De Massiac, 1652, *MMA* 11: 256.
[187] Luís de Cácegas and Luís de Sousa, *História de S. Domingos* (Lisbon, 1662), part II, book IV, chapter XIII, *MMA* 5: 608.

with the sword but presented them in the form of a dance.[188] It was the experience of dancing in *sangamentos* that probably informed the performance that the three Kongolese ambassadors that Garcia sent to Count Mauritz van Nassau in Brazil in 1643. Their physical capacity impressed Johan Nieuhof so much that he wrote that they "were elegant and strong, very agile" and danced and leaped marvelously and "handle a sword wonderfully."[189]

As they did with other elements of European culture, Central Africans introduced European music into the local fare. By mid-century at least, trumpets of European design (introduced by the Portuguese) joined the traditional ivory and wood trumpets (*mpungu*) at Kongo's court.[190] Cavazzi also noted a dance performed by the nobility and matrons called *Maquina ma Fuete*, "which is called a royal dance" because it was done in the presence of the king and high-ranking officials. To Cavazzi, the dance was performed with so much reserve and seriousness that it appeared to be Castilian, and he even noted that the dancers carried little baskets with stones inside to resemble castanets.[191]

The music of Angola was made not only with African musical instruments but also European instruments. When Njinga entered Luanda in 1622, she was greeted "with the sound of various instruments both abbondo [Mbundu] and European."[192] Again, when Pedro Tavares married the Manisonsa (a local Mbundu ruler) at the church near Lake Quilunda off the Bengo in 1632, the celebration attracted people from several miles around, including European settlers Simão Nunes, who played viola, and João Fernandes, who played the drum for the dance that all performed. The evidence of musical appropriation was not limited to the core areas, for the small bells the people of Libolo wore around their waists were said to have been adapted from the Portuguese, who "introduced them for grandiosity."[193] The appropriation of musical instruments was not a one-way process, for Portuguese and Luso-African also relied on African musicians to indicate their status. For example, African musicians were prominent members in the households of the Portuguese and Luso-Africans and accompanied their masters, playing local instruments like

[188] Cavazzi, *Istorica Descrizione*, Book I, no. 314.
[189] Johann Nieuhof, *Gedekweerdige Brasilianse Zee – en Lantreise* (Amsterdam, 1682), p. 56.
[190] Cavazzi, *Istorica Desscrizione*, I, no. 332.
[191] Cavazzi, *Istorica Descrizione*, I, no. 334.
[192] MSS Araldi, Cavazzi, "Missione Evangelica," vol. A, Book 2, p. 24.
[193] Cavazzi, *Istorica Descrizione* I, no. 353.

marinbas, chucalhos (rattles), *pandeiros* (tambourines), and local violins. Cadornega noted that those Portuguese and Luso-African masters who did not have such a retinue were dismissed as being poor and not "the lord and macota a mindele [white nobleman]."[194]

European musical influence often came in through the Church. From early times, Portuguese and Luso-Africans resident in Kongo or in Luanda organized religious celebrations in which European religious music was played. For example, the kings of Kongo, like Álvaro III, went to church accompanied by musicians playing "instruments of music and war in their fashion," but in the church might hear an organ play, in all probability tuned to European scales. Certainly, the same bishop who complained of royal behavior admitted that the "Ethiopians sing well and are expert in musical arts."[195] Jesuits in Kongo in the 1620s sent their students into the streets singing songs about the "mysteries of the Faith." They reported, optimistically to say the least, that this new music had come to replace secular songs and, moreover, prevented wild animals from coming at night to attack farm stock and even people.[196]

The feast of Saint Francis Xavier, which was held in Luanda in 1620, provides an excellent example of the penetration of European music and the participation of Africans in it. Governor Luis Mendes de Vasconcellos, fresh from his victories in Ndongo, and the Jesuits organized the festival to imitate similar events in Portugal and were so satisfied with the results that they concluded that the quality of the performance was so high that it could have been done in Lisbon "to the amazement of the blacks." The procession included giant effigies and a pygmy they had captured in the war against Ndongo, who was dressed in an elaborate costume. The recently founded Brotherhood of Our Lady of the Rosary, populated by the Africans, also marched in the procession. As if in imitation of the *nsanga*, the festivities included Mbundu, who performed a "dance of swords as good as the best in Portugal." Although the prominent participants were the governor, the white settlers, and the members of the religious orders and clergy, the festival also included the "principal people of the country and the common people." The part of the celebration that revealed core elements of the emerging Atlantic Creole culture was represented by the floats that portrayed the kings of Kongo

---

[194] Cadornega, *História* 1: 210.
[195] Soares Report, 1619, *MMA* 6: 377; on the organ, see Manuel Baptista Soares, "Visita ad sacra limina," 16 November 1619, *MMA* 6: 420.
[196] Franco, *Synopsis Annalium*, no. 14, p. 245.

and Angola both richly dressed in European style and the king of the empire of Ethiopia "dressed in rich country cloth." Each of these kings had a song composed for him by students at the college of Luanda that welcomed the saint and thanked him for bringing Christianity to Africa. Mbundu slaves of the college also played a part: dressed in red velvet, they performed music according to the sequences they had learned from the missionaries. The Mbundus and Kongos who participated in the festivities were not simply passively learning European music and dance or simply in European styles. Many added their own variant, successfully, in bullfights "because they were good dancers" and to demonstrate their musical skills.[197]

In addition to the intermixing of Christian and Central African traditions in religious services, names, baptisms, burials, and public festivals, Africans living in the core Atantic Creole areas, and others outside the core, also became familiar with a wide range of other Iberian cultural practices, including foodways, dress, and the like. Although most Africans in the region grew a variety of local crops, including various millets, sorghum, and beans, they accepted the various European and American crops that were introduced into Africa from the beginning of the "Columbian Exchange." In Kongo, for example, American corn, called "masa ma Mputu" or "grain of Portugal," had become a staple along with the indigenous grain products.[198] In addition, by at least the middle of the seventeenth century, Kongolese as well as Mbundu farmers and workers on the plantations on the Bengo, and probably others, were routinely preparing manioc flour and it became a regular part of their diet, alongside the four kinds of African grain.[199] To consume manioc, Central Africans had to adopt the processing system, derived ultimately from American techniques, to extract poison.[200] New American crops were not exhausted by these examples, for in Kongo people ate a type of bean that was known as *lukanza lua Brasil*, or Brazilian bean, and from Europe they had naturalized radishes and onions.[201] In the middle of the

[197] "Relação das Festas que a Residençia de Angolla fez na Beatificação do Beato Padre Fran^{co} de Xavier da Companhia de Jezus," Felner, *Angola*, pp. 531–41. For an interpretation of the festival in the light of more recent Carnivals in Luanda, see David Birmingham, "Carnival at Luanda," *Journal of African History* 29 (1988): 93–103.
[198] ARA OWIC 46, fol. 4, Capelle to Maurits, "Corte beschrijvinge"; Da Roma, *Breve Relatione*, p. 82.
[199] Barthélemy d'Espinchal de Massiac, 1652, *MMA* 11: 250.
[200] Da Roma, *Breve Relatione*, pp. 82–4; Cavazzi, *Istorica Descsrizione*, I, no. 286.
[201] Da Roma, *Breve Relatione*, pp. 89–90.

seventeenth century, sugar cane was grown in great abundance and the Capuchin missionary Giovanni Francesco da Roma believed that at one time there were actually sugar mills as in Brazil, but in Kongo "now they only crush it and suck out juice."[202]

Portuguese settlers in Angola, and often those resident in Kongo or even in the more distant markets, introduced a wide variety of European fruit, including pears, peaches, and almonds.[203] They may also have introduced chickpeas as well, for Cardonega reported in his time that in the Dande region the local people grew both rice and chickpeas.[204] Although grains were often prepared in the traditional way, whereby they were ground in mortars and then boiled to make a sort of porridge, called *nfundi*, the Kongolese had also started to make a sort of bread, following Portuguese influence, called *mbolo*, from the Portuguese term for "cake," which Italian missionaries thought very "tasty and easy to digest."[205] Cadornega also noted that cakes of this sort were made of bananas and eaten by both European settlers as well as Africans.[206] Even Europeans critical of African foodways found *mwamba*, the popular Central African gravy that was eaten with the ground and cooked grain, tasty and easy to digest. Most people made the dish from peanut oil and peppers, although those who could afford it might add meat or fish.[207] In fact, during the seventeenth century an African Creole cuisine was developing in Luanda among the Portuguese and Luso-African residents and was being consumed by "blacks as well as whites, whites native to this country and some from Portugal." This creole dish called "macaça caça, ingilhos, maquecas, or gingombos," consisted of meat or fish, with *nkasa* leaves, black beans and palm oil (for lack of Portuguese olive oil) and was cooked in a *nkasa* leaf."[208]

Tobacco was also an important America crop that had become indigenous to Central African agronomy. Samuel Brun, visiting Soyo in 1611, observed, "They are industrious and they can bear hunger for a considerable time, as long as they have magkay [*makaya*, leaves in Kikongo] or tobacco, whose leaves they grind and ignite, so that a strong smoke

---

[202] Da Roma, *Breve Relatione*, p. 90. There is no documentary evidence that there were sugar mills in seventeenth-century Central Africa.
[203] Cadornega, *História* 3: 375–6.
[204] Cadornega, *História* 3: 55, author's note 84.
[205] Da Roma, *Breve Relatione*, p. 83; Cavazzi, *Istorica Descrizione*, 1, no. 286 (largely based on da Roma).
[206] Cadornega, *História* 3: 372.
[207] Cavazzi, *Istorica Desscrizione* I, no. 287.
[208] Cadornega, *História* 3: 357–8.

is produced, which they inhale for thirst and hunger," suggesting a long familiarity with the plant.[209] When Mateus Cardoso crossed Mbamba province in 1625, his carriers demanded tobacco, because they also believed it relieved hunger and made work easier.[210] By mid-century the crop was ubiquitous in Kongo, where it was both smoked and chewed.[211] In fact, tobacco smoking was so much a part of the culture in the Dembos region that high-ranking people were buried with it in their tombs to smoke in the afterlife.[212] Dutch merchants in Loango observed that tobacco was one of the products commonly traded on the coast from the interior, as local merchants went many miles into the interior to deal with them.[213] Njinga was an avid smoker, and in fact tobacco smoking was common in her lands.[214] Slaves awaiting shipment in Luanda could not be maintained in health, Dutch officials believed, "if they were not given tobacco of the type that is called macaya."[215]

The palm wine that Africans in the region made by fermenting the sap of trees, which was consumed daily, passed beyond the African producers and consumers as African rulers shared the drink with Europeans traders, officials and missionaries. But the process of consuming alcoholic beverages among Atlantic Creoles was not limited to African-produced beverages, for Africans in the Atlantic Creole zone consumed European beverages as well, and wine drinking was well established throughout much of the area.[216] Central Africans imported and drank considerable quantities of European wine. Dapper, describing the situation in 1641–1642, noted that the Kongolese were "much inclined to drink, especially Spanish wine and brandy," and often even commoners held parties for their friends that involved heavy wine consumption.[217] Cavazzi believed that even poor people might sell one or two of their children to pay the costs of buying European wine to give to guests at their wedding feasts.[218] Father Giovanni Francesco da Roma thought grapes could grow in the

[209] Samuel Brun, *Schiffarten* 27.
[210] Mateus Cardoso, "Relação da 2a ida que o Pe. Mat...fez ao Reyno de Congo," 14 September 1625, *MMA* 7: 372–3.
[211] Da Roma, *Relatione* 123.
[212] Cadornega, *História* 1: 425.
[213] ARA OWIC 46, fol. 9, Capelle to van Nassau. "Corte beschrijvinge."
[214] Gaeta, *Meravigliosa Conversione*, pp. 176, 184.
[215] ARA OWIC 58, Cornelis Nieulant to High Council of Brazil, 17 December 1642.
[216] On wine consumption in central Africa, see the pathbreaking work of José Curto, *Enslaving Spirits: The Portuguese-Brazilian Alcohol Trade at Luanda and its Hinterland, c. 1550–1850* (Leiden, 2004).
[217] Dapper, *Naukeurige Beschrijvinge*, p. 198.
[218] Cavazzi, *Istorica Descrizione* I, no. 282.

region, and indeed would yield two harvests a year, but that the only reason they did not have grape wines was because the Portuguese prevented the importation of vines so as to keep the market to themselves.[219]

Imported wines were already important products by the start of the seventeenth century. Portuguese fiscal officers complained in 1612 that Canary wines were in high demand, because "without [them] one cannot buy slaves in the ordinary feiras of Angola," and that the wines were often stolen by *pombeiros* for their masters.[220] Portuguese paymasters imported vast quantities of wine, especially Canary wine, to pay the Imbangala, who would not fight without having it. Imbangala, both leaders and common soldiers, were especially interested in drinking European wine at any festival or gathering. Queen Njinga continued this custom during her Imbangala years, though even in 1625 she was demanding wine from the Portuguese.[221] Gaeta, who knew her later in life, also noted her habit of drinking Canary wine, of which he said, "each barrel cost a slave."[222]

The dominant members of the Atlantic Creole zone also adopted new clothing styles that set them apart from the bulk of their kinsmen, who continued to wear the traditional single cloth (sometimes made of palm fibre) wrapped around their waists. Leading members of Atlantic Creole society could choose from a range of African and European fabrics and dress. Capelle observed that the nobility of the Kongo "ordinarily wear long mantles in the Portuguese fashion" that were made from fine linen cloth and other fabrics brought from Luanda by the Portuguese. When the Dutch fleet of Piet Heyn visited Soyo in 1624, he found the count and his wife dressed in Portuguese clothing. Other noble ladies in Soyo's court wore long clothes that covered both the top and bottom part of their bodies, whereas the serving maids wore a cloth that only went up to the waist.[223] A distinctive feature of upper-class Kongolese clothing was *nkutu*, a finely made netted top covering that Antonio Manuel prominently displayed on his diplomatic mission to Rome and that is shown on his bust in Santa Maria Maggiore in Rome.[224] (See Figure 6.) Some of the clothing was made by local tailors, but the slipper-type flat shoes with

---

[219] Da Roma, *Breve Relatione*, p. 58.

[220] Memorials of Pedro Sardinha to Conselho de Estado c. 1612, *MMA* 6: 105.

[221] Curto, *Enslaving Spirits*, p. 150–1; 198–9.

[222] Gaeta, *Meravigliosa Conversione*, p. 175.

[223] De Laet, *Jarlijck verhael*, p. 66.

[224] ARA OWIC 46, fol. 5, F. van Capelle to Count Jan Maurits van Nassau and Directors, "Corte beschrijvinge van de principaelste plaetsen gelegen in Angola te weten Commo, Goby, Maiomba, Loango, Cacongo, Molemboe, Zarry, Sonho, Congo, en anderen omleggende plaetsen..." March 1642. Da Roma records give a slightly more

FIGURE 12. Dembo Ambuilla. Photograph by authors from original at the archive of the Academie das Cienças, Lisbon.

decorations that some Kongo men wore were manufactured in Luanda and sold in Kongo for a high price.[225]

Imported cloth was used extensively in burials. When a Christian Kongolese died, "one or two of the most faithful slaves remain perpetually in service of the dead." One slave prayed for the deceased every Saturday and on All Souls Day, lighted lamps, and dressed the body in new cloth.[226] The custom of dressing the dead in imported cloth had become

elaborate description of the dress of the Kongolese nobles. See Da Roma, *Breve Relatione*, p. 68; Cavazzi, *Istorica Descrisione*, book 1, no. 343–6.

[225] Cavazzi, *Istorica Descrizione* I, no. 345. Cavazzi noted that apart from the queen and her children, who wore slippers, other ladies in court were barefooted; Cavazzi, *Istorica Descrizione* I, no. 347.

[226] Cavazzi, *Istorica Descrizione* I, 261.

so widespread that even in areas of the interior where there was little Christianity or where local customs still prevailed friends and servants of deceased used a great deal of imported European cloth.[227]

Other elements of the Atlantic Creole world, such as housing and crafts, are less visible in the records and in any case did not affect local practices as those linked with religion and religious rituals. Central African approaches to housing showed limited influence from contact with the Portuguese as only the king of Kongo and a few nobles adopted the European-style housing that was common among the Portuguese settlers throughout West Central Africa. In the Kongo capital São Salvador, for example, Portuguese settlers often built European-style houses in stones covered with earth and decorated with local plaster with rooms that were "well supplied with small tables, chairs and draperies in the European fashion."[228] However, the royal residence revealed a mixture of both African and Portuguese style. The pattern of enclosing a large area (more than a mile and a half) with multiple dwellings illustrated more of the African style but the enclosure also contained the European-style house of the king. He lived in a wooden house with a second floor, and the missionary da Roma, who was in Kongo from 1645 to 1646, observed that "in all Congo there is not another who owns a second floor like the king."[229]

Most people in Kongo, including the majority of the nobles, lived in much simpler buildings that could be constructed in a few days and in rural areas were abandoned frequently.[230] Nevertheless, even those higher status nobles who chose not to follow European building techniques still lived in large enclosed areas with many small buildings. Their own residences were larger and had finished floors, contained palm cloth hangings and tapestries with imported silk curtains, and were furnished with European-style chairs covered in velvet, parasols, and wardrobes, so that they are "the paragon of civil people, to be distinguished as lords of great bearing."[231]

Africans who lived in Luanda and around the other Portuguese presidios were familiar with Portuguese-style buildings, and if they were

---

[227] Cavazzi *Istorica Descrizione* I, 262.
[228] Da Roma, *Breve Relatione*, pp. 106–8.
[229] Da Roma, *Breve Relatione*, pp. 106–8. The Jesuits also had a two-story building, but their upper floor was only a library. BN Madrid, MS 3533, Teruel, "Descripcion narrativa," p. 180.
[230] Da Roma, *Breve Relatione*, pp. 106–8.
[231] Cavazzi, *Istorica Descrizione* I, 294; Igreja da Conceição de Luanda, 4 December 1635, *MMA* 8: 337.

household servants, they lived in them with their owners. In Luanda Africans helped build the houses that were constructed with stone covered with plaster in the Portuguese style, some of them with large courtyards. Around the European houses the Africans built their settlements composed of many straw houses.[232] In the presidios and other settlements Portuguese residents also built their own Portuguese-style houses, which also had large courtyards where they kept their slaves.[233] Pedro Tavares, who traveled throughout the presidios outside of Luanda and in the more scattered Portuguese settlements in the Bengo region, observed African-style housing, including the encircled settlement made of wattle and daub belonging to the *soba* Nambacalombe, who lived with his wife and "40 women his concubines," each one of whom occupied a house with her children.[234] Tavares frequently visited but never stayed in the houses of the Portuguese, preferring the small, private African one-room quarters.

In the areas of Ndongo and Matamba African-style structures prevailed. At Njinga's kilombo at Senga a Cavanga there were several large structures, including an enclosed stockade on one side of the plaza or central square. The stockade was made from great logs tied together from behind and completely open to the front, where various public business took place. The kilombo also boasted a more formal "great house where ambassadors were received, principally those of the King of Congo . . . for whom she had a seat on the side of the wall, which she had covered with velvet and silks, both the seats and the walls." The house was big enough to allow quite a large number of people to sit on rich carpets used for state occasions.[235] Njinga's more permanent dwelling in Matamba was constructed in a similar fashion but was even more elaborate and was located within a two-square-mile enclosure.[236]

Enslavement and Atlantic Creole Culture

As this and the preceding chapter have made clear, between 1607 and 1660 Central Africans exhibited varying degrees of Atlantic Creole culture in religion, naming patterns, burial practices, foodways, material culture, and music. The circumstances of war, banditry, commerce, domestic slavery, and tribute led a significant number of these people to be sent as slaves to the Americas. A few thousand of the hundreds of thousands

[232] ARA OWIC 56, Pieter Moortamer and C. Nieulant, 17 September 1641.
[233] ARA OWIC 58, Mortamer Report, 14 October 1642.
[234] ARSI 55, fol. 96, Tavares to Vogado.
[235] Cadornega, *História*, 1: 413–14.
[236] Gaeta, *Meravagliosa Conversione*, pp. 192–4.

who made the crossing from Luanda and other West Central African ports to Brazil and the Spanish Indies were diverted by English and Dutch privateers to the emerging colonies in the Americas. It was these Atlantic Creoles who became the founding group of Africans in those colonies.

An analysis of the wars, banditry, and judicial and other developments outlined in the Chapter 3 reveals that, although the mixture varied from year to year, Atlantic Creoles always represented a significant proportion of the captives exported to the Americas. We have attempted to describe enslavement by war in a series of maps. These maps, which represent the situation in Angola in five-year intervals beginning in 1615, display events from both a cultural dimension and a military perspective. Shadings on the maps reflect the degree to which Atlantic Creole culture had developed. The darkest shading indicates the areas where the greatest creolization had taken place, whereas the lightly shaded regions represent the areas with intermittent or superficial creolization. Unshaded areas represent the locations with very little creolization. The gradual spreading and intensi-fication of creolization from 1615 to 1660 are represented by the changing area of shading. For example, the intensification of Christianization under Capuchin guidance in eastern Angola in maps after 1650 is represented by an intensification of the shading in that region.

Wars are represented by an intensification of shading or outlining in the areas from which people were enslaved. For example, the maps indicate the approximate areas of recruitment of the losing side in a war. Thus in the 1615–1620 wars, heavy shading east of Massangano represents the enslavement of people during Mendes de Vasconselhos's campaigns, which continue on the 1621–1625 map. Moreover, in the 1615–1620 map in Kongo additional heavily shaded areas represent Álvaro III's campaigns against the rebel Duke of Nsundi in 1616 and Duke António da Silva in 1619–1620.[237]

The maps illustrate that campaigns often took place in the core Atlantic Creole areas (heaviest shadings) and frequently occurred in intermedi-ate Atlantic Creole zones (lighter shaded areas). Several wars did occur in areas with little exposure to Atlantic Creole culture (the Portuguese campaigns in Benguela in 1617–1618, and the wars between Kasanje and Njinga in the 1650s) and thus would have yielded captives with no familiarity with Atlantic Creole culture. Most of the campaigns, however,

---

[237] For a full explanation and documentation of the events on which these maps are based see Chapter 3.

involved the capture of fully creolized central Africans or those partially familiar with Atlantic Creole culture. For example, many of the soldiers and support personnel captured and enslaved during the Dutch occupation (1641–1648), or again in the Portuguese wars against Kongo or Kongo's several civil wars, involved people from the core Atlantic Creole regions who would have brought with them to the Americas the Central African Atlantic Creole culture.

The Angolan records contain a range of descriptions about the cultural background of the captives. For example, during the war that João Correio de Sousa waged against the Kongo provinces of Bumbi, Kazanse, and Nambu a Ngongo in 1622, at least 80 Christian Kongo nobles and thousands of ordinary Christian Kongoles were captured and deported to Brazil. The Jesuits, in a complaint against the governor, noted the "cruelties that were done to the Christians of the Congo," and Pedro II, Kongo's king, complained to his representative in Rome that Correia de Sousa had "destroyed and desolated many provinces in the kingdom... where they are infinitive Christians" who were made slaves."[238] Moreover, as Kongo armies included large numbers of *adargueiros* ("shield bearers"), who were of noble status and often members of the Order of Christ, in the civil wars, the number of nobles captured and enslaved could number in the hundreds.[239]

The slaves who were exported during the 1620s and who came from Ndongo or from the core were also familiar with Atlantic Creole culture. Not all of them came through violent capture, as the Portuguese received Africans that subject *sobas* paid as taxes "according to the condition of each one."[240] A report of 1624 listed 94 from such payments, though the number rose to the 300s in following years. Most *sobas* paid only a few slaves, but Ndongo was expected to pay 100.[241] Those who were reduced to slavery for crimes or disobedience in Portuguese-controlled territories might be individuals of high status who were quite familiar with Atlantic Creole culture. Among them were high-ranking people, including "two macunzes, companions of mani lumbo" from Ndongo kept in prison until they could be "embarked abroad in the form of a sentence."[242] De Sousa, in 1629, sent out as exiles a number of military officers who were captured in the war against Njinga, including *soba* Sonde, the kiambole

[238] Pedro II to Giovanni Battista Vives, 28 November 1623, *MMA*, 7, 161.
[239] Thornton, *Warfare*.
[240] Fernão de Sousa to Antonio de Castro, 29 December 1629, *FHA* 2: 241.
[241] Heintze, "Angolan Vassal Tributes," on the numbers and nature of this tribute.
[242] Fernao de Sousa to Sons, 1630, *FHA* 1: 300.

of Matamba, and another "war negro" taken in the assault.[243] In 1629 Azevedo de Araújo advised the governor "that the sovas of province of Aire are all risen up, and their payments of baculamentos are two years behind, for which they are to be beheaded or shipped out, and other lords put in their lands who would obey." De Sousa ordered the soba branded on the chest with "two marks of mine and they would be sold...as my pieces" until later.[244] In 1631, de Sousa exiled the soba of Cambambe to Brazil. He had been thrown out by his subjects, but he continued to harass the newly elected *soba*.[245]

During the period of Dutch occupation, the cultural background of captives reflected the wars that took place between the Portuguese and Njinga as well as the conflicts between the king of Kongo and the Count of Soyo. One group of captives represented people from the core Creole Atlantic zone (Kongo and Soyo), whereas the other group comprised a mixture of captives, some of whom were familiar with Atlantic Creole culture, whereas others were not. The Dutch officer Pieter Mortamer observed in 1642 that the Portuguese got "few slaves other than Ambondesche [Mbundu] and Chingasche [Njinga's] exports." He noted that although they received captives from Loango and Congo, "they keep with them until they were habituated to poverty and slavery," because the group included "nobles taken in wars" and that if they were immediately exported "they neglect themselves and die on route."[246]

The fact that captives and slaves were drawn from areas with widely varying exposure to Atlantic Creole culture explains the differing reactions that observers of the time had of the background of the people who were shipped to America. In 1617, for example, a Jesuit report from Bahia noted that "the people from Angola are mostly unenlightened in the doctrine and the things that pertain to their salvation."[247] The Jesuits did seek to improve the situation, and Capuchins augmented this effort after they began work in Angola in the 1650s. Cavazzi noted that missionaries worked hard to "in order that they be instructed and baptized, checking (invigilandosi) in the ports, to know, if on the embarkation to America they are truly Christians."[248]

---

[243] Fernão de Sousa to Lopo Soares Lasso, 10 December 1629, *FHA* 2: 315.
[244] Letter of CM to Governor, 17 September 1629, and his undated response, summarized in Fernão de Sousa to Sons, 1630, *FHA* 1: 326–7, 2: 335.
[245] Informação de Fernão de Sousa to Government, n.d. (between 7 and 11 December 1631, *FHA* 2: 335.
[246] Mortamer, "Schriftlijk Raport," fol 13.
[247] ARSI Brasilia 8, 250–1, as quoted in Sweet, *Recreating Africa*p. 198.
[248] Cavazzi, *Istorica Descrizione* I, 331.

Another example comes from a report published in 1624 by Alonso de Sandoval. Writing of conditions in Cartegena regarding newly arrived captives, he remarked that Angolans were considered Catholic because "when we examine these Angolans it is not to baptize them, but to see if there are any who have not received water or have not received it by heart, or for other causes... or they have not been baptized." Indeed, de Sandoval contrasted the fate of these Angolan captives with those who came from "Caboverde and the Rivers of Guinea (and at times San Thomé)."[249] De Sandoval's own research among the sea captains and responses he received from Jesuits in Luanda confirmed that the carelessly executed mass baptisms in which Holy Water was thrown over large groups of captives preparing to embark were not sufficient and that the captives should be re-baptized.[250] The Jesuit's response did note, however, that "some come well baptized and others not."[251] Other reports concerning the religious and cultural background of central Africans captives during the period describe people with no familiarity of Christianity or other elements of Atlantic Creole culture.

The observations of Jesuits and others concerning the mass baptisms that took place in Luanda should not be the basis on which the religious and cultural background of the captives is judged.[252] As the preceding chapters have demonstrated, Atlantic Creole culture with its religious core had spread, with varying degrees of intensity, in Kongo and Angola over a long period of time. The wars, raids, commercial transactions, and the like that led to enslavement brought people from all over the region, and for some, mass baptisms in Luanda were their only exposure to Atlantic Creole Culture, but certainly they should not stand in for the entire group.

The 1617 Jesuit report that described Angolan captives as "unenlightened in the doctrine" probably referred to the slaves captured in the wars waged at just that time by Manuel Cerveira Periera south of the Kwanza and in Benguela among peoples with very little contact with the Afro-Atlantic world. Pedro Travares's comments concerning the captives with whom he sailed from Luanda to Rio de Janiero in 1635 reveal the mixed cultural identities of the Central Africans. He observed that of the 600 captives on board, "... most were already baptized, but knew nothing of

---

[249] De Sandoval, *Natureza*, book 2, cap. 5, fol. 255v.

[250] De Sandoval, *Natureza*, book 3, cap. 4, fols. 243–6.

[251] De Sandoval, *Natureza*, book 3, cap. 4, fols. 243–6.

[252] See James Sweet, "Spanish and Portuguese Influences on Racial Slavery in British North America, 1492–1619," paper given at the 5th Annual Gilder Lehman Center International Conference, "Collective Degradation: Slavery and the Construction of Race," November 7–8, 2003, pp. 27–9.

the faith" and that they had come from 200 leagues in interior or had "just as arrived in city" and then were baptized and embarked.[253] The captives from the far interior were undoubtedly captured during the wars waged by Njinga to conquer Matamba and against Kasanje in an area with very few Atlantic Creoles.

This pattern of sending out captives with varying levels of exposure to Atlantic Creole culture continued after the Portuguese restoration in 1648. During this period, the Portuguese war against Mbwila would bring out Atlantic Creoles, whereas those against Kisama would represent people from the outer zone. Similarly, the wars of Kasanje against Njinga in the 1650s would send out both captives who were familiar with Atlantic Creole culture, especially its religious dimension, as well as people who had no familiarity with it. The rebellion in Kongo that broke out in 1657–1658, Kongo's continuing wars with Soyo, and Portuguese invasion of Kongo would yield captives from a core region who would be much more familiar with Atlantic Creole culture.

[253] ARSI Lusitania 55, fol. 106.

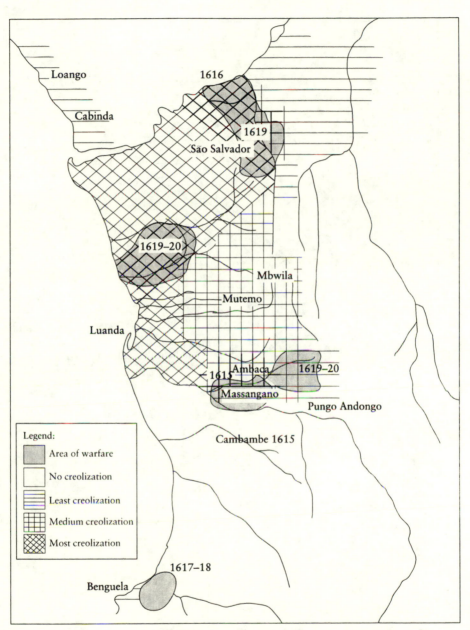

Loango

Cabinda

1616

São Salvador

1619

1619–20

Mbwila

Mutemo

Luanda

Ambaca   1619–20

1615

Massangano

Pungo Andongo

Cambambe 1615

Legend:

Area of warfare

No creolization

Least creolization

Medium creolization

Most creolization

1617–18

Benguela

War in Angola, 1615–20

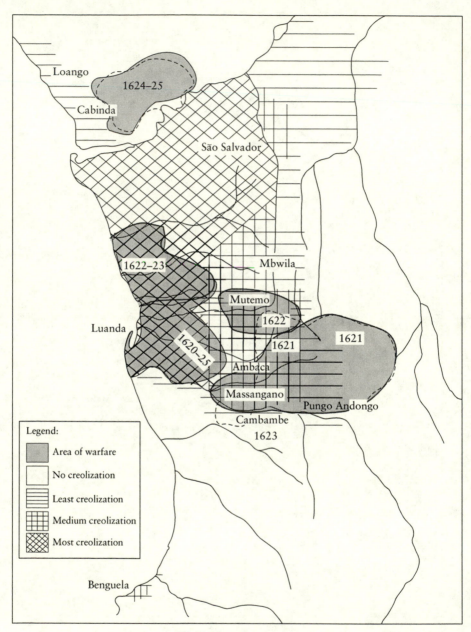

Loango

1624–25

Cabinda

São Salvador

1622–23

Mbwila

Mutemo

1622

1621

1621

Luanda

1620–25

Ambaca

1621

Massangano

Pungo Andongo

Cambambe
1623

Legend:

Area of warfare

No creolization

Least creolization

Medium creolization

Most creolization

Benguela

War in Angola, 1621–25

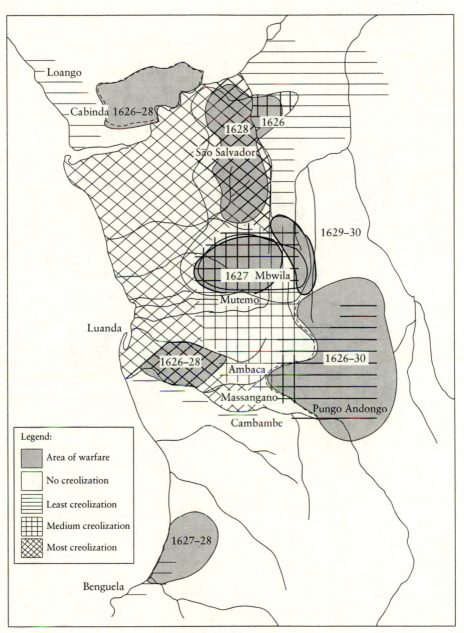

Loango

Cabinda 1626–28

1628   1626

São Salvador

1629–30

1627 Mbwila

Mutemo

Luanda

1626–28

Ambaca

1626–30

Massangano

Cambambe

Pungo Andongo

Legend:

Area of warfare

No creolization

Least creolization

Medium creolization

Most creolization

1627–28

Benguela

War in Angola, 1626–30

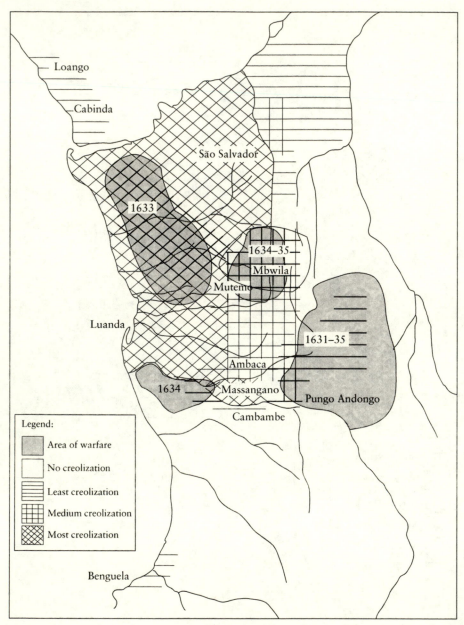

Loango

Cabinda

São Salvador

1633

1634–35

Mbwila

Mutemo

Luanda

1631–35

Ambaca

1634

Massangano

Pungo Andongo

Cambambe

Legend:

Area of warfare

No creolization

Least creolization

Medium creolization

Most creolization

Benguela

War in Angola, 1631–35

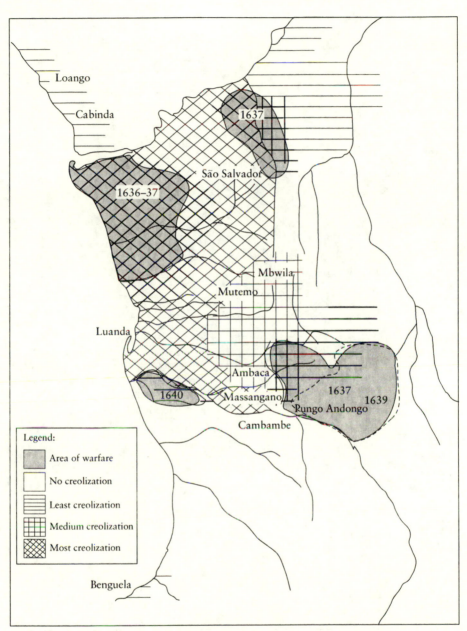

Loango

Cabinda

1637

São Salvador

1636–37

Mbwila

Mutemo

Luanda

Ambaca

1637

1640

Massangano

1639

Pungo Andongo

Cambambe

Legend:

Area of warfare

No creolization

Least creolization

Medium creolization

Most creolization

Benguela

War in Angola, 1636–40

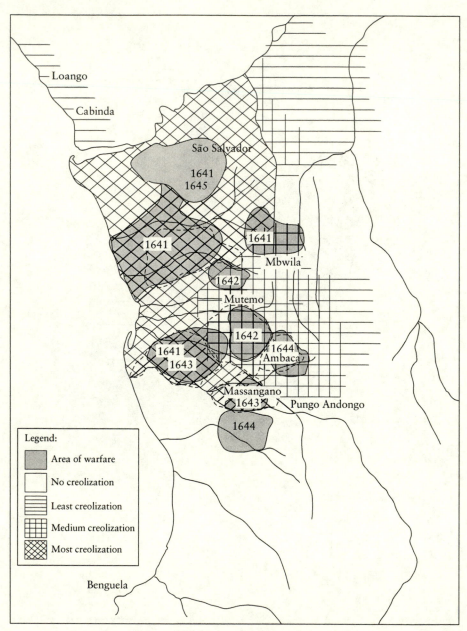

Loango

Cabinda

São Salvador

1641
1645

1641

1641

Mbwila

1642

Mutemo

1642

1644
Ambaca

1641
1643

Massangano

1643

Pungo Andongo

1644

Legend:

Area of warfare

No creolization

Least creolization

Medium creolization

Most creolization

Benguela

War in Angola, 1641–45

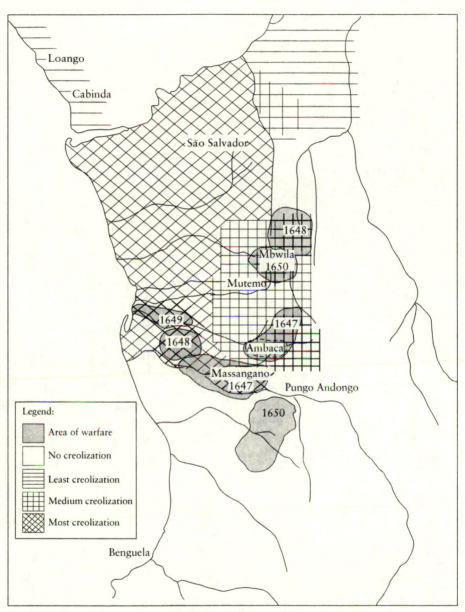

Loango

Cabinda

São Salvador

1648

Mbwila
1650

Mutemo

1649

1648

1647

Ambaca

Massangano
1647

Pungo Andongo

1650

Legend:

Area of warfare

No creolization

Least creolization

Medium creolization

Most creolization

Benguela

War in Angola, 1646–50

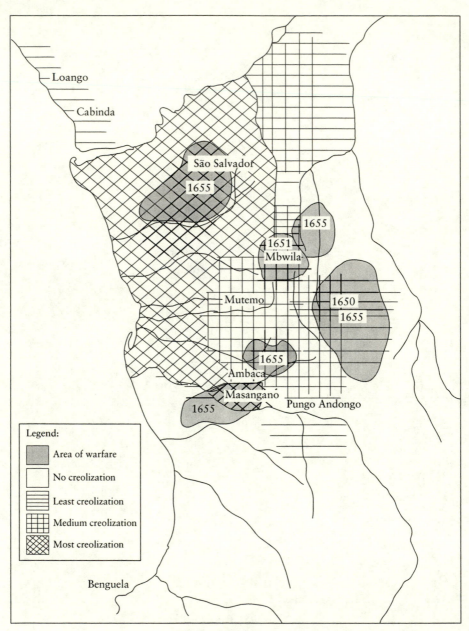

Loango

Cabinda

São Salvador
1655

1655

1651
Mbwila

Mutemo

1650
1655

1655

Ambaca

Masangano

1655

Pungo Andongo

Legend:

Area of warfare

No creolization

Least creolization

Medium creolization

Most creolization

Benguela

War in Angola, 1651–55

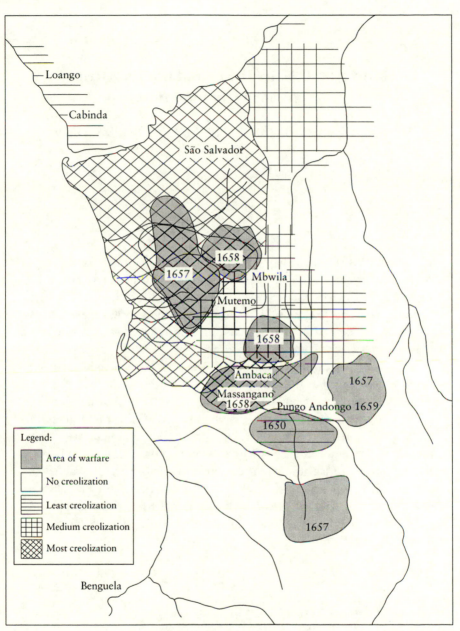

Loango

Cabinda

São Salvador

1658

1657   Mbwila

Mutemo

1658

1657

Ambaca

Massangano
1658   Pungo Andongo 1659

1650

1657

Legend:

Area of warfare

No creolization

Least creolization

Medium creolization

Most creolization

Benguela

War in Angola, 1656–60

5

Shifting Status and the Foundation of African American Communities

Atlantic Creoles in the Early Anglo-Dutch Colonies

In his innovative and widely influential interpretation of the origins of African American culture, Ira Berlin argued that the first Africans, whom he called the Charter Generation, who came to the Anglo-Dutch settlements were Atlantic Creoles. However, he contended that these Atlantic Creoles who possessed both the skills and cultural predisposition to make their way in the new colonies came from the environs of European trading posts in West Africa or the Caribbean.[1] Berlin has been rightly taken to task for claiming that the Africans who lived around the posts in West Africa or the few who might have been taken from the Spanish possessions in the Caribbean were vulnerable enough to enslavement and numerous enough to influence the emergence of African American culture.[2] These objections are removed once one accepts, as we have demonstrated earlier, that the vast majority of the Charter Generation had West Central African and not West African roots. The West Central Africans are a much more likely source of Atlantic Creole culture than West Africans could have been because of their vast numbers and the regularity with which they were enslaved.

---

[1] Berlin, *Many Thousands*, pp. 17–26. Berlin first introduced this idea in "From Creole to African: Atlantic Creoles and the Origins of African American Society in Mainland North America," *William and Mary Quarterly* 53 (1996): 254.

[2] For the best criticism, see, Robin Law and Kristin Mann, "West Africa in the Atlantic Community: The Case of the Slave Coast," *William and Mary Quarterly* 56 (1999): 310; see also Sweet, "Spanish and Portuguese Influences," pp. 25–30. The source of their criticism is the small size and relatively limited "creolization" in this early period, a critique which Sweet extends even to the Angolans.

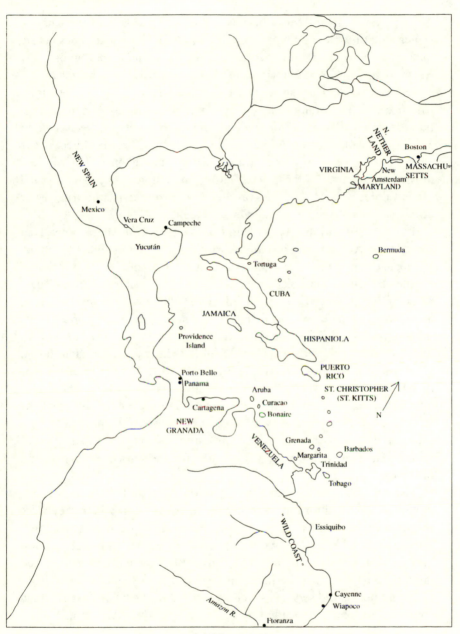

NEW SPAIN

Mexico •

Vera Cruz
Campeche •

Yucután

N.
NETHER
LAND

VIRGINIA

New
Amsterdam
MARYLAND

Boston •

MASSACHU-
SETTS

Bermuda

Tortuga •

CUBA

JAMAICA

Providence
Island

HISPANIOLA

PUERTO
RICO

Porto Bello
Panama •

Aruba

Cartagena •

Curacao

Bonaire

ST. CHRISTOPHER
(ST. KITTS)

N

NEW
GRANADA

VENEZUELA

Grenada

Margarita
Trinidad

Barbados

Tobago

"WILD COAST"

Essiquibo

Cayenne •
Wiapoco

Amazon R.

Ftoranza •

Caribbean Basin

The West Central African origins of the vast majority of the Charter Generation of Africans who arrived in English and Dutch colonies before the mid-seventeenth century, whether in New England or Barbados, New Amsterdam or the Amazon region and Guianas, made them distinct in several crucial ways. They spoke just two closely related Bantu languages, Kikongo and Kimbundu, and many knew a creolized version of Portuguese as well. There is little evidence of ethnic enmity between the two groups that would have inhibited social interactions between them in the Americas. As we have demonstrated earlier, the violence that resulted in their enslavement almost never pitted one ethnic group against each other. Conflicts that led to wars resulted either from dynastic struggles or Portuguese wars of conquest and enslavement.[3]

The common cultural background of West Central Africans involved very similar African religions and worldviews, which included for many an engagement with Christianity and a deep connection to Atlantic Creole culture in outlook, dress, cuisine, and agricultural knowledge. These traits, enhanced and modified to suit the new American environment, would provide a crucial cultural model for the waves of captives, mostly from West Africa brought in by the slave trade after 1640 who were not Atlantic Creoles, whom Berlin has designated the "Plantation Generations," which followed them in the mid to late seventeenth century.[4] The Atlantic Creole Charter Generation was thus the most homogenous group of Africans to enter the Americas in the whole history of the slave trade. This homogeneity may well have allowed them, even though they were not numerous, to have a substantial impact on the formation of African American culture that would influence the subsequent generation of Africans.

The Atlantic Creole Charter Generation possessed the means to set down their own cultural pattern in the Americas, even where they were subsequently outnumbered by new arrivals with no Creole background. They had enough contact with each other to avoid simple absorption into the world of their masters and Euro-America neighbors, established families to pass on their heritage, and worked at skilled and supervisory tasks and household service as well as labored in the fields or performed construction labor alongside the newly arrived West Africans. A good

---

[3] The only instance when an Mbundu army faced a Kongo army occurred in 1622 when the Portuguese João de Sousa invaded Kongo and relied on Mbundu-speaking soldiers. See Chapter 2 and the map and discussion of this war in Chapter 4.

[4] Berlin, *Many Thousands*, pp. 93–216, see pp. 95–108 for an overview.

number would become free and establish their own communities and estates, and some of them would disappear into the larger Euro-American community through intermarriage or migration to the frontier. A few even founded families that became powerful. For those who remained in slavery, their strategic position made them the cultural models for the more numerous non-Creole arrivals, reinforced by the cultural role of the free African American community.

Because the Atlantic Creole background of the Charter Generation was what made it distinctive, the fact that large numbers of Central African Atlantic Creoles were still included in the waves of new Africans that made up the Plantation Generation (about one in five on the English ships and even more for the Dutch) meant that the Creole elements of the older Central African Charter Generation's influence were reinforced.[5] Thus, no matter whether a colony was long established or newly founded, there would always be a Central African component in the makeup of the African population. The fact that later arrivals continued to have an Atlantic Creole background meant that their particular cultural blend would continue to inform the Plantation Generation when it became demographically dominant.

This interpretation of the role of the Atlantic Creole Charter Generation elaborates on another of Berlin's contentions, that is, that in some parts of America, notably in the Chesapeake (and later the Carolina Low Country), the Charter Generation was overwhelmed numerically by the Plantation Generation, whose origins were more from the interior parts of Africa, beyond the Atlantic Creole fringe. Berlin claimed that the Plantation Generation "Africanized" the Charter Generation, "whose members sank swiftly into historical oblivion." Plantation society isolated these new arrivals who "turned inward making the plantation itself... the site for reconstruction of African life." Although Berlin's model of the Charter Generation giving way to the Plantation Generation might work best for Barbados, where a very small Charter Generation was overwhelmed by a vast, new Plantation Generation after the late 1640s, it is less effective for other parts of the Anglo-Dutch Americas, including the Chesapeake, from which he derives this model.

However, Berlin recognized that in some other parts of North America, such as New Netherland/New York or New England, a smaller number

---

[5] David Richardson, "Slave Exports from West and West Central Africa, 1700–1810: New Estimates of Volume and Direction," *Journal of African History* 30 (1989): 17. Dutch slavers had higher numbers of Central Africans.

of imports and the absence of plantations made a lesser impact. It was enough to transform it from a "society with slaves" to nearly a "slave society." In these places, Berlin contended that although a substantial number of non-Atlantic Creole Africans arrived, they did not displace the Charter Generation, so that the Charter Generation managed "to extend its influence into the late eighteenth century."[6]

The Charter Generation: Demography and Settlement

The most important factors guaranteeing the influence of the Charter Generation were its size relative to the European settler population, its capacity, regardless of its size, to maintain some semblance of community and networking through proximity to each other and intermarriage, and its ability to exploit its Creole background to maintain influence in the new slave communities that formed during the Plantation period. Studying the relationship between the first Africans in the English and Dutch colonies and the subsequent arrivals occasioned by the growth of the Anglo-Dutch slave trade shows a variety of patterns and relationships among the Charter Generation and its successors.

Two dominant patterns emerge among the Atlantic Creoles who made up Charter Generation, depending on whether they were a small or large proportion of the whole settler population. In Barbados, the Chesapeake, New England, and the rural parts of the Dutch colony of New Netherland, the Charter Generation comprised a small faction, typically less than 1 in 20, of the larger settler group. However, in Bermuda, Tobago, the "Wild Coast" of South America (the Guianas), the urban center of New Amsterdam, and several failed colonies in South America and the Caribbean, the Charter Generation made up a much larger proportion of the total population, ranging from one fifth to over half. Either way, however, this group would have a substantial cultural impact on the less homogeneous and less Creole subsequent generations of Africans.

The significance of this impact would be determined in part by the size and rate of the arrival of the Plantation Generation. In some cases, as was most notable in Barbados, this generation was very large relative to the Charter Generation and arrived within 20 years. This comes closest to Berlin's model of "re-Africanization" of the pioneering first generation, limiting its Creole impact in the formation of later Afro-Barbadian culture. The situation in the Chesapeake, Berlin's main example of the

[6] Berlin, *Many Thousands*, pp. 107–8; 187–8.

impact of a non-Creole Plantation Generation, was less dramatic. The numbers of new arrivals were smaller relative to the Charter Generation than in Barbados, and they came in much more slowly, over more than half a century. In the Dutch colonies of Tobago and the "Wild Coast," a substantial Plantation Generation of diverse Africans met a large initial population of Central African Atlantic Creoles. In these areas the cultural influence of the Charter Generation would be more evident than their much less numerous compatriots in Barbados.

In contrast, in Bermuda, the Dutch islands of Aruba, Bonaire, and Curaçao, and New Amsterdam, the Charter Generation formed a much larger proportion of the total initial population, and moreover, there was not as large an influx of non-Atlantic Creoles to weaken their influence as in the case of the Chesapeake or Barbados. In New England and New Netherland (the rural hinterland of New Amsterdam) the Charter Generation was small, but there was no Plantation Generation to overwhelm them.

The Charter Generation: Low Population Settlements

For many writers, the earliest Africans in the Dutch and English settlements in the Americas were not sufficiently numerous to maintain their own identity and cultural practices. Living near Europeans and sometimes sharing their homes, the Charter Generation was absorbed by European culture as it grew in America, especially as so many were already Creole. Later, however, as Berlin argued, the larger and more demanding plantation regime "destroyed" the Charter Generation and forced the Plantation Generation into separate quarters, sometimes barracks, usually located at some distance from the quarters of the owners. Isolated from interaction with Europeans, they shaped a neo-African culture whose outlines are becoming evident in archaeological, linguistic, and folklore research.

Although not disagreeing with the idea that the creation of separate slave quarters with its own cultural elaborations was a fact of the later period, our research suggests that the Charter Generation managed to keep an Atlantic Creole identity even though they lived in close quarters with Europeans. The crucial factor was their ability to maintain a wide range of social interactions among themselves, which did not require whole separate villages to be kept up. Their common Central African background made even small groups a community – two or three people who shared language, worldview, and other cultural expectations might be sufficient to keep a cultural tradition. Their separate social, ethnic, and legal status tended to both push them away form the Europeans with whom they might live and pull them together as a group.

A. *Virginia*

Virginia is the best documented case of colonies that possessed a small number of Central Africans relative to the overall population and can serve not only as an illustration of the pattern for its own region (the Chesapeake) but also as a model for other, less richly documented regions. Virginia's sparse African population is revealed as early as in the census of 1620, taken after the first group of Africans arrived, which showed 32 of a population of 917 (3.5 percent). These numbers changed only a little in subsequent years. A pamphlet of 1649 provided another estimate, "That there are in *Virginia* about fifteene thousand *English*, and of *Negroes* brought thither three hundred good servants."[7] Africans had thus fallen to only 2 percent of the overall population. But this ratio may be a bit low, for a study of the 21 land patents listed for 1647, the period when data for the pamphlet was compiled, revealed some 8 "negroes" among the 218 people transported, accounting for 3.7 percent of the overall number of people claimed in these patents.[8] Both the estimate and our test cannot be considered anything more than suggestive, but in any case, the African population of the Chesapeake area was a very small percentage of the overall population in the colonial region.

Although the African population of the Chesapeake region was less than 5 percent of the total, residential patterns that tended to concentrate them in specific locations still allowed for a regular contact and a sense of community among them. John Coombs's study of the Chesapeake shows that the wealthiest and politically best-connected Virginians concentrated the largest number of Africans on their lands.[9] If three Africans living together is a minimum for forming a cultural community, then the muster list of 1625, which indicated the residence of 23 Africans in the Virginia colony, showed that only 3 people lived in groups of less than 3 (13 percent), whereas 16 lived in groups larger than 5 (69.5 percent). Abraham Piercy held 8 Central Africans at James City, making it

---

[7] [John Farrer] *A Perfect Description of Virginia* (London, 1649), p. 3.

[8] Data derived from abstracts in Nugent, *Cavaliers*, 1: 168–74. Patent data is far from definitive, so this estimate must be considered suggestive only.

[9] John Coombs, "Building 'The Machine': The Development of Slavery and Slave Society in Early Colonial Virginia," Ph.D. dissertation, College of William and Mary, 2003, pp. 79–82.

the largest concentration.[10] A decade later, when there were more Central Africans, this pattern continued. In the lists of servants claimed as headrights in patents recorded between 1637 and 1641, 101 persons were listed as "negroes." Groups claimed for headright that contained only one African made up less than 10 percent of the total, whereas 78 percent of the Africans claimed for headright were listed in conjunction with at least 5 other Africans, and almost half (46.5 percent) were in groups larger than 10. Of the 11 claims that had slaves in 1637, there were a total of 29 African and 240 European indentured servants, so that Africans were 12.1 percent of the total in such claims.[11] There were even greater concentrations, though, as Captain Samuel Matthews in 1649 had no less than 40 African servants on his land, which made up 13 percent of the Africans in Virginia at the time.[12]

Some idea of these concentrations can be gained from examining the distribution of Africans on the larger estate holders of the Eastern Shore of Virginia, the only area to have substantial records before the mid-seventeenth century.[13] Nathaniel Littleton, to take one example, accumulated 24 African servants, 12 adults and their 12 American-born children, between 1635 and 1656. Of this group, 8 had been together for between 15 and 20 years in the same location.[14] Littleton lived near four other prominent slave-owning families, the Charletons, the Kendalls, the Vaughans, and the Potts, whose members freely traded, worked, and intermarried

[10] "Musters of the Inhabitants in Virginia, 1624/5," in Annie Lash Jester and Martha Woodroof Hiden, *Adventurers of Purse and Person, 1607–1625* (1964). In another muster of 1624 there were greater concentrations, 11 at Flowerdew Hundred, but these were probably refugees from the war with Powhatan, which caused the population to be redistributed. We have therefore used the 1625 muster list as the most representative.

[11] Data derived from abstracts in Nugent, *Cavaliers*, 1: 56–129. There is a considerable literature on the statistical use of headrights, because many claims were fraudulent. However, this range comes from an early period when headright claims were more accurately assessed and looked into. See Edmund Morgan, "Headrights and Head Counts: A Review Article," *The Virginia Magazine of History and Biography* 80 (1972): 361–71; and Wesley Frank Craven's reply, p. 371 [the review and its reply concerned use of the data that Craven made to write his book, *White, Red, and Black: The Seventeenth Century Virginian* (Charlottesville, 1971)]. See also Russell Menard, "Immigration to the Chesapeake Colonies in the Seventeenth Century: A Review Essay," *The Maryland Historical Magazine* (1973): 323–9.

[12] Farrer, *Perfect Description*, p. 15.

[13] The Eastern Shore community and its interrelationships, well documented in the surviving records, has been the subject of several detailed historical studies, which have been used to reconstruct the next paragraphs, see for the most recent, Breen and Innes, *Myne owne Ground*, Deal, *Race and Class*, and Heinegg, "Free African Americans."

[14] Deal, *Race and Slavery*, pp. 367–9, has carefully worked out these relationships.

with each other. When hard times pressed them, these masters often sold
Africans to each other, selling them back in better times.[15] A good number of these bondsmen were also freed in one way or another (as many
as one third had gained freedom by 1670), but generally they retained
contacts and patronage arrangements with their former masters, though
many of these families still had slaves in their numbers. Two thirds, however, remained bound though they had many relations with their now-free
compatriots.

Holding their slaves together in groups was important to the early
owners. Francis Pott, for example, once told his nephew, who was managing his affairs while he was off in England, that "I had rather parte
with any thinge, or all that I have besides, then with my Negroes."[16] It
seems clear that the Littletons were also anxious to preserve the families of
their slaves, even when estates were sold, passed on, or divided amongst
heirs.[17] William Kendall, another of the early Eastern Shore masters, left
an estate to his son in 1684 along with eight negroes, Will (probably
Driggus), Charles, Great Jack, Little Jack, Harry, Tom, Bessie, and Mary
(Driggus), were not to be alienated from the land "but there to be and
remain as an appendant and an appendix to the freehold...."[18] Will
Driggus's family had been in this network since at least the 1630s.

Even when families were broken by division of estates, they tended
to stay in groups among the heirs, often over generations. Giles Brent
in August 1656 gave his son "my Negro woman called Joane" with the
proviso that "if my son shall dye before the age of 21 years then the Negro
is to be mine during mine and my sister Margaret Brent's life...and her
children if she shall have any."[19] Similarly, the will of Thomas Speke left
one half of his servants "excepting negroes" to his wife and the rest to
his son; although his wife would receive an unnamed "negro woman"
but her progeny would be divided between the two. This division ensured
that Speake legally bound his heirs to keep his "Negroes" together.[20]

Slave quarters that would dot Virginia's landscape during the Plantation Generation were not present during the period of the Charter Generation. Some Africans lived in their master's homes, along with European

---

[15] Deal, *Race and Slavery*, pp. 281–2, for the vagaries of slave families and their sale and resale within the group.
[16] Northampton County, Deeds and Wills, 1645–1651, fol. 95.
[17] Deal, *Race and Class*, p. 368.
[18] NCODW&C 1680–1692, p. 97, Deed of Gift WK Senior to WK Junior, 6 June 1684.
[19] Court of 6 August 1656, John Frederick Dorman, *Westmoreland County Records, 1658–61* (Washington, DC, 1970), p. 112.
[20] Court of 1 December 1659 in Dorman, *Westmoreland County*, p. 48.

servants and Native Americans,[21] creating an environment that in some ways replicated the conditions that some Atlantic Creoles had experienced in the households of the Portuguese in Luanda. In 1639, for example, a Northampton court allowed that "Francis the negro shall have his trunk, which he claimeth, now being in the h[ouse] of [Englishman] John Foster," with whom he was presumably living.[22] When Piscataway Indians entered Daniel Gookin's house on his farm in the South River section of Maryland in 1652, they found three of his African American servants, Jacob Warrow, his wife, Mary, and seven-year-old son, Jacob, "being then in the Said house where they dwelt being Servants to the said Capt Gookine." The intruders murdered Jacob and his son, left the wounded Mary for dead, and pillaged the house of "Gunns powder Shott, Apparell and other Goods of a good Value" that were stored there.[23]

But in many places, Africans occupied separate houses within the larger community, if not yet quarters, especially on the estates of richer planters, where they tended to be concentrated. In Virginia and Maryland servants of all sorts, African and European, also appear to have lived, at least on some, probably larger, estates, in "quartering houses." For example, in 1645 Thomas Taylor went to the quartering house on his land to get "Anthony the negro" in order that they might make a division of the corn.[24] Simon Overzee, a Maryland planter, kept slaves in "a quartering howse" in 1656. This house had multiple rooms, as one of his negro female servants was in the house when he beat negro Simon Antonio to death, whereas on another occasion Antonio was himself in an "inward room" of the "quartering howse" illicitly eating hominy.[25] In all likelihood, separate quarters for servants and Africans would only be built in holdings where there were a significant number of dependants. Evidence from Flowerdew Hundred, whose Africans eventually became a part of Samuel Matthew's estate of 40 Africans in 1648, suggests that servants lived in houses that held somewhere around 5 people each.[26] Thus any group of more than 5 Africans might well be housed together, as appears was the case on Overzee's plantation in Maryland.

---

[21] Coombs contends that servants often lived with slaves in crowded quarters in the masters' dwelling, "Building 'The Machine'," pp. 12–19.

[22] Susie Ames (ed.), *County Court, Northampton, 1632–40*, p. 158.

[23] Court of 26 September 1653, *Maryland Archives* 10: 293–4. When Gookin took out a patent for land in Lancaster County, Virginia, in 1642, he listed "Jacob a Negro" among the people he transported (Nugent, *Cavaliers* 1: 139).

[24] Susie Ames, *County Court Records of Accocomack-Northhampton, Virginia, 1640–45* (Charlottesville, VA, 1973), p. 457.

[25] Court of 2 December 1658, *Maryland Archives* 41: 190–1.

[26] Deetz, *Flowerdew Hundred*, pp. 44–5.

Just as masters' movements and concentration of resources might bring Africans together for long periods, so a web of association among Africans connected them to each other.[27] In Northhampton, the center of the Eastern Shore community, one freed former bondsman, John Francisco, served as a witness in the will of a fellow former slave, Sebastian Cane. Francis Pane and Emmanuell Driggus, two other freedmen, agreed to support, if necessary, yet another enslaved African American, Hannah Carter, so she could be freed. Sebastian Cane's wife's petition was confirmed by John Francisco.[28] Driggus also adopted two children of other Africans, and when his son, Thomas, lost his children Driggus adopted them and obtained their freedom. When a court deprived Thomas Driggus of his children because he abused others, including John Franscico, at the same time it recognized the community by awarding Driggus's children to Francisco. The networks in the community are well illustrated by the activities of William Harman, another bondsman, in the 1660s. Harman, who was probably born of African parents in America, married Emmanuell Driggus's daughter, Jane Gossal, was friendly with John Francisco, who entertained him at his home, and bought a gun from Francis Pane (another African).[29]

The formation of a visible African and African American community on the Eastern Shore has attracted a great deal of attention from historians, thanks to its abundant documentation, and it is possible that the mainland had similar communities, though the lack of documentation prevents a thorough examination of it. The earliest muster for the Jamestown area already showed a concentration of Africans in the hands of George Yeardley and Abraham Piercy, whose connections with the Earl of Warwick may have given them better access to purchase slaves from his privateers. Thus, the 11 Africans found at Piercy's Flowerdew Hundred in 1624 represent a significant concentration of Africans – almost half of the total in the colony – most of whom were brought to Virginia on the first privateers, the *Treasurer* and *White Lion*, in 1619. They were originally held by George Yeardley and then acquired by Abraham Piercy in 1624 and eventually found their way to Captain Samuel Matthews's estate, Matthews' Manor, in 1629. Twenty years later, Matthews was said to have 40 Negroes on his estate, 1 of every 8 Africans in the colony, many of whom had been "brought up to trades."

---

[27] Breen and Innis, *Myne owne Ground*, pp. 102–3.
[28] Heinegg, "Free African Americans," Pane Family; Deal, *Race and Class*, pp. 265–78.
[29] Paul Heinegg, "Free African Americans," Harmon Family, 1.1; Deal, *Race and Class*, pp. 336–55.

Matthews's near neighbors included William Evans and Robert Sheppard, both of whom also owned slaves. Evans was patenting land in 1619–1648 along the James River, especially in the creeks around Hog Island, in what would become Surry County.[30] That Africans on these neighboring estates had personal and social relations with each other is demonstrated by the case of John Gaeween, one of Evans's slaves who was raising pigs for his own benefit and who had "a young child of a negroe woman belonging to Lieut. Robert Sheppard," whose freedom Gaeween bought from Sheppard in 1641.[31] Two years later, in 1643, when Evans patented more land in James City, Gaeween was listed (as John Grasheere) as one of Evans's dependants along with several other Africans named Michael, Katherine (Gaeween's wife), and Mathew.[32] During this period, a number of the Africans from the Hog Island area were moved northward to developing Lancaster County. Denis Conniers transported Africans there, as his Lancaster County patent of 1653 lists John Grasheare, along with fellow Africans Kate, Peeter, Dorothy, and Christopher, for his own land, whereas he transported three other Africans, Edward, Susan, and Martha to the neighboring patent of Elianor Brocas.[33]

Virginia did not experience a rapid shift to the Plantation Generation. Even as late as the 1650s, most Africans reported in headright documents were found in groups rarely exceeding 10 or 15, delivered in all probability by privateers as before. The first evidence of the arrival of the Plantation Generation was reflected in a land patent of 1656, when Tabath and Matilda Scarburgh are listed as having imported 41 Africans in a single lot.[34] These Africans, along with perhaps an equal number of others, had been purchased by their father, Edmond Scarburgh, in New Amsterdam from among the cargo on the Dutch slaveship *Witte Paert*.[35] More important, they had been brought directly from Africa and were from Calabar and Allada in West, and not Central, Africa.[36] But if these Calabars represented the start of a Plantation Generation, they were not so numerous as to displace or destroy the Charter Generation. For the next 50 years, until 1705, Africans arriving in larger lots, frequently from West Africa,

---

[30] Summary of patents in Surry County Wills, Deed, 1652–1673.

[31] Court, 17 October 1640, McIlwaine, *Minutes*, 468.

[32] Nugent *Cavaliers*, 1: 146.

[33] Nugent, *Cavaliers* 1: 245.

[34] Virginia State Archives, Land Patent Book, no. 4, 26 March 1656, p. 23.

[35] See "Edmund Schareburch's" petition to the Council of New Amsterdam to export slaves to Virginia, 29 August 1655, *Council Minutes, 1655–56*, p. 77.

[36] Directors in Holland to Stuyvesant, 23 November 1654, Fernow, *Colonial Records* 14: 304 (the slaves were from the "Bight of Guinea").

were still not numerous and came irregularly, primarily from Barbados.[37] Some 50 Africans arrived in Virginia during the summer of 1661, according to an English visitor, though 32 were dead at Christmas.[38] Even still, a significant number were from Central Africa, such as the cargo of slaves from Angola brought out in 1659 or the 84 slaves captured from a Dutch ship, the *Waepen van Amsterdam*, bound from Angola to Curaçao in 1663 and carried to Virginia.[39] Their numbers were augmented by the equally diverse population of the English Caribbean colonies, especially Barbados.[40]

Archaeological and documentary evidence suggests that this group of West Africans, however small, created a Plantation Generation, for separate slave quarters appear in the record around 1670. Material remains suggesting cultural connections to the Calabar region, such as the pipe stems that become ubiquitous in slave quarter remains, present the first evidence of a strong West African component in Virginia's new Plantation Generation population.[41] This changed status and perception was perhaps noted by the Virginia Assembly in 1670, which now described the Afro-Virginians as having "their owne Nation."[42]

B. Barbados

Although Berlin argued for the Chesapeake as the classic model for the transition from Charter to Plantation Generation, in fact, Barbados is far closer to the model than any North American location. However, unlike Virginia, there is relatively little documentation on developments for this early period. Barbados, often regarded as England's first slave society, began with a larger percentage of Africans than that in Virginia, for in 1628, one year after its first settlement the island held 100 Englishmen and 40 slaves, both African and Native Americans, and thus the percentage was perhaps as high as 25 percent.[43] But this did not last, as a flood of

---

[37] Coombs, "Building 'The Machine,'" pp. 40–68.

[38] BL Add MSS 11410, fol. 19, "Account of Col. Doyley upon his Return from Jamaica ... " 1662.

[39] Charles R. Boxer, "English Shipping in the Brazil Trade, 1640–65" *Mariner's Mirror* 37 (1951); New York Historical Society, NYC Box 1, New York and Virginia, 1663, "Proceedings upon a compliant of governor Stuyvesant to Governor Berkeley ... " (Copied from the records of the General Court of Virginia). See also O'Callaghan, *Documents* 1: 122.

[40] Anthony Parent, *Foul Means: The Formation of a Slave Society in Virginia, 1660–1740* (Chapel Hill, 2003), pp. 75–95.

[41] Deetz, *Flowerdew Hundred*, pp. 365–6.

[42] Hening, *Statutes* 2: 281.

[43] Henry Winthrop to Emmanuel Downing, 27 August 1627, in *Winthrop Papers* 1: 357.

indentured servants changed the ratios dramatically. In 1638, according to estimates made by Gary Puckrein, there were some 200 Africans of a total of 6,000 people, or about 3 percent of the population, thus more or less matching the ratio in Virginia.[44]

What material there is shows an initial pattern of local concentration similar to that of Virginia's. Deeds for the years 1643–1644, the first such series of documents for the island, reveal that of the 53 Africans held there, 30 (56.6 percent) were in groups of 5 or larger, 12 (26 percent) were in groups of 4, and none were by themselves.[45] This was the pattern on the eve of the Sugar Revolution, when the Plantation Generation would soon arrive to overwhelm the Charter Generation. One of the first shiploads of this latter group of Africans comprised more than 229 slaves delivered in 1644 by George Richardson and Richard Parr of the *Marie Bonaventure* of London to Edward Crostle and Josias Hart in exchange for tobacco, not yet sugar. These Africans were then sold to some 41 different persons, most of whom received small lots of one or two, eight at most, so that these newcomers did not initially overwhelm the Charter Generation.[46]

It was only after the Sugar Revolution, and the arrival of the Plantation Generation, which began at that point, that the ratio of African to English changed dramatically, for by 1655 the African population made up 46 percent of the 43,000 inhabitants of the island.[47] In 1670 Governor Lord Willoughby, with scant exaggeration, estimated the island had 5,000 English and 70,000 Africans (93 percent).[48] The pattern of concentration of Africans in groups of five or six was transformed by the new arrivals, and by the end of the 1640s they were much larger concentrations.

Richard Ligon was already observing this level of concentration in 1648 or 49, for he lived on an estate with 96 "negroes ... with their children."[49] The distinctive settlement pattern of the Plantation Generation

---

[44] Puckrein, *Little England*, p. 33, and no. 29, p. 199. Puckrein apparently adopted this estimate based on ratios of slaves to indentured servants in NAB, RB. But there is only one known deed that includes such numbers in or before 1638; that being the Ketteridge inventory of 1635, for the RB only includes inventories after 1640. However, our investigation of RB 3/1 and 3/2, which covers this period and beyond, confirms the very small numbers of Africans listed on them; most in fact have no Africans at all.

[45] NAB RB 3/1, pp. 55, 61, 68, 71, 92, 94, 151, 289, 337, 607.

[46] NAB RB 3/1, Contracts, 30 July 1644 and 31 July 1644, p. 419; also 15 August 1644, p. 439.

[47] Dunn, *Sugar and Slaves*, p. 87.

[48] BL Egerton, 2395 fol. 490, Lord Willoughby's interest in the island of Barbados, 17 March 1670.

[49] Ligon, *True and Exact History*, p. 22

was already evident. The slaves on the estate where Ligon resided were
then living in groups of "little houses" that were only for them, and he
went on to say that though these houses were small, they might subdi-
vide their houses into multiple rooms, "none above six square feet."[50]
Slave quarters, like little villages, were thus in existence in 1648 on larger
estates that had made the transition to sugar plantations, such as those of
Thomas Modyford or James Drax. It is doubtful that any observer before
Ligon's time in Barbados could have witnessed "the sight of a hundred
handsome negroes, men and women, with every one a grass-green bunch
of these fruits [plantain] on their heads...all coming in a train one after
another."[51]

C. *New England, New Sweden, and Rural New Netherland*

New England had the smallest population of Africans in North America,
and the lowest percentage of the total population. The first Africans to
be mentioned in New England records arrived sometime before 1633.[52]
Loose estimates of the population of Africans living in all of New England
in the period propose that there were some 200 Africans of a total population of about 13,500 in 1640 (1.5 percent), 400 of 22,500 by 1650 (1.8
percent), and 600 of 33,200 by 1660 (1.8 percent).[53] Even in 1680, Governor Bradstreet of Massachusetts estimated the population of Africans
or African Americans in his colony at only around 120.[54]

This early group probably originated in the activities of the Providence
Island Company, which had close connections with New England, and
indeed an early shipment of slaves came from Providence Island in 1637.
That they were probably Angolan is suggested by a mysterious reference
to "Canniball Negroes" (possibly Imbangala) being sent from the colony
to Providence Island in 1638.[55] These "Canniball Negroes" may have been

---

[50] Ligon, *True and Exact History*, pp. 22, 47.
[51] Ligon, *True and Exact History*, pp. 43–4.
[52] Wood, *New England's Prospect*, p. 66.
[53] John McCusker and Russell Menard, *The Economy of British America, 1607–1789*
(Chapel Hill, 1985), p. 103. This table is created from U. S. Bureau of the Census, *Historical Statistics of the United States, Colonial Times to 1970* (Washington, DC, 1975)
2: 1168. There is little direct evidence for these figures, which should not be taken as any
more than suggestive.
[54] Governor Bradstreet to Privy Council, 1680, quoted in James Savage, "Gleanings for
New England," *Collections of the Massachusetts Historical Society* (3rd series, 8, 1843),
p. 337.
[55] For a fuller treatment, see Linda Heywood and John Thornton, "The Removal of 'Canniball Negroes,' from New England to Providence Island," paper presented at the conference "African American Slave Trade to New England," Boston, 22 April, 2004.

part of the group of Africans bought by Mr. Peirce "in the Salem ship, the Desire," which had returned from the West Indies after seven months and had brought "some cotton, and tobacco, and negroes."[56] In fact it was only in 1638 that the earliest detailed reference identified at least three Africans (a man and two women) living on the lands of Samuel Maverick on Noodles' Island (now East Boston). They formed something of a small community, for one of the women acted "as a maid" for another who claimed "to be a Queen in her own countrey," and the other was a man who was forced to sleep with the "queen."[57]

Although there are no documents that allow us to guess at the distribution or living arrangements of the New England Africans systematically, the scattered references for the 1640s and 1650s suggest that many lived in their master's houses. One of these was Mr. Stoughton's "Negro maid," who was admitted to the Dorchester church in 1641 and who was "well approved by divers years' experience, for sound knowledge and true godliness." Another, reported in the same year, was the unfortunate maid of Bridget Pierce who carelessly let her mistress's fine linen burn.[58] Other African women also served as maids, as did Hope in 1652 or Katherine, who had two illegitimate children in Salem in 1650 and 1653.[59] At least one man was free in Plymouth, for a muster list of 1643 reveals the presence of a "blackamore" there.[60] In fact, there were enough Africans in New England that in 1652 they were required to serve in the militia until the Massachusetts Bay Colony banned their service four years later. In New Haven, Connecticut, there was another small community. Lucretia, living in her master's house in New Haven, testified that she saw English servant Thomas Hogg engaging in an "act of fylthyness with his hands."[61] Some of these Africans socialized with each other, for the next

---

[56] Dunn, Savage, and Yeandle, *Journal*, p. 246. The *Desire* arrived in Boston on 26 February 1638 and the order to remove the cannibal Negroes was issued from London on 3 July of the same year.

[57] John Josselyn, *An Account of Two Voyages to New-England: Wherein you have the setting out of a ship ... to the year 1673* (London, 1675), p. 28.

[58] Dunn, *Winthrop Papers*, pp. 347, 352.

[59] Court of 17 July 1650, Records and Files of the Quarterly Court of Essex County, Massachusetts (Salem) 1636–1656, vol 1: 196 (Katherine); Court of 1 May 1653 *Records and Files of the Quarterly Court of Essex County, Massachusetts, 1636–56*, vol. 1, p. 287, and Court of 21 August 1653, *ibid* 1: 323; Court of 26 December 1652, *Suffolk Deeds Liber 1*, p. 290; 26 December 1652 (Hope).

[60] There is considerable controversy as to whether this freeman was named Abraham Pierce, which occasioned a major dispute raised by Pierce's descendants when he was identified as the blackmore and included in the living history section of the Plimouth Plantation.

[61] Court of 2 February 1646, Hoadly, *New Haven* 1: 296.

year a certain Anthony was unexpectedly overcome by drinking "stronge watter" served up by his African friend Matthew.[62] In Rhode Island there was at least some small community as well, for Peter Tollman owned a number of "negers" when his property was seized in 1649.[63]

Swedish Delaware had the lowest percentage of Africans, only one; "Antony," an "Angoler," appeared in a 1648 roll of inhabitants in the colony.[64] Antony's background was not dissimilar to those of other Africans of the Charter Generation, as he had been captured from a Portuguese slave ship in 1638, came from Angola, and like so many others eventually won his freedom.

The colony of New Netherland, along the Hudson up to Fort Orange (Albany), Long Island, and what is today coastal New Jersey and Delaware, formed the rural hinterland of New Amsterdam. There were few Africans in the early years, in spite of the Company's promises, made in 1634, to provide "12 black men and women out of the prizes in which Negroes shall be found."[65] On the lands controlled by the van Rensselaer family, a private holding near present-day Albany, there were some Africans. In 1630, for example, the ship *Bruynvis* delivered no less than 50 Africans (20 men and 30 women) to Pavonia, one of Rensselaer's holdings, suggesting that he might have had ample Africans to employ on his farms, but it seems that these and most others went to the West India Company's holdings in Manhattan. The surviving van Rensselaer documents, although mentioning Africans, record few in their rural farms. Two surveys, in 1632 and 1634, do not mention any African workers on several Rensselaer farms and provide only that "a farm laborer to be engaged ... and also another laborer or a black in his stead" on one new project.[66] However, at least eight more Africans were introduced between 1644 and 1664, and probably there were still more.[67] Even in 1664, only

---

[62] Hoadly, *New Haven*, 1: 335.

[63] Court of 1 December 1649, *Rhode Island Court Records*, vol. 2? 1662–1670 (Providence, 1922), p. 10.

[64] Pennsylvania Historical Society, Amandus Johnson papers, 55/4 German list of people, 3 January 1648, p. 4.

[65] New Project of Freedoms and Exemptions, n. d. (c. 1634), no. 31, O'Callaghan, *Documents* 1: 99.

[66] A. J. F. van Laer (ed.), *The Van Rensselaer Bowier Manuscripts* (Albany: SUNY, 1908), pp. 222 and 277. Both letters refer to the same plans, though the second one mentions another farm that could be worked by "a boy or a negro," p. 277.

[67] Jan Folkerts, "Kiliaen van Rensselaer and Agricultural Productivity in his Domain: A New Look at the First Patroonship and Rensselaerswijck before 1664," in Nancy Anne

about 6 percent of the African population of the Dutch colony lived outside the immediate vicinity of New Amsterdam.[68]

Some of the Africans laboring in the rural areas had, and sometimes retained, ties to the larger New Amsterdam community, because the West India Company sometimes supplied slaves from its New Amsterdam settlement to holdings elsewhere in the colony. In 1644, for example, the Company indentured Maria (daughter of the Angolan-born Groot Pieter), who was sent from her home in New Amsterdam to work in the household of Nicholas Coorn at Renselaerwyck (near Albany). She was to work in his house for four years and at the end to be restored to the Company.[69]

Martin Krigier (Crigier), who had property on Long Island at Amesfoorde, held quite a few slaves apart from those he held in New Amsterdam, for in 1654, he complained that an English pirate named Thomas Baxter had abducted three to four of his Africans who had been sent to recapture some runaways.[70] In another rural holding near Middleburg on Long Island, a small holder named Taelman was robbed in 1646 by Englishmen who wanted to take his tobacco. As they could speak Algonquian, they hoped to frighten the African servants who were living there or, failing that, kill them. The thieves, John Smith, "Samuel Salis and Pasque," noted "there are only two Negroes there whom we shall kill and take the tobacco."[71] Here as in other sparsely inhabited colonies, the Africans, though not numerous, seem to have been concentrated in groups sufficiently large to retain some cultural continuity.

The Charter Generation: High-Population Settlements

Other areas possessed much higher initial populations of Africans, which increased the possibilities of longer lasting and stronger communities. In such a setting the Plantation Generation, if it came at all, could not

---

McClure Zeller and Charles Gehring (eds.), *A Beautiful and Fruitful Place: Selected Renselaerwijck Seminar Papers* (Albany, 1993), pp. 303 and 307, no. 77. Folkerts claims that Africans were not fully counted in the numerous unpublished papers of the manor.

[68] Van den Boogart, "Servant Migration," p. 58.
[69] Indenture of service of Maria, a young Negro girl to Nicholas Coorn, 25 May 1644, van Laer 2, *Register of Provincial Secretary*, p. 223.
[70] Pieter Stuyvesant, 8 April 1654 decree, *Council Minutes, 1652–54*, p. 130. One of these men may have joined his gang, for a negro is mentioned among his cohorts in vs. Thomas Gridy, 25 February 1656, *Council Minutes, 1655–56*, p. 245–6.
[71] Cornelies van Tienhoven, fiscal against Jan Smith from Willickschier in old England, post 15 January 1656, *Council Minutes, 1655–56*, p. 200.

be as overwhelming as in Barbados or even Virginia. However, in some places, because the settlements were transitory, these developments were not visible, though it is quite clear in Bermuda and New Amsterdam.

A. The Transitory Colonies: The Amazon and the Caribbean

In several of the early Caribbean colonies and the Amazon where privateers often left the bulk of their captives, Africans might be quite numerous. English, Dutch, and Irish colonies in the Amazon basin show this early transitory pattern. English and Irish settlers working in close cooperation with Dutch merchants (though the Dutch West India Company did establish some colonies as well) founded a number of settlements in the Amazon after 1611. The Portuguese from Brazil finished many of them in 1623–1625 and subsequently reestablished colonies between 1629 and 1633, which were also were wiped out.[72] While they were occupied, the Amazon colonies acquired slaves for a precocious sugar industry as well as tobacco production. For example, in 1623 Wallon visitors to the Wanari found Henry Foster working there with "three negroes."[73] The earliest Dutch forts, established on the north section of the river, contained "negroes of Angola," no doubt taken from prizes when the Portuguese destroyed them in 1623.[74] The surviving documentation gives no indication of the number, though the Portuguese commander did note the capture of some 116 people including both Native Americans and Africans.[75]

Caribbean settlement had a similar history and sometimes had substantial African populations, as warfare between the Spanish and the Dutch and English interlopers resulted in these colonies being short lived. St. Martin, for example, was occupied by the Dutch in 1631, but when Spanish forces conquered the island in 1633, they found an African population of some 30–40 of a total of about 140 people or somewhere between 20 and 30 percent of the population.[76] The Providence Island Company,

---

[72] Lorimer, *English and Irish Settlements*, pp. 35–125.

[73] "Journal of the Voyage . . . of heads of families . . . " Mrs. Robert W. de Forest, *A Walloon Family in America: Lockwood de Forest and His Forbearers 1500–1848 . . .* (2 vols., Boston, 1914), 2: 237.

[74] Luis Aranha de Vasconcelos to Crown, post April 1625; *Anais da Biblioteca Nacional de Rio de Janeiro* 36 (1904): and Antonio Vicente Cochado, Guedes, *Costa da Norte*, pp. 37 (both translated in Lorimer, *English and Irish*, pp. 245 and 248).

[75] A report from Luis Aranha de Vasconcelos, 1625 in Lorimer, p. 244; and Report of António Vicente Cochado . . . 1623, Lorimer, *English and Irish* p. 250.

[76] AGI SF, 233, Letter of 1 July 1633; Marquis de Cadereita to King, 15 July 1633, in Wright (ed.), *Zeevaarders*, p. 291; same to same, 1 July 1633, p. 233.

England's leading privateering venture after 1631, supplied its colonies with Africans from its prizes. In Tortuga (Association), the Company's eastern base and well supplied by its privateers, the Spanish found 200 Africans of a population of 950, also a little above 20 percent, when they conquered it in 1633.[77] Just a few years later, in 1641, another Spanish force captured Providence Island itself and found 381 Africans and 350 Englishmen on the island, so that the Africans were over half of the population. But the island, the pearl of English privateering since 1635 had sent off a significant number of Africans to other colonies for fear of revolt earlier that year, so that at some point the African population must have made up a much higher percentage.[78]

B. Bermuda

Bermuda was one of these early colonies that did survive, and from very early onward, the island had a substantially higher number and proportion of Africans than was ever found in either Virginia or Barbados. This was not because of any great economic strength or vibrancy but because Bermuda, as the main privateering base for the English prior to 1635, naturally acquired a large number of Africans of the Charter Generation. The island's early success as a tobacco-growing colony, tobacco's collapse in the late 1630s, and, unlike their Barbadian counterparts, the Bermudans' inability to develop a lucrative plantation crop made it unable to attract the English slave trade that would bring in the Plantation Generation elsewhere. Those slaves who ended up in Bermuda after 1650 were not connected to a revolution in sugar or tobacco, the development of large estates, or the creation of separate slave quarters of newly arrived Africans. Instead, they were integrated piecemeal into a substantial and demographically expanding Charter Generation.

Bermuda may well have had a much higher percentage of Africans than the 1 in 14 (7 percent) that Virginia Bernhard guessed for 1622. The fact that Bermuda authorities thought to issue an act to restrain the movement of Africans and to limit their carrying of weapons as early as 1623 suggests that it was facing problems holding a large African population.[79] However, Bermuda authorities never thought to issue orders or

---

[77] BL Add Mss 13 992, "Relacion sumaria del estado presente en que se halla la Isla Espanola...c. 1650, printed, fol. 500v. The population included 250 Native American slaves as well.

[78] Kupperman, *Providence Island*, p. 172, citing AGI Santa Fe, 223, Francisco Diaz Pimienta to King, 11 September 1641.

[79] Lefroy, *Memorials* 1: 308–9.

discuss removal of Africans to achieve a more favorable ratio of Europeans to Africans as Providence Island's leadership did in decreeing that a ratio of two whites to every African was essential, and so it is doubtful that Bermuda's African population could have exceeded about a third. Healthy demography played a role in maintaining the African component, for Bernhard goes on to suggest that both Africans and Europeans had good reproduction and survival rates, unlike so many other tropical colonies. Detailed records are lacking on the proportions of African to Europeans and a 1684 census provide the first data of the racial breakdown of the population, showing that people of African descent made up 1,737 of a population of 7,626 or 22.8 percent.[80] By 1691, the African descended population accounted for just over 30 percent of the total.[81]

The Bermuda Company monopolized the initial store of slaves, brought to it by its own privateers, and it rented or lent them out to private persons. But soon private persons acquired their own African servants, breaking up this early concentration. Bernhard's study of slaveholding on Bermuda in 1663, the end result of this process of evolution, shows that ownership of slaves was very widespread.[82] Bernhard's careful examination of inventories reveals that even smallholders had one or two African servants, though the wealthier probably also had more servants. No general pattern of slave quarters emerged and most "slaves slept in the slaveholder's house, usually in the kitchen, sometimes in another room."[83] Although this might suggest a lack of sufficient concentration to allow the Charter Generation to achieve some sort of community, focusing on concentration by owner is misleading on an island of only 21 square miles. Given the small size of properties and their clustering together on even less arable land, no one African could have been very far from others.

In the absence of the deeds and patent records that allow us to determine patterns of residence as in early Virginia and Barbados, the formation of families provides the best guide to early Bermudian community

---

[80] Mike Jarvis, "'In the Eye of All Trade': Maritime Revolution and Transformation of Bermudian Society, 1612–1800," Ph.D. dissertation, College of William and Mary, 1998, unpaginated appendix.

[81] Bernhard, *Slaves and Slaveholders*, p. 98.

[82] Bernhard, *Slaves and Slaveholders*, pp. 101–8. Bernhard gives her statistics, based on a detailed study of 107 wills between 1663 and 1707 of people listed in the 1663 survey, in terms of numbers of slaves per owner in a range of ownership, work we cannot duplicate. Nevertheless the pattern as Bernhard observes is similar to that of mainland North America.

[83] Bernhard, *Slaves and Slaveholders*, pp. 108–9.

patterns. African families appeared very early; as early as the 1620s there was a strong complaint against a Somers' Island Company manager's, Daniel Elfrith's, attempt to move "ould Francesco" and "James the Negro and their wives" from Company property.[84] Likewise, Lieutenant Buckely sued for the wages of Francisco and his wife, Anthonia, when he left for England in 1628.[85] As the geography of Bermuda required closer contact, a number of legal wrangles arose over the formation of families across ownerships lines but did not slow family formation down. In 1630 a Company servant named Paraketo's wife, Katulina, was owned by a private individual, leading to a dispute that was resolved by allowing the couple to live together but splitting the ownership of their two children, Alice and Ann.[86] In 1631, another Company African servant, "Sander" (Alexandre?), and his wife were living together.[87] But when Sander's child was sold by Mr. Winter, an overseer the next year, Sander sought redress from the Company, which instructed its agent to use "all lawful office of favour ... whereas he petitions that his wife may live with him, I will have you take what course you can countenance for satisfaction of his desire, it seeming to me a request full of reason."[88]

Addressing another problem of split ownership, in this case between his own servant Sambo and Sambo's wife, owned by another settler, Roger Wood revealed that the Company had "this blacke crewe" that at that time had several (at least five) families and thirteen children under the age of 10 in 1632. Wood recognized the problems of this formation, for the women and children were "lyving vpon my charge, for they [the women] doe little else than to looke to theire children for no man willbe troubled with them." Nurturing children had thus pushed labor aside, and although the Company was concerned with its profit, it allowed such matters to stand, as it did not have (and would not develop) the plantation system that would use older females to see to the children of working mothers. To resolve his own problem, Wood sent one of his men who was married to Sambo's wife's owner in exchange for Sambo's wife, not "to deprive you of your negroe for my own benefit ... as that thereby I or myne may euer be able to wage with him ... in hise plea and measure his corne by

---

[84] Ives, *Rich Papers*, pp. 17, 58–9, 214–15, 233–4.
[85] Council Table, Bermuda, 10 February 1628/9, Lefroy 1: 483.
[86] Council 27 July 1630, Lefroy, *Discovery* 1: 505.
[87] BRC, vol. F, Roger Wood Letter Book, no. 60 (no foliation).
[88] BL Add MSS 63854 B, Mr. Jessop's Letter Book, transcript, fol. 11, Earl of Warwick to Hugh Wentworth, 19 July 1634.

his owne bushell, his man having marryed my woman, my man having marryed his."[89]

Bermuda did not participate in the new slave trade of the 1640s and 1650s, provoked by Barbados' entry into the trade. However, thanks to the fall of Providence Island in 1641, Bermuda once again became the port of choice for privateers like Henry Jackson, who brought the fruits of his 1645 raids in the Caribbean to Bermuda. Other privateers supplied the majority of the arrivals, and brought their prizes only in small lots,[90] as did John Wentworth in the *Charles* in 1665 with slaves taken from the Dutch at Totola.[91] Bermudan sailors also took direct voyages to Africa to buy slaves but often sold their profits in Virginia and North Carolina and only a residue in Bermuda. Thus in 1672, a ship went from Bermuda to Calabar but sold only half of its 125 slaves in Bermuda; the rest went to North Carolina and Virginia. In 1683 another ship, "Comanded by one Capt. Stone (her name not remembered) and brought back abt. 90 slaves. But most of them was carry'd to North Carolina, Virginia and places on the continent."[92]

C. Dutch Curaçao, Tobago, and the Wild Coast
The Dutch establishments at Curacao and Bonaire, taken from the Spanish in 1634, were conceived as a privateering base for the western end of the Caribbean. The Dutch had already been anchoring their privateering on the island and exploiting its salt and hoped to acquire Africans to "use them for all kinds of labor on the land."[93] There were no Africans on the island in 1635 (and only three in 1638), according to Spanish reports, but it was soon being used as a transfer point for captured slaves.[94] Many slaves

[89] BCR, vol. F, Roger Wood Letter Book, no. 88. We have been aided in reading this fragmentary and fragile text by the conclusions of others, Lefroy, p. 539, and Berhard, p. 38.

[90] On Jackson's raids, see ... ... on the sale of his captives, or rather their indentures for 99 years each, see BCR 2, fols. 102–3 and *passim*.

[91] The sales of this prize were sold and enumerated in BCR 5a, fols. 69v–81v *passim*. Wentworth held a Portuguese marque, suggesting that he was among the freebooters of Tortuga, on the private men of war, see BL 11410, fol. 9, "A Brief Account of the Island of Turtudos..." 1662.

[92] Calendar of State Papers (August 4 1708) quoted in Smith, *Slavery* p. 20

[93] Goslinga, *Dutch in Caribbean*, pp. 129–40; 343 (quote from Johan van Wallbeeck) the plan to use it was already being developed as soon as the island was taken, ARA OWIC 2, 2 September 1634.

[94] According to a Dutch mariner captured by Native Americans in Spanish service on the island, there were no Africans on the island in 1635, AGI Indifferente General 1869, Deposition Martin Pietersen, 10 February 1635; ARA OWIC, 54 Jacob Pietersz Tolck

were also held for shorter times before being sold or transferred elsewhere. Frederick Roeberge made an agreement in 1639 for two years to take some 25 Africans held on the island to St Christopher.[95] An Irish solider noted that on Bonaire in 1641 there were 13 Africans of 60 inhabitants (22 percent), and at Curaçao 40 Africans of 200 residents (20 percent).[96] In 1643, the directors of the West India Company believed that Africans "come ashore in large numbers, especially during the months of May and June."[97] There were enough Africans on Curaçao by 1643, however, to warrant special provisions to prevent their revolt or escape to Native Americans.[98] Many of these slaves became a labor force for the island in the salt pans and also worked as farmers and fishers. Instructions to the first governor specified that Company slaves would be placed under supervision for their work.[99] However, the labor of the salt mines soon absorbed a substantial number of the Africans, for a resolution of 1644 required the use of "all the negroes, to work the salt pans, "because there is nothing more profitable and beneficial" that could be done.[100]

Curaçao and its neighbors experienced no rapid development of population as a result of any production revolution and thus no Plantation Generation. In later years, its role as a transshipment point for Dutch slavers supplying Spanish and Dutch colonies elsewhere (including New Amsterdam) overshadowed its role as a producer of salt or other local products. Thus, for example, when *Den Coninick Salomon* arrived in Curaçao with a cargo of 331 slaves from "Guinea" in 1659, 300 were immediately sold to a Spanish merchant and most of the rest were distributed as gifts to people going to Europe; only a handful remained on the island. The group that remained on the island, mostly children, were sent to work at the salt pans, probably on Bonaire.[101]

Another region of substantial African density was the "Wild Coast" (Surinam and Guiana), where both the English and Dutch founded

to XIX, Curacao 6 September 1639 (privateering base); AGI SD 194, Declaracion de los Olandeses de Curassao, 5 July 1638 (three negroes in that year).

[95] ARA OWIC 22, Resolutions of Zeeland Council, 22 and 31 August 1639.

[96] AGI SD 215, "Declarasion de vn soldado yrlandes (Onofre Brien) que se quedo en el Puerto de Cauello..."14 December 1642.

[97] Resolution of 14 April 1643 in Charles Gehring (ed. and trans.), *Curacao Papers, 1640–1665* (Interlaken, NY, 1987), pp. 22–3.

[98] Resolution of 19 May 1643, in Gehring, *Curacao Documents* p. 43.

[99] Instructions to Tolck, 1638, cited in Page, *Dutch Triangle*, p. 113.

[100] Resolution of 18 July 1644, Gehring, *Curacao Papers*, p. 42.

[101] Matthias Beck to Pieter Stuyvesant, 23 August 1659, in Gehring, *Curacao Papers*, pp. 124–7.

colonies, though on this coast sugar production led to massive imports of Africans from diverse origins to make a Plantation Generation. Given the fairly large Charter Generation, however, the impact of these later arrivals may well have been lessened. Early Dutch colonies on the Wild Coast were established at various places, notably at Essequibo, Wiapoco, Berbice, and Cayenne, though only the Essequibo colony, founded by Cornelius Groenwegen in 1616, lasted beyond a few years.[102] Indeed, Africans seem to have been very significant in the development of the region, for when the West India Company was considering developing a slave trade in 1626, they noted the need for slaves in their colonies on the Amazon and the Wild Coast.[103] A Dutch statement of liberties and exemptions for colonists on the "Wild Coast of Brazil or the Islands lying there" in 1628 made it clear that the West India Company should "take pains to furnish the colonists with as many Negroes as shall be possible."[104] However, the slave trade did not yet develop, and capturing Portuguese vessels was still the primary means of acquiring Africans. David de Vries noted that in his short-lived colony on the Wild Coast, they managed to capture a slave ship that had stopped to water.[105]

Slightly after the formation of the settlements on the Wild Coast, the Zeeland merchant Jan de Moor established a colony on Tobago in 1627. Initially he planned to rely on privateering to supply African laborers. The settlers, including the earliest Africans, set about producing ginger, which was already arriving in the Netherlands by 1630.[106] It also produced sugar, and Africans were a substantial portion of the population. When the Spanish attacked and dislodged the colony in 1637, they captured some 100 people, among French and Dutch settlers, and "36 Negroes."[107] Africans therefore might have made up as much as a third of the population by that time.

[102] Goslinga, *Dutch in Caribbean*, pp. 79–80; 409–11.
[103] ARA OWIC 20, 21 December 1626, cit. Martin, *Loango Coast* p. 54, no. 3.
[104] "Liberties and Exemptions accorded and granted by the Chartered West India Company... on the Wild Coast of Brazil or the islands... 22 November 1628, article 25, American Boundary Commission Documents, no. 40.
[105] De Vries, *Korte Verhael*, p. 144.
[106] ARA OWIC 21, fol. 241v, Minutes of Zeeland Chamber, 5 August 1630.
[107] BL Add MSS 36324, Venezuela Arbiration Papers, vol. 11, 1637–1638, fol. 74–74v, transcript of AGI Miscellaneous, Council of War 147/5/21, Consulta 10 November 1637, citing letter of Juan de Eulate, 29 December 1636; also AHC Buenos Aires, transcript 9, no. 215, "Sobre el soccorro que el gobernador de Guyana enbio a quella audiencia...." A number of Africans were among those captured, and the Spanish, lacking shipping to remove all the English, Dutch, and French found there, had them strangled, sparing only 19 boys because of their age.

But the colony was not totally lost, for the survivors fled with their African servants to the Wild Coast, greatly reinforcing the Dutch settlements at Berbice and Essequibo (modern-day Guyana).[108] Spanish reports for 1637 related that these colonies had substantial African populations; at Berbice there were 40 Dutchmen with 25 Africans (38.5 percent of the population) and in Essequibo "120 Dutchmen and many Negroes."[109] The Dutch retaliated by sacking the Spanish settlement of Santo Tome on the Orinoco and carried off "all the slaves, both Indians [Negroes] and Indian natives," belonging to the Spanish.[110] In addition to the reinforcement from Tobago, the Guiana region was also augmented by former plantation owners, primarily Jewish, who came to the coast following 1644, and then those who fled Recife upon its fall in 1654, bringing with them many slaves from their Brazilian holdings.[111]

Sugar production on the Wild Coast allowed a Plantation Generation to be brought to the Dutch settlements. In 1656 the Dutch renamed the region "Nova Zeelandia" and sent out a ship with colonists, and the next year a second ship went to Africa to acquire slaves, in accordance with its charter.[112] The Spanish reported in 1657 that two settlements of Dutch numbering 430 near the Orinoco had already imported enough Africans that they numbered more than 1,500, thus outnumbering the Dutch by three to one, to work their sugar plantations (*ingenios*).[113] By the early 1660s, the settlement at Pomeroon had some 600 Dutch and Native Americans and 1,000 African slaves (62.5 percent); in 1662 the Spanish believed the Dutch there to have 1,000 Dutch and 400 Indians "and a greater number of negroes founding a new Brazil."[114] The future development of that region would be connected to large-scale slavery supported by direct slave trading from Africa.

[108] Cabildo of Trinidad to King, 27 December 1637, American Boundary Commission, doc. 53.
[109] Juan Desologuren Memorandum, 19 November 1637, American Boundary Commission Document 51. Information about the geography was taken from "Juan" a "negro of the Santome nation," who was taken in the raid on Tobago.
[110] Letter on destruction of Santo Tome by Dutch, 1638, American Boundary Comission, doc. 57.
[111] Herbert Bloom, *The Economic Activities of the Jews of Amsterdam in the Seventeenth and Eighteenth Centuries* (Bayard Press, PA, 1937), pp. 145–7.
[112] Goslinga, *Dutch in the Caribbean*, pp. 427–9.
[113] BL Add MSS 36321, Venezuela Arbitration Documents Transcripts, vol. 8, fol. 127v, Governor of Guyana to Marquis de Montealegre, 18 January 1657.
[114] Pedro de Viedma to King, 20 March 1662, American Boundary Commission Documents, no. 85.

Permanent English colonies, following several failed attempts by Sir Walter Raleigh, and short-lived colonies founded by Robert Harcourt in 1618 or Mr. Marshall in 1643, finally appeared at Surinam in 1650, and in 1652, Anthony Rous, a prominent planter in Barbados, brought "300 people of the English Nacion" there.[115] Initially, at least, there seem to have been relatively few Africans in the colony, for a plea issued by Lord Willoughby in 1655 spoke of the transportation of servants and mentions the supplying of "servants, English and Negroes."[116] His plea must have been successful for in 1657, the Spanish governor of Guyana believed that more than 1,500 Africans were working for French and English masters in Surinam.[117] In 1662, the governor of Trinidad, Pedro de Viedma, noted that the 36 English settlements in Surinam included "a great number of Negroes."[118] Given the development of the slave trade in Barbados, it is likely that such Africans derived from the direct slave trade, in fact, in 1663, there were ships bringing slaves arriving straight from Africa.[119] This group would form the Plantation Generation, but unlike the earlier Africans, they were of diverse origin and much more heterogeneous than their predecessors.

D. New Amsterdam

Dutch New Amsterdam, the core of a very sparsely inhabited New Netherland, had a relatively large and concentrated Charter Generation, in fact the highest proportion of any area in North America. By 1638 there were perhaps 100 Africans in New Amsterdam, around 30 percent of the total population in the city.[120] This proportion appears to have remained stable; marriages between Africans made up 28 percent of the marriages in the Dutch Reformed Church in New Amsterdam in the period 1639–1652,

---

[115] Scott, in Harlow, *Colonizing Expeditions*, p. 142; Scott conflated an advance colony in 1650 with a small number of settlers with the larger one sent out by Lord Willoughby in 1652, see "Reasons Offered by the Lord Willoughby..." c. 1656, in *ibid.*, pp. 177–8, 180–1.

[116] "Certain Overtures made by ye Lord Willoughby...," in Harlow, *Colonizing Expeditions*, p. 176.

[117] BL Add MSS 36321, Venezuela Arbitration Documents Transcripts, vol. 8, fol. 129, Governor of Guyana to Marquis de Montealegre, 18 January 1657.

[118] Pedro de Viedma to King, 20 March 1662, American Boundary Documents, no. 85.

[119] William Yearworth to Robert Harley, 27 January 1663, Harlow, *Colonizing Expeditions*, p. 190.

[120] Ernst van den Boogaart, "The Servant Migration to New Netherland, 1624–64," in Pieter Emmer (ed.), *Colonialism and Migration; Indentured Labour before and after Slavery* (Dordrecht, Boston, and Lancaster, 1986), p. 58.

especially in the earlier years.[121] A great many of these obtained their freedom. In 1643 Governor Krieft granted a limited freedom to a group that probably represented close to half the population of Africans.[122]

This concentration was not only because New Amsterdam was the recipient of many African slaves from the West India Company's raids on Portuguese shipping but also because the Company insisted on keeping them together in its rapidly growing capital town. This decision to concentrate its Africans led to the development of a fairly substantial village near the "Fresh Water" (Kalkhook) in what would be today the Lower East Side near the site of the former World Trade Center and including Washington Square.[123] Here, Central Africans often worked as a group under a Dutch supervisor, doing public projects like building the fort but also many other types of work, including mobilizing to fight against local Native Americans.[124]

The African community seems to have consisted of a group of houses constructed by them and scattered alongside the "Fresh Pond," a marshy area near the former World Trade Center.[125] This community was already in existence in 1639, when Thomas Valaren was convicted of committing

---

[121] Sherill Wilson, *New York City's African Slaveowners: A Social and Material Culture History* (1994), p. 38, citing Samuel S. Purple (ed.), *Records of the Reformed Dutch Church in New Amsterdam and New York: Marriages from 1639 to 1801* (New York, 1890) (transcript of original Dutch register).

[122] New York State Archives, Dutch Records, Laws and Ordinances, fol. 183, Willem Krieft's response to petition of 11 named Africans, 25 February 1643. The petition mentions both that the petitioners were married and that they were "burdened by many children" (*vervallen in veel kinderen*). Allowing two to three children per couple, the total must have been close to 50. English translation in van Laer, 1: 212.

[123] The location of this community is problematic, largely because Vingboon's map of Manhattan in 1639 showed a camp of Company slaves quite some distance up the island. The documentary material cited here and below makes it clear that a large company had to be living around the Fresh Water, at least in 1643. Thelma Foote has proposed that the group was moved there temporarily about the time the map was drawn, perhaps to serve against the threat of the Native Americans, *Black and White Manhattan: The History of Racial Formation in Colonial New York City* (Oxford, 2004), p. 38.

[124] Deposition Concerning the Erection of Fort Amsterdam and Other Work Done by the Company's Negroes, 22 March 1639, in O'Callaghan, *Documents* 14: 18; on their military service, see articles submitted by the honorable director and council of New Netherland to the heads of families or householders, van Laer, 1: 124. Later uses, see Stuyvesant to alderman, n. d., entered in Council Minutes, 12 February 1652, in *Council Minutes* 14: fol. 19.

[125] Goodfriend contends that the Africans were housed in large barracks, "Burghers and Blacks: The Evolution of a Slave Society at New Amsterdam," *New York History* 59 (1978), p. 130, based on Stokes, *Iconography* 2 and 4, the underlying documentation, unfortunately incorporates early mistranslations of *huysen* as "house."

violence in the "houses of the blacks" (*Swarte huysen*) and condemned to pay 12 florins.[126] Land grants to Europeans from 1643 mention this settlement: a grant to Evert Duyckinghe finds the "Negroes' lot" (*'t hof van Negroes*) on its west side, a grant to Touchyn Briel simply mentions "the Negroes" as living along a thicket in delineating her border, and Thomas Nysen's grant in 1647 refers to the area as the "Negroes' plantation" (*d'negroes plantagis*).[127] It appears that this property consisted of several houses; in a grant dated to 1654 the area near Duyckinghe's land is referred to as "the houses of the Negroes" (*de huisen van de Negroes*).[128]

The community, those who were free and others who remained slaves of the company, had considerable solidarity. They had their own leader, a "Captain of the Negroes," named Bastayen in 1644.[129] When eight of them were tried in 1641 for the murder of a fellow African, Jan Primeiro, they "voluntarily declared and confessed that they did it jointly [*gecompaereert*]," and when asked who was the leader (*aenvoerder*) and who gave the death blow, they said "they themselves did not know they had done it together [*samentl(ijck)*]."[130] They exhibited a similar spirit of solidarity in 1646 when an anonymous group turned in Jan Creoly, another member of the community, for sodomizing 10-year-old Manuel Congo.[131]

Not all Africans in New Amsterdam lived in a large community that could provide opportunities for networking. These would include Company slaves who were hired out as private workers, some who were occasionally sold, or others in the hands of private people. Thomas Hall used three African workers on a farm the company leased to him in 1647,[132] and in 1652 he also employed a single African man from the

[126] New York State Archives, Council Minutes, 22 September 1639, fol. 50, see Van Laer, *Council Minutes* 4: 61.
[127] New York State Archives, Land Patents, GG 67 (Evert Duckinghe), GG 77 (Touchin Briel), GG 208 (Tonis Nysen) (translations in Gehring, *Land Papers*).
[128] New York State Archives, Land Papers, HH 11, 19 June 1654.
[129] Evans, ed. "Doop–Boek (DB) of the Reformed Church of New Netherland" in *New York Genealogical and Biographical Society Record* 2 (New York, 1890) 17/ 261 as "Captain of the Blacks" [*Capt van de Swarten*] or later as *Captyn van de* Negers, DB 18/263.
[130] New York State Archives, Council Minutes, "Cornelio vander Hoykens fiscael eyscher c. Cleyn Antonio Paulo d'angola, Gracia d'angola, Jan de fort Orange, Manuel de Gerrit de Reus, Antony portugees, Manuel minuit Simon Congo, ende manuel de Groote over homisidie begaen aen Jan premero mede Negro," 14–15 January 1641, fols. 83–4, translated in van Laer, vol. 4.
[131] New York State Archives, Council Minutes, 25 June 1646, fol. 262 (translation in van Laer, 4).
[132] 30 November 1641, Fernow, *Colonial Records* 14: 35.

FIGURE 13. Francisco Angola, a free Angolan in New Netherland. Source: Ira Berlin and Leslie Harris, eds., *Slavery in New York* (New York: New Press, 2005).

Company on another farm he leased.[133] These arrangements were not unusual, and even Dutch colonists indentured their children this way, as Tobias Peaks indentured his stepdaughter Annetje Patricks in 1649 as a "servant girl" to do housework to Cornelis Tienhoven for two consecutive years.[134] The Company also lent out the children of their freedmen: three were in various locations in 1650, including the households of Governor Stuyvesant and Marten Krigier, who would later become mayor.[135]

Others in small groups were in private hands, such as Louruiso Barbosse, a young black boy (*Swarte jongen*) who was cooking in the house of his owner, Gysbert Opdyck, in 1639, when Opdyck killed him (accidentally, he claimed) in the course of punishing the youth for bringing him a

---

[133] Directors to Stuyvesant, 26 April 1651, Fernow, *Colonial Records* 14: 139.
[134] Indenture contract, Van Laer 3: 86.
[135] Answer to the Remonstrance delivered by the Delegates from New Netherland, on the 27 January 1650, point 43, O'Callaghan, *Documents* 1: 343. On Krigier in 1661, see DB 62/316.

dirty pot.[136] Another group of privately owned Africans was composed of a company of African and Native Americans brought by Captain Jan de Vries from Brazil to New Netherland in 1644 to assist in "Krieft's War" war against the Native Americans. They stayed in a company, and when de Vries left in 1647, he ordered Michiel Jansen to take care of "his free Negroes and Brazilian women."[137] De Vries had a child named Jan by a woman known only as "Swartinne" (Black Woman) while his estate was left in the hands of Paulo d'Angola and Clara Criollo (formerly Dorothe van Angola), members of the local community who also looked after his child's interest.[138]

One of the largest groups of privately owned Africans was the eight Africans whose ownership was disputed between Geurt Tyssen and Judich Verlettes in 1652.[139] The fate of the slaves brought by Juan Galliardo's ship in 1652 reveals the existence of small-scale ownership and selling of slaves among a wide variety of owners. Four years after the arrival of the ship, a report noted that "some of these negroes are already dead; some have run away: some are still on hand here, with divers inhabitants, as bond slaves, purchased and paid for, but most of these have been two, three or more times resold, and have changed masters."[140] Pieter Stuyvestant himself, although governor, owned slaves independently of the Company; in 1660 he had no less than 40 Africans working for him on one of his farms at the Bowrie (the Bowry), which might have accounted for 1 in 10 Africans on the island.[141]

By 1650 there was therefore a large and well-established Central African Charter Generation in New Amsterdam. Shortly after that, the Company granted New Netherlanders the right to import slaves directly from Africa. Such shipping frequently tapped markets at Allada and Calabar, as did the *Witte Paert*, the first such vessel to arrive in New Amsterdam in 1655. At least 10 slaving voyages stopped in New Amsterdam

---

[136] New York State Archives, Council Records, Court of 9 November 1639, English translation in van Laer, *Colonial Records* 4: 66.

[137] Stokes, *Iconography* 4: 111–12.

[138] This history is first traced out in David S. Cohen, *Ramapo Mountain People* (New Brunswick, NJ, 1974), pp. 26–7. Cohen has Paulo d'Angola and his wife coming from among a group that de Vries brought from Brazil, but in fact, they were already in the colony when he arrived. Perhaps these people were "his free negroes" and had been ordered to do him service, through their obligations to the Company.

[139] Geurt Tyssen vs. Judich Verlettes and Anna Heckx, 9 September 1652, in Gehring, *Council Minutes, 1652–54*, 5: 37, 41, 50.

[140] O'Callaghan, *Documents* 2: 28, 6 September 1656.

[141] Henricus Selyns letter, 4 October 1660, *Ecclesiastical Records*, 488.

between 1655 and 1664 when the English took over the colony, bringing in many as 800 slaves; in fact, the *Gideon* arrived in 1664, carrying 291 slaves.[142] Looking at raw numbers this influx might have doubled the population of African descent in New Amsterdam, and they might constitute a sort of "Plantation Generation" without forming the classic plantation complex of Virginia or Barbados.

In fact the impact of the West Africans was much more limited. Many came sick or had already been rejected for poor health at Curaçao, where the ships typically stopped first, and surely died rapidly. Many of those who came on the *Musch*' were quite old, having been rejected by the Spaniards, while the *Gideon*'s cargo was "half-starved" and had "many who were infected with scurvy," forming a "a very poor lot" being overaged and thus sold for a low price.[143] Many more were sold immediately outside the city; for example, a sizable portion of the *Witte Paert*'s Africans were bought by Edmund Scarbourgh and taken to Virginia. Furthermore, after the English took over, the slave trade to New York dropped considerably, with only relatively small shipments coming from the West Indies providing many Africans until the end of the seventeenth century.

Quite apart from the effect that the newly arrived Africans had on the demography of the city, the majority of them came from Central Africa and were thus Atlantic Creoles. Indeed, initially the West India Company intended that once direct slave trading with Africa began, those slaves taken from the Allada-Calabar area were to go to Brazil, and New Netherland was to receive slaves from Angola, whose trade would be open to all. The colony of Curaçao was conceived as a way station for the furthering of the Angola trade.[144] Thus when the *Gideon* went on a trading venture to Africa it stopped first at Elmina (not then a slave-trading post, dealing primarily in gold) and continued to Loango before stopping at the Dutch colonies on the Wild Coast and then delivering 291 slaves to New Amsterdam in 1664.[145] Therefore, the vast majority of the new arrivals, far from being diverse and not of Creole origins, were in fact from the same Atlantic Creole roots as the Charter Generation.

[142] Foote, *Black and White*, pp. 36–7, though we have identified a few other voyages not mentioned in her text, for example, the *Vogelstruijs*, master Sijmen Cornelisz Gilde, went from Amsterdam directly to the West Indies; it then brought slaves from Curacao to New Netherland, GAA NA 1309 fol. 7, 25 January 1658.

[143] Documents collected in Donnan, *Documents* pp. 429, 433; also O'Callaghan, *Colonial Documents* 2: 430.

[144] Proceedings of the XIX, 1645, O'Callaghan, *Documents* 1: 157–8; see Report of Affairs of the West India Company, January 1648, O'Callaghan, *Documents* 1: 230; 235.

[145] Donnan, *Documents*, pp. 422–5; 429–33.

The Plantation Generation as Founders: Heterogenity
and Demographic Dominance

The varying patterns of the Charter Generation were not evident in the settlements that welcomed the Plantation Generation. Africans came in overwhelmingly large numbers to a booming sugar economy or labored in emerging economies based on lucrative crops like indigo and rice that created the classic plantation settlement patterns from the very start. They were, moreover, brought by the existing slave trade to Africa and thus less homogenous than the earlier Central African Charter Generation. Central Africans probably made up only a quarter of their numbers, the rest being drawn from a wide variety of West African sources.

Jamaica stands out as a case in point here. When the English took the island from the Spanish in 1655, they met an existing small community of "Spanish Negroes," most of whom had fled to runaway settlements to avoid the violence of the English conquest. By 1662, the island held 3,653 Europeans and 552 Africans (18 percent of the total), mostly brought from Barbados by the conquerors, and the Plantation Generation was already arriving, because the English had received 244 slaves from a Dutch ship shortly after their arrival. The residual of the Afro-Spanish residents formed a community of 150 people resident in a "pollinck" (*palenque*, a self-governing runaway settlement) under Juan Bulo.[146] By 1677, the African portion had reached half of the total population, and by 1739 the revolution was complete: 99,000 Africans lived on the island with just 10,000 Europeans.[147] As a measure of the diversity of the Plantation Generation, the English were now well aware of the variety of origins of the Africans in the Caribbean, Lord Willoughby wrote to London that, happily, the diversity of Africans "whose different tounges and animosity in their own country has hitherto disposed them from insurrection."[148]

Tobago represents a variant of this pattern, but unlike Jamaica, the colony was short lived. Here, the Charter Generation was also the Plantation Generation following the resettlement of the island by the Dutch in

---

[146] BL Add MSS 11410, fol. 12, "A brief account of the island of Jamaica in America," n. d., c 1662; the arrival of the Dutch ship is noted in "Relation Concerning the Expedition to the West Indies, 1654–[1664]," fol. 138; the Royal African Company was promising more, fol. 307.

[147] Philip Sherlock and Hazel Bennett, *The Story of the Jamaican People* (Princeton and Kingston, Jamaica, 1998), pp. 92–3.

[148] PRO CO 29/1, fol. 58, Willoughby to Lords of Council, 9 July 1668.

the 1650s as they recouped the loss of Jan de Moor's pioneering colony. A Dutch-financed company representing the Duke of Kurland (modern-day Latvia) created a colony on Tobago in 1659, and this in turn was taken over by a Zeeland-based company in 1665. Slaves to work in the new settlement came directly from Africa and from a variety of places. The Duke of Kurland had already founded a colony on the Gambia River before turning to Tobago and used its commercial relations in Africa to supply the island with slaves.[149]

M. Lamsin, the Dutch proprietor of the colony when Dutch interests superceded those of Kurland, followed up on the Duke's lead and provided slaves from "time to time." According to estimates made in 1666, the island consisted of some 12,000–13,000 inhabitants "not counting the Negroes...who it is believed, are a much greater number."[150] Like Barbados, Tobago went through a rapid agricultural cycle, focusing first on tobacco and then, when prices fell, diversifying into other crops, such as sugar cane, indigo, cotton, and ginger, and moving directly into a pattern that would have been characteristic of a Plantation Generation.[151] The short-lived settlement in Tobago also resembled the classic Plantation Generation pattern in the rapid development of separate slave quarters. In the Lampsins's main settlement was a village for more than 80 Africans who worked on his nearby estate and sugar mill.[152] But Dutch Tobago, like its predecessor, was eliminated by Spanish and Caribs, and by the early eighteenth century the island was abandoned by Europeans.

The Americanization of the Central African Atlantic Creoles

In contrast to the later Plantation Generation, whose religious outlook and cultural practices are well documented by traveler's accounts and more recently by studies in material culture and archaeology, the universe of the Atlantic Creoles who formed the Charter Generation is poorly described. Before 1660 visitors to the colonies made passing references to Africans in

[149] Otto Mattiesen, *Die Koloniale- und Überseepolitik der Kurländischen Herzöge im 17. und 18. Jahrhundert* (Stuttgart, 1940) pp. 236–272; 446–510.

[150] Charles de Rochefort, *Relation de l'île de Tabago, ou de la nouvelle Oüalcre une de les illes Antilles de l'Amerique* (Paris, 1666), p. 71. The earlier history, and its charter, is recounted on pp. 59–64.

[151] Rochefort, *Relation*, pp. 51–7.

[152] Rochefort, *Relation*, p. 82. Quarters with large numbers of Africans were also found elsewhere, p. 84.

the community but almost never described their lives and customs. This may well be because their numbers were sufficiently small and their Creole lifestyle sufficiently similar to that of the lower-class European population; they did not stand out as exotic enough to warrant special attention. In fact, such writers were not blind to non-European peoples, for they left vivid descriptions of Native Americans and of African societies when they visited the continent.[153]

Without having accounts similar to those describing the later Plantation Generation, which began appearing in travelers' accounts in the later seventeenth century – we must rely on the more limited evidence provided by wills, deeds, inventories, and court and church records to understand the cultural world of the Charter Generation. This limited information is somewhat offset by the wealth of description that is available on their manner of capture in Africa. The range of cultural information that can be found in seventeenth-century sources on Africa, and especially the well-developed accounts of religious life, makes it possible to complement and augment the limited American source material. Using this approach, some aspects of their religious behavior, naming patterns, a few agricultural skills, and some elements of their cultural behavior can be explored and reconstructed in the American colonies.

One of the most important and striking aspects of the Central African Charter Generation's Atlantic Creole background was that a significant number of them were Catholics. In-depth descriptions of how this Catholicism informed the everyday life of members of the Charter Generation is hampered by the fact that many Dutch and English settlements left little in the way of ecclesiastical records, as often the European population itself was not very observant and were frequently without sufficient clergy. This probably explains the relative paucity of references to Africans in the church records of Bermuda.[154] However, where records do exist, as in the case of New Amsterdam, we find a very active African population participating fully in its recorded sacraments.

---

[153] This may be a factor of the type of writing as well. For example, the early English colonies are mostly described in prospectus literature that focused mostly on natural resources (though rarely neglects to say something about native peoples). For the Dutch, there are more descriptive accounts; the most revealing is Andrian van der Donck's description of New Netherland, which contains no mention of the African inhabitants, whereas Barleus and Nieuhoff's descriptions of Brazil do have sections dealing with the African poplation.

[154] Bernhard, *Slaves and Slaveholders*, p. 44 (for the situation in Bermuda and Virginia).

The numbers of these Africans who were Christian and the depth of their knowledge and conviction varied according to the time and place of their enslavement in Central Africa, because, as we have seen, they were not uniformly spread over the whole region. For example, Africans who came to Virginia in 1619 on the *White Lion* and *Treasurer*, captured in Vasconcelos's campaigns against Ndongo and in the civil war in the southwest Kongo province of Mbamba the same year, included some with fairly substantial exposure to Christianity from Kongo and around the Portuguese posts and settlements. The shipment also included others from around Ndongo's capital of Kabasa who would have had much less contact with Christianity or even no contact at all. Captain Guy's *Fortune*, which supplied the only other recorded shipment to Virginia in 1628 of "manie Negroes" taken from an "Angola man... intended for the Spanish of the West Indies," would also have carried West Central Africans with different exposure to Christianity.[155] This would also be the case for "20 men and 30 women, Negroes, who were captured in the last prize" in 1630 and who the West India Company factor in Pernambuco sent to its colony in Pavonia, New Netherland. These Africans were in all likelihood captured in the Portuguese/Njinga wars in eastern Angola, as well as the factional war between King Ambrósio and Duke Manuel Jordão of Nsundi. As such, the captives from these wars included a substantial mix of people with both Christian and non-Christian backgrounds.[156]

As we have noted, some ships carried Central Africans who had very little Christian background, as was the case on the slave ship that the Jesuit missionary Pedro Tavares sailed with from Angola to Brazil in 1634, whose slaves were unfamiliar with Christianity.[157] The Africans taken in 1636 by Dutch privateers from the *Nossa Senhora do Rosario e as Animas* on its way to Cartagena were probably from Kongo, where a civil war that year caused many people to be enslaved. The privateers probably sold them to Tobago or perhaps to the English in Providence Island. In this case, probably the majority would have been Catholics.[158] Other

[155] PRO State Papers. Domestic. Charles I, letters and papers 16/103.

[156] ARA OWIC 44, Servatius Carpentier to the directors of the WIC Zeeland, 25 September 1630, English translation quoted in Phelps, *Iconongraphy*, p. 944. According to de Laet, *Iaerlijck verhael*, 2 p. 147, the last prize was taken on 8 June 1630 by the *Overijssel*, an Angola man carrying 280 captives.

[157] ARSI 55, fol. 106, Pedro Tavares to Jeronimo Vogado, 29 June 1635 (Jadin's French translation ["Pero Tavares... "] marks the pagination of the Rome version, this section is lacking in the Evora version).

[158] Vila Vilar, *Hispanoamerica*, Appendix, quadro 4.

casualties of that civil war were likely to have been on the "Spanish" slave ship that the men of David de Vries' private colony on the Wild Coast captured and subsequently took to Barbados the same year. However, the "cannibal negroes" that the Providence Island Company ordered removed from New England in 1638 might have had very little engagement with Christianity. These mysterious captives were probably Imbangala, whose outlook was even anti-Christian and who were taken prisoners in the war between Njinga and Kasanje.[159]

Although to missionaries like Pedro Tavares the Christianity of the Central Africans was deficient or fell short of expectations, those Africans who did claim to be Christian exhibited certain core elements of Christian practices. One of the most important ways that they exhibited their Christian identity was their desire to have their children baptized. Another, which also revealed their Christian background, was their having Christian names in Iberian form and bestowing such names on their children. Central Africans in the Charter Generation also used the practice of selecting godparents (usually a fellow member of the community) to be witnesses at the baptism of their children. They were also inclined to have their marriages sanctified by the Church and to participate fully with their European counterparts in Christian ceremonies.

Thus to these Atlantic Creoles what mattered was the assertion of a Christian identity rather than a sectarian Catholic one. Although in Kongo the elites might vigorously assert their Catholic identity in the face of Dutch Catholic proselytizing, most ordinary Kongolese Christians did not face this problem. Moreover, in Central Africa they showed no reluctance to mix African elements in their Christian beliefs and practices, and when confronted with a Protestant church structure and liturgy that were more similar than different to the core Catholic liturgy, they did not reject it.

The willingness of the Central Africans to seek baptism is revealed in early Virginia. The muster of 1625 lists "Antoney Negro: Isabell Negro: and William their child baptised," living in Elizabeth City.[160] This Antoney, probably the same Anthony Johnson who became both free and prosperous in his later days, was sufficiently interested in the formal marks of Christian identity to offer his child for baptism and have his offer accepted, even though he had been in the colony only a few years. John Graweere, who may have arrived in the colony not much later, in

---

[159] Linda Heywood and John Thornton, "Removal of 'Canniball Negroes,'" ...
[160] Muster of Inhabitants of Virginia, January–February 1625 (ed. Jester and Hiden), p. 49.

1641, "had young child of a negro woman ... which he desired should be made a christian and be taught and exercised in the church of England," and he purchased her freedom to ensure that the child was raised this way.[161] Similarly, at about the same time, Emanuel Driggus wanted to ensure that his children would be brought up "in the feare of god and in the knowledge of our Saviour Christ Jesus."[162]

Although very little is known of the role of Christianity among the early inhabitants of Bermuda, they probably did have their children baptized. In 1647 the Bermuda assembly ordered that all children be baptized immediately, as a means to stamp out Anabaptism, but excluded "Bastards or Negroes children" from this requirement, probably reflecting the sense that they were not caught up in this particular heresy but that they were regularly baptizing their children.[163] One Afro-Bermudan named "ould Saunders," perhaps reflecting a more general sentiment among the African population, gave up his child Ellicke to John Stowe Marshall in 1648 or 1649 for a term of 20 years to ensure that he was brought up "in the fear of god and to reading as far as the understanding of the bible ... "[164]

There is even less to be said of New England, with its small population of Africans. In 1641 the "Negro maid servant to Mr. Stoughton," whom Puritans in Dorchester, one of the independent towns of the Massachusetts Bay Colony, considered "well approved by divers years' experience, for sound knowledge and true godliness," resolved that she should be "received into the church and baptized."[165] Perhaps the maid's willingness to participate in a religious environment that required so much from her originated as much from previous exposure to Christianity in Central Africa as from the ministrations of her Puritan mentors.

Undoubtedly English reluctance to see their slaves as Christians, as Ligon noted that the planters' interpretation of English law made them believe that "being once a Christian, he could no more account him a slave, and so lose the hold they had of them as slaves,"[166] hampered both their willingness to report the Christian background of their slaves as well

[161] Court of 31 March 1641, McIlwain, p. lost.
[162] NCHR Deeds, Wills..., no. 3 (1645–1651), fol. 82.
[163] "An act for enforcing...children," c. July 1647, in William Golding, *Servants on Horseback*... (London, 1648), p. 13. This law clearly did not prohibit Africans from baptizing their children, as Bernhard, *Slaves and Slaveholders*, p. 37, contends.
[164] Lefroy, *Memorials* 1: 645. It is possible that Saunders came in the early batch of Africans who began arriving in 1617, or about 30 years earlier, because his designation as "old" might make him no more than 50.
[165] Dunn, *Winthrop Papers*, p. 347.
[166] Ligon, *History*, p. 50.

as any efforts at evangelization. In this uniform reluctance to acknowledge the Christian background of their slaves, some Atlantic Creoles did what they could to maintain their Christian identity. Contemporary documents tell us nothing about the religious orientation of the Charter Generation in Barbados, but there was a group whose Catholic background was visible. The French priest Antoine Biet, who visited Barbados in 1654, confirms the Christian identity of some of the slaves on the island when he observed that some of the slaves "contented themselves by baptizing the children in the house, and if any of them have any tinge of the Catholic Religion which they received among the Portuguese, they keep it the best they can, doing their prayers and worshipping God in their hearts."[167] Other slaves, such as Samuel Drew's "nigger, called Anthony seemed to have a desire to become a Christian" in 1655, may have been seeking opportunities to become part of a Christian community.[168]

No other area reveals the depth of Africans' desire to maintain a Christian identity than New Amsterdam, where there was more readiness to include slaves in a multicultural Christian community. Records of the Reformed Church's baptisms and marriages kept from 1639 onward show this fully. Thus on 7 July 1641 Jacom Anthoney van Angola presented his daughter, Catharina, to be baptized, and the witnesses included Clyn Anthony van Angola and Susanna van Angola (the last probably the child's mother).[169] Indeed, during the 1640s the registers show almost one in three baptisms in New Amsterdam were of Africans, which closely parallels their percentage in the whole community. Such a high percentage suggests that the entire African community presented their children for baptism. It was more likely that changes in church policy rather than a change in the attitude of the Africans caused the number of African baptisms to drop off precipitously in the 1650s. In fact, the idea that the African community had become Christian was sufficiently well accepted in the colony that Dutch dissidents, writing to the Netherlands to complain of the Company's behavior, specifically challenged the custom of

---

[167] Antoine Biet, *Voyage de la France Equinoxiale en la isle de Cayenne* (Paris, 1664), p. 291. An English translation, that marks the original pagination is in Jerome Handler, "Father Biet's Visit to Barbados in 1654," *Journal of the Barbados Historical Society* 32 (1967): 56–76.

[168] Cambridge University Library, Darnell Davis Papers, Box 2, no. 19, "Pages from the Early History of Barbados," drawn from MSS in the possession of the Duke of Portland, release of 23 February 1655.

[169] DB 11/252.

reenslaving the children of the free African community, denying "that anyone born of a free Christian mother should still be a slave and must remain in service."[170]

One of the most visible ways that Atlantic Creoles in the Charter Generation demonstrated their Creole and Catholic background was in their names. This is best revealed in the giving of Iberian names as is readily evident from the names that are recorded in various wills, deeds, and other inventories in the English and Dutch colonies. These documents show that Atlantic Creoles bore Iberian names or English or Dutch equivalents of the same names. Transforming Iberian names to their English or Dutch equivalents was common throughout the colonies, as we see in the case of Nicholas Silvedo, listed as a Portuguese indentured servant laboring in Virginia whose Anglicized name probably translates to the birth name Nicolau Silveira.[171] Because neither the English or Dutch masters would bestow Iberian names on their slaves, these Africans must have brought them from their original homes.[172]

In the deeds and other records where such names appear, they represent a significant percentage of the population, even though a large number of Africans are listed simply as "Negro." The unnamed "negroes" present a number of possible interpretations: it could be that they were from the non-Christian portion of the African population and did not have Christian names (they could not remember the name hastily given to them during mass baptisms in Luanda), they were known among themselves by Kikongo or Kimbundu names that did not have a corresponding European equivalent (though both English and Dutch managed to reproduce very complex Algonquian names), or simply that some servants were not listed by names in registers and rosters. Occasionally Scotch and Irish were listed

---

[170] *Vertoog van Nieu-Neder-Land Weghens de Gheleghentheydt, Vruchtbaerheydt, en Soberen Staet desselfs* (Haguel, 1650), p. 32. We have modified the translation in O'Callaghan, *Documents* 1: 302.

[171] Paul Heinegg, "Free African Americans," Harmon Family, 1.1; Deal, *Race and Class*, pp. 336–55.

[172] James Sweet, for example, challenges the idea that these names were Creole, arguing that such names were routinely given to first-generation slaves, sometimes even before they left Africa (but only referencing in this latter case the baptismal ceremony of non-Creoles in Luanda). Although it is true that a typical Iberian slave name would include a national marker, like Maria Angola or Pedro Congo, this was not English custom, though it appears to have been used by the Dutch. In any case, they would not have chosen Iberian as opposed to English or Dutch names, Sweet, "Spanish and Portuguese Influences," pp. 27–8.

simply as "Scot," "Irish," or "servant," just as Africans were recorded as "Negroes."

The largest sample of names of enslaved Africans in the Charter Generation comes from Virginia. For this colony, thanks to the legal requirement that people wishing to patent land list their servants by name, there is a large sample of names, even though the majority of the Africans were listed on these records as simply "negroes" without any name at all.[173] A survey of names from patents, deeds, inventories, and court records covering the period 1635 to 1660 reveals a total of 285 names. For the period up to 1650, of a total of 98 named people, some 25 percent had Iberian names (for example, Antonio, Manuel, and Maria). Another, Galatia, had a name that represented a typically Central African pronunciation of Graça; similarly "Bashaw" appears to be a localization of Sebastião.[174] Seventy-five percent had English names that had a ready Iberian equivalent (John, Michael, or Ann but not William, Sarah, or Jenny), typical English names of the period. A few had names that were identifiably Central African, such as Andolo, Palassa, Congo, or Cassango.[175]

A new pattern of naming appears in the 1650s as the first generation of Atlantic Creoles gave way to their American-born children, and some parents decided to give them purely English or Dutch names. This trend was started by the first known baptized African American child, William, the son of Antoney and Isabell, in 1625. Thus names like Margery, Jane, and Sarah, which have no Iberian equivalents, began to appear, though some parents clearly continued with Iberian names as well. Thus, the Iberian or Anglo-Iberian pattern still held, for during the period from 1650 to 1660, of 165 names, 72 (43 percent) had such names, 20 (12 percent) had names that were purely Iberian, and 2 (Palassa and Angora; .01 percent) had names from Central African languages. At the same time, however, the first names of the Plantation Generation start to appear. Matilda and Tabatha Scarborough, who used 41 recently arrived Africans purchased in New Amsterdam from the *Witte Paert* to patent land in Northumberland

---

[173] The study of these records is problematic, as study of the European people in the lists reveal that many times the same servant was listed more than once in various patents requests. We have sought to eliminate double counting by checking masters' names and lists to ensure that this does not effect our statistics. It is, however, impossible to rule out double counting in some cases. Fortunately, our statistical case is well demonstrated even if one allows for this double counting.

[174] Deal, *Race and Class*, 254.

[175] See list in appendix for sources and our lisiting. We made other equivalents: Mingo = Domingo, Bashaw = Sebastião.

County, Virginia, in 1656, gave their African names, among them names such as Ufodor, Chigidra, Ambe, and Ogombo.[176] Given their origins in Allada and Calabar, these names are probably drawn from Fon, Ewe, Igbo, and Kalabari roots.

In no English or Dutch American colony does the Central African origin of naming show up more than in New Netherland. Virtually all of the 172 names that are found in Dutch records, including court records and petitions, and those names that appear in the baptismal and marriage registers of the Dutch Reformed Church, are of Iberian origin or are close Dutch equivalents.[177] Only 11 (6.4 percent) are names of uniquely Dutch or of unknown origin (Evert, Abraham, or Barent, for example).[178] A few names appear to be of Central African origin, probably Kimbundu, such as Palassa, a name that can be found in records of Bermuda, Virginia, and New Netherland.[179] Most of the New Netherland Africans also bear an ethnic marker, such as Simon Congo or Anthony van Angola, and those who do not are usually designated as "neger" or "swartinne."[180] The overwhelming majority carry the origin designation of Angola, and only a few are Congo. Three (2 percent) carry the ethnonym of "Portugies" (but also "Neger"), indicating an origin in the African part of the Atlantic world. Three more are indicated as Santomee (2 percent) and one is indicated as being of Cape Verde, which are the only markers that

---

[176] Virginia State Archives, Land Patent Records, vol. 4, p. 32.

[177] The Dutch Reformed Church began keeping records in 1639, but suddenly and abruptly stopped recording any of African origin in 1654; see the records in Thomas Grier Evans (ed.), *Baptisms from 1639 to 1730 in the Reformed Dutch Church in New Amsterdam and New York* (New York, 1901) (transcript of original Dutch register) and Purple, *Records*. Children continued to be baptized, as Stuyvesant's wife was arranging for children of his farm to be baptized in the 1660s, but these do not appear on the record letter of Vice President Beck to Stuyvesant, 15 November 1664, O'Callaghan, *Voyages of the Slavers St John and Arms of Amsterdam*, pp. 226–7.

[178] These names include Samuel, Gerasÿ, Pernante, Leen, (might be Helena) Phizithien, Lare (might be Hilaria), Lucas (rare but not impossible in seventeenth-century Portuguese), and Janneken.

[179] Council Meeting Minutes, 1655, pp. 267–8; Purple, *Marriages*, 11/573 DB 15/257, New Netherland, Pallas, Palass, Palasse; BCR book F, no. 88, "Polassa" the wife of Mingo Grande on Bermuda (1634); York County, Deeds and Orders, p. 122, Palassa. We learned of Palasa as a Kimbundu name in an interview with the *sobas* of Dondo, Angola, August 2004.

[180] This pattern of giving ethnic names as a sort of surname was common practice in Spanish colonies and often attested in Portuguese as well. See the usage in AGI Contadura 1056, letters of 2 January 1613, 15 November 1614. For general statements, see Gonzalo Aguirre Beltrán, *La población negra de México: Estudo Etnohistórico* (3rd ed., 2 vols, Mexico City, 1989), 2: 99–103.

suggest an African origin other than Central Africa and could conceivably be ultimately of West African origin.[181]

Some of the Atlantic Creoles bore double first names, such as Jan Francisco, Fernande Marie, Joachem Anthony, or Catalina Anthony, suggestive of the common Central African naming pattern of giving a father's first name as the child's second name. This practice is documented directly in New Netherland; in 1644 when Emanuel van Angola and Phizithiaen d'Angool had a son named Claes Emanuel, his second name was his father's first name. Claes Emanuel then married Lucretia Louyse in 1680. She was the daughter of Lovys Angola (and hence carried her father's first name as her second name) and Hilary Criolyo (married 1660); other children of the same union were Lysbeth Louyse and Anthony Louyse. Their children were then named after their paternal and maternal grandparents and godmother.[182] Naming children after grandparents could also be found in Virginia; William Harmon named his son Manuel, probably after Emmanuel Driggus, his grandfather.[183]

The Atlantic Creoles had no problem, then, in adopting the Dutch system of naming, which was very similar to their own custom of giving a father's name as a second first name, though the Dutch system usually included the ending *–zoon*, *–zen*, *–sz*, or *–s*. For example, the African Manuel Trompetter (that is, Manuel, the trumpeter) and his wife, Anthonya, baptized their daughter Christina in 1645, and although her birth record simply records her name as "Christina" she appears later, when she married in 1663, as Christina Emanuels.[184] This modification to fit the Dutch system is probably the origin of the several names Pieters, Pietersz, Sanders, and Samuelsen found among the Afro-New Netherlanders of the later period.

A few of the Atlantic Creoles probably also had Portuguese language surnames; for example, Domenico Deis, who baptized his child Tÿntie

---

[181] See our list in the appendix. We tried to be conservative, combining many of the ambigious entries under each other, for example, "Francisco Neger" is just one person unless compelling reasons make us believe there are two.

[182] DB 339/142; Purple, *Records*, fol. 603, p. 26, see Goodfriend, "Black Familes in New Netherland," *Selected Rensselaerswijck Seminar Papers*, p. 153, for the working out these relationships, but clearly missing the Angolan rather than Dutch origin of this system.

[183] Paul Heinegg, "Free African Americans," Harmon Family, 1.1; Deal, *Race and Class*, pp. 336–55.

[184] Birth record, 18 February 1645, DB 18/263; her later appearance is in O'Callaghan *Calendar* 256; Fernow, *Records* 4: 41–2.

in 1639, was probably originally Domingo Dias.[185] Anthony Matthyszen van de Camp, a "Neger," who baptized his son, Cosmus, in 1651, probably bore a name translating the Portuguese name de Campos. When the English took over the colony in 1664, some of the Dutch subsequently Anglicized their names, as did members of the Atlantic Creole community. Hence, Maria d'Angola, who appears in marriage registers three times, eventually was listed as Mary d'Angola in 1684 under the English.[186] Similarly, Dorothe d'Angola eventually became Clara Creole in her later years.[187]

Bermuda might have revealed a similar pattern, given its large and early African population, but the legal records of the colony did not preserve large name lists, and only a small number appear in wills and court records. The existing records reveal more of an English pattern of names. A search of records discovered 93 names recorded between 1617 and 1660.[188] For the earlier period, up to 1650, there are 52 names; of these 21 (40.3 percent) are purely Iberian, such as Antonio or Maria, and if we include English names that have Iberian counterparts, such as Anthony and Mary, the number rises to 31 (59.6 percent) of the total. A sizable number of Bermudans, however, bore English names that had no clear Iberian equivalent, such as Jane, Richard, and Rebecca. However, it should be noted that the records of Bermuda have very few names before 1630, when a great many children would have been born on the island to the first largely nameless generation of Africans who came in the rush of the late 1610s and early 1620s. In their choice of English names, the Atlantic Creoles in Bermuda did not turn to the kind of slave names that were found everywhere in the English-speaking world during the Plantation Generation, so there were Rebeccas and Janes but no Catos and Caesars. In the later period, from 1650 to 1660, the number with Iberian names declines, 12 of a total 41 names (29.5 percent) are either Iberian or English with an Iberian equivalent, following what was probably a trend of giving "typical" English names to children of Africans.

---

[185] DB 10/249 from 1639. In 1700 Susanna De was the wife of Pieter Francisco, Neger, DB 266/247 baptizing their son Jan (with Willem De as a witness). Although it is a generation late, this name might be a transformation of Dies.

[186] Richard Dickenson, "Abstracts of Early Black Manhattanites," *The Record* 116 (1985): 104.

[187] Dickenson, *Abstracts*, p. 104.

[188] A list is included in the appendix.

No name list exists for the period of the Charter Generation in Barbados, as the earliest records that list names date from 1643, two years after the arrival of slave ships from West Africa bringing large numbers of people. What the first named list shows is that Africans bore a variety of names, including Iberian names, plantation names, West African names, and English names. Thus, it is not surprising that any Charter Generation Africans might be overwhelmed by these heterogeneous newcomers who came in the hundreds off the ships that arrived primarily from Allada and Calabar. A fine example of this mingling of people of various origins is found in an entry from 1643, just two years after the first massive arrival of West Africans. On 21 December 1643 Daniell Fletcher bought one half of an estate called Charles Fort with the following eight named Africans: Tony Mingoe, Grange, Mall, Butler, Maria, Judy, Nell, and Illumah.[189] This mixture includes Iberian names like Tony (Antonio), Maria, and Mingoe (Domingo); English names like Judy, Mall (Moll), and Nell; a West African name (Illumah), and finally Butler, a plantation name. Three hundred eighteen named Africans appear in the records of the period from 1643 to 1660, primarily from wills and indentures. In the earliest periods, until about 1650, most Africans (and the majority of the European servants) in these documents were unnamed; there were over 400 unnamed "negroes" before 1647. Of those named only 23 (7.2 percent) had Iberian names and 55 (17.3 percent) had English names with an Iberian equivalent. The most common names were ones that were apparently West African, accounting for 117 (36.8 percent) of the names.[190] Seventy-five (23.6 percent) were purely English percent and 40 names were of uncertain origin; a few, such as Butler, Tamerlain the Great, and Samson, were tacked onto the Plantation Generation by capricious overseers and masters. Such names later became common throughout the English-speaking Americas. Many of the names are neither English nor Iberian, and a good many sound phonologically African. When Nathaniel Sylvester transported slaves from Barbados to a new estate on Shelter Island, off Long Island, in 1654, their names, as revealed in a will 25 years later, show only a few of Iberian origin (Tony) and a pattern that

---

[189] RB3/1 Deeds, p. 92. See also p. 33 where an earlier list also include a wide mixture with a number of Christian servants.

[190] We have not attempted to define specific West African ethnic names from our list and are operating on the assumption that names that not English or Iberian and have phonological patterns consistent with West African languages, for example, Ago, Aga, Cushoe, Fumfum, Obree, and Effe (but are not Central African) are assumed to be West African.

resembles the Barbados of the time, Grace, Hannah, Jacquero, and Nanny, for example.[191]

The sparse New England records reveal only 10 named Africans between 1634 and 1660 (9 more are identified only as "negroes"), too small a sample to be able to have much statistical weight. Of this small group half had either an Iberian name or its English equivalent. Of the remainder 3 had African names (Angola, Moniah, and Mungaly), one had an English name (Hope), and the last one had a name of uncertain origin, Jugg, but which is found in both Virginia and Barbados lists, perhaps reflecting the type of name that masters assigned to slaves. Later records in New England show a high prevalence of such names, for example, Cesar, Silvanius, Nimrod, or Juniper, all in 1670.

Other traces of the Catholic background of the Atlantic Creole population rest on less secure evidence. There are scattered references suggesting that Africans followed the practice of having godparents witness the baptism of their children. Although church records for New Amsterdam listed such individuals as witnesses, not godparents, their parents regarded these witnesses as godparents. On 30 August 1643, for example, Emmauel Pietersen, a free negro, was the husband of the freewoman Dorothe d'Angola and guardian of Reyrory, in her petition on behalf of the orphan son of Kleyn Anthony of Angola and Louwize (both free negroes), she swore that she had stood as "godmother or witness" at the Christian baptism of the child, whose parents had died soon after the ceremony. Dorothe d'Angola also stated that (as was expected of a godparent), out of "Christian affection," she had immediately adopted and reared the child as own child "without asking assistane from anyone, but maintained him at her own expense from that time until this day.[192]

In Virginia a handful of godparentage cases might point to a larger but less well documented process. In 1641 John Graweere put his child in the charge of its godparent to ensure that the child would receive an education and be freed at the end of a set period.[193] In his will, probated

[191] Shelter Island Historical Society, Will of Nathaniel Sylvester, 19 March 1679/80, pub in Grania Bolton Marcus, *Discovering the African-American Experience in Suffolk County, 1620–1860* (Mattituck: Ameron House for Society for Preservation of Long Island Antiquities, 1988 rep 1995), pp. 79–80.
[192] Register of Salomon Lechaire, 21 March 1661, in Kenneth Scott and Kenn Stryker-Rodda (eds.), E. B. O'Callaghan (trans.), *New York Historical Manuscripts: Dutch. The Register of Salomon Lachaire, Notary Public of New Amsterdam, 1661–1662* (Baltimore, 1978), p. 22.
[193] Court of 31 March 1641, H. R. McIlwaine, ed., *Minutes of the Council and General Court of Colonial Virginia* (Richmond, 1924), p. 477.

in 1673, African-born Francis Pane, who had been in the colony since at least 1637, left goods to some of his godchildren, giving "each a cow and also a pigg when they attaine to lawfulle age," as he lacked children, but excluded one of the godchildren, Derrick Driggus, whom he appears to have disliked.[194]

Being Atlantic Creole, and especially being Christian, gave many members of the Charter Generation greater access to freedom; it also made it easier for them to prosper and to feel comfortable in the world of European settlers. In addition, it allowed them to become leaders of the emerging African American population and ultimately act as teachers of the Plantation Generation.

In this regard, a number of members of the Charter Generation stood out. Anthony Johnson, perhaps the best known and studied of the group, became the most successful Atlantic Creole on the Eastern Shore, and one of the only ones to win a fairly secure place in the larger society as a landowner. He was among the earliest Africans in Virginia, attesting to 30 years of residence in a deposition in 1652 and was probably mentioned in the 1625 muster list.[195] He patented 250 acres at great Naswattock Creek in Northampton in 1651, while his son received rights to 450 adjacent acres in 1652 for the transport of 16 people between them. In 1652 the colonial government granted his wife and daughter tax exemption, thus freeing them from the burden that African American women uniquely faced of being titheable.[196] He interacted with the other free Atlantic Creoles, such as Francis Payne, to whom he sold a colt in 1652. Johnson owned at least one servant or slave, an African named John Casor. He was a prosperous man, compared to his other Atlantic Creole peers, when he decided to take his herd of livestock and move to Somerset County, Maryland, in 1665.[197]

In the decades that followed, as land passed from one generation to another, some memory of the connection to Central Africa still remained.

---

[194] Deal, *Race and Class*, pp. 272, 277, no. 35, Deal likens this to godparentage in Latin America and suggests it acted vertically as well as horizontally. Payne was first claimed as a headright in 1637, Nugent, *Cavaliers and Pioneers:* I:74 and thus must have entered the colony with the earliest Africans.

[195] On the 30 years' residence NCoDW 1651–1654, p. 123. Several scholars disagree about which of the various Anthonys on these lists was Anthony Johnson, the most convincing one is that of Deal, who links him with his future wife; see *Race and Class*, pp. 217–18, though Deal also suggests that none of these might be true.

[196] Breen and Innis, *Myne owne Ground*, p. 12.

[197] Heinegg, "Free African Americans," Johnson Family; Deal, *Race and Class*, pp. 217–50.

In 1667 John Johnson, son of Anthony Johnson, purchased 44 acres, which he called "Angola," on the east side of the Chesapeake Bay and south side of Wicomico River.[198] He and other free African Americans moved to Sussex County, where their settlement came to be know as Angola Neck, mentioned in the will of Major William Dyre, proved in 1688, "I give and bequeth to daughter mary Dyre land known by the name of Whitehorse...land lying in Angola Neck...some time the land of Richard Shoutster."[199] Place names referring to Angola, including Angola Neck, are still found in the area, near Rehoboth, Delaware, today. Another group followed the frontier south of the James River and into what would become North Carolina.[200] Many of these African Americans came to be known as "Indians" in the hostile racial climate of the eighteenth and nineteenth centuries. It was from such groups that the modern-day "Melungeons" or the "Nanticokes (or Moors)," "Lumbees," and "Piscataway" emerged, as genealogical research has shown.[201]

Just as Anthony Johnson was the success story of the Eastern Shore communities, and well known thanks to extensive documentation, so the mainland's most famous early African was John Pedro. His name, with its two first names shows its Central African roots and perhaps his origins as a minor Kongo nobleman. Probably captured in 1619 and thus one of the Africans taken by the *White Lion* and *Treasurer*, he was sidetracked to New England, to the Earl of Warwick's brief colony at Westo, before arriving in Virginia in 1623, a fact mentioned in the census of 1625.[202] We know nothing more of him until he arrived in Lancaster County in the late 1640s as a free man and as much a man of property as Anthony Johnson. John Pedro already held land in Lancaster County by 1650 for Bertran Obert's land boundary was defined by "marked trees of John Pedros."[203] He supplied land to William Brocas, husband of Elianor Brocas, when that family arrived. Between 1651 and 1656 John Pedro received land from and assigned land to a variety of English landowners in the country, including

---

[198] Thomas Davidson, *Free Blacks*, p. 29.
[199] William Dyer will, 4 July 1688, *Some Records of Sussex County, Delaware* (Philadephia: C H B Turner/Athens, Lane and Scott, 1907–1909), pp. 141–2.
[200] Heinegg, "Free African Americans," introduction.
[201] Heinegg, "Free Africcan Americans," Families of Delaware, Maryland, and Virginia, introduction.
[202] For the later history of John Pedro's descendants, under various names but nowadays Peatross, see Virginia Davis, *Tidewater Virginia Families: A Social History* (1989), pp. 127–56.
[203] Nugent, *Cavaliers* 1: 204.

Evan Davis, Obert, and Conniers, and also bought and sold properties.[204] While residing in Lancaster, John Pedro undertook to performing work, perhaps construction, for English colonists, although he was sometimes sued for failing to perform it.[205] He also took up land in Maryland, for in 1654 his attorney, Richard Collett, acknowledged his loss of a suit to William Chaplyn.[206]

John Pedro's activities involving landholding and economic pursuits did not end when he arrived in Maryland, as his interests extended to politics as well. He was associated with a faction led by William Eltonhead, who had left Virginia for Maryland during the troubles that beset the English colonies with the establishment of the Commonwealth in England. In 1655 he joined a number of other Maryland planters in Anne Arundel County to oppose the anti-Catholic Governor William Stone, perhaps supporting Catholic issues, probably because he was a Catholic himself. In 1655 the two factions came to blows at the Battle of the Severen, in which Eltonhead's faction lost. The victors decided to execute the leadership, though they spared many, but John Pedro was not among them, as he was executed along with Eltonhead and two others.[207] John Pedro's descendants in Virginia, starting from his son, Matthew, eventually became the Peatross family, which counted a number of prominent people.[208]

Mathias de Sousa presents an intriguing case of an Atlantic Creole who did not come as a slave and became prominent in spite of an African background. He arrived in Maryland in 1634 with the first group of settlers who came with the Jesuit priest Father Richard White. White subsequently cited him as a "mulatto" in an account he gave of the settlers who came with him, and he may have met the priest in Portugal where White had served for a time, because his name might be either Portuguese or perhaps Kongo, where there was also a de Sousa family. In 1641 de Sousa attended the Maryland Assembly as a freeman, though as far as can be ascertained did not engage in any business of record.[209] He had skills as a mariner and was appointed in 1642 as skipper and trader to go to trade with the

---

[204] Lancaster County Court Orders, 1652–1655, in VCA 118, 175, 216, 231.
[205] Lancaster County Court Orders, 1652–1655, in VCA 215.
[206] Court of 5 December 1654, *Archives of Maryland* 10: 407.
[207] John Hammond, *Leah and Rachael, or the Two Fruitful Sisters, Their Present Condition, Impartially Stated and Related* (London, 1655), p. 25–6.
[208] Davis, *Tidewater Virginia Familes*, pp. 127–56.
[209] Maryland Assembly Proceedings, Liber MC, p. 178, *Maryland Archives* 1: 120.

Susquehannocks, with authority to hire men to be under his authority, and he "would write to Mr Brent to assist him in it."[210] However, unlike John Pedro, the records are silent on his fate after 1642.

John Pedro and Mathias de Sousa's familiarity with the world of the European and Euro-Americans of Lancaster County and Maryland mirrored the type of relationships that more humble Atlantic Creoles formed with the settlers who held them in servitude. In Virginia it appears that such close relationships were formed both by those who had obtained their freedom and those who remained in servitude. Often these relationships protected them and made it easier for them to move from bond to free.

Francis Pane (also mentioned as Francisco a Negro) made a typical arrangement with Phillip Taylor, who claimed him as a headright in 1637. Instead of having Pane as a simple worker in his fields, Taylor seems to have let him have lands to work on his own. In 1640 Pane declared in court, that "Mr Taylor and I have divided our corne and I am very glad of it now that I know myne . . . owne ground I will work when I please and play when I please."[211] When Taylor died, his widow Jane continued the arrangement, and the relationship evolved when she moved to Maryland in 1648, because she decided to leave Pane on her former lands with control over the crops he had planted and to manage the land and "use the best meanes lawfully hee can for the further betteringe of the said cropp." She gave him right to use land "from tyme to tyme" in exchange for payment of 1,500 pounds of tobacco.[212]

In spite of differences in their demographic and legal status, some Atlantic Creoles in New Amsterdam had as much success as did their counterparts in Virginia. The fact that the "the strongest and fleetest [*sterckste ende belopenste*] were required to serve in the militia, armed with a hatchet and a half pike [*een handtbijl ende een halff pieckjen*]," from at least 1641 may have put them in close touch with the European settlers, especially if this meant service in Krieft's War (1643), the most serious combat of the period.[213] Settlers felt sufficiently at ease with the presence of Atlantic Creoles that they not only let them fight alongside them but even allowed them to manage their affairs. When Stuyvesant

[210] Court and Testimentary Business, November 1642, *Maryland Archives* 4: 138.
[211] NoC O 1640–1645, fol. 457.
[212] NoC DW 1651–1654, fol. 118.
[213] Articles submitted by the honorable director and council of New Netherland to the heads of families or householders, van Laer, 1: 124.

went up to Kingston in 1660, he left orders to "let the free and the company's Negroes keep watch on my bowrie."[214]

The New Amsterdam community also had its success stories like those of Anthony Johnson and John Pedro. By 1643, Cleyn Manuel owned livestock and horses when he and two other Africans, Manuel de Gerrit de Reus and Manuel de Groot, successfully accused Dutch settler Jan Celis of wounding one cow and driving "many cows and horses" into the swamp.[215] Manuel de Gerrit de Reus eventually received land that encompassed much of what is now Washington Square Park.[216] The suit made against him by the Dutchman Barent Hendricksz for wages in the amount of 6 florins in 1645 shows that he was hiring whites to work for him.[217] Anthony Fernando, another member whose son's baptism was witnessed by the supervisor of the Company's negroes, rented land from Jacob van Corlaer, where he kept hogs and grew corn "for his children," and he worked it with "his people."[218] In fact, present-day Chatham Square was more or less directly owned by these landowners, whose vibrant community was visited by Jaspar Danckaerts in 1679.[219]

The New Amsterdam group also exploited their cultural backgrounds to forge close relationships with the Dutch, as did Susanna Anthony Robberts, when she apprenticed her brother to Wolphert Webber for three years in 1664 in order that he learn "reading and writing" as well as be "decently clothed."[220]

As in Virginia and Maryland, some members of the successful New Amsterdam community moved to the frontier. When the Dutch briefly recaptured New York in 1673, a large number of the Afro-Dutch community swore allegiance to the Prince of Orange. Later, some members of the de Vries, Emmanuels, and van der Donck families moved from New York into the Upper Hackensack River, settling in the Tappan Patent in the early 1680s. They continued to buy land, expanding their families and keeping close ties with each other. Eventually they would become a community

---

[214] Stuyvesant to van Ruyven, 18 March 1660, quoted in Page, p. 192.
[215] New York State Archives, Dutch, Council Minutes, fol. 180, 19 November 1642, translation in van Laer, *Council Minutes* 4: 208.
[216] Dickenson, "Abstracts," p. 170.
[217] Barent Hendricksz, plaintiff vs. Emanuel de Gerrit de Reus, 1645, van Laer, 4: 256.
[218] William Bekman, vs. Anthony Fernando, 1655, Fernow, *Records* 1: 255.
[219] Jaspar Danckaerts, *Journal of Jaspar Danckaerts, 1679–1680* (New York, 1913), p. 65.
[220] *Register of Lechaire*, p. 9, further details in Goodfriend, "Black Families," p. 103.

known locally as the "Ramapo Mountain People," which survives to the present day, clinging to its older Dutch ways, such as remaining with the Dutch Reformed Church and following Dutch American folkways.[221]

Elsewhere in North America a fortunate handful of early Africans managed to win freedom and a certain degree of autonomy though landholding. The only known African in Swedish Delaware, Antonio, the Angolan, a "bought slave" in 1644, made purchases from the company that suggested that he was a man of modest means and perhaps free.[222] He was also a personal and trusted servant of the governor.[223] In New England, there are also traces of such a class. Boston Ken (Sebastian Cane) owned land in Dorchester (now in Boston) by 1656 and used this to set another African named Angola free by bonding property before he moved to Virginia.[224] Angola eventually owned land of his own in Boston.

In the Caribbean, Bermuda provides enough information to allow a glance of the life of the Charter Generation. Africans there may have been the earliest and most fully integrated into the European community, although this did not guarantee the kind of success evident among Africans in New Amsterdam and the Chesapeake. In a small island, where its agricultural sector was never very successful and where livelihoods were made in fishing, whaling, and salvaging wrecks, there was less scope for someone not in the elite to do much, whatever their race or origin. Perhaps some of the early Africans obtained their freedom but there are few records of free people before the 1650s, and no notable free families as can be traced in the Chesapeake or New Netherland (and Bermuda records are quite extensive).[225] They were sufficiently numerous that by the early

---

[221] Cohen, *Ramapo Mountain People*, pp. 32–59.
[222] Johnson, *Swedish Settlements*, p. 722. Johnson cites only documentation in the Swedish archives without giving specifics. We were unable to trace these among his (incomplete) papers in the Pennsylvania Historical Society.
[223] Pennsylvania Historical Society, Amandus Johnson, 55/3 "Relation to the Worshipful West Company in Old Sweden, sent from New Sweden, sent in June 16, 1644."
[224] This story can be followed, as well as Bostian Ken's in *Suffolk Deeds* 2: 297, 3: 78; 7: 22, 144, 8: 298–9 (Angola); Morison, *Suffolk Court Records* 2: 598; Bostian Ken also known as Sebastian and Bus Bus. See *Suffolk Deeds* 2: 297, 4: 111, 113. His estate comprised, in 1662, "1 barrell liquor, 1 barrell sugar, 1 barrell mackerel, 1 barrel codfish, one third of Hopwell, burden 10 tons," which Cane handed it over to his friend Francis Vernon, Sebastian Cane note, 6 October 1662 in *Suffolk Deeds* Lib 4, 113–14.
[225] Bernhard suggests that there were a number in the earlier period, citing, for example, James Sarnando. But the record of his life she gives does not suggest that he was ever free, and her strongest evidence seems to be that he (and others she believes may have been free) had a second name, Bernhard, *Slaves and Slaveholders*, pp. 74–82.

1660s the island assembly passed a series of enactments that denied Afro-Bermudans the rights of natural privileges and restricted their associations with whites. A further elaboration of this trend in 1664 required that all able-bodied free negroes either leave the island or "spend the remainder of their days with such masters or mistresses as myself and the council shall think fit to appoint."[226]

This legislation was symptomatic of a larger interest of company officials who wanted to control all Africans and their descendants and were concerned about the private manumissions, because it appears that most of the earliest Africans were held by the Company and let out to individual masters only for long and easy terms. Although these masters might set the servants free, the Company never recognized their right to do so, nor did it acknowledge the freedom of the former slaves. This situation might help to explain the practice of long indentures and the apprenticeship of children by parents. In 1639 or 1640, James Sarnando indentured his child to Hugh Wentworth and his wife in the following manner. "James did take the said Childe by the hand and delivered it into the hande of Mr. Wentworth saying here Master mee give you this Childe take her and bring her up and mee give her to you freely. And then in like manner hee did take the sayd Childe by the hande again and putting the Childes hand into Mistress Wentworths hande sayd, heer Mistirs mee give you this Childe take her and bring her up and mee give you her freely."[227] Similarly in 1662 Hannah Bestiana, then a free woman but in a "sick and weake condicion," gave two of her children as apprentices, one for 21 years and the other for 30 years, with the understanding that she was to "carefully Educate or cause [them] to be educated and brought up... " This arrangement was noted to be customary in the country and thus took place more often than we see in records.[228]

Not only did some members of the Charter Generation experience economic success and develop various interactions with Europeans, but a few of the men married European-descended women, thus linking themselves more permanently with the white community. Five of the 10 known Atlantic Creole freemen in Northampton County, Virginia in 1664

---

[226] Proclamation of Governor Florencia Seymour, 26 July 1664, Lefroy, *Memorials* 2: 216.

[227] BCR 2 (1636–1661), p. 85, attestation June 1644, citing incident of four or five years earlier.

[228] Apprenticeship of Free Negro Children, 19 April 1662, Lefroy, *Memorials* 2: 155–6 (original in BCR, 5a, fol 22). The signature of Sibila Rightly and Bestiana occur together as we read the document.

married women of European descent.[229] John Pedro, the mainland's most successful African, did so as well.[230]

African women, however, did not have the same opportunities, and very few free families are descended from the union of African American women and European men. There was certainly interracial sex between European men and African women, though it was harshly punished. But marriages were rare, and in fact, none are documented for this period. In 1630 the Virginia authorities symbolically and formally announced their disapproval of this sort of sexual contact by sentencing Hugh Davis in 1630 to be "soundly whippd before an assembly of negroes and others for abusing himself of the dishonor of God and the shame of Christians by defiling his body in lying with a negro, which fault he is to acknowledge next Sabbath Day."[231] In 1640, another Englishman resident in Virginia, Robert Sweat, had a child by an African servant (probably named Margaret Cornish) and was made to do public penance for it.[232] Similarly, in 1638 in New Netherland, the West India Company thought to prevent its people from certain negative behaviors that included "fighting, adulterous intercourse with heathens, blacks or other persons, mutiny, theft, false swearing, calumny and other immoralities."[233] Rather, African-descended women married members of their own community.[234]

Although there may have been as much interracial sex in Bermuda as Virginia, thanks to the larger number of Africans and the close proximity they had with Englishmen, the pattern was quite different. One does not find any African or African-descended men marrying English women as took place in North America, and the interracial sex noted in the record involves illicit relationship between Englishmen and African women, which, though punished as fornication, was not as symbolically distained as in North America. In 1652, the Bermuda assembly thought

---

[229] This finding, surprising for many who have imagined that the free African American mixed people originated in relationship between masters and slaves, is amply documented in Heinegg, "Free African Americans."

[230] Davis, *Tidewater Families*, p. 157.

[231] Hening, *Statutes at Large* 1: 146.

[232] Mcilwaine, *Minutes* 4: 77, General Court, 17 October 1640.

[233] *Laws and Ordinances of New Netherland* (Albany, 1868), p. 12.

[234] Brown, *Good Wives*, p. 126. Brown believes that this was due to a degradation of African-descended women; it might be equally be a way of insuring freedom to the offspring where legal status was still held to descend though the female line. Later some slaves also married free European-descended women, founding many lines of free African Americans, see Heinegg, "Free African Americans," Introduction.

that it might examine the behavior of one Henry Gaunt for "being unnecessarily conversant with negro women, that he had given them guifts, and if he hath not left his familiarity with such creatures, it is desired that such abominations be inquired into."[235] A number of mulattoes appear in the records of the 1650s as well: in 1657 George Tucker gave Henry Tucker, his uncle, an interest in two mulatto girls named Marie and Sarah.[236] Guidelo, a negro, and a Scotsman had a child named Jane, who was apprenticed for 21 years in 1661.[237] John Davis, an English mariner, married the mulatto Penelope Strange in 1660, one of the very few records in the colonial world of a marriage between a European man and an African-descended woman.[238] It was only in 1663 that the assembly of Bermuda prohibited free-born subjects of the island from "mary with, or haue any *commerce* with any negroes, molattoes, or mustises [mixed Native American-European people]" subjecting those to being banished.[239]

Their familiarity with Christianity, their naming and family patterns, and their general comfort with European culture made Atlantic Creoles appear to be part of the emerging settler world. However, Atlantic Creoles also brought with them from Central Africa some cultural practices as well as expertise in the production of some tropical crops that set them apart from the Europeans who held them as servants and slaves.

Ligon, one of the only early witnesses to give any sort of cultural description of Africans in the English and Dutch colonies before the 1660s, provides an important portrait of one aspect of the lives of the Charter Generation even as they were being swallowed by the arriving Plantation Generation. These were the Africans "bred up amongst the Portugalls," who he contended had "some extraordinary qualities which the others [West Africans] have not," particularly their fencing. Those who he saw on James Drax's plantation were both artful in their use of the rapier and dagger and also highly skilled, which Ligon, having been a fencer himself, thought he was competent to judge as an expert. He saw staged fencing, in which they marched to each other, embraced in a friendly way, and then commenced the fight in earnest, a ritualized battle reminiscent of the *nsanga* in Kongo or the Mbundu military exercises. These skills in fighting

[235] Lefroy *Memorials* 2: 30 Assize 8–13 June 1652.
[236] BCR, vol. 52, fol. 63.
[237] BRC, 5a, fol. 21.
[238] Assizes 1 December 1660, Lefroy, *Memorials* 2: 141.
[239] Account of General Assembly, 27 January 1663, Lefroy, *Memorials* 2: 190.

were unlikely to have been imparted to them by their European masters and even in Central Africa were marks of nobility.[240]

Ligon also considered their singing remarkable, and although he thought he had heard better singing in Europe, he believed their approach comparable and praised some of the individual voices.[241] No doubt he was also hearing the Creole influence of European church music, performed for over 100 years in Kongo and around the Portuguese colonies.

The Atlantic Creoles left few other traces of its presence in Barbados other than a place name. As early as 1647 the question arose as to the origin of the name "Conger Rode in parish of St Phillip," mentioned in a land sale, as well as a "Conger Rock," where some held that they were so called "in consequence of new Negroes from Congo being there in abundance on the neighboring plantation."[242] Not only does the early date rule out the possibility of the name being given because of new arrivals but it also points out the rapidly vanishing legacy of the Charter Generation.

Aside from these intriguing cultural notices, the Charter Generation's presence was attested to by references to some of their skills in tropical agriculture, including Caribbean crops that had been introduced into Central Africa by Portuguese commerce in the sixteenth century. It is probably safe to say that Fernando, an African whose skill in "West Indy plants," including tobacco, warranted Robert Rich's urgent request of 1617 that he be purchased at whatever price necessary, was an Atlantic Creole.[243] There were undoubtedly other Africans with similar skills who would follow in subsequent groups from Angola, where tobacco was commonly grown.

In Africa, women performed most of the agricultural labor in Central Africa, and American planters recognized this and quickly put the women to work in the fields, where their skills in growing maize and tobacco, honed in Africa, paid off. As early as 1643, African women were held to

[240] Ligon, *True and Exact*, p. 52.

[241] Ligon, *True and Exact*, p. 52.

[242] Andrew Laskley to Thompson, 8 May 1647, in "The Lucas Manuscript Volume in the Barbados Public Library," *Journal of the Barbados Museum and Historical Society* 22–23 (1954–1956): 74, 150. The name created confusion at the time, though one opinion held that it represented as "some have imagined, in consequence of some accidental circumstance of new negroes from Congo being in the neighboring plantations in abundance." The writer, however, dismissed the other explanation, that it related to a fish name. The early spelling was clearly "Conger" and not "Congo" as the writer pointed out, but in English pronunciation, such a confusion does not necessarily contradict an ultimate derivation from "Congo."

[243] Robert to Nathaniel Rich, 22 February 1617/8, Ives, *Rich Papers*, p. 59.

be titheable, reflecting their use as laborers in agriculture, whereas other women were not.[244] It comes as no surprise that African women were hard at work growing tobacco in Virginia, where in 1646 sheriff John Paul, was ordered to seize so much tobacco "as is due from a Negro woman" to pay for the support of orphans.[245] Central African men also worked in agriculture, and the Dutch identified Angola as a source that could provide laborers for the agriculture of New Netherland; consequently the contract for the *Gideon* specified that the slaves it was to take in Angola would be used for agriculture.[246]

Atlantic Creoles were probably also responsible for introducing the exploitation of palm trees and the making of palm wine, given their experience of exploiting the palm wine tree and making and consuming palm wine in Kongo and Angola. A 1652 inquest in Bermuda detailed the great and grievous destruction that Africans had caused to the "Palmeto trees for the making of a drink called Bibby wch doubless was at the first innocently done by them who would drink a cupp or the like." The inquest noted that the practice was so common that the Africans cut down the tallest trees, which gave the sweetest bibby to distill the palm wine. The inquest identified the "Idle negros in all parts of the Islands" as being responsible for cutting down most of the trees and accused the settlers of encouraging the destruction and making "a prfitt of Bibby by aquaevitae, despite knowing well of what great vses these palmetto trees are of in this plantaion and that wee could not liue without it."[247]

Englishmen learned, in fact, to exploit special agricultural skills that Africans possessed, mostly strikingly the capacities that Senegambians had for growing rice, as soon as the slave trade made people of such origin available. William Berkeley, the able and energetic governor of Virginia, for example, sought a wide range of innovations to make the colony's agriculture more viable, including the introduction of rice growing. To assist he used Africans, probably brought to Virginia by New England ships from Barbados, an island he much admired.[248] Thus an account of 1649 noted that the governor "caused half a bushel of Rice (which he

---

[244] For the use of African women as opposed to European or Euro-America, see Coombs, "Building the 'Machine,'" pp. 75–6.

[245] York County, VCA 3 (13): 63–4.

[246] Amsterdam Chamber to Council of New Netherland, 20 January 1664, O'Callaghan, *Documents*, 1: 222.

[247] Assize 8–10 June 1652, Lefroy, 2: 28.

[248] *Perfect Description*, p. 14. That New Englanders were visiting Senegambia is revealed in the *Rainbow* incident of 1645.

had procured) to be sowen, and it prospered gallantly, and he had fifteen bushels of it, excellent good Rice, so that all these fifteen bushels will be sowen again this yeer; and we doubt not in a short time to have Rice so plentiful as to afford it at 2d a pound if not cheaper, for we perceive the ground and Climate is very proper for it as our *Negroes* affirme, which in their Country is most of their food, and very healthful for our bodies."[249] Although Central Africans were familiar with rice cultivation, only Senegambians had it as "most of their food." Senegambians could then be found on Barbados; as Ligon noted, among the various places that the new Africans came from included "Catechew [Cacheu]" and "River Gambia," both well-known rice growing regions.[250]

Despite the differences in agricultural knowledge and outlook, the Atlantic Creoles of the Charter Generation were culturally much closer to the Europeans than to the Africans of the Plantation Generation that would follow. Atlantic Creoles became members of the existing Christian religious institutions and followed many of the cultural practices of their European counterparts, such as having Christian names and passing these on to their offspring. This made them less exotic to their European masters and fellow workers than the West Africans who would follow them. They would use this cultural proximity to their advantage as they became integrated into colonial society and economy.

[249] Farrer, *Perfect Description*, p. 14.
[250] Ligon, 46.

6

Becoming Slaves

Atlantic Creoles and the Defining of Status

The exploration of the Atlantic Creole background of the Charter Generation in the English and Dutch colonies opens up an opportunity to reexamine questions about race, slavery, and the status of Africans in the early Americas that have dogged historians of North America since the early 1950s and perhaps earlier. Recent scholarship has refocused attention on these questions, identifying in particular racial slavery as a cultural as well as an economic system as unique in the Atlantic world, largely reacting toward the predominant paradigm that saw African slavery in New World societies and racism as being economically determined by the rise of capitalism.[1]

In 1997, Robin Blackburn, for example, in a comprehensive study of slavery in the various European colonies in the Americas, argued that Europeans found it easier to subject Africans to slavery, an institution that had greatly declined in their own societies in Europe, than to subject Europeans to it. Blackburn believed that the interpretations of the Biblical Curse of Ham found Africans to be degraded and thus suitable to be enslaved.[2] In the same year James Sweet, addressing specifically slavery in the Iberian world, also pointed to hostile attitudes toward dark-skinned

---

[1] The economic paradigm was pioneered by the 1944 publication of the West Indian historian, *Capitalism and Slavery* (Chapel Hill, NC, 1944); see also work of Andre Gunder Frank, *World Accumulaiton, 1492–1789* (London, 1978); essays in Joseph E. Inikori and Stanley L. Engerman, *The Atlantic Slave Trade: Effects on Economies, Societies and Peoples in Africa, the Americas, and Europe* (Durham and London, 1992).

[2] Robin Blackburn, *The Making of New World Slavery: From the Baroque to the Modern* (London and New York, 1997), pp. 64–79.

people derived from the heritage of the war against the Muslims and Christian teachings about the curse of Ham to explain racism and racial slavery in the Spanish and Portuguese Americas.[3] David Eltis produced a systematic, economically driven analysis in 2000, arguing counterfactually that that it would have been both cost-effective and legal to use Europeans (convicts, vagabonds, and prisoners of war) as slaves in the Americas. However, Europeans did not take this option, he contended, because they considered the institution to be too harsh for cultural insiders, but they were willing to impose it on Africans, who they considered to be outsiders.[4] Cultural studies and postcolonial literature have also contributed to the discussion by locating an ever wider range of ways – physical appearance, susceptibility to disease, skill, technology, and social and cultural norms – by which early modern Europeans distanced themselves from other peoples of the world.[5]

This recent set of Atlantic-focused studies actually revised and modified the work of Winthrop Jordan, whose landmark 1969 book, *White over Black*, on the origins of slavery in colonial North America (but actually the Chesapeake region) identified preexisting European racism as the primary cause of the institution.[6] In the historiography of North America as in the discussion of slavery in general, however, Jordan's position was largely counterbalanced in the 1980s and 1990s by economic-driven arguments presented by Edmund Morgan, Russell Menard, and David Galenson (among others) that linked the origin of slavery in North America to the relative cost of indentured European and enslaved African labor or to issues of productivity.[7]

---

[3] James Sweet, "The Iberian Roots of American Racist Thought," *William and Mary Quarterly* 54 (1997), pp. 143–66.

[4] David Eltis, *The Rise of African Slavery in the Americas* (Cambridge, 2000), pp. 57–84.

[5] See, for example, Joyce E. Chaplin, *Subject Matter: Technology, the Body, and Science on the Anglo-American Frontier, 1500–1676* (Cambridge, MA, 2001).

[6] An excellent historiographical summary, for Virginia, where the debate has been most developed, is found in "The Origins Debate: Slavery and Racism in Seventeenth Century Virginia," *Virginia Magazine of History and Biography* 97 (1989): 311–54, a modified and revised version was published in Alden T. Vaughan (ed.), *Roots of American Racism: Essays on the Colonial Experience* (Oxford, 1995), pp. 136–74;

[7] Edmund S. Morgan, *American Slavery/American Freedom: The Ordeal of Colonial Virginia* ((New York, 1975) Douglas Deal, *Race and Class in Colonial Virginia: Indians, Englishmen, and Africans on the Eastern Shore During the Seventeenth Century* (New York and London, 1993); Berlin, *Many Thousands Gone*; Russell Menard, "From Servants to Slaves: The Transformation of the Chesapeake labor System," *Southern Studies*, 16 (1977), pp. 355–90.

The historical dilemma that engendered this debate concerned two central issues: the status of labor in the early settlement period in English North America (especially the Chesapeake), from roughly 1607 to 1676, and the role of racial prejudice in emergence of slavery. During this period, most workers were indentured servants of European origin, who served for limited periods and enjoyed some legal rights, giving way by the end of the period to an enslaved African labor force with very few rights. The legal conditions of the Africans who came during the early period seemed to the historians to resemble those of indentured servants more than slaves, and indeed some even argued that the Africans were simply regarded as indentured servants who were enslaved only later.[8] For historians such as T. H. Breen and Stephen Innes or Douglas Deal, in the early period Africans were relatively well treated, shared space with European workers, and were frequently manumitted, and then could participate in the life of the community by bearing arms, appearing in court, and owning land. Because of the apparent ease of interaction and ability to improve one's status, many scholars saw this period as one that challenged the idea that Africans were from the beginning held as slaves and accorded a degraded position.[9] There were some, however, most notably Alden Vaughan, who argued that despite these exceptional cases, Africans were always held as slaves in a degraded and dehumanized position because of existing prejudicial racial attitudes.[10]

The historiography of regions outside of the Chesapeake has been determined by specific developments in those areas. In Bermuda, for example, where a similar long period of coexistence between European and African workers took place as it did in the Chesapeake, writers such as Cyril Packwood, Virginia Bernhard, and Clarence V. H. Maxwell followed the discussions of their North American counterparts. They also

---

[8] The importance of this situation was first elaborated on by Oscar and Mary Handlin, "The Origins of the Southern Labor System," *William and Mary Quarterly* 7 (1950): 199–222.

[9] T. H. Breen and Stephen Innes, "Myne Owne Ground," in *Race & Freedom on Virginia's Eastern Shore, 1640–1676* (Oxford, 1980); Douglas Deal, *Race and Class in Colonial Virginia: Indians, Englishmen and Africans on the Eastern Shore during the Seventeenth Century* (New York and London, 1993) highlighted this period as one of relative social fluidity for some Africans.

[10] A situation first advanced by Carl Degler, "Slavery and the Genesis of American Race Prejudice," *Comparative Studies in History and Society* 2 (1959): 49–66, and advanced in the work of Jordan, *White over Black*, and continued in the writing of Vaughan, most recently in Vaughan (ed.), *The Roots*.

discussed the social fluidity of this early period while acknowledging the role of racism in a harsher subsequent slave regime. Packwood, for example, although arguing that the early Africans in Bermuda "had the same status as white indentured servants," wrote that "their black color and high visibility made them stand out as something different, and they were treated as subhuman."[11] They based their conclusions on a relatively well-preserved set of court and other records that pointed to the fact that the earliest Africans in Bermuda were treated much the same was as their counterparts in the Chesapeake were.[12]

In Barbados, the scarcity of records for the early period and the transformation caused by the Sugar Revolution made it difficult for historians to discern a period of fluidity as was the case for North America and Bermuda.[13] Thus the relationship between racism and slavery has never been as prominent as in these two areas. Students of the Caribbean argued that economics and not race was responsible for the debasement of Africans and that slavery was present from the very beginning. Richard Dunn, who placed his own research directly against that of the Chesapeake scholars, pointed out that slavery in Barbados flowed from economic origins, whereas Gary Puckrein concurred, finding little evidence of a period of African limited service for that island.[14] Hilary Beckles's detailed research on servants and slaves in Barbados unhesitatingly declared that Africans had always been regarded as slaves and were treated as such, and Barbadian racism followed from that.[15] Larry Gragg, although acknowledging that racism was present, discounted it as a cause of slavery in favor of an economic explanation.[16] Karen Ordahl Kupperman, one of the few scholars to work on Providence Island records as well as those of Virginia, also argued that slavery was the mode of labor

---

[11] Cyril Outerbridge Packwood, *Chained on the Rock: Slavery in Bermuda* (Hamilton, 1975), p. 6.

[12] Packwood, *Chained*, pp. 1–9; Virginia Bernhard, *Slaves and Slaveholders in Bermuda, 1616–1782* (Columbia, Missouri, 1989); Clarence V. H. Maxwell, "Race and Servitude: The Birth of a Social and Political Order in Bermuda, 1619–1669," *Bermuda Journal of Archaeology and Maritime History* 11 (1999): 39–65.

[13] Richard S. Dunn, *Sugar and Slaves: The Rise of the Planter Class in the English West Indies, 1624–1713* (Chapel Hill, 1972), pp. 224–7.

[14] Gary Puckrein, *Little England: Plantation Society and Anglo-Barbadian Politics, 1627–1700* (New York and London, 1984).

[15] Hilary McD. Beckles, *White Servitude and Black Slavery in Barbados, 1627–1715* (Knoxville, 1989), pp. 59–78.

[16] Larry Gragg, *Englishmen Transplanted: The English Colonization of Barbados, 1627–60* (Oxford, 2003).

for Africans on Providence Island from the beginning and did not link the institution to racism.[17]

Scholars of Dutch North America have not taken up this debate. Although noting the unusual features of Dutch slavery, such as ease of manumission, regularity of baptism, and legal rights enjoyed by Africans, Joyce Goodfriend, writing in 1978, did not link this to debate for the English colonies. In 1984 Peter Christoph went so far as to argue that "there was no prejudice against blacks and a good deal of matter of fact acceptance of them," though he has not proposed that this meant they were not slaves.[18] Graham Hodges, whose work began appearing from the mid-1980s, agreed that the Dutch regarded the Africans as slaves from the beginning but contended that the position of the Dutch Reformed Church and economic and demographic factors rather than racial ones dictated the nature of slavery.[19] More recently, Thelma Foote traced the emergence of slavery strictly to economic issues and argued that Calvinist theology counterbalanced the role of racism in the treatment of dependents, including slaves.[20]

Ira Berlin's contention that the first Africans were Atlantic Creoles, which he advanced in 1997, changed the nature of the debate, as he argued that whatever notions Europeans might have had about Africans in general, those whom the Dutch and English brought to the early colonies appeared much more like insiders and some were treated as such. This attitude had an important impact on the institution of slavery, for he argued that the early period represented a society with slaves, rather than a slave society, and thus with greater access to freedom and rights. This, however, was not the case with the Africans who would follow them in the Plantation Generation. The relative insider status of the Charter Generation allowed members to negotiate pathways to freedom and relative political and legal equality in colonial North America.[21]

Although we disagree with Ira Berlin on some of the specifics of his argument, we believe that his ideas concerning the relative ease of social mobility of the Charter Generation are correct. In the rest of the chapter

[17] Karen Ordhal Kupperman, *Providence Island, 1630–41: The Other Puritan Colony* (Cambridge, 1993).

[18] Peter R. Christoph, "The Freedmen of New Amsterdam," *The Journal of the Afro-American Historical and Genealogical Society* 5, nos. 3&4 (Fall and Winter 1984).

[19] Graham Hodges, *Root and Branch: African Americans in New York and New Jersey, 1613–1863* (Chapel Hill and London, 1999), pp. 6–25.

[20] Thelma Wills Foote, *Black and White Manhattan: The History of Racial Formation in Colonial New York City* (Oxford University Press, 2004), pp. 34–52.

[21] Berlin, *Many Thousands*, pp. 25–9.

we address the contention that Europeans held uniformly negative attitudes about Africans and that this would contribute to their treatment
by examining some of the most relevant of English and Dutch writings
on Africa between 1450 and 1660. We show that they displayed a broad
range of views, both positive and negative, which runs counter to the
idea that European writing represented Africans in an entirely negative
way and, moreover, that with regard to Central Africa, where most of the
Charter Generation originated, their writings portray the people (especially in Kongo) very sympathetically. The following section contends that
although the English and Dutch colonists did regard the first Africans as
slaves and not as indentured servants, they had not yet defined slavery as
lifelong, inheritable servitude but only as indefinite service, which might
explain their opportunities for expanded rights, including freedom, social
acceptance, and mobility. Finally, we suggest that the Christian background of many Atlantic Creoles may have been the key that made these
opportunities more attainable.

English and Dutch Travel Literature and Racial Attitudes

In the view of some scholars, deep-seated European negative attitudes
toward Africans led them to treat Africans as a separate and distinct
group and to regard them as natural slaves whose outsider status warranted different treatment from European servants. Many have been
influenced by Jordan's classic work, contending that Englishmen thought
Africans to have a defective (non-Christian) religion, to be beastly by
diet and behavior, possibly akin to the apes, sexually uncontrollable
and uncontrolled, and perhaps stained black by sin or by Ham's curse.
Englishmen conceived the Devil to be black as Africans were. Although
Jordan occasionally mentions sympathetic statements by English travelers, the overall thrust of his analysis is to emphasize an overwhelming
negative assessment of Africans. Vaughan, for his part, quoted the early
Chesapeake governor John Smith, referring to the Africans as coming
from "those fried regions of blacke brutish negers" as an example of the
type of racial attitude that Englishmen held about the Africans arriving
on their shores.[22]

To assess the European view of Africans as a way of unraveling the
development of racial attitudes and its role in the evolution of slavery

[22] Vaughan, "Origins Debate," p. 147, quoting from his earlier study, *American Genesis:
Captain John Smith and the Founding of Virginia* (Boston, 1975). See also Sweet, "Collective Degradation."

in the English and Dutch colonies, we need to evaluate these attitudes as they developed. In particular, we need to see how the recognition of the Charter Generation as Atlantic Creoles may have shaped the development of slavery. Unfortunately, the colonial records of the English and Dutch colonies do not shed much light on racial attitudes. There are few unambiguous theoretical statements in legislation or court decisions, and narrative accounts rarely speak of the Africans at all when dealing with the new colonies, other than to note their presence or describe their work. This stands in marked contrast to the treatment of Native Americans, who are regularly described and evaluated by European visitors.[23] Similar evaluations about Africans in America figure in this literature only in the post-1660 period, with the notable exception of Richard Ligon, who visited Barbados in the late 1640s.[24] Ligon's descriptions, furthermore, relate to the Plantation Generation rather than the Charter Generation, given the early emergence of this group in Barbados.

In the absence of direct local testimony, most of the scholars who favor the idea that racism determined the development of slavery consult a wide range of religious and cosmological treatises, literary works, and travelers' accounts published in Europe and use these as a proxy for uncovering the attitudes of the settlers. However, often their analyses rely selectively on those sections of the works that portray negative attitudes, while overlooking the more positive materials. Since the early 1990s, Emily Bartels, in perusing a wide range of travel, creative, and literary works, has argued that the English had ambiguous attitudes toward Africans, especially as reflected in travel literature. She has further contended that postcolonial theory has assigned modern colonial attitudes to earlier periods.[25] Likewise, P. E. H. Hair, reading early English accounts of Africa, has pointed out that many of the generalizations about European attitudes are based on a selective reading of literary and travel accounts and are more intended to address North American readers "concerned with North American social problems."[26]

[23] See Chaplin, *Subject Matter, passim.*
[24] Ligon, *The True and Exact History.*
[25] Emily Bartels, "Imperialist Beginnings: Richard Hakluyt and the Construction of Africa," *Criticism* (34), 1992; "Making More of the Moor: Aaron, Othello, and Renaissance Refashioning of Race," *Shakespeare Quarterly*, 41 (1990), pp. 433–54; "Othello and Africa: Postcolonialism Reconsidered," *William and Mary Quarterly* 54 (1997), pp. 45–64.
[26] P. E. H. Hair, "Attitudes to Africans in English Primary Sources on Guinea up to 1650," *History in Africa* 26 (1999): 45.

Our examination focuses especially on this travel literature, rather than on imaginative works, for the Dutch and English, as they were written by the very category of people who would settle in the Americas and own slaves and make the laws that governed slavery. This literature was supplemented by orally transmitted information from ships' officers and missionaries who could give eyewitness testimony of conditions in Africa.[27] Settlers and slave owners who read this travel literature probably regarded it as an accurate representation of conditions in Africa.

The earliest literature in English to present first-hand information on Africa was published by Richard Eden in 1555 as an appendix to a translation of Peter Martyr's description of America and then separately printed in 1577. Eden's book represented two trends in English writing; first was the classically based cosmographical and speculative treatment of Africa.[28] This cosmological literature did present a very negative image of Africa and has been the source of works by the Vaughans and others. However, the travel literature relied on observers' careful testimony. Eden's started with a description taken from the German writer Sebastian Münster (1544) based on medieval cosmological literature and ended with a second, similar account by Robert Gainsh, also drawn from Münster, that described the negroes as "a people of beastly livinge, without a God, lawe, religion, or commonwealth."

Subsequent development in British travel literature, however, generally omitted the classical cosmological details with their speculative and negative tone and replaced it with more objective, informative information.[29] Richard Eden also represented the new trend. His account of "the Kingdom of Guinea," which identified three sub-Saharan African kingdoms, came directly from an account published in 1505 by Alvise da Mosta, an Italian visitor.[30] Eden also published the travelogue of Englishmen Thomas Windham and John Lok's voyages to the Gold Coast and Benin in 1553–1555.

---

[27] Samuel Purchas, for example, when writing Battel's account of his voyage in Angola included information he had gained in conversation with Battel.

[28] Eden, *Decades*, p. Hakluyt, *Principal Navigations* vol. 2, book 2, p. 331.

[29] Jorge Cañizares-Esguerra, *How to Write the History of the New World: Historiographies, Epistomologies, and Identities in the Eighteenth Century Atlantic World* (Stanford, 2001).

[30] Richard Eden, *The Decades of the Newe World of West India...* (London, 1555), p. Sebastian Münster's *Cosmographia universalis* (1544, translated into German, French, and into English by Eden himself in 1553), which in turn was based on the account of Alvise da Mosto (1455–1462, published in 1505).

Eden's entire work was subsequently placed at the start of the African section of Richard Hakluyt's collection of travels in 1589 and became an important source for colonial leaders and was thus positioned to inform their attitudes and decisions toward Africans. In addition to Eden's work, Hakluyt also published a more substantial corpus of travelers' accounts for the period after 1555. Hakluyt's *Principal Navigations* became a standard reference book for Englishmen interested in colonial expansion.[31] In publishing this work, Hakluyt broke with the tradition of including medieval cosmological literature and developed his work from eyewitness accounts, reflecting probably the demands of his clientele for accurate description of African trade rather than learned classical notions.

Shortly after Hakluyt's first edition, Englishmen would obtain a much fuller description of an African country when Abraham Hartwell published his translation of Filippo Pigafetta's *Relatione del Reame de Congo* in 1597 (first published in 1591). To this was added John Pory's 1600 translation of the account of Muslim-turned-Christian traveler Leo Africanus, first published in 1526.

In 1613 Samuel Purchas began publication of his world history, which eventually would be seen as a continuation of Hakluyt's great work. *Purchas, His Pilgrimmage* contained a synthetic account of world history and geography that, although it incorporated classical and Biblical sources, was mostly based on eyewitness accounts from Hakluyt and from manuscripts that Hakluyt had collected but not published. Purchas augmented these sources by including translations of sources from other languages and from information gleaned from interviews with sailors and adventurers who knew sub-Saharan Africa first-hand. This work went through several editions and rapidly supplanted Hakluyt as the standard source for information on Africa that English nobles, merchants, and colonists would consult.

In 1625, Purchas then published what amounted to all his original source material in the first edition of *Purchas, His Pilgrims*, a massive, 2,000-page tome. Purchas chose accounts for the African section that represented what he thought to be the best description of each subregion in the continent, reprinting Pory's translation of Leo Africanus's account of North Africa and the Western Sudan, Richard Jobson's diary of his visit to Gambia in 1620–1621 (a book length account of the voyage was published separately in 1623),[32] Dutch traveler Pieter de Marees' account

---

[31] For African materials in Hakluyt and their impact, see Hair, "Attitudes."

[32] Richard Jobson, *The Golden Trade, or a Discovery of the Rio Gambra*...(London, 1623).

of the Gold Coast, first published in 1602, and the account of his friend and "neere neighbor" Andrew Battel's "Strange Adventures" in Angola and Loango, written about 1610, and finally Hartwell's translation of Pigafetta. Purchas remained the standard reference for Englishmen on Africa, as no other significant English account was published again until the late 1660s.[33]

As eyewitness testimony replaced the earlier speculative cosmologies in travel literature, a new set of evaluations of Africa based primarily on cultural criteria emerged. For example, Eden's account of the kingdoms of Guinea contended that the inhabitants lived in "no cities, but onely in certain low cottages made of boughs of trees," and were "pure Gentyles and Idolatrous, without profession of any religion or any knowledge of God, then by the lawe of nature."[34] Similarly, Leo Africanus's account of sub-Saharan Africa drew on Islamic tradition as old as the Christian medieval one that denigrated non-Muslims. He believed there was "no Nation under Heaven so prone to Venery."[35] After a litany of evils committed by the Numidians of North Africa, Leo went to note that "the Negroes likewise, lead a beastly kind of life, being utterly destitute of the use of reason, of dexteritie of wit, and of arts, yea, they so behave themselves as if they had continually lived in forest among wild beasts."[36] Further, he added in another aside for his Christian readers that "neither is there any Region in all the Negroes Land which hath in it this day any Christians, howbeit those which dwell neereunto the Ocean Sea are all of them very gross Idolators."[37]

Although such passages certainly focus on the traits that Jordan and the Vaughans credit with informing English attitudes, the same work might easily reinforce a much more positive outlook, as when Leo noted of Mali that "the inhabitants and governors thereof are most rich, great lovers of Iustice and Equitie, albeit some lead a brutish kind of life."[38] They lived in cities and had rulers and even empires. He went on to

---

[33] For Purchas's treatment of Africa, see P. E. H. Hair, "Africa (other than the Mediterranean and Red Sea lands) and the Atlantic islands," in L. E. Pennington (ed.), *The Purchas Handbook: Studies of the Life, Times and Writings of Samuel Purchas, 1577–1626* (2 vols, London, 1997), 1: 194–218.

[34] Richard Eden, *The Decades of the Newe World of West India...* (London, 1555), p. Sebastian Münster's *Cosmographia universalis* (1544, translated into German, French, and into English by Eden himself in 1553), which in turn was based on the account of Alvise da Mosto (1455–1462, published in 1505).

[35] Purchas, *Pilgrims* 2, p. 765.

[36] Purchas, *Pilgrims* 2, p. 767.

[37] Purchas, *Pilgrims* 2, p. 761.

[38] Purchas, *Pilgrims* 2, p. 751.

write that there were "professors" who "read lectures."[39] The rulers of the region of Timbuktu were also very rich and, moreover, "hither are brought divers Manuscripts, or written Bookes out of Barbary, which are sold for more money than any other Merchandize."[40] Even in Lok's diary that accompanied Eden's account, there was depicted an orderly life, with "princes and gentlemen" and whose women went "laden with collars, bracelets hoops, and chaines, either of gold, copper or ivory," and on the Gold Coast Africans had towns, governed by captains.[41] During William Towerson's voyage in 1555, the Englishmen met the ruler of a town who they felt was worthy of removing their caps and bowing down before.[42] Such views did not close the door on Africans as humans with familiar cultural norms.

A reader of Purchas's collection thus learned of Africans being of a different color than Europeans, but practicing agriculture and raising stock, living in towns under rulers, and living in different named countries. European travelers found things to criticize among the Africans in his accounts, more tellingly because they were eyewitness observations rather than speculations. But here, too, they were counterbalanced by more positive images that worked against a tone that was "critical of the Africans' bodies and beliefs, customs and character."[43] Condemnations in Purchas's collection were fairly specific: Africans were thievish, lecherous, and libidinous and practiced erroneous religious beliefs inspired by the Devil, and some of them were horrible and bloody cannibals.

Travelers like Pieter de Marees, whose account informed readers about Africans in the Gold Coast and Benin, reflected the point of view of a merchant who had daily commercial interactions with Africans. He often accused Africans of being cunning thieves and believed that "for stealing among all the Nations in the World, they have not their masters." Yet he immediately tempered this observation by noting that they "esteeme it to be a shame to steale from one another," but "esteeme it to be a credit unto them and brag thereof," when they stole from the Dutch.[44]

---

[39] Purchas, *Pilgrims* 2, p. 827.

[40] Purchas, *Pilgrims* 2, p. 828.

[41] Hakluyt, *Principal Navigations*, vol. 2, part 2, 333 (princes and gentlemen), 29 and 330 (living in towns, with captains). N.B. page numbers vary in this section of *Principal Navigations*

[42] Hakluyt, *Principal Navigations*, 2, part 2, p. 32.

[43] Vaughan and Vaughan, "Before *Othello*," p. 44.

[44] Purchas, *Pilgrims* 2, p. 952.

Furthermore, De Marees was more generous when describing courts and justice on the Gold Coast, as they worked according to procedures that Europeans could accept. He noted that "although they bee wild men, and without any civilitie or good behaviour, yet therein they use a very good and laudable custome."[45] He also observed that Africans in Benin were less inclined to steal, and their law carried draconian punishment for it. According to de Marees, the people "will doe no wrong one to another, neither will take anything from strangers, for if they do they should afterward be put to death."[46]

As for African sexual mores, de Marees was more critical. He described the inhabitants of Cape Verde as being "very greedie eaters, and no lesse drinkers, and very lecherous and thievish and much addicted to uncleanenesse" as evidenced by their having many wives, and the women "also are much addicted to leacherie," whereas Gold Coast men were also "very lecherous, and much addicted to uncleanesse; especially with yong women."[47] Jobson, however, took a more complex approach when he noted that Mandingo men in the Gambia had "such members as are after a sort burthensome unto them," a result of Ham's curse; he did so to explain why they abstained from intercourse with pregnant wives and as an explanation of polygamy, "which may seeme not overstrange unto us, in that our Holy Writ does make mention therof."[48] As Jordan noted in quoting this passage, the relationship between the Curse of Ham and the Mandingo's physiology was rooted in medieval concepts relating to African libidinousness, but in fact, Jobson's presentation explains their actual behavior in terms drawn from Scripture and deliberately undermines any reader's inclination to see the Africans as overly libidinous.[49]

Of all the traits that Africans displayed, the most troubling to Purchas's authors, and perhaps his readers, was their non-Christian religion. Because post-Reformation Europe had no tolerance for even European divergence of opinions on matters of faith and went so far as to kill fellow Christians, it would be expected that Europeans would show no

[45] Purchas, *Pilgrims* 2, p. 950.
[46] Purchas, *Pilgrims* 2, p. 966.
[47] Purchas, *Pilgrims* 2, pp. 927, 933.
[48] Jobson, *Golden Trade*, p. 55. Ham's curse in this period was not linked, as it would be later, to blackness or slavery but to sexuality.
[49] Jordan, *White over Black*, p. 35. For a full explanation of the curse of Ham and its background, as well as its connection to racial ideology, see Benjamin Braude, "The Sons of Ham and the Construction of Ethnic and Geographical Identities in the Medieval and Early Modern Periods," *William & Mary Quarterly* 54 (1997): 103–42, esp. pp. 135–8.

sympathy to African religion. Battell's account of the Imbangala represented an excellent example of a thoroughly negative face of African
religion, lent credence by his own experience of living with them and
actually participating in their rituals, which he described from first-hand
knowledge. He knew the Imbangala to be the "greatest cannibals in the
world," led by a pagan who "took the Devils counsell" and "warreth
all by enchantment."[50] Needless to say, the Imbangala as described by
Battell worshipped the Devil and spoke with him, though they would not
let Battell witness their acts as he was a Christian.[51] His description of
infanticide among them inspired Purchas to write "generation of Vipers"
in the margin.[52]

Battell's description of religion at Loango, although not as shock-
ing as his account of the Imbangala, depicted it in a negative light. He
informed Puchas that in Loango the inhabitants were all "Heathens and
observe many superstitions." His most telling criticism of Loango practices was the "Tyranicall Custom" in which a 12-year-old son of the
king of Loango was killed for witnessing his father drinking.[53] Purchas,
however, tempered these judgments by inserting his own commentary on
Battell's description of the use of judicial ordeals in Loango by comparing
them to ordeals described in the Bible.[54]

De Marees' description of religion on the Gold Coast is even more
balanced. The people of the Gold Coast, he wrote, were "Idolatrous and
very superstitious in their Religion" and "altogether wild, rough, and
uncivill, having neither Scripture nor Bookes, not any notable Lawes that
might be set downe, or declared. . . ."[55] However, de Marees does describe
piety in the religious life of the inhabitants of the Gold Coast and dealt
with it at length, showing that they believed in an afterlife and had a
theology, because when they die "they know that they goe into another
World, but they know not whither, and that therein they differ from brute
beasts . . . ," and for all that they keep a sort of Sabbath, resting on "Dio
Fetissos," which was "their Sunday."[56] Some, according to de Marees,
had been in touch with the Portuguese, were already Christian, and even
know to read and write.[57]

---

[50] Purchas, *Pilgrims* 2, p.
[51] Purchas, *Pilgrims* 2, pp. 975, 977.
[52] Purchas, *Pilgrims* 2, p. 977.
[53] Purchas, *Pilgrims* 2, p. 980.
[54] Purchas, *Pilgrimmage* 2, p. 586; see also the description in *Pilgrims* 2, pp. 982–3.
[55] Purchas, *Pilgrims* 2, pp. 932, 941.
[56] Purchas, *Pilgrims* 2, pp. 941, 943.
[57] Purchas, *Pilgrims* 2, p. 941.

Purchas chose to publish Pigafetta's account of Kongo in his section on Central Africa, perhaps the most positive description of any African kingdom written in the era. This is not surprising because Duarte Lopes, the source of Pigafetta's knowledge, was a knight in the household of King Álvaro II and served as his ambassador to Rome, where he sought to advance Kongo's status within Christendom by obtaining an Episcopal See. Lopes was thus enjoined by Álvaro to put the best possible face on the country. First and foremost, Lopes presented Kongo as a Christian kingdom and recounted an edifying history of the church in Kongo since the fifteenth century, from the miraculous victory of King Afonso over his heathen brother in 1509 through Divine intervention through the pious overtures of Álvaro to Rome in 1588.

English readers of Purchas would read not only that Álvaro was a pious Christian but also that he was civilized, commanding a country of vast extent, with multiple provinces, a capital city named São Salvador with 100,000 inhabitants, and many churches. His land was fertile and its people prosperous and modestly dressed, often in Portuguese style. His overview presented a Kongo as close to Europeans as it was possible to get and a long way from heathen barbarians worthy of enslaving.

The earliest Dutch descriptions of Africa resemble the English ones in general, in part because they relied heavily on English travel literature. Dutch readers read the English literature, for copies of books by Hakluyt and Purchas are often mentioned in library inventories and book sales of the time in the Netherlands.[58] In addition to the English literature that included Dutch writers like de Marees, the Dutch were more likely to read travel literature written in German. The Dutch literature, like the English, especially focused on material culture, sexuality, and religious practices, among others.

These accounts were particularly concerned about what they perceived as the limited and primitive African material culture. The German Samuel Brun, who served in the Dutch West Indian Company and published his travel account in 1624, noted that the people of Gabon made houses "of very poor quality," and they "have no bed but lay on the ground, very plain [*wild*] and poor," whereas those around Mayombe (near Loango) made houses that were made of "wickerwork [*reyszwerck*] woven together and are so light and poor in quality [*schlecht*] that one can carry them where ever one wishes.... all night long they sleep

---

[58] Ernest van den Boogaart, "Books on Black Africa. The Dutch Publications and their Owners in the Seventeenth and Eighteenth Centuries," *Paideuma* 33 (1987): 121.

on the ground."[59] Brun also commented that in Mayombe people were scantily clad.[60]

Brun, a doctor, was troubled by African sexuality, although more often it concerned the loss of Dutch men to venereal diseases than it served as a comment on the libidinousness of Africans, though de Marees clearly told Dutch men, as he had told the English, of African lechery, primarily on the Gold Coast.[61] He blamed Africans, as well, for promoting sexual license, "for they bring their own daughters into the ships in order to get something from our people."[62] Pieter van den Broecke, who visited West and Central Africa three times between 1605 and 1612 and whose accounts of his travels were published in 1634, followed suit when he observed that the people of Cape Verde were quick to "offer the virginity of their children" to Dutch travelers who would pay with rice, but added it was in time of need.[63] However, Brun noted without disapproval that some Dutch factors married African women.[64]

Brun was shocked by cannibalism, believing that people at Gabon were man-eaters because they had filed their teeth to points.[65] Stories of the "Jagas" from Pigafetta probably inspired him to write about cannibalism. He noted that the people of Kongo fought against enemies who were cannibals, who, on achieving victory "kill all their enemies and eat them for they are cannibals [*Menschenfresser*]."[66]

Their writing gives the impression that Africans were familiar with Europeans and had adjusted to their ways. Africans also had fine cities; de Marees found Benin's main street "seven or eight times as wide as the Warmoes Street in Amsterdam," and van Wassenaer made similar comparisons for Loango.[67] They had great manufacturing skills; for example, Brun brought beautiful textiles from Loango, "such clothing is so

---

[59] Brun, *Schiffarten*, pp. 8–9 and 40.

[60] Brun, *Schiffahrten*, p. 7.

[61] Brun, *Schiffahrten*, p. 41

[62] Brun, *Schiffahrten*, p. 44.

[63] Van den Broecke, *Korte historiael end journaelsche aenteyckeninghe...nae Cabo Verde, Angola...* (Amsterdam, 1634), p. 4, October 1606 entry in K. Ratelband, *Reizen naar West-Afrika van Pieter van den Broecke, 1605–1614* (Hague, 1950), the Dutch edition marks pagination of original manuscript, English translation of James D. LaFleur, *Pieter van den Broecken's Journal of Voyages to Cape Verde, Guinea and Angola, 1605–1612* (London, 2000) provides only entry dates.

[64] Brun, *Schiffahrten*, p. 51.

[65] Burn, *Schiffahrten*, p. 42.

[66] Brun, *Schiffahrten*, p. 29.

[67] De Marees, *Beschrivinge ende historische verhael vant Gout Koninckrijck van Gunea...* (Amsterdam, 1602, mod. Ed. S. P. L'Honoré Naber, Hague, 1911, with original

beautiful and brilliant that it looks like the most exquisite velvet" and was "very artistically woven with beautiful figures and tapestry. I brought one of them home with me and still have it at hand."[68]

Travelers had positive comments to make about African societies, for example, that they had well-ordered governments. Just as de Marees praised the judicial customs of the Gold Coast, so Brun, otherwise so critical of religion in the area, noted that the people of Cape Mount, "have a good system of justice," which was, in fact, consultation with the same "Devil" that he condemned elsewhere.[69] He had similar comments about the Gold Coast, "They also exercise good justice in their manner..." and "are very upright to each other."[70]

The most extensive negative comments of Dutch writers were related to African religious practices, of even greater concern to them than to English writers, perhaps because of their strict Calvinism. Linschoten, the first Dutch traveler to write on Africa in any detail, criticized the religion of Gabon, in his influential book of 1596, calling their beliefs "idolatrous and pagan" so that they "they had no God, nor humanity, or order" not recognizing God "or divine things," some adoring "some trees or the land even as mother and nourisher of all things."[71]

Dutch visitors clearly believed that African religion had efficacy, but that its power derived from the Devil. They condemned Africans, however, for being misguided by the Devil and not as the result of some ancient curse, like the Curse of Ham. Brun noted that though it was "terrible to say" the people in Loango "believe in wicked Satan." Satan apparently drove them, in some visitors' eyes, to terrible customs; Pieter van den Broecke related that the king of Loango killed his favorite nephew because the child touched him while drinking, explaining this act, similar to one also described by Battell, by saying that the Devil told him if he did not kill the child, he would die. Van den Broecke went on to say that the king of Loango was also a great sorcerer who knew the Dutch were coming before they arrived because he had conjured it from the Devil.[72] When pressed by Van den Broecke to explain why they worshipped the Devil, "and not our Savior Jesus Christ, they answer that they do not know him,

pagination marked), p. 115a; this passage also occurs in Purchas's English translation, *Pilgrims* 2; Van Wassenaer, *Historisch verhael*, 8th part, fol. 26v, October 1624.

[68] Brun, *Schiffahrten*, p. 13.
[69] Brun, *Schiffahrten*, p. 53.
[70] Brun, *Schiffahrten*, p. 76.
[71] Linschoten, French, pp. 251, 254.
[72] Van den Broecke, *Korte historiael*, p. 16, October 1612, La Fleur pp. 95–6.

but do indeed know the Devil [*duyvel*] well ... so it is a terrible thing that these people are so blind."[73] Nicholaes van Wassenaer, whose newspaper regularly published stories drawn from the sailors of the West India Company between 1622 and 1631, reported in 1623 that the "Priests" of the Gold Coast had actually made a contract with Satan, who then helped them.[74] Brun and his companions believed that the Devil himself had stirred up a crowd against them when they went to spy on some ceremonies on the Gold Coast.[75] Van Wassenaer was sufficiently interested in the subject to provide very long and detailed accounts of African religious practices and sought the opinion of a learned Dutch academic, Johannes Isaac Pontanun, on the meaning and significance of "Fitischi," which van Wassenaer thought was an African word but was actually just a local adaptation of the Portuguese word *feitiço* ("object of witchcraft") as Pontanun explained, from its Latin roots.[76]

In spite of their negative outlook regarding African religion, Dutch and German travelers nevertheless commented positively on some aspects of the religion. Brun, after praising the people of Cape Mount for being "very modest, both men and women," went on to add that "they worship the evil spirit [*bösen Geist*] and make sacrifice to him as often as he requires."[77] Similarly when describing Gold Coast religion, Brun wrote that "these wretched people ... worship the Devil [*Teuffel*] and yet keep some good things in order," for as de Marees had noted a few years earlier, they kept what amounted to a Sabbath, "Tuesday is their Sabbath ... and strictly adhered to it since their God Fitysi has forbidden them to do so."[78]

Like the English, the Dutch knew of the Christianity of West Central Africa through both Pigafetta's work, available in Dutch since 1596, and the writing of other travels. For example, Pieter van den Broecke noted, as we saw earlier, the depth of religious practices that he witnessed in Soyo (Kongo) when he was there in 1612, such as the widespread attendance at religious service, literacy, and public devotions. Because they did not only rely on Pigafetta, Dutch readers also knew the non-Christian elements in Atlantic Creole culture, most tellingly revealed by Barleus, who modified Pigafetta's account by noting that in Kongo "when it is convenient to them they simulate the religion in the presence of Christians, but most of

---

[73] Van den Broecke, *Korte historiael*, p. 17, October 1612, La Fleur, p. 99.
[74] Nicholaes van Wassenaer, *Historisch verhael*, 5th part, fol. 54, May 1623.
[75] Brun, *Schiffahrten*, p. 50.
[76] Van Wassenaer, *Historisch verhael* 6th part, fol. 68, 1623.
[77] Brun, *Schiffahrten*, p. 49.
[78] Brun, *Schiffahrten*, p. 73.

them are heathens and idolators, who adore the king more than god."[79] Yet, on the whole, Dutch readers, like the English, became familiar with a Creole, Christian Central Africa.

Both English and Dutch colonists often recognized that the Africans living in their midst originated in the same West Central regions described so positively in the travel literature. Dutch sea logs routinely noted the provenance of the ships they captured, and English knew enough that Captain Guy's prize ship taken to Virginia in 1628 was an "Angola man." In New Netherlands, Africans' origins were noted in their names and in official documents like baptismal records. They had a large store of knowledge about this region from available travel literature supplemented no doubt by oral accounts from the sailors and captains of English and Dutch ships. What they learned from reading, they might either confirm or reinforce this knowledge.

Colonists surely knew West Central Africa to be the region most integrated into the Atlantic culture of any region of Africa, that the Portuguese had a large colony there and the people often spoke Portuguese, that many were Christians and had been a part of this larger Atlantic world for over a century. Many of them, after all, came bearing familiar names like Antonio and Maria, which, though smacking of Catholicism, were not so strange that they renamed them, other than perhaps to translate the names from Portuguese to English, as Anthony and Mary. In short, rather than seeing Central Africans as polar opposites of themselves, they may well have seen them as a part of their world, and more like their European servants than their Native American neighbors.

Given this knowledge and the ambiguity of attitudes reflected in the travel literature and the specific knowledge they had about West Central Africa, it seems that scholars have overdrawn the degree to which the English and Dutch perceived the first Africans as complete outsiders and therefore suited to be slaves. Breen and Innis were correct to say that "ethnocentrism was probably a more powerful force shaping human relations than racism."[80] It also seems unlikely that deep-seated prejudice led to the formalization and finalization of slave legislation for Africans, making them uniquely disparaged in the eyes of colonial leaders. John Smith's often hostile view of Africans as coming from "those fried regions of blacke brutish negers" or being "as devilish and idle people as any in the

---

[79] Casparis Barlaei [Caspar Barle], *Rerum per Octennium in Brasilia* (Amsterdam, 1647), p. 246.
[80] Innis and Breen, "*Myne Owne Ground*," p.

world" must have at least somewhat been tempered by his own knowledge based on Pigafetta that the people in Kongo were Christian.[81]

Atlantic Creoles and Changing Status: The Legal Origins of Slavery

In our view, both the English and Dutch regarded the majority of the first Africans they brought to their colonies as slaves, not as indentured servants, though a few did come as servants from Europe or the Caribbean. However, neither people defined slavery in the way that would become the norm for African forced labor after the mid-seventeenth century. The definition of slavery as lifetime, heritable servitude would develop only with the Plantation Generation.

The key to understanding the Africans' legal status lies in the terminology most often used to describe them in English and Dutch legal sources. Sources in both languages most often referred to the Africans they took from Portuguese slave ships as "negroes" or a variant of it ("negar" and "neger"). This term, which was borrowed directly from the Portuguese, had no meaning in Dutch or English until the middle of the sixteenth century, when speakers of both languages began visiting those areas in Africa frequented by the Portuguese.

In Portuguese the basic term *negro* means nothing more than "black," derived from the Latin root *niger*, and it was used in 1448 when the Portuguese first came to the *terra dos negros* ("land of the negroes" or "land of the blacks") near the mouth of the Senegalese River and employed it as a regional or ethnic name.[82] At some point during the sixteenth century the term *negro* took on a second meaning of "slave" when referring to people that might even be independent of skin color.

By the late sixteenth century Europeans active in the Atlantic world adopted the Portuguese term *negro* as the common term for black Africans. For example, in the sixteenth century the English referred to people from Africa as "blacks," "Moors," or "Blackamores" and sometimes "Aethiopians" and these terms continued to appear in literary texts, especially in England proper. But in the Atlantic world, where the English were sailing out to trade, raid, and eventually settle, *negro*, borrowed from the Portuguese, soon supplanted all other terms for Africans. Thomas

---

[81] On "devilish people," see John Smith, *Advertisement for the Unexperienced of New England or Elsewhere* (London, 1629), p. 30; on Kongo, see John Smith, *The True Travels, Adventures and Observations of Captaine Iohn Smith* (London, 1630), pp. 37–8.
[82] Zurara, *Crónica do Descobrimento*, Chapter 31.

Windham, who led the first English voyage to Africa in 1553, was guided by a renegade Portuguese pilot named Antonio Pinteado, who knew the lands and their commerce from previous visits as a Portuguese sailor, probably introduced the term to his English employer.

Richard Eden, who published the first account of Windham's voyage in 1555, added a general introduction incorporating this knowledge when he informed readers that the inhabitants of Africa were "Blacke Moores, called Aethiopians or Negroes."[83] In Windham's own account, he used only the former term, when he described the king of Benin as "a Blacke Moor (though not so blacke as the rest)."[84] Robert Gainsh gave the full range of terminology in an interpolation into John Lok's voyage of 1554, referring to "Moores, Mooren, and Negroes."[85] John Hawkins, visiting Cape Verde in 1564, noted that "these people are all blacke, and are called Negroes."[86] Richard Madox described people he saw around Cape Mount in Sierra Leone in 1582 as "negroes" when writing in English and as "Ethiopians" when writing in Latin.[87] It is fairly clear that by the 1560s, at least in the travel literature published by Hakluyt, the prevalent term to describe Africans was "Negroes," usually not linked with any specific reference to their color or to slavery, and it did not mean that all Africans were slaves. Rather it was an ethnic or national term, rather like "Africans" might be used today (though this term was rarely employed in early literature to describe inhabitants of the continent).[88] Hakluyt's usage continued in Samuel Purchas, beginning with his first universal geography, *Purchas, His Pilgrimmage*, published in 1613, and many subsequent editions. It is possible that this usage carried directly to English colonies, for Bermuda documents record an "Indian Negroe girle called Nan" in a will of 1675.[89]

---

[83] Richard Eden, *The Decades of the Newe Worlde . . .* (London, 1555) reprinted in Hakluyt, *Principal Navigations*, vol. 2, part 1, p. 10.

[84] Hakluyt, *Principal Navigations* 2, part 2, p. 12.

[85] Hakluyt, *Principal Navigations*, 2, part 2, p. 331

[86] Hakluyt, *Principal Navigations*, 3, p. 503.

[87] The Diary of Richard Madox, in Elizabeth Stono, fol. 35, p. 164, "I judge the Negroes . . . come down either to fysh . . ." and fol. 27, p. 167, "Farma, King of the Negroes." Madox kept part of his diary in Latin, and in using that language he called Africans "Aethoip –, fol. 40, p. 172, and fol. 184, p. 197.

[88] This is based on a reading of the accounts published in the second book of Hakluyt's 1599–1600 edition, devoted to Africa, which reproduces material through the early 1590s.

[89] BRC Wills, vol. 1, p. 261, Berhard, *Slaves and Slaveholders*, p. 60, believes her to be a mixed-race child.

The Dutch were later than the English in visiting Africa, and their nomenclature was also influenced by the Portuguese patterns but not as much as the English. When a prize ship carrying 130 Africans arrived in Middelburg in the Netherlands in 1596, its cargo was consistently referred to as *Mooren* ("Moors"), the medieval European term for Africans.[90] The first Dutch travelers' accounts of Africa, dating from the same period, quickly employed "negroes," also clearly borrowed from Portuguese as a simple and generic designation for Africans.[91] Jan Huygen van Linschoten, traveling to India in 1595–1596, referred to the inhabitants of Mozambique as "negroes" as were the inhabitants of "Cape Verde, the island of San Thome, and all parts of Ethiopia," also including Angolans and the inhabitants of Gabon.[92] Pieter de Marees, an early Dutch trader on the Gold Coast, whose book was published in 1602, and Dierick Ruiters, who traded in Africa and Brazil between 1600 and 1618 and published his book in 1623, both used "negros" most often and "blacks" (*swarten*) occasionally to refer to Africans, without modifying the Portuguese spelling. Ruiters even respected the feminine ending in calling African female slaves in Brazil "Negras."[93] The Dutch States General learned that when Elias Tripp was trading in Guinea in 1609 the Portuguese governor sent "canoas ende Negros" (canoes and negroes) to attack him.[94] In 1615, Dutch traders complained that the "negros" on the Gold Coast were blocking their trade in gold, in both cases referring to free Africans, though using the Portuguese term.[95] Ruiters showed some variation,

[90] Japikse (ed.), *Resolutiën*, 9: 423; H. de Stoppelaar, *Baltasar de Moucheron: Een bladzijde uit de Nederlandsche Handelgeschiedenis tijdens den Tachtigjarigen Oorlog* (Hague, 1901), pp. 61–2; the same term, "mooren vt Indie" is used in documents in a burial archive, lost in the Second World War. Our thanks to Deinke Hondius of the Erasmus University in Rotterdam for discussion and some references on this group.

[91] Alison Blakely, in a careful study of Dutch terminology, notes the use of this term and discounts its origin from the Low Countries' connection to the Spanish Empire. *Blacks in the Dutch World: The Evolution of Racial Imagery in a Modern Society* (Washington, DC, 1994), pp. 32–4.

[92] Jan Huygens van Linschoten, *Itinerario: voyage ofte schipvaart van Jan Juhgen...naar Oost ofte Portugaels Indien* (3 parts, Amsterdam, 1995–1996, mod. ed. H. Terpstra, The Hague, 1955–1957). He employes a more varied terminology in referring to Kongo, but the section is a summarized translation of Pigafetta and thus governed by his language.

[93] Pieter de Marees, *Beschryvinge ende historische verhael vant Gout Koninckrijck van Gunea* (Amsterdam, 1602, mod. ed. S. P. l'Honoré Naber, the Hague, 1912); Dierick Ruiters, *Toortse der Zee-vaert: verlichtende de West-Indien, Brasilien, Guinee en Angola* (Vlissigen, 1623, mod. ed. S. P. l'Honoré Naber, the Hague, 1913), p. 4 (original pagination, marked in modern edition) for the reference to "Negras."

[94] ARA St Gen Loketkas, Admir. 33: 2.

[95] ARA Resol St Gen, 18 September 1615.

for example, referring to an African merchant in Sierra Leone, named Francisco Mendes, as "a Black" (*een Swerte*) from whom he bought salt, but in the next line continued, "this Negro, Francisco Mendes" (*Desen Negro Francisco Mendes*).[96] However, the use of *Swart* continued as well, for Nicholaes van Wassenaer used the term almost exclusively to describe the Africans he reported about in his newspaper, which gave news from the Atlantic world from 1622 to 1635.[97] Germans, such as Johann van Lübelfing and Samuel Brun, who worked in the Dutch West India Company, showed the same evolution as the Dutch, with Lübelfing calling the Africans he met in "Barbary" Moors (*Moren*) from his voyage of 1599–1600, whereas Brun (who traveled in 1611–1620) used *Schwartzen* ("blacks") as his term of choice.[98]

As in the case of descriptions of Africa, the term of choice for Africans in the English colonies was almost always "negroes." In English, it was employed almost exclusively in legal texts like deeds and court records.[99] Spelling of this foreign term varied widely, "negar" and "neger" also being reported, and in 1655 the variant "nigger" first appeared in Barbados.[100]

The use of "negro" in legal texts suggested primary employment as an ethnic term as in Portuguese, much as Irish, French, Portuguese, or other European ethnicities were often noted in such documents, as, for example, in the Virginia muster list of 1624, Anthony Bonall and "La Geurd" are bracketed as "Frenchmen," Symon is identified as an "Italien," and James and John are bracketed as Irishmen, whereas Peter, Anthony, Frances, and

---

[96] Ruiters, *Toortse*, p. 295.

[97] van Wassenaer, *Historisch verhael*, 5th Part, , fol. 54v, 8th part fol. 26v–28, and *passim*.

[98] Johann von Lübelfing, *Ein schön lustig Reissbuch* (Ulm, 1612), p. 26; Samuel Brun, *Samuel Brun, des Wundartzet und Burgers zu Basel, Schiffarten* (Basel, 1624), *passim*. Both are published in English translation in Jones (ed.), *German Sources*, with the original pagination, Lübelfing's German version is printed in appendix, Brun's original text was published in a modern edition, with original pagination, S. P. L'Honoré Naber (ed.), Hague, 1913.

[99] This is our observation from examining hundreds of legal documents in Virginia, Bermuda, Barbados, and Providence Island, as well as less volumuous records for other more ephemeral or poorly documented colonies such as the Amazon colonies or Caribbean islands like St Christopher (St Kitts). The term *negro* is so overwhelming in its usage that there cannot be more than one or two exceptions.

[100] Darnell Davis papers, release found in Duke of Portland at Wellbeck MSS, 23 February 1655, of his "nigger" called Anthony, who seemed to have a desire to become a Christian, in lieu of another "nigger" called Samson delivered to him by Penn. Darnell Davis, "Pages from the Early History of Barbados, 1627–52," in *Barbados Agricultural Report*, 28 September 1909, p. 2.

Margarett, are bracketed as "negroes."[101] To construct a muster list in 1629, Virginia householders were instructed to make a "general muster of all the inhabitants, men, woemen, and children, as well Englishe as negroes inhabiting within the same."[102] This nomenclature system was still much in use later, too, for in 1650 Richard Turney received 600 acres in Virigina for transporting servants among whom were "Lyn the Turk" and "Manuel the Negro," and as late as 1661 Richard Parrot transported "Anthony a Portugal" as well as "Peter, Margaret and Maria, three negroes."[103] In general, those people who were not English were known as much by an ethnonym as by any other name, so that Irish were often not listed with a surname, just as Africans were usually not. Thus we have "Elionor, an Irish mayd," "David a Welchman," and "William an Irishman." Furthermore, Irish were often listed with no name at all; for example, in 1654 Col. John Moltrom received 250 acres "for ye trans of 2 Scots and 3 Irish brought out of Mr. Warren's ship and Capt. Swauley's ship" as were a number of anonymous "negroes."[104] In one instance we have "five Irish servants" and "David, a Negro."[105] One can observe the same process in Barbados: Irish also often appear without surnames, as in 1660 the "ye Thomas the Irishman" was given away in a will.[106]

Dutch usage in America was more varied than English, employing a wider range of terms for Africans, including "African" "Swarte" (blacks), or "Negros" (and variant spellings). In 1629, the Dutch West Indian Company promised to send the colonists of its new colony on the Hudson with "soo veel Swarten . . . als haer mogilelijck wesen sal" (as many blacks . . . as it possibly can).[107] As in English, *negro* to the Dutch was something of an ethnic marker, for when land was granted to Domingo Antony, he was presented as "Domingo Antony, Negro" as was "Catelina wodinger van Jochem Antonij, Negro" (Catelina widow of Jochem Antonij, Negro).[108]

---

[101] State Paper Office, Colonial, vol. 3, no. 2, "Lists of the Livinge & Dead in Virginia, February 16th, 1623," fols. 48–49, 50.

[102] General Court of Virigina, 8 April 1629, McIlwaine, *Minutes*, p. 196.

[103] W. Preston Haynie, *Northumberland County, Virginia, Records of Indentured Servants, 1650–1795* (Heritage Books, MD, 1996), pp. 26; Lindsay Duvall, comp. *Virginia Colonial Abstracts* 2, vol. 2 (Lancaster County Court Orders and Deeds, 1656–1680) (Southern Historical Press, SC, 1979), p. 14.

[104] Haynie, *Indentured Servants*, p. 34.

[105] Based on a study of names found in the patent lists, for several years, 1637, abstracted in Nugent, *Cavaliers and Pioneers*, pp. 353, 385.

[106] NAB, RB 6/14, p. 385.

[107] A. J. F. van Laer (ed.), *The Van Rensselaer Bowier Manuscripts* (Albany: 1908), p. 152.

[108] New York State Archives, Albany, Dutch MSS, Land Records, GG, 80 and 81.

When describing their raiding on Portuguese commerce, the Dutch used the term *negros* regularly to refer to the people found in the cargos of slave ships, though it coexisted with *swarte*, for example, in Johannes de Laet's chronicle.[109]

Although all used *negro* as an ethnic marker, the Portuguese also used it to mean "slave," perhaps as early as the early sixteenth century.[110] This was the case when the Portuguese employed the term to refer to Native Americans enslaved in Brazil, where they were called regularly *negros da terra* or "native negroes" and sometimes just plain *negroes*. In the inventory of governor Mem de Sa's sugar mills Sergipe and Sant'Ana in Bahia in 1572, *negros da guiné* were distinguished from *negros da terra*, and in another inventory of 1574, *escravos da guiné* were distinguished from *escravos da terra*.[111]

Negro was not the only word for slave, however. The Portuguese called enslaved people by various terms, such as *escravos* and *peças* ("pieces" referring to the accounting unit, *peça de India*, which meant a healthy adult male slave). Africans who spoke or wrote in Portuguese adopted this usage very early. Afonso I of Kongo, writing in 1514, referred to people he was exporting as either "peças" or "spravos [escravos]."[112] In her first letter to the Portuguese commander Bento Banha Cardoso in 1626, Queen Njinga complained of being robbed of *peças* she was sending to market, but she was careful to distinguish her dependants, *quizicos*" (kijiko), as different from these slaves.[113]

In Portuguese Africa, *negros* had also come to mean slaves. For example, in Angola, *negros* referred to slaves as a unit of value, for when Maria de Távora, widow of the governor Manuel Pereira, accused Manuel de

---

[109] De Laet, *Iaerlijck verhael*, passim.

[110] For a discussion of this term in the Portuguese context see Sweet, "Iberian Roots."

[111] Inventario do engenho de Sergipe por Morte de Mem de Sa, in Instituto do Açúcar e Alcool., *Documentos para a História do Açúar* (3 vols., Rio de Janeiro, 1963), 1: 40, 89–94; Inventario 1574, pp. 341–8; for more on "negros da terra," in the southern part of the country, see John Monteiro, *Negros da terra: Índios e Bandeirantesnas origiens de São Paulo* (São Paulo, 1994).

[112] Afonso to Manuel I, 5 October 1514, MMA 1: 295 (spravos), 297 (spravos), 300 (peças que fosem spravos – pieces that would be slaves).

[113] Queen Njinga to Bento Banha Cardoso, 3 March 1625 [ed. 1626], quoted in Fernão de Sousa to Gonçalo de Sousa and his brothers, c. 1630, FHA 1: 244–5. It might have been possible that the Kikongo or Kimbundu terms of slave that could be exported (*mvika* in Kikongo, *mubika* in Kimbundu) might have been employed, but in fact it did not. *Moleque*, from the Kikongo term *nleke* meaning "a young person," was employed throughout the Portuguese Atlantic and in Spanish territories to mean a young slave, valued less than a peça da India.

Rocha in 1612 of spoiling his goods, she referred to "seis centos banzos de fato que he o mesmo que seis centos negros" (six hundred *banzos* of cloth, which is [worth] the same as six hundred negros).[114] The meaning of *negro* and *slave* also became linked in the minds of Africans, for by the middle of the seventeenth century, Kongolese were insulted to be referred to as *negros*, a term only used for slaves, insisting that foreigners, when referring to skin color, use the alternate Portuguese term for black, *pretos*.[115] When Richard Jobson visited Gambia in 1623 he met quite a few Portuguese residents who he thought to be black and "Negro," yet he noted "be they never so blacke, to be called a Negro," perhaps in response to the other resonances of the term.[116]

Escravo, a term with Roman roots, referred to a perpetual hereditary condition of complete dependence on a master and defined a legal condition well established in Iberian law. To what degree did the English and Dutch who borrowed the term *negro* from the Portuguese as an ethnic marker for Africans also adopt the legal meaning of *escravo*? Although speakers of both languages also used the Portuguese equivalent of *escravo* ("slave"), which both come from common medieval linguistic roots, the actual meaning of *slave/slaven* in English and Dutch is different in important ways. Although the term retained the meaning of complete dependence, it lacked the reference to perpetual dependence, which the Portuguese term retained.

The term *slave* was seldom used to refer to Africans brought to any English possession in the Americas before the 1650s.[117] There are a few exceptions; Henry Winthrop described Native Americans and Africans in Barbados as "slaves" in 1627 (though not a legal document), and this term was also used in Maryland in a case of 1642 where Leonard Calvert sold John Skinner various items, including "fourteene Negro men-slaves and three women slaves."[118] Notwithstanding these few examples when the term *slave* was used, the overwhelming majority of the documents do not use the term when referring to African dependants. The rarity of usage of

---

[114] AHU, Cx 1, doc. 17, Petition of Maria de Tavora, 26 January 1612.

[115] Biblioteca Nacional de Madrid, MS 3533, Antonio de Teruel, "Descripcion Narrativa," APF: SOCG 250, Giacinto Brugiotti da Vetralla, "Nelli schiavi che si cōprano e vendero..." (c. 1650).

[116] Jobson, *Golden Trade*, p. 30.

[117] There are occasional uses of the term *slave* in early English literature. For example, John Lok referred to Africans he carried to England in 1555 as slaves; Hakluyt, *Principle Navigations*, 2, part 2, 22.

[118] Bill of Sale, 1 March 1642, *Archives of Maryland* 4: 189.

the term *slave* has been the source of much of the discussion concerning whether the status of Africans in the early English settlements was that of indentured servants or slaves.

Although the English were aware of Portuguese and Spanish practice of slavery and the legal condition of slaves in their lands, they did not necessarily see slavery exactly as the Spanish and Portuguese did. They might view it as a long (perhaps even life-long) contract as seen in the act of the Barbados Assembly passed in 1636 that declared "negroes and Indians that came here to be sold, should serve for life unless a contract was before made to the contrary."[119] Lord Mandeville, a member of the Somers Island Company that controlled Bermuda, wrote to Thomas Durham, "For the negroes I see no reason why they should deserve freedom from their service," clearly seeing their term as indeterminate and possibly indefinite.[120] In fact, Robert McColley has argued that in the seventeenth century, *servant* meant both "slave" and "indentured servant."[121] Indentured servants could be sold, exchanged, or passed on from one owner to another, and sometimes they, too, were acquired through capture. In 1640, Barbados received some kidnapped Frenchmen who were sold for 900 pounds of cotton a head.[122] However, they had definite terms of service and in theory would be freed.

The idea that slavery was a permanent condition restricted to Africans was not firmly established in the English legal mind either, in spite of the Portuguese model. When Captain Jackson brought about a dozen Africans to Bermuda in 1637–1638, he sold them all to Hugh Wentworth with the stipulation that they serve 99-year indentures, certainly lifelong but not heritable.[123] That same year, a certain Maria was sold to serve for 19 years.[124] When Jackson returned to Bermuda in 1644 after a year-long privateering raid in the Spanish territories, he stipulated that another group of Africans he had taken were to serve shorter terms, some for 4,

[119] [William Duke] *Some Memoirs of the First Settlement of the Island of Barbados and Other Caribee Islands*...(London, 1743), p. 20 (from now lost records).
[120] BL Add MSS 63854, fol. 242, B Mr. Jessop's letter book, transcript of a coded copy found at BL Add MSS 10615 no. 177, Lord Mandeville to Thomas Dunham, 24 May 1638.
[121] Robert McColley, "Slavery in Virginia, 1619–1660: A Reexamination," in Robert H. Abzug and Stephen Maizlich (eds.), *New Perspectives on Race and Slavery in America: Essays in Honor of Kenneth M. Stampp* (Lexington, KY, 1986), pp. 12–14.
[122] Darnell Davis, *Pages from the Early History of Barbados, 1627–1652* (Barbados, 1909), p. 143.
[123] BCR 2: 9–10.
[124] Packwood, *Chained*, p. 8.

others for only 7 years.[125] In his will of 1650, a Barbados man wished that "as for my negro he shall serve 21 years after the date hereof. And then to be free."[126]

The fact that some Africans did come to the colonies as indentured servants has confused the issue of slavery as well. "John Phillip A negro Christened in England 12 yeers since," who appeared in a Virginia court in 1624 to testify, was probably serving as an indentured servant or perhaps as a sailor on an English ship.[127] "Brase," a "Negro" pilot taken from a Spanish vessel in the West Indies in 1625, was also treated more or less as an indentured servant in Virginia.[128] Jack, who came to Charles City County, Virigina, in about 1636, claimed indentured status and showed the court a contract, dated 1653, specifying 11 years more service and may thus have come from England.[129] John Casor argued in 1655 that he had come into Virginia in 1641 as an indentured servant and that Anthony Johnson, the prosperous Atlantic Creole, had held him illegally, though Johnson argued that Casor had no indenture and was thus his for life.[130] Another Atlantic Creole, Fernando, argued in 1667 that prior to coming to Virginia he had lived several years in England and he "should serve no more than any Englishman."[131] But these Africans were exceptions, and the bulk of those people labeled negroes were probably regarded, as the Portuguese usage implied, as slaves.

But in English, the word *slave* did not have a fixed legal meaning of life-long, inheritable servitude in early-seventeenth-century America. English colonists often used the term *slave* as meaning "totally dependent," as when Francis Newman petitioned in 1620 that although he was "sent a freeman" to Virginia, he was "sustayinge great bondage and slavery" at the hands of Captain Argoll.[132] Lewis Hughes of Bermuda similarly complained in 1621 that he will not be "merchant's slaves" with regard to the

---

[125] BCR 2: 102–3, 22 January 1644.

[126] Cambridge University Library, Davis Papers, Box 7, Env. 22, citing extracts from nonextant book of Wills and Deeds, vol. 4, fol. 629.

[127] H. R. McIlwaine (ed.), *Minutes*, 33; see also Vaughn, "Blacks in Virginia," p. 470, for further discussion.

[128] Vaughn, "Blacks in Virginia," pp. 470–1, based on McIlwaine, *Minutes*, pp. 66–68, 72.

[129] Billings, *Old Dominion*, p. 169–70. He must have won his suit as he was in court as a free man the next year, York County 1661–1664, VCR 3 (12), p. 331.

[130] Billings, *Old Dominion*, p. 155.

[131] Billings, *Old Dominion*, p. 169.

[132] Petition of Friends of Francis Newman, 8 April 1620, Kingsbury, *Virginia Company* 1: 337.

extension of credit.[133] Elsewhere, Bermuda settlers complained in 1622 that "children [were] dying like slaves."[134]

Although these were hyperbolic complaints they expressed the idea of degradation and total dependence; in several English colonies, courts gave slavery more specific meaning when they imposed it as a punishment for crime on any settler of any origin. Bermuda records frequently mention terms of temporary enslavement for crimes, and in addition to the one decision when "Symon the Negro" was condemned to slavery at the governor's pleasure in 1617 "for having to do with a child in carnall copular," most of the miscreants were English. In the same year, Nicholas Gabriell, for example, was sentenced to be a "slave unto the colonie" for publicly criticizing the governor.[135] The records of New England also include this type of slavery: on 4 October 1638 William Andrews was condemned for an assault on Henry Coggan "to be delivered as slave to whom the court shall appoint" and was released a year later. In 1639 John Kempe was also "committed for a slave to Leift Davenport "for filthy vncleane attempts with 3 young girles." Likewise, Thom Savory was sentenced to be "sould for a slave until hee has made double restitution" for housebreaking in 1640.[136] English and Scotch might also be enslaved in England for crime and sent to Barbados, as a Barbados deed stated in 1640, "the prisoners of the Tower shall 'tis said bee Barbadozzed."[137]

The pattern of enslavement of Europeans and their sale to America continued well into the seventeenth century, even after the concept of African slavery was institutionalized. The English sold prisoners of war taken in the Civil War (1641–1651) to lifetime servitude in America. In 1648 New Englander Roger Williams wrote to John Winthrop, "it is said that Cromwell has discomforted the Welch...of whom he toke 9,000 prisoners, great score of Scots and Welsh and sent and sold as slaves in other parts."[138] In 1649, Irishmen who continued to resist after the

---

[133] Magdalene College, Oxford Ferrar papers 1475a, Grievances by Lewis Hughes, 23 May 1621, fol. 1v.

[134] Magdalene College, Oxford Ferrar Papers 1475c, various grievances, 1622.

[135] Lefroy, *Memorials* 1: 127 (summary only), BRC 1: no page, illegible today, read as this by Packwood. Lefroy notes this legal instrument in providing summaries of these cases, some of which are no longer legible.

[136] John Noble (ed.), *Records of the Court of Assistants of the Colony of Massachusetts Bay, 1630–92* (Boston, 1904), pp. 78–9 (enslavement of William Andrews); p. 89 (Andrews' release); p. 86 (John Kempe); p. 94 (Thomas Savory).

[137] Cambridge University Library, Davis Papers, Box 7, envelope 22, quoted from the old Barbados Archives, Deeds, vol. 1, fol. 746 (no longer extant).

[138] Williams to Winthrop, 3 December 1648, *Roger Williams Correspondence*, p. 260.

storming of Drogheda "when they submitted, these officers were knocked on the head, and every tenth man of the soldiers killed, and the rest shipped for Barbados."[139] A deed in Barbados in 1654 mentions "Christian servants for their respective terms... all the Negroes, Indians, and other slaves...," suggesting that some prisoners might be included in the "other slaves."[140]Although these slaves were often freed after a certain term, often 6–8 years, where no term was mentioned the slavery was understood to be for life, until 1681, when Charles II decreed that such people could not be enslaved for life.[141]

This custom of enslaving defeated oponents continued in various risings and other campaigns that followed Cromwell's victory. Heinrich von Uchteritz, a German lower noble serving in the Loyalist army, was sold in 1652 along with hundreds of others to Barbados for 800 pounds of sugar to a "count" in Barbados who held "one hundred Christians, one hundred Moors [*Moren* or Africans], and one hundred Savages [*Wilden* or Native Americans]" as "slaves" (*Sclaven*).[142] In 1659 a number of prisoners taken in the Salisbury Rising of 1654 petitioned the Crown for release from what they described as "uncondemned" slavery in Barbados, which appears to have been conceived as at least a lifelong servitude. Among these, one nobleman pleaded for the "Redemption of the Innocent Slaves at Barbados, and the prevention of the further slavery of England (Our case is but your Touchstone, by which you may discover whether English, be Slaves or Freemen)."[143] In 1664, when the English took over New Amsterdam, they sent a force to take over the colony of New Amstel on the South (Delaware) River Even though the English met no resistance. the inhabitants of New Amstel (which included only one African) "were invaded, stripped, utterly plundered, and many of them sold as slaves to Virginia."[144]

[139] Cambridge University Library, Davis Papers, Box 1, envelope 39, Letter of George Honorable Lenthal, Esq, 17 September 1649, in A. B. Ellis, "White Slaves and Bondservants," *Popular Science Monthly in the Argosy* (5 June 1893).
[140] BAR, RB 3/2, p. 638, 12 March 1654.
[141] Cambridge University Library, Davis Papers, Box 1, envelope 39, Letter of John Cotton to Cromwell and commentary in Ellis, "White Slaves."
[142] Heinrich von Uchteritz, *Kurtze Reise-Beschreibung auf der Insul Barbados* (Weissenfels, 1712), p. 9.
[143] *Englands Slavery or Barbados Merchandize; represented in a petition to the High and Honourable Court of Parliament, by Marcellus Rivers and Oxenbridge, Foyle Gentlemen on behalf of thmselves and three score and ten more Free-born Englishmen sold (uncondemned) into slavery...* (London, 1659).
[144] "Report of the Honble Peter Stuyvestan, late Director-General of New Netherland, on the Causes which led to the Surrender of that Country to the English, 1665" in J. Franklin Jameson, *Narratives of New Netherland, 1609–1664* (New York, 1909), p. 465.

These varied and flexible notions of status eventually gave way, for Africans, to a concept closer to the Portuguese model of perpetual and inheritable service wherever the Plantation Generation came in sufficiently large numbers to overwhelm the Atlantic Creoles of the Charter Generation. The Barbados legislature's decision that "negroes and Indians" who had no other contract in 1636 established that lifetime servitude awaited them on the island. In 1639 Maryland fixed all indentures at four years for "all Christian inhabitants" but added, parenthetically, "slaves excepted," allowing longer terms in these cases but not necessarily defining Africans as slaves, because a variety of other people could also be slaves.[145] In 1661 courts in Virginia ruled that Negroes who ran away could not have their terms increased as they "are incapable of making satisfaction by the adding of time," implying that at least lifelong servitude was customary.[146] In 1664 the Maryland Assembly drew up an act obliging Negroes to serve "durante vita" and later in the same act spoke of "negroes or other slaves."[147]

Although the courts increasingly defined the status of Negroes as life-long slaves, even in the 1660s they still had not resolved whether it was perpetual. A Virginia court freed Elizabeth Key in 1656 because, among other reasons, she was the daughter of a free man, "that by the Common law the Child of a Woman slave begott by a freeman ought to bee free."[148] Similarly, when the Maryland Assembly of 1664 debated whether the issue of children born to free mothers by "negroes" should be free and decided that they were to serve for 30 years, they fell short of making the condition permanent.[149] Moreover, a Virginia court ruled in 1662 that all people born there "shall be held bond or free only according to the condition of the mother," including those children born to Englishmen by a "negro woman, be she slave or Free."[150]

From the beginning the Dutch in America unhesitatingly regarded Africans as slaves, even though, like the English, their definition of slavery diverged from that of the Portuguese. Johannes Michaelius, who as the first person to write about Africans in New Netherland had spent some time in West Africa, referred to *Angoolischen slavinnen* ("Angolan slave women") in New Amsterdam in 1628, whereas on another occasion

[145] General Court, 1638/9, *Archives of Maryland* 1: 80.
[146] Grand Assembly of Virginia 32, March 1660/1, Henning, *Statutes* 2: 26.
[147] Upper House Journal, Assembly Proceedings, 1664, *Archives of Maryland* 1: 526–27.
[148] Report of A Comittee Concerning the freedome of Elizabeth Key, 21 July 1656, Billings, *Old Dominion*, p. 157.
[149] Upper House Journal, Assembly Proceedings, 1664, *Archives of Maryland* 1: 527.
[150] Billings, *Old Dominion*, p. 172.

he observed that Native Americans did not scoff the Creator, *als d'Africa-nen wel duuven doen* ("as the Africans certainly do").[151]

Perhaps because of their deep involvement in the Portuguese world in Brazil after 1629 and in Angola after 1641 the Dutch had borrowed the idea that "negro" was equal to "slave" more than the English had. In instructions given to the Dutch attackers in Luanda in 1641, the directors of the West India Company mixed the usages, first by referring to all the inhabitants of Angola as "negros" but then by telling their agents that they must use Angola to bring negros to the lands of Brazil (*van lands negros t'commen*). Not wishing to alienate the Angolans, the Company's officials were enjoined not to enslave the free people by raiding, so that *dat geen negros din vrijs inbevondert sijn* ("so that no negros will be taken from the free people"), but to take only those who were truly enslaved before the Dutch came. Such slaves, "negros," would be certified slaves (*alsgesert is*).[152]

The Dutch usage in America is confirmed in the 1641 court record of the trial of the group of Africans who murdered one of their own in 1641. The defendants were referred to on 17 January as *alle negros* ("all negroes") and on the 24 January as *alle negros ende slaven* ("all Negroes and slaves").[153] Furthermore, a group of 11 "negroes and slaves" [*negros ende slaven*] in 1644 who petitioned Governor Krieft of New Amsterdam claimed that they had served the company for 18 to 19 years and demanded their freedom, arguing that even this service was excessive as they had long been promised their freedom.

This passage has formed the linchpin of the argument for those who take the position that the Dutch did not regard slavery as lifetime servitude, because they clearly did regard them as slaves. But Krieft, apparently without any difficulty, granted their request for freedom. However, their freedom was limited for the terms of their manumission specified that they had to pay 30 schepels of wheat and other dues to the company and their children were "bound and obligated" (*gehouden ende verplicht*) to serve

---

[151] Joanas Michaëlius to Adrianus Smoutius 11 August 1628 in Albert Eekhof, *Jonas Michaëlius Founder of the Church in New Netherland*...(Leyden: A W Sijthoff, 1926), p. 120, 123 (Dutch), translation modified.

[152] ARA OWIC 56, doc. 24, point 13, "Instructie van Wegis Sijn Excie Johan Maurits grave van nassau...voorde Heer Admirael Cornelis Cornelisz Jol De Haeren pieter Morthamer ende Cornelis Nieulant politique Raden ende de h.Overste Lieutenant James Hinderson...van de Stadt Loanda de St. Paulo ende desse Lffs omleggen de forten," 28 May 1641.

[153] New York State Archives, Albany, Dutch MSS, Council Minutes, 1638–1649, ff. 83 and 84. Truncated translation of these documents can be found in AJF van Laer, *New York Historical Manuscripts* 4: 97–8.

the company as "serfs" (*als lijff Eygenen*). The newly manumitted also had to serve the company (*sullen gehouden wesen ten dienste te sijn*) in some unspecified way.[154] No indentured servant faced these restrictions at the end of their term of service, but neither did slaves, for these people owned property and sued in court.

Indeed, at the time some Dutch settlers recognized the inconsistency in the situation. In a remonstrance to the Company in 1649, they complained about Krieft's arrangement, arguing that these Africans were free "but their children remain slaves" (*haer kindern blyven slaven*), which was "contrary to all public law" (*teghens aller Volcken recht*).[155] In their reply the Company did away with the inconsistency, ruling that the Africans' "children remain slaves" (*de kinderen slaven blijven*), but contended that only three of the children performed some service (*eenige dienst*).[156] The nature of the services that the freed Africans were expected to perform is revealed in an order of 1653 when citizens were to repair the fort, and the "Free Negroes" formed one of the four teams into which the labor was divided, the others being composed of Dutch citizens, on pain of losing their rights as citizens.[157]

Individual settlers also used this form of "half-freedom" in their dealings with Africans, for when Johannes Megapolensis, the minister, following an earlier promise, granted Jan Francisco his freedom in 1646, "in view of the long and faithful service rendered by him," he stipulated that Francisco would also have to render 10 schepels of wheat annually.[158] The Company continued to use this method of half-freedom until the British took over. On 28 December 1662, for example, Stuyvesant granted manumission to three Negro women who claimed that they were imported into New Netherland in 1628 and thus had served the Company for 34 years. Like their compatriots, they were required to continue in service, in this case to "weekly do housework" for Stuyvesant.[159] As late as 1662, one of

---

[154] New York State Archives, Council, 25 February 1644, fol. 183, Van Laer, *Council Minutes* 1: 212 (we have modified van Laer's translation, in particular the translation of *lijff Eigenen* as "serfs" rather than "slaves").

[155] *Vertoogh van Nieu-Neder-Land* ... (The Hague, 1650), p. 32. In a response the company maintained that only three were so held.

[156] ARA St. Gen., 12564, doc. 38 "Corte bericht ofte antwoorde op eenige poncten, begrepen inde schrifte deductie van Adriaen van der Donck ... " 24 November 1650, a translation is in O'Callaghan, *Documents*.

[157] Council Minutes, 20 April 1653, in Gehring, *Council Minutes, 1652–54*, pp. 69–70.

[158] Van Laer, *New York Colonial Manuscripts* 4: 365.

[159] Albert Eekhof, *De Hervormde Kerk in Noord-Amerika, 1624–1664* (2 vols., Hague, 1913), 2: 148, 159.

these children, Anthony, the son of Cleyn Anthony, who had been adopted by other Africans, was the subject of a petition by his adopted parents to obtain full freedom, so that he could inherit "his or the petitioners' temporal [goods]."[160]

Not all Africans in New Netherland were granted half-freedom because of long service, and some did serve for life. This was revealed in the sale of a certain Anthony by Frederich Lubberstein to Richard Lord, who was "to employ the said Negro during his lifetime in all such work as the said Richard Lord shall think proper." Luberstein surrendered "all ownership of the said Negro."[161]

Whether slave or half-free, Africans were always regarded as "The Company's negroes" and forced to engage in such undesirable and hard labor that condemning Europeans to "labor with the Company's negroes" was a severe punishment to inflict on them. A court in New Netherland ruled that a habitual troublemaker who had wounded a solider, Gysbert Cornelissen Beyerlandt, in 1639 be sent back to the Netherlands, but until a ship could come to take him, he had to work with the Company's negroes.[162] Jan Habbensz was condemned to be "put in irons and forced to labor with the Honorable Company's Negroes as an example to all others of that kind."[163] This type of punishment was sufficiently harsh that it was written into a decree in 1642 that warned that "no one shall draw a knife, much less to wound any person under penalty of a fine of 50 florins, or in default to work for three months in chains with the Negroes."[164] Lesser offenses were eventually punished in this way, as in 1654 when Elias Emmens was sentenced to work with the Company's negroes for one year for insolence.[165] Deserters faced serious punishments, not only being subject to physical discipline but also being sentenced to serve with the Company's negroes, as happened to Claes Michielson, who in 1658 was to have his "hair clipped, then publicly flogged, ears pierced with a hot iron and afterwards to work one year with the Negroes."[166]

---

[160] Petition of Emmanuel Pietersen, 21 March 1661, Scott-Rhoda, *Register of Salomon Lechaire*, p. 22.

[161] Bill of sale, 28 November 1646, Van Laet, *Register of the Provincial Secretary* 2: 365.

[162] Council Minutes, 3 February 1639, Van Laer, *Council Minutes* 4: 37

[163] Minutes 22 November 1641, Van Laer, *Council Minutes* 4: 128, fol. 108.

[164] Minutes, 11 July 1642, van Laer, *Council Minutes* 4: 151, translation altered per the original New York State Archives, Council Minutes, fol. 129, so that his labor is performed only in chains and not in a chain gang.

[165] Council Minutes, 3 October 1654, Gehring, *Council Minutes*, p. 185.

[166] O'Callaghan, *Calendar* p. 8. Two other men suffered variants of the same punishment in the same year.

Therefore, both the English and the Dutch always regarded the Africans taken from Portuguese slave ships, or later purchased in Africa, as slaves, though during the earlier periods they had not yet determined exactly how long the servitude would last (though certainly longer than the usual time for an indentured servant). In any case, early colonial masters seem to have shown an unusual propensity to grant manumission to Africans and, as we have shown, some of whom appear to have been quite successful as landowners and community builders.

Atlantic Creoles and Manumission

Atlantic Creoles seem to have attained freedom remarkably easily, considering the later history of American servitude. This issue, the frequency with which they were manumitted, has been a key topic in the debate about the status of the Charter Generation. In 1972 Edmund Morgan, after examining the 1668 titheable list for Northampton County, Virginia, supported this idea when he reported that 29 percent of the Africans in that county were free, a figure that far exceeded the percentage of free African Americans at any subsequent point in American history.[167]

Most of the discussion on the status of the first Africans in the English and Dutch colonies has centered on English and Dutch law and racial attitude. What the above discussion has revealed, however, is that the question is much more complex. A significant percentage of the first Africans were Atlantic Creoles and their ability to demonstrate that they were Christians facilitated their transition from slavery to freedom. Thus the best explanation that accounts for the large percentage of free people among the Charter Generation in the Dutch and English settlements may be more related to this fact than to loopholes in the law or the development of slavery. In contrast to the assumptions that the arriving Christians were converted in America, Ira Berlin identified the Creoles familiarity with European culture, including religion, and Graham Hodges specifically notes the connection between the Christian background of the Angolans coming to New Netherland and the high percentage who obtained manumission.[168]

---

[167] Edmund Morgan, "Slavery and Freedom: The American Paradox," *Journal of American History* 59 (1972–1973), p. 18, no. 39.

[168] See, for example, Berlin, *Many Thousands Gone*, pp. 29–63, *passim*; Hodges, *Root and Branch*, pp. 22–5.

Both English and Dutch popular wisdom, if not law, maintained that a Christian could not hold another Christian as a slave. The Synod of Dort, which was convened in 1618 to resolve theological differences among Calvinists (including English and Dutch), discussed the issue of the obligation of a Christian master to free a Christian slave, although there was no official decision. Samuel Rishworth, a Providence Island official and committed Puritan, for example, opposed Christians holding slaves, but the Company argued in 1635 that it was morally defensible to "keepe such ᴾsons in a state of servitude during their strangeness from Christianity," implying that once they had become Christians they could no longer be slaves.[169] This attitude reflected the long-standing position of Christian Europe that Christians could enslave Muslims and non-Christians. The Dutch theologian Godefridus Cornelisz Udemans, writing in 1638, argued that "Heathens and Turks" might be used as slaves by Christians, "provided that they have been caught in a Just War, or purchased for a correct price from their parents, or other competent Masters." He felt that these conditions were met, at least for non-Christians, "as related that this ordinarily occurs in Angola. For this accords with the Divine Law."[170] He wrote nothing, however, about Christian slaves coming from Angola, but did say that it was not permissible for a Christian to hold another as a slave.[171] In fact when Krieft freed some of the West India Company's slaves and still kept them "half-free," the stinging complaint that some settlers stressed that anyone "born of a free Christian mother could not be held as a slave" (much as the English would later determine).[172] That they had done so in the specifically Calvinist form is revealed in the Reformed church's marriage and baptismal registers.

Many Anglicans also believed that Christian Africans could not be held as slaves. In 1648, when the non-Christian West African Sambo expressed his desire to become a Christian, Richard Ligon, who was visiting Barbados at the time, intervened with Sambo's master on his behalf, but his

[169] PRO 124/1 fol. 75, Providence Island Company to Capt Philip Bell, Gov of the Island of Providence, London, 20 April 1635.
[170] Godefridus Cornelisz Udemans, *'t Geestlijck Roer van't Coopmans Schip* (Dodrecht, 1638, 2nd ed., 1640), Chapter IV, point 10, fol. 183.
[171] Udemans, *Geestelyk roer*, cap IV, fol. 183v.
[172] *Vertoogh*, p. 32. Graham Hodges quotes in this respect another document that adds "if they want to submit themselves to the lovely yoke of Our Lord Jesus Christ, Christian love requires that they be discharged," citing this same source in its English translation O'Callaghan, *Documents*, 1: 302, but this passage is not located there.

master reminded his fellow Englishman that English law made it so that "we could not make a Christian a slave" and to make a slave a Christian would be to threaten the whole institution of slavery.[173] If Ligon never met any Christian slaves during his stay in Barbados, Father Antoine Biet, a visiting French priest, met them. He reported that during his stay in Barbados those Africans who had "the Catholic religion which they have received amongst the Portuguese... keep it as best as they can, saying their prayers and worshiping God in their hearts."[174] At about the same period the French priest Jean-Baptiste du Tertre reported that the English and Dutch would not convert their slaves to Christianity as they would no longer be slaves.[175] These ideas still prevailed as late as the 1680s, when James II made a resolution that "the negroes upon the plantations should all be baptized, declaiming against that impiety of their masters prohibiting it since they believed that they would be ipso facto free."[176]

Occasionally, mixed-raced individuals petitioned for their freedom on the basis of their upbringing among Christians. Doll Allen, a mixed-race woman of Bermuda, claiming freedom from being a "perpetuall slave" in 1652 asked to be set apart as "God set a distinction between her and heathen Negroes, by prouitentially allotting her birth among Christians."[177] Elizabeth Key lodged a similar complaint in 1656, also counting her baptism as grounds for obtaining freedom and, like Allen, Key was born of an English father.[178]

Africans who were Christians when they arrived were able to take advantage of the belief that Christians could not be held in slavery. In the English colonies, their names provide some indication of their Christian status. A clear case of this comes from the two early Jamestown censuses in which some Africans are listed with Iberian Christian names or English versions of them and others are listed just as "Negroes." A remarkable number of the manumitted Africans on the Eastern Shore bore Christian names. That "Antonio and Isabell" on the 1625 census are revealed to

---

[173] Ligon, *True and Exact History*, p. 50.
[174] Antoine Biet, *Voyage de la France Equinoxiale en l'isle de Cayenne* (Paris, 1654), 292.
[175] Du Tertre, *Histoire* 2: 503.
[176] John Evelyn *Diary* (2 vols, London, 1685) 2: 479.
[177] Lefroy, *Memorial* 2: 34–5.
[178] Billings, *Old Dominion*, p. 165–57; Warren K. Billings, "The Cases of Fernando and Elizabeth Key: A note on the status of blacks in 17th century Virginia," *William and Mary Quarterly* 30 (1973): 467–74.

have "their child baptized" without further comment, it suggests that their Christian background was not questioned.

Records of Dutch manumissions in New Netherland reveal a similar pattern for the freed Africans. The names show that the Africans clearly brought the Iberian names with them, were self-identified and must have received the names through being raised in a Christian community (Kongo, Portuguese Angola, and the pockets of Christian communities as far east as Matamba) and not just through the nominal baptism in Luanda. In fact, the Dutch Classis of Amsterdam thought Luanda baptisms did not change the status of heathens, "even if they were baptized in gross by the Papists in Africa," and that their children could not be baptized "until parents pass over into Christianity."[179] Although the records are less helpful, Bermuda seems to have followed a similar course, with the early emergence of free people and a significant proportion of Iberian names among those few who belonged to the group.

Those Central Africans who were not Christians, like their West African counterparts who arrived later, could not claim their freedom on such grounds. By the 1650s in Barbados and the 1660s in the Chesapeake, legal changes connected with the expanding slave economy and the growth of the plantation system closed this important route to freedom for all Africans. The Maryland Assembly passed legislation in 1664 holding slaves to service "durante vita," giving as a rationale "thinking it very necessary for the prevention of the damage of such slaves may sustain by such slaves pretending to be Christian and so plead the law of England."[180] The arrival of West Africans in New Netherland also had significant repercussions as well, even in the absence of a plantation transformation. In 1664 Henricus Selijns, a pastor in New Amsterdam, refused to baptize negroes on the grounds that he believed they sought it only for "freeing their children from material slavery."[181] He was surely referring to the newly arrived West Africans, because Christian Africans of the Charter Generation were already baptized and would have presented babies for baptism.

The hardening of the laws in the 1660s explicitly excluded African Christians from using their religion to obtain manumission and also closed

[179] C. Schulz, pastor, 1661, *Ecclesiastical Records*, p. 508.
[180] Upper House Journal, Assembly Proceedings, 1664, *Archives of Maryland* 1: 526–7.
[181] Henricus Selijns, 9 June 1664, van der Linde (ed.), *Old First Dutch Reformed Church*, 231/Dutch 230.

the avenue for freedom by excluding converts from using Christianity as a means to gain freedom. In Virginia and New Netherland they did so in the environment of the arrival of large numbers of West Africans, whose culture was different and more alien to Euro-American expectations. This influx of West Africans came with economic changes that eventually would affect law and close the door even for Central Africans, including the descendants of the manumitted Charter Generation.

APPENDIX

Names of Africans Appearing in Early
Colonial Records

Inventories, court records, and other documents contain a substantial number of names borne by the earliest African inhabitants of the English and Dutch colonies in the Americas. These names can give us some idea of the origins of the people, their sense of themselves, and connect in a few cases to their Angolan and African past. We have compiled as exhaustive a list of names as we can using the resources that we examined during the course of research on this project. A full discussion of the implications of this name list is found in Chapter 5.

Names in Barbados Records

The first chart shows names found in the earliest detailed records of Barbados, RB 3/1, whose entries cover the period 1640–45, which refers to Africans in the colony just after the start of the large-scale importation of slaves from West Africa (which began in 1641). It is as close as we can come to a list of the earliest names of Afro-Barbadians.

Names	Source (RB 3/1)
Gonye	1643 p. 61
Nangoe	1643 p. 61
Tony	1643 p. 92
Mingo	
Grange	
Mall	
Butler	
Maria	

(*continued*)

(continued)

Names	Source (RB 3/1)
Judy	
Nell	
Illumah	1643 p. 92
Tom	1643 p. 94
Tony (different)	
Mingo (different)	
Stinner	1643 p. 205
Sib	1642 p. 276
Maragarita	1644 p. 439
Judith	1643 p. 666
Catherine	1643 p. 666
Domingo	1645 p. 692
Culley	
Bainell	1643 p. 33
Iebell	
Manuell	
Tussey	
Jabon	
Curley	
Branke	
Zackeri	
Peter	
Lazarus	
Jone	
Lattey	
Granbell	
Cuddey	
Suckey	
Wally	
Toney	
Tyre	

Note: There are 388 people listed as "Negro" in the document; only 39 are listed with names.

The second chart shows names of people who appear in later records and reflect more fully the names given after the commencement of large-scale slave imports, primarily from West Africa.

Name	Source
Alle	1647 RB 3/2 p. 9
Agoe	1647 RB 3/2 p. 10
Toney	1647 RB 3/2 p. 63

Name	Source
Tobu	
Maga	
Judge	1647 RB 3/2 p. 63
Tony	1662 RB 3/2 p. 540
Sambo	
John Tackey	
Mingo	1662, RB 3/2 p. 540
Margaret	
Grane Bass	
Maria	
Virgoe	
Nall	
Hannah	
Mary	1662 RB 3/2 p. 540
Jack boy	1662, RB 3/2 p. 540
Tom	
Robin	
Anatta boy	1662 RB 3/2 p. 540
Catherine girl	1662, RB 3/2 p. 540
Toney Waringa	1665 RB 3/2 p. 555 (men)
Toney Trebaley	
Grasse	
Jaw	
Mathew	
Damon	
Oga	
Cova	
Tom Ebo	
Dye Browne	
Sandy Papa	
Bill (boys)	
Jems	
Baldy	
Richard	
Black William	
Sama	
Saco	
Joania	p. 556 (women)
Katsy	
Judith	
Catacoy	
Ada	
Honar	
Jugg	

(continued)

(continued)

Name	Source
Nan	
Ankin	
Ago	
Cafaway	
Isabell	
Bess	
Catalina	
Malonga	
Magarita	
Maria	
Acia	
Mary	p. 556 (girls)
Baasha	
Nancy	
Maiaa	
Benay	
Washaw	
Civa	
Katherina	
Robin Comite	1663 RB 3/2 p. 566 (men)
Sambo	
Caran	
Wallo	
Tom	
Grandy Nanglged	(women)
Oeu	
Saya	
Bess	
Popo Minhan	
Bray	
Budgay	
Chauma	
Uuima	
Margarita	
Darry pichaninies	p. 567
Jack	
Sarah	
Minlian	
Ogua	
Vunia	
Nan	
Oea	
Robin	1653 RB 3/2 p. 612 (men)

Name	Source
Toney	
Andrew	
Mingoe	
Simmony	
Miqueria	
Agenye	
Paunch	
Thom	
Amunga	
Michaell	
Jack Geudge	
Jesse	(women)
Inuoue	
Braccoe	
Jugg	
Andacco	
Abescha	
Ambo	
Besu	
Aleck	
Dawn	(boys)
Dambo	
Harry	
Mingo junior	
Wlm junior	
Hickie	
Savudie	
Abigall (girls)	
Obee	
Hagar junior	
Hagar Junior	
Maria	
Kett	
Simmey	1654 RB 3/2 p. 641 (women)
Oversee	
Peco	
Abida	
Cultibulo	
Grandy Marea	
Little Maria	
Old Marea	
Innam	
Mocongo	
Grandy Oneba	

(continued)

(continued)

Name	Source
Little Oneba	
Gillian	
Gandy Jugg	
Lillell Jugg	
Hoobora	
Umina	p. 642
Moone	
Bucka	
Black Negro	
Onebo	
Shu	
Lilly	
Obree	
Away	
Fumfum	
Acame	
Neeta	
Jone	
Pevida	
Meta	
Sara	
Ellina	
Fafawn	
Jane	
Madline	
Cate	
Acco	
Toby (men)	
Effee	
Grigg	
Goulder	
Pidgim	
Old Phillip	
Grandy Tom	
Ambota	
Gee	
Old Harry	
Peetar	
Gy	
Tim	
Bim	
Maa	
Marca	(pickaninny girls)

Name	Source
Bo	
Baby	
Bessee	
Willmot	
Man	
May	
Oggo	
Omnia	
Umkia	
Little Jack	
Gindy Man	(pickaninny boys)
Tom	
Fill	
Leffy	
Wayshey	
Robin	
Hugh	
Tony	(children)
Jones	
Peg	
Babb	
Mall	
Dick	
Venda	
Nan	
Bess	
Haobara	
Nan	
James	
Jack	
Frank	
Frante	
Mary	
Jone	
Ferdinando	
Little Griff	
Chaga	
Gilliam	
Comtax	
Will	
Tamberlayn the Great	1654, RB 3/2 p. 671
Robyne the Great	
Jeffrey	
Mingo	

(continued)

(continued)

Name	Source
Hanger	
James	
Ned	
Tomy	
Symon	
Tonye	
Joche	
Tym	
Deck	
Jacke	
Little Mingo	
Powell	
Munday	
New Robin	
Roger	
George	
Will	
Chill	
Rattle	(boys)
Rolan	
Congerman	
Grubb	
Judith	(women)
Ingebo	
Jila	
Kate	
Bell	
Black Mary	
Cushoe	
Marya	
Lady	
Cataline	
Monday	
Minykin	
Dulo	
Yambo	
Sara	
Franke	
Sib	
Beo	
Booman	
Mye	
Doll	

Name	Source
Jane	
Sambo	1647 RB 3/2 p. 80
Bonnie Basse	1647 RB 3/2 p. 80
Jugg	1656 BR 6/13, p. 144 (freedom)
Will id	
Battee id	
Latti	1654 BR 6/13 p. 64 (freedom)
Benta	1654 BR 6/12 p. 157 (freedom)
Sarah	1657 BR 6/30, p. 12 (freedom)
Arabella mulatto	1658 RB 6/14, p. 344
Nango id*	
Jack	1652 RB 6/11, 510 (freedom)
Cousoc	1659 RB 6/14, p. 333 (freedom)
Sam + wife	1654 Davis 7/15 (3, f 100)
Peter + wife + 3 pickaninnies	
Bessie + picaninnies (= 2)	
Dick + wife + 2 pickaninnies	
Adam + wife + 2 pickaninnies	
Abala boy	1654 Davis (3 f 100)
Sambo	c 1648 Ligon 50
Cooke	1658 JBMHS Lucas 73 L 164 males
Robin	
Grig	
Guy	
Dick	
Little Tom	
Sampson	
Surley	
Roger	
Jeffery	
Peter	
Callibar	
George	
Harry	
Dane	
Ferdinando	
Tom Bosou	
Anthony	
Ould Gilliam	(women)
Mingo	
Bess	
Pugam	

(*continued*)

(continued)

Name	Source
Aquary	
Alice	
Joane	
Jane	
Rose	
Eeley	
Nan	No date JBMHS Lucas MS 164

Sources: BR *Barbados Records. Wills and Administrations* (3 vols., 1 (1639–80), vol. 2 (1681–1700), vol. 3 (1701–1725). Houston, TX: Sanders Historical Publications, 1979, 1980, 1981).
Davis Darnell Davis Papers, Cambridge University Library
Ligon Richard Ligon, *A True and Exact History of the Island of Barbados* (London, 1657).
JBMHS Lucas MS, "The Lucas Manuscript Volumes." *Journal of the Barbados Museum and Historical Society* 12 (May 1945).

Names in Bermuda Records

Bermuda Records are older than those found in the other colonies, yet they contain very few names. This is surprising, especially when one considers the relatively large number of Africans and their descendants on the island.

Name	Source
Antonio mother Philass	1636 EBR p. 11
Susan	1639 EBR p. 11
Ann mulatto Richard Laycraft	1646 EBR p. 11
Mary mother Penny mulatto	1648 EBR p. 12
Susan father Simon	1654 EBR p. 12
James	1657 EBR p. 12
Jane	1657 EBR p. 12
Anthony	1657 EBR p. 12
John Daniel Simonsen (child)	1642 EBR p. 13
Daniel	1649
Rebecca Elizabeth	1649
Anthony Hernandris	1643 EBR p. 17
Amis Hernandris marries Anthony	
Joao Whom [Whern] m Ellon Hernandris	1643, EBR p. 18
Hannah Manena moth Priscilla	1660 EBR p. 18
John fath Peter moth Catherine	1647 EBR p. 18

Name	Source
Sarah same as John	1648
Sarah fath Thomas	1660 EBR p. 18
John Akerhurst	1655 CR 2: 249
No first Attwood	1651 CR 2: 249
Elon daugh John Whom bapt	1644
Ann mulatto bapt	1646
Sander dcd	1648
Mary bpb daugh Penny mulatto	1648
Rebecca dt of Simon Simonsen, bp	1649
Ann dt Elizabeth Simonsen, bp	1649
James bp	1657
Jane bp	1657
Anony bp	16
Anthony	1616
Maria	1650 BCR Bk of Wills I,. 77
Thomas boy	
Symon	
Grace	
Richard	
Robert infant	
Noomia free until 30 yrs	1653 p. 23
Roger free at 30	
Anthony man	1653 p. 31
Isabella	1653
Sander + wife	1647
Old Samba + wife	1647
Chelme negro maid	1647
M Burrows (free)	1658 p. 51
Francisco (free)	
Framico + wife (free)	
John (free)	
Williams (free)	
Nodd mulattos (free)	
Timothy mulatto (free)	
Iosias Simon	1659 p. 51
Bongo	
Ellick s of Old Sauders	1649 Lefroy 645
Francisco	1628 Lefroy 483
Anthonia, wife of Francisco	1628
Paraketo male	1630 Lefroy 1: 585 BCR Bk E.
Catulina wife of Paraketo	1630
Alice eldest daughter of C and P	
Ann younger daughter	

(continued)

Name	Source
Sambo	1634 Lefroy 1: 539 BCR vol. F Roger Wood letters, no. 60, 24 Dec 34
Justina d of Sambo	
Mingo grande	1634 BCR F, no. 88
Polassa wife of Mingo grande	
Mingo	
Isabella wife of Mingo	
Anthonio the long	
Anthonio the ould	
Katalina	
Katalina	
Isabella	
Bridget	
Maria	
Amra dtr of Katalina	
Saray dtr of Maria and William	1632 BCR F Ltr Book of Roger Wood
Dorothy dtr of Maria and William	
Lucretia wf of Manano	
Susan dtr Thomas Bar	
Guindolin dtr Thomas Bar	
Priscilla dtr Thomas Bar	
Manano	
Bridget wf of Manano	
William sn of Manano and Bridget	
Sarah dtr Manano and Bridget	
Richard sn Manano and Bridget	
Sambo	
Catale wf of Sambo	
John sn Catale and Sambo	
Maria dtg Catale	
Penelope dtr Catale	
John son Catale	
Sander	1634 BL Add 63854 f 11
James Sarnando	1639/40 BCR 2: 85
Hanna dtr of James Sarnando	
Maria had bastard	1638 Bernhard 46
Ann bast by Bowley	1639 Bernhard
Mingo Woman For w Daniel	164? Bernhard 46
Daniel Forn w Mingo	1641/7 Bernhard 46 CR 1: 193b
Maria Adult with Span	1641/7 Berhard 46
Anthony marr. Adul w Paraketo	1641/7 Bernhard 46

Name	Source
Paraketo woman adult with Anthony	1641/7 Bernhard 46
Phillip woman witness	1639 Bernhard 47 Lefroy 1: 553
Alexander, 99 year term	1638 BCR 2: 9
Maria 99 yrs	1637
Jasper	1637
Maria 99 yrs	
Txrter	
Christopher	
Maria	
Peter	
Alexander 99 years	1637
Peter	1637 PRO CO 124/2 f. 150v
Christopher	1637 PRO CO 124/2 f. 150v
Elizabeth	1642 BCR 5a 55v
Gonsallio given for 3 yrs	1645 BCR 3: 102
Whan	
Sander	1646 BCR 2, 130
Blacke Moll	1647/8 Lefroy 633
Menena (man)	1647 BCR 3, 11
Elizabeth Sayles	1647 BCR 3, 11
Peeter	1648 BCR 2: 146
Sarah	1648 BCR 2: 145
Tony	1649 BCR: 146
Doll Allen not a heathen negro or slave?	1652 Lefroy 2: 34–5
James the Negro	1655 Lefroy 2: 61
Elizabeth girl	1656 Lefroy 2: 70
Cabilecto conspiracy	1656 Lefroy 2: 95
Blacke Anthony conspiracy	1656 Lefroy 2: 94
Ffranck Jeames conspiracy	1656 Lefroy 2: 95
Black Tom	
Willi Fforce	
Black Robin	
Tony	
Black Jacke	
Black Harry, conspirator	1656 Lefroy 2: 95
Marie, mulatto	1657, BCR 52, f. 63
Sarah, Mulatto	1657 BCR 52, f. 63
Samuel father of Salvadoro	1659 Lefroy 2: 127
Salvadoro, son of Samuel	1659 Lefroy 2: 127
John Deuale	
Whan alias John	1659
Anthonie	

(*continued*)

(continued)

Name	Source
Plenthento	1659 Lefroy 2: 127
Penelope Strange mulatto	1660 Lefroy 2: 141
Guindelo m of Ruth	1659 BCR 5a f 21
Ruth dtr of Guindelo	1659 BCR 5a f 21

Sources: EBR Bermuda Archives, *Early Bermuda Records 1619–1826 Guide* (Juniper Hill Press, Bermuda, 1991).
BCR Bermuda Colonial Records.
Lefroy J. H. Lefroy (ed.) *Memorials of the Discovery and Early Settlement of the Bermudas or Somers Islands, 1515–1685* (London, 1877, 3rd edition, Toronto: University of Toronto Press, 1981).
Bernhard Virginia Berhnard, *Slaves and Slaveholders in Bermuda, 1616–1782* (Columbia, MO and London, 1999).

Names in New Netherland Records

Court records and land deeds join with extensive marriage and baptismal records to give us a fairly full record of names and naming patterns in the Dutch colony. Double dating in the source column indicates our opinion that a person who appears twice in the records is the same person. We have also recorded relationships between some of the people in order to determine their identity and avoid double counting.

Names	Source
Negro Mayken/Mayken van Angola	1628 Calendar, 246, DB 18/263
Anthony (New Sweden)	1637 Johnson
Pedro Negretto	1639 Van Laer 4: 53 (f 44)
Louriso Barbosse	1639 Van Laer 4: 66 (f 53)
Pieter St. Anthony f. Barent Jan, Jacob	1639 DB 10/249, 11/252
Barent Jan s Pieter St Anthony	1639 DB 10/249
Jacob s Pieter St Anthony	1641 DB 11/252
Domenco Anthony	1639 DB 10/249
Jan Francoys aka Jan Francisco	1639 DB 10/249; 1648 Purple 15/580
Susanna de Angola aka Susanna Simons van Angola	1639 DB 10/249; 12/253
Domenco Deis	1639 DB 10/249
Trÿntie s Domenco Deis	1639 DB 10/249
Samuel Angola f Laurens h Catharina de Angola 1644	1640 DB 10/250 Purple 13/576
Catharina de Angola w Samuel van Angola	1644 Purple 13/576

Names	Source
Laurens s Samuel Angola	1640 DB 10/250
Marie d'Angole w Jan Francisco	1640 DB 10/250; 1648 Purple, 15/580
Isabel d'Angola	1640 DB 10/250
Catelina van Angola w Anthony v A	1641 Dickenson 103
Gosman de Neger	1641 DB 11/252
Cleyn Antonio Paulo [van Angola] aka v Angola aka Anthony de Angola h Catelina v A h Lucie de Angola f Anthony	1641 Van Laer 4: 97 (f. 83 Dickenson 103).
Anthony s Cleyn Antonio	1643 DB 15/258
Jan Augustinus	1643 DB 15/258
Victorie Paulus Negrinne	1643 DB 15/258
Paulo d'Angola wf Dorothe/Clara de Angola	1641 Van Laer 4: 97 Dickenson 104
Anthony Blind	Dickenson, 104
Gracia d'Angola h Maria Santomee	1641 Van Laer 4: 97 Dickenson 103
Maria Santomee [aka Maria d'Angola] wf Gracia d'Angola wf Christoffel Santomee wf Manuel Sanders 1671	1641 Dickenson 103
Christoffel Santomee h Maria Angola, s Pieter ST? aka Christoffel Crioel van Santomee	1641 Dickenson, 103,173 Purple 21/594
Maria Angola w Gerasÿ Angola w Christoffel van Santomee	1656 Purple 21/594
Gerasÿ van Angola h Maria Angola pre	1656 Purple 21/594
Pieter Portugies f Elizabeth	1643 DB 15/257
Elizabeth d Pieter Portugies	1643 DB 15/257
Sebastiaen Neger	1643 DB 15/257
Jan de Fort Orange m wid Jan Primeiro f Maria	1641 Van Laer 4: 97; DB 10/250
Maria d Jan de Fort Orange	1640 DB 10/250
Manuel de Gerrit de Reus vab Angola aka Manuel Swagger f Dominicus, Michiel, Barber, Elizabeth, Dominicus	1641 Van Laer 4: 97 Dickenson, 170, 172 DB 17/262
Dominicus s Manuel de Gerrit de Reus	1641 DB 11/252
Michiel s Manuel de Gerrit de Reus	1642 DB 12/253
Barber s Manuel de Gerrit de Reus	1642 DB 12/253
Elizabeth d manuel de Gerrit de Reus	1644 DB 17/262
Dominicus	1648 DB 24/271

(*continued*)

(continued)

Names	Source
Antony Portugees [aka Willem or Willem Anthony P f Antony and Maria twins, f Jochem	Dickenson, 169; 172
Jochem s Antony Portugees	DB 15/258
Antony s Antony Portugees	1641 DB 11/ 252
Maria d Antony Portugees	1641 DB 11/252
Magdaleen d Antony Portugies	1646 DB 20/266
Manuel Minuit [see Emmanuel Pieterson]	Van Laer 4: 97; Dickenson, 170
Simon Congo Aka Simon Congoÿ Augustyn	1640 Van Laer 4: 97 Dickenson, 169 DB 10/250; 22/269
Johan Francisco f Philip	1640 DB 10/250
Maria grande h v.	1640? DB 10/250
Francisco Neger	1641 DB 11/252
Grache Negrinne	1641 DB 11/252
Laurens de Angola h Lucie de Angola d pre	1641 Dickenson 103
Catharina d Jacom Anthony van Angola	DB 11/ 252
Laurens de Angola s of Laurens	1643 Dickenson 103
Lucie [Louize] de Angola wf Laurens, wf cleyn Anthony Angola	1641 Dickenson 103 Purple 10/572
Manuel de Groot/ Groot Emanuel f Philip	1641 Van Laer 4: 97 (f. 83)
Philip s Groot Emanuel	1645 DB 19/264
Jan Primeiro	1641 Van Laer 4: 97 (f. 83)
Maria dtr Jan van Fort Orange	1640 NYGBSR 6 1: 34, DB 10/250
Magdalena van Angola m Maria	1641 NYGBSR 6: 34
Emanuel van Angola f Pernante, Michiel, Nicolaes, Suzanna	1642 Goodfriend, 103, DB 10/252
Emanuel de Angola h Christina de Angola	1644 Purple, 13/576
Pernante s Emanuel van Angola	1640 DB 10/252
Michiel s Emanuel van Angola	1645 DB 19/264
Nicolaes, s Emanuel van Angola	1649 DB 26/275
Suzanna d Emanuel van Angola	1651 DB 28/278
Emmanel Pieterson [aka Emmuel Minuet] h Dorothe de Angola	1643 Dickenson 103; 170, 172
Anthony Ferdinando (from Caiscais, Ptg) h Maria van Angola f Marye 1642	1642 DB 13/255; 1642 Puple 12/575
Marye d Anthony Ferdinando	1642 DB 13/255
Elizabeth d Pieter Portugies Neger	DB 13/255

Names	Source
Phizithiaen d Angool wf of Leen Laurens wf Emanuel de Angola	1642 Goodfriend 103, Purple 11/573
Leen Laurens h Phizithiaen d'Angool	Purple, 11/573
Domenicus s Fernande Maria van Angola	1642 DB 13/255
Fernande Maria van Angola	1642 DB 13/255
Susanna Pieters	1643 DB 13/258
Groot Pieter f Maria	1644 Van Laer 2: 223,
Maria d Groot Pieter	1644 Van Laer 2: 223
Nicholas Emanuel s Emanuel	1649 Goodfriend 103
Chrystan van Angool	1649 Goodfriend 103
Lovys Angola	1649 Goodfriend 103
Hilary Cirolyo	1646 Goodfriend 103
Elary was slave of Juan Antonio	Van Laer 4, 333, f 226
Domingo Antony/Antonio	1643 Gehring, 24 GG 80
Anthony van Angola h Catalina van Angola pre h Lucie van Angola	1641 Purple 10/572
Catelina Antony wid Jochem	1643 Gehring, 24, GG 81
Jochem/Jochim aka Jacom Anthony van Angola h Catelina	pre 1641 Gehring, 24, GG 81
Dorothe Angola wf Emanuel Pietersen aka Clara Criolo wf Paulo d'Angola aka Etory or Retory	1653 Scott-Rhoda Lachair, 22–3 Dickenson, 172 Purple 18/588
Antony s of cleyn Antony and Louize adp E pieterson	1643 Scott-Rhoda, Lachair, 22–3
Louize	1643 Scott-Roda, 22–3
Lovyse	1643 DB 15/258
Cleyn Manuel	1644 Dickenson, 170
Phillippe Swartinne aka Philippe Swartinne van Angola (m of Anna) m Emanuel	1644 DB 17/261 Purple 14/579
Emanuel	1646 DB 21/267
Emanuel Congo	1644 DB 17/261
Lucretie d'Angola	1644 DB 17/262
Anneken Grande	1645 DB 20/266
Francienne [aka Mandeere Angola] m Domingo Angola	1652 Dickenson, 103, Purple 17/587
Paulo Negro h Anthonia Negrinne	1653 Purple 18/588
Anthonia Negrinne w Paulo Negro	1653 Purple 18/588
Domingo Angola h Francienne Mandeere f Christina Angola 1664	1652 Purple 17/587
Pieter Santomee f Christoffel?	Van Laer 1: 212, f 183 Dickenson, 173
Jan Francisco f Jan Francisco	Van Laer 1: 212, f 183 Dickenson 170
Maria dtr Big Peter	Van Laer 2: 223, f 11b

(continued)

(continued)

Names	Source
Manuel Trompetter d. Christina wf Anthonya d pre 1664	1643 Gehring, p. 34, GG 117
Christina d Manuel Trompetter	1645 DB 18/263
Anthonya wf M Trompetter	Dickenson, 103
Anthony Trompetter	1644 DB 17/261
Lare Swartinne m Jochem	1644 DB 17/261
Jochem s Lare Swartinne	1644 DB 17/261
Susanna Congo	DB 18/263
Anna Negra	1645 Gehring, p. 36, GG 125. Dickenson, 170
Jan Creoly	1646 Van Laer 4: 326, f 262
Manuel Congo	1646 Van Laer 4: 326, f 262
Jan Francisco Jr	1646 Van Laer 4 342, f 271 Dickenson, 170
Anthony	1646 Van Laer 2: 365, f 151
Jan de Neger (Renssalerwick)	1646 VRBM 835–6
Anna negerinne	1647 Gehring 48 Dickenson, 171
Peter van Campen/Pieter Tamboer, 1647	1645 Dickenson, 169
Anthony Chongo h Francisco de Angola?	1644 Dickenson, 170; Purple 13/577
Francisco de Angola h/w Anthony Chongo	1644 Purple 13/577
Francisco de Angola h Lucretia Albiecke van Angola	1646 Purple 14/579
Lucretia Albiecke van Angola	1646 Purple 14/579
Andries d'Angola/Andrie van Angola h of Anna negrerine [van Angola] f Tryntie, Evert	1647 Gehring 48 Purple 11/574
Anna Negrinne aka Anna van Angola w Francisco Capo Verde aka Anna van Capo Verde, w Andries van Angola	1642 Purple 11/574
Francisco Capo Verde h Anna van Angola	1642 Purple 11/574
Tryntie s Andies van Angola	1645 DB 18/263
Evert, s Andries de Neger	1649 DB 26/275
Francisco (second brief 62?)	1647 Gehring 55 Dickenson, 171
Antony Congo	1647 Gehring 56
Bastien van Angola Negro f Francisco Bastien	1647 Gehring 56 Dickenson 102, DB 17/261
Frans/Francisco Bastiensz/Bastien	Dickenson, 169

Names	Source
Jan 1647 aka Jan van Angola f Sebastiaen h Philippe Swartinne van Angola	1646 Gehring 56 Dickenson, 171 DB 22/269; Purple 14/579
Sebastien s Jan van Angola	1647 DB 22/269
Marie Anthony	1645 DB 18/263
Paulo de Angola d. pre 1653 h Dorothe	pre 1653 Dickenson, 103
Anthony Fernando f Susanna, Anthony	1646 Fernow 1: 255
Anthony s Anthony Fernando	1649 DB 26/275
Susanna d Anthony Fernando	1646 DB 20/266
Susanna bapt at 17	1647 DB 22/269
Emmanuel van Angola (baptized)	1646 DB 20/266
Lange Anna	1646 DB 20/266
Adam s Emanuel Neger	1647 DB 22/269
Eva d Emanuel Neger	1647 DB 22/269
Cecilia	1647 DB 22/269
Palasse aka Pallas van Angola aka Palassa van Angola	1643 Council Mtgs 1655, p. 267–8 Purple, 11/573 DB 15/257
Bastayen/Sebastiaen Captÿn van de negers	DB 18/263; 19/264
Christina Angola Domingo Angola d 1664	1664 Dickenson, 103
Christina van Angola w Emanuel de Angola, 1649 wit	1644 Purple, 13/576; DB 26/275
Simon, s of Emanuel Neger d. Lucretia	1649 DB 26/275
Claesje s Anthony de Neger	1649 DB 26/275
Domingo Angola h Francienne h Christina h Marycke [Maykie] pre 1664 adp Chistina Trompeter	1643 Dickenson, 103
Marycke [Maykie] wf Laurence, wf of Domingo A	1643 Dickenson, 104
Anthony Antonnys [aka of bowery]	1660 Dickenson, 169
Claes de Neger	Pre 1667 Dickenson, 170
Lucas Pieters br Soloman s Pieter Santomee? h. Anna Jans	1656? Dickenson, 171 Purple 22/596
Pieter Santomee/St Thome f Mathias	1645 DB 18/263
Mathias s Pieter Santomee	1645 DB 18/263
Paulus Neger aka Paulus van Angola f Jannekin, Jacob	1649 DB 26/275
Jannekin s Paulus Neger	1649 DB 26/275
Jacob	1653 DB 34/286
Lucretia d of Emanuel Neger	1649 DB 26/275

(continued)

(continued)

Names	Source
Marie d'Angola	1651 DB 28/278
Anthonÿ Matthÿszen van de Camp Neger aka Anthony Matthÿs f Abraham Isaacq, Cosmus, Cecelia	1651 DB 29/279
Abraham Isaacq	1651 DB 29/279
Cosmus s Anthony Matthyszen vd Camp	1654 DB 36/288
Cecelia d Anthony Matthys	1655 DB 38/292
Mattheus de Angola f Augustyn	1655 DB 38/291
Augustyn s Mattheus de Angola	1655 DB 38/291
Lisbeth Francisco wit not id as Negerinne	1651 DB 29/279
Emmanuel van Spangien f Andries (blacks as witnesses)	1653 DB 34/286
Andries s Emanuel van Spangien	DB 34/286
Maria Portugies	1654 DB 36/288
Franciscus Neger h Catherina Negrinne	1659 Purple 24/601
Catherina Negrinne w Franciscus Neger	1659 Purple 24/601
Louÿs Angola h Hilarÿ Criolÿo	1660 Purple 26/603
Hilarÿ Criolÿo w Louÿs Angola	1660 Purple 26/603
Solomon Pietersz bowrey	1667? Dickenson, 171

Sources: Calendar O'Callaghan, *Calendar of Historical Manuscripts in the Office of the Secretary of State, Dutch Manuscripts* (Albany, 1855–1856).

Council Meetings, 1655 Charles Gehring (ed. and trans.) *Council Minutes, 1655–56* (Syracuse, 1995).

DB *Doop-Boek* of the Reformed Church of New York, published in "Baptisms in the Dutch Reformed Church of New Amsterdam and New York City, 1639–1730," *New York Genealogical and Biographical Society Record* 2 (1890): 10–41.

Dickenson Richard Dickenson, "Abstracts of Early Black Manhattanites" *New York Genealogical and Biographical Record* 116 (1985).

Fernow Berthold Fernow, ed. *The Records of New Amsterdam from 1653 to 1674* (7 vols., New York, 1897).

Gehring Charles Gehring (ed. and trans.), *New York Historical Manuscripts: Dutch. Land Papers, Volumes GG, HH and II* (Baltimore, 1980).

Goodfriend Joyce Goodfriend, "Black Families in New Netherland," *Journal of the Afro-American Historical and Genealogical Society* 5 (1984): 95–108;

Johnson Amandus Johnson, *Swedish Settlements on the Delaware, 1638–1664* (2 vols., Philadelphia, 1911).

NYGBSR *New York Genealogical and Biographical Society Record.*

Purple Samuel S. Purple, *Records of the Reformed Dutch Church in New Amsterdam and New York: Marriages from 11 December, 1639, to 26 August, 1801* New York, 1890).

Scott-Rhoda, Lachair Kenneth Scott and Kenn Stryker-Rodda (eds). New York Historical Manuscripts: Dutch. The *Register of Salomon Lachaire, Notary Public of New Amsterdam, 1661–1662* translated by E. B. O'Callaghan (Baltimore, 1978).

Van Laer A. J. F. van Laer, *New York Historical Manuscripts: Dutch* (4 vols., Baltimore, 1974).

Names in the Virginia-Maryland Records

Virginia names come primarily from the land patent documents, which specified that persons wishing to patent land in Virginia had to certify that they were bringing a certain number of people with them, and often they were named in the documents, although a considerable number of "negroes" were only cited as "Negro." A few names also appear in court records.

Names	Source
Anthony Johnson	1623 Deal, 217
John Philip	1624 McIlwain, 33
Anthony	Census 1624, 40
William	
John	
Anthony	Census 1624, 40
Angelo (woman)	Census 1624, 40
Edward, Neck of land	Census 1624 45
John	Census 1624, 46–7
Anthony (Eliz City)	Census 1624, 51
Isabell (Eliz City)	Census 1624, 51
Thomas Guine? Dead	Census 1624, 57
Brase (sailor)	Court 3/10/25, McIlwain, 73
Angelo in Treasurer	Census 1625, f 24
John Pedro in Swan 1623	Census 1625, f 52
Edward (Neck of L)	Census 1625, f 29
Antonio (Warrosq)	Census 1625, f 39
Mary (Warr) in Margaret and John	Census 1625, f 39
Antoney (Elis Cittie)	Census 1625, f 41
Isabell	Census 1625, f 41
William s Ant and Is (Eliz Cittie)	Census 1625, f 41
Antho	1635 Nugent, 25
Mary	1635 Nugent, 25
Anthony	1635 Nugent, 28
Cassango wf Anthony	1635 Nugent, 28
Mary	1635 Nugent, 29 (diff)
Bashaw	1635 Nugent, 31
Juliana	
Andrea	
Maydelina	
Cesent	1635 Nugent, 31
Anthony	1635 Nugent, 31
Solon	1635 Nugent, 32
Mary	1635 Nugent, 35

(continued)

(continued)

Names	Source
Mathias (Cheesman)	1635 Nugent, 35
Mathias (Cheesman)	1636 Nugent, 69
Emmanuel Driggus	lt 1630s Deal, 279
Jo:	1637–40 Accomack (Fleet) 32, 199
Francis	1637–40 Accomack (Fleet) 32, 202
Augt:	1637 Nugent, 73
Francisco	1637 Nugent, 74
Andolo	1637 Nugent, 81
Mario	1637 Nugent, 81
Mingo	1637 Nugent, 61
Franc:	1637 Nugent, 61
Fr:	
Anth:	
Alexander	
Joh	1637 Nugent, 61
Austin	1637 Nugent, 66
Bashaw	1638 Nugent, 2: 84 (see 31)
Jabina (Juliana, Nugent 31?)	1638 Nugent, 2: 84
Andrea	
Cesent	Nugent, 84
Magdelina	1638 Nugent, 84
Bass	1638 Nugent 2: 94
Domingo	1638 Nugent 2: 101
Saconyo	1638 Nugent 2: 101
Tonie	1638 Nugent 2: 105
Gereen	1638 Nugent 2: 105
Joan	1639 Nugent 2: 112
Anthony	1638 Johnson
Domingo	1640 Marshall, 18
Francis	1640 Nugent, 2: 119
Matias de Sousa (mulatto from Portugal)	1634
John Graweere	1640 Court 1641 McIlwain
Emanuella w	1642 Nugent 2: 133
Jacob	1642 Nugent 2: 138–9
Catalina	1642 Nugent 2: 141
Tony	1642 Nugent 2: 141
Susan	1642 Ames 2: 324
John the Nagro wife and family	1643 L Norfolk Bk A, f 24, p. 177
Basteans Nagro	1643 L Norfolk Bk A, fol 27, p. 177
Michael	1643 Nugent 2: 146
Catherine w of Michael	1643 Nugent 1: 146
John Grashere (see Graweere)	1643 Nugent 1: 146

Names	Source
Mathew	1643 Nugent 2: 146
Peter	1643 Nugent 2: 152
Martin	1643 Nugent 2: 154
Antonio	1644 Nugent 2:
Michaell	1644 York Cnty DO 2
Couchanello	1644 York Cnty DO 2
Palassa	1644 York Cnty DO 2
Mary (girl)	1644 York Cnty DO 2
Elizabeth (3y)	1644 York County DO 2
Mingo	1645 Nugent 2: 158
France	1645 Nugent 2: 158
Domingo	1645 Nugent 2: 158
Scourgoa	1645 Nugent 2: 158
Peeter	1646 VCA 3: 46
John	1646 VCA 3: 46
Galatia	1646 Deal, 254
Grace aka Grace-Susana	1646 VCA 3: 46 Deal 252–4
Katherin	1646 VCA 3: 46
Temperance	1645 Marshall, 42
Susan	1645 Marshall, 42
Jane	1645 Marshall, 42
Mary	1645 Lower Norfolk A, f 17, p. 255
Black Jack	1646 L Norfolk B, p 23
Marchant	1646 NCo DW 1651 p. 28
Will (boy)	1646 NCo DW 1651, p 28
William (boy)	1646 NCo DW 1645 p. 51
Prew (gril)	1646 NCo DW 1645 p. 51
Elizabeth	1647 Nugent 1: 170
Anthony	1647 Nugent 1: 173
Michaell	1647 Nugent 1: 173
Mary	1647 Nugent 1: 173
Luce	1647 Nugent 1: 173
Anthony (child)	1647 Nugent 1: 173
Francisco from Barbados	1647 L Norfolk B, p. 109
Amanuell	L Norfolk B, p. 109
Antonio	L Norfolk B, p. 109
Maria	1647 L Norfolk B p. 109
Emmanuel Driggus h aka Manuel Elizabeth	1645 NCo DW 1651, fol 82; NCo DW 1645 f 95 (Manuel)
Francis Driggus w Emannuel Driggus	1645 NCo DW 1651, f 82
Elizabeth adopted by Emmanuel (8)	1645 NCo DW 1651, f 82
Jane Driggs bought by Emmanuel Driggus	1645 NCo DW 1651, f 82

(*continued*)

(continued)

Names	Source
Edward Driggs (b 1650) h Elizabeth s Thomas, Francis	1657 NCo DW 1655 p. 74
Elizabeth Driggus, w Edward Driggus	NCo DW 1657 p. 115
Bashaw Farnando	1645 NCo DW f 82
Emmanuell	1648 York Cty 302 VCA 3 (14) 105
Mingo	1648 York Cty 302 VCA 3 (14) 105
Sibiria	1648 Nugent 2: 177
John	1648 L Norfolk B, 50
Tonny	1649 Nugent 2: 184
Basse	1649 Nugent 2: 184
Philip Mongun	1650 NCo DW 3, f 217 cit Breen-Innis
Sarah	1650 Nugent 2: 208
Susan	1650 Nugent 2: 208
Manuell	1651 Nugent 2: 218
Joane	1651 Nugent 2: 218
Kate	1651 Nugent 2: 219
Mary	1651 Nugent 2:219
Tom	1651 Nugent 2: 219
John Cole	1651 NCHR 4: 38
Mary 3 mayd	1652/Marshall Abst f 32
Edward	Nugent 1: 245
Susan	Nugent 1: 245
Martha	Nugent 1: 245
Jacob Warrow	AM 10: 293ff
Jacob s of Jacob Warrow	AM 10: 293
Mary Warrow w Jacob Warrow	AM 10: 293
Mingo Matthews	1645 Deal, 383–93
Peter	1654 Surry Cnty Deeds, 14
Tony Longo	1655
John Casar	1655 NCo, Billings 155–56
Ann Drigges	1656 NCHR Deeds, 1x no. 7, f. 63 Marshall, 63
Negro Sandee	1656 NCo DW 1655, p. 59
Black Robert, aka Robin h Fallassa	1656 NCo DW 1655, p. 59
Fallassa aka Pallassa aka Prossa m. Francis, Sandee w Black Robert	1656 NCo DW 1655, p. 59; Nco DWO 1657 p. 16
Francis s of Falassa and Robert	1656 NCo DW 1655, p. 59
Peter George Negro	1661 NCo DW 1657, p. 133
Jean George aka Jane d Peter George	1661 NCo DW 1657, p. 133
Joane	1656 Duvall 2/2, p. 2
Shaha	1657 Duvall, p. 4

Names	Source
Roma	1657 Duvall, p. 4
Simon Antonio aka Tony	1658 AM 41: 190–91
Abraham	1658 Weisiger, p. 123
Michael	1659 Surry County Deeds, 34
Henry	1659 Duvall, p. 9
Peter	1659 Duvall, p. 9
Mena	1659 Duvall, p. 9
Nanne	1659 Weisiger York p. 26
Winfred	1660 Weisiger p. 34
Anthony, boy	1660 Weisiger p. 34
Joseph	1660 Weisiger, p. 34
Maree	1660 Weisiger, p. 44
John	1660 Weisiger, p. 34
Witt (old)	1660 Weisiger, p. 62
Robin (old)	Weisiger, p. 62
George (boy)	Weisiger, p. 62
Tom (boy)	Weisiger, p. 62
Judy	Weisiger, p. 62
Moll	Weisiger, p. 62
Bridgett	Weisiger, p. 62
Ann (girl)	Weisiger, p. 62
Bess (girl)	Weisiger, p. 62
Peg (girl)	Weisiger, p. 62
Lawrence (old)	Weisiger, p. 62
Sue (girl)	Weisiger, p. 62
Jane (girl)	Weisiger, p. 62
Margery (girl)	Weisiger, p. 62
Bessie w Lawrence	Weisiger, p. 62
Sarah (girl)	Weisiger, p. 62
Nanne (girl)	Weisiger, p. 62
Besse (girl)	1660 Weisiger, p. 62
Cuttee	1660 Weisiger p. 75
Anthony	1664 VCA 1(1): 148 (new ed)
Alkamy	
Cooper	
Congo	
Guy	
James	
Accrue	
Robin	
Sisly	
Katherine	
Francis	1664 VCA 1(1): 148

(continued)

(continued)

Names	Source
Jack	1636/53/64 Billings, p. 169–70
John Francisco	1664 NCo DW 1664 f 52
Francis Paine	1664 NCo DW 1664 f 52

Sources: Accomack (Fleet)
AM *Archives of Maryland*
Ames Susie M. Ames (ed), *County Court Records of Accomack-Northhampton* (Charlottesville, 1973)
Billings Warren M. Billings (ed.), *The Old Dominion in the Seventeenth Century: A Documentary History of Virginia, 1606–1689* (Chapel Hill, 1975)
Census 1624 PRO CO 1/3, pub. in *Colonial Records of Virginia* (Richmond, 1874)
Census 1625 PRO CO 1/3, published in Annie Lash Jester and Martha Woodruff Hiden eds. *Adventurers of Purse and Person: Virginia 1607–25* (Princeton, 1956), pp. 5–69
Deal J. Douglas Deal, *Race and Class in Colonial Virginia. Indians, Englishmen, and Africans on the Eastern Shore During the Seventeenth Century* (New York and London, 1993)
Duvall Lindsay O. Duvall, *Virginia Colonial Abstracts. Series 2, vol. 2. Lancaster Country, Virginia. Court Orders and Deeds, 1656–1680* (Easley, SC, 1979)
Johnson Amandus Johnson, *The Settlements of the Swedes on the Delaware*
L Norfolk Bk A Alice Grantley Walker, *Book "A" Lower Norfolk County, Virginia, 1637–46*, Baltimore: Geneological Publishing Co., 1994
L Norfolk B Alice Grantley Walker, *Book "B" Lower Norfolk County, Virginia, November 1646–15 January 1651/2* Baltimore: Geneological Publishing Company, 1978
Marshall James Handley Marshall, *Abstracts of the Wills and Administrations of Northhampton County, Virginia 1632–1862* (Camden, ME, 1994)
McIlwain Henry Read McIlwaine (ed.) *Minutes of the Council and General Court* (Richmond, 1924)
NCo DW Northhampton County Court Records Deeds and Wills
York Cnty DO York County, (Virginia) County Deeds, Orders, Wills 2, 1645–49
Nugent Nell Marion Nugent, *Cavaliers and Pioneers: Abstracts of Virginia Land Patents and Grants, 1623–66* (Baltimore, 1983)
Surry Cnty Deeds
VCA Beverly Fleet (ed.) *Virginia Colonial Abstracts* (3 vols., Baltimore: Geneological Publishing Co., 1988, originally published 1937–49)
Weisiger Benjamin Weisiger, *Henrico County Deeds*

Names in New England Records

There are too few names from New England records to be able to make any statistical statements; however, what little can be gleaned from them is presented here.

Names	Source
Hope	1652 Suffolk Deeds, I, 290
Angola	1656 Suffolk Deeds 2, 97–8 and 7, 22
Anthony the N	1671 Suffolk Deeds 7 114
Mariae (Hartford)	1667 Hartfort Land Rec 2: np
Samuel Reeps	1672 Early Records of Providence 3: 226
Sebastian Cane aka Buss a negro aka Bostian Ken aka Buss Buss Negro	1662 Suffolk Deeds 4, 113
Lucretia	1646 Hoadly, *New Haven* 1: 296, fol. 176
Anthony	1647 Hoadly, *New Haven*, p. 335
Matthew	1647 Hoadly, *New Haven*, p. 335
Katherine	1650 Essex Records 1: 196
Kate	1653 Essex Records 1: 323
Moniah	1659 Essex Records 2: 183
Mungaly	1659 Essex Records 2: 183
Jugg	1670 Essex Records 2: 247
Anthony a Negro	1661 Suffolk Deeds 4: xi
Seasar	1670 Essex Records 4: 322
Silvanus	1670
Nimroid	1670
Grace	1674
Juniper	1674

Sources: Essex Records: George F. Dow, ed. Records and Files of the Quarterly Courts of Essex County, Massachusets (Salem, 1911-21).

Early Records of Providence: Horatio Rogers, et al. The Early Records of the Town of Providence (19 vols., Providence, 1883–1906).

Hartfort Land Rec: George Burnham and Levi Woodhouse, General Index to the Land Records of the Town of Hartford (Hartford, 1873).

Hoadly, New Haven: Charles Hoadly, Records of the Colony and Plantation of New Haven (2 vols., Hartford, 1857).

Suffolk Deeds: John T. Hassam, Suffolk Deeds (12 vols, Boston 1896–1902).

Index

Tunda, 74, 131
Tyssen, Geurt, 45, 266

Uchteritz, Heinrich von, 322
Udemans, Godefridus Cornelisz, 328
ukisi, 63, 171
Ungaro, Bernardo, 207
Upper Guinea, 39, 49
Utica, 63

van Caerden, Paulus, 21
van Caerden, Pieter, 21
van Capelle, Frans, 43, 207
van den Broecke, Pieter, 19, 106, 170, 171,
    308, 309, 310
van der Hagen, Pieter (ship's captain), 19
van Geel, Joris, 177
van Pere, Abraham, 37
van Uytgeest, Dirck Simonszoon, 36
Vasconcelos da Cunha, Francisco de, 134
Vaughan, Alden, 295, 296, 299, 304
Vaz, Duarte, 192
Veas, Francisco de, 178, 202
Venezuela, 16, 22, 27, 47, 260, 261, 262
Venice, 17, 51
Vera Cruz, 5, 6, 39, 40, 161
Vergulden Craen (ship), 25
Vetralla, Giacinto da, 166
Viedma, Pedro de, 261, 262
Virgin Mary, 66, 152, 171
Virginia, i, ix, xi, xii, xiii, 5, 6, 7, 8, 20, 23,
    28, 31, 40, 45, 46, 48, 161, 242, 243, 244,
    245, 246, 247, 248, 249, 254, 255, 256,
    258, 267, 270, 271, 272, 275, 276, 277,
    278, 281, 282, 283, 284, 285, 286, 287,
    289, 292, 295, 296, 297, 299, 311, 315, 316,
    319, 320, 322, 323, 327, 329, 331

Vlissingen, 6
Vogado Sottomaior, Manuel, 119, 120
Vogado, Jeronimo, 120, 191, 197, 198, 271
Vunga, 75
Vungu, 55, 106, 144

Waepen van Amsterdam (ship), 248
Walsingham (English captain), 27
Wandu, 133, 150, 151, 152, 155, 171, 202, 203
Warner, Thomas, 29
Wembo, 91, 141
wene, 57
West Indies. *See* Spanish Indies
White Lion (ship), 6, 7, 28, 161, 246, 271,
    283
White, Richard, 284
Wiapoco, 21, 24, 37, 260
Wild Coast, 20, 21, 22, 24, 25, 37, 240, 241,
    258, 259, 260, 261, 267, 272
William of Orange, 14
Williams, Roger, 321
Windham, Thomas, 301, 313
Windhout (ship), 41, 42
Winthrop, John, 32, 46, 321
Witte Paert (ship), 45, 247, 266, 267, 276
Wyndham, Thomas, 11

Xilonga, 115
Xingu River, 21

Yardley, Francis, 46
Yeardley, George, 246

Zeeland, 19, 24, 30, 34, 36, 37, 41, 42, 43,
    259, 260, 269, 271
Zelotes dos Reis Magros, Calisto, 202
Zenza River, 56, 84, 116, 127, 149, 205